CREATING WILDERNESS

The Environment in History: International Perspectives

Series Editors: Dolly Jørgensen, *Umea University;* David Moon, *University of York;* Christof Mauch, *LMU Munich;* Helmuth Trischler, *Deutsches Museum, Munich*

Volume 1
Civilizing Nature: National Parks in Global Historical Perspective
Edited by Bernhard Gissibl, Sabine Höhler, and Patrick Kupper

Volume 2
Powerless Science? Science and Politics in a Toxic World
Edited by Soraya Boudia and Natalie Jas

Volume 3
Managing the Unknown: Essays on Environmental Ignorance
Edited by Frank Uekotter and Uwe Lübken

Volume 4
Creating Wildnerness: A Transnational History of the Swiss National Park
Patrick Kupper

Creating Wilderness
A Transnational History of the Swiss National Park

Patrick Kupper

Translated by Giselle Weiss

berghahn
NEW YORK · OXFORD
www.berghahnbooks.com

Published by
Berghahn Books
www.berghahnbooks.com

English-language edition
©2014 Patrick Kupper

German-language edition
©2012 Haupt Bern
Wildnis schaffen. Eine transnationale Geschichte des Schweizerischen Nationalparks

All rights reserved. Except for the quotation of short passages for the purposes of criticism and review, no part of this book may be reproduced in any form or by any means, electronic or mechanical, including photocopying, recording, or any information storage and retrieval system now known or to be invented, without written permission of the publisher.

Library of Congress Cataloging-in-Publication Data

Kupper, Patrick.
    [Wildnis schaffen. English]
    Creating wilderness : a transnational history of the Swiss National Park / Patrick Kupper ; translated by Giselle Weiss.
        pages cm. — (The environment in history : international perspectives ; volume 4)
    Translation of: Wildnis schaffen : eine transnationale Geschichte des Schweizerischen Nationalparks. Bern : Haupt, 2012.
    Includes bibliographical references and index.
    ISBN 978-1-78238-373-4 (hardback : alk. paper) —
    ISBN 978-1-78238-374-1 (ebook)
  1. Schweizerischer Nationalpark (Switzerland)—History. 2. Nature conservation—Switzerland—History. I. Title.
    SB484.S9K88 2014
    333.7209494—dc23

2013044896

British Library Cataloguing in Publication Data

A catalogue record for this book is available from the British Library

ISBN: 978–1-78238-373-4 hardback
ISBN: 978–1-78238-374-1 ebook

Contents

List of Figures	vi
Acknowledgments	viii
List of Abbreviations	ix
Introduction	1
Chapter 1. Global Parks: National Parks, Globalization, and Western Modernism	15
Chapter 2. National Natures: The Swiss National Park and the Conservationist Internationale	38
Chapter 3. Local Landscapes: Political Spaces, Institutional Arrangements, and Subjective Attitudes	70
Chapter 4. Total Protection: Philosophy and Practice of Freely Developing Nature	107
Chapter 5. Ecological Field Laboratory: The Park as a Scientific Experiment	137
Chapter 6. Wilderness Limits: Natural Dynamics and Social Equilibrium	175
Conclusion	219
Bibliography	226
Index	255

Figures

Charts

Chart 1. Population development in the regions of the Upper Engadine, Lower Engadine, Val Müstair, and in St. Moritz and the five national park communities, 1850–2000 — 78

Chart 2. Yearly number of researchers and the number of workdays spent in the park, 1918–60 — 169

Chart 3. Annual overnight stays in the Cluozza hut, 1926–2008 — 190

Chart 4. Number of visitors to the Swiss National Park, 1955–2008 — 195

Chart 5. Development of stocks of chamois, ibex, and red deer in the Swiss National Park, 1915–2010 — 204

Chart 6. Cost of damage caused by wildlife in the area of the Swiss National Park and for feed in the area of Zuoz-Brail, 1962–99 — 206

Maps

Map 1. Location of the Swiss National Park in the Rhaetian Alps and the southeastern corner of Switzerland (GIS-SNP, Swiss National Park, Spatial Information Department) — 2

Map 2. Southeastern Switzerland (GIS-SNP, Swiss National Park, Spatial Information Department) — 76

Map 3. Changes in the park area. (GIS-SNP, Swiss National Park, Spatial Information Department) — 88

Map 4. Hydraulic installations. (GIS-SNP, Swiss National Park, Spatial Information Department) — 183

Illustrations

Illustration 1. Switzerland? Promotion of Glacier National Park by NPS in 1933. (US National Park Service, George A. Grant Collection)   23

Illustration 2. Paul Sarasin and Fritz Bühlmann, ENPK president and secretary, at the entry to Val Cluozza, c. 1920. (Swiss National Park)   57

Illustration 3. Carl Schröter and Steivan Brunies on Murtèr ridge in 1912. (Staatsarchiv Graubünden, Swiss National Park Photograph Collection)   81

Illustration 4. Park map published in the March 1910 issue of the journal Heimatschutz. (Heimatschutz 3/1910, annexe 2)   84

Illustration 5. Fallen trees decaying "in peace," Munt la Schera, c. 1920. (Swiss National Park, Collection Hermann Langen)   110

Illustration 6. Introduction of ibex at Murtèr above Val Cluozza in the 1920s. (Swiss National Park, Collection Hermann Langen)   114

Illustration 7. SBN membership promotion of 1909. (Pro Natura)   127

Illustration 8. Figure from Schütz et al. 2000a. Combination of the two time-series.   167

Illustration 9. Cover of the 1942 guide to the Swiss National Park (Verkehrsverein Graubünden 1942)   193

Illustration 10. Dead red deer at the train station of Lavin in spring 1951, attracting children and photographer Rudolf Grass. (Rudolf Grass)   203

Tables

Table 1. Changes in the park area, 1910–2010   86

Table 2. Recalculation of annual compensation, 1959   88

Acknowledgments

This book has been five years in the making. For me it represents a very rewarding period out of which emerged experiences and encounters that will stay with me always, along with the memory of the support and friendship that I received. For their generous encouragement of my work throughout this time I would like especially to thank David Gugerli, Christof Mauch, and Thomas Scheurer. Another big helping of thanks goes to Brigitta Bernet, Harald Fischer-Tiné, Bernhard Gissibl, Lea Haller, Sabine Höhler, Jon Mathieu, and Daniel Speich. Their constructive criticism benefited me enormously. I am deeply grateful to the many people who provided countless bits of information, suggestions, and tips both in person and in writing. Thanks also to those who provided help with my research: the archivists and librarians in Zurich, Bern, Basel, Chur, Munich, and Washington, DC, as well as the staff of the communes of Scuol and Zernez and the Swiss National Park. I would like in particular to express my appreciation to Flurin Filli, Heinrich Haller, Ruedi Haller, Hans Lozza, Isabelle Mauz, Jürg Paul Müller, Mario Negri, Jonathan Putnam, and Erika Zimmermann. Finally, I owe my deepest debt of gratitude to my family and to everyone who stuck with us through the not-infrequently chaotic days.

This book was made possible by a generous grant from the Swiss National Science Foundation. Preliminary studies in 2006 were funded by the Research Council of the Swiss National Park and the professorship for History of Technology at ETH Zurich, which also offered me a stimulating working environment from 2006 to 2011. In 2007 a fellowship from the *Schnitter-Fonds für Technikgeschichte* made possible a four-month research stay at the German Historical Institute in Washington, DC. In 2010 an invitation to the Rachel Carson Center in Munich allowed me to focus intensively on writing for six months. To these institutions and their staffs I extend my heartfelt thanks.

Producing the translation naturally entailed a reworking of the text, which I have adjusted and updated where necessary without fundamentally changing the structure or argumentation. The translation was funded by the Research Council of the Swiss National Park and the professorship for History of Technology at ETH Zurich. I would like to thank my translator, Giselle Weiss, for her skilled and sensitive work and Franziska Hupfer and Markos P. Carelos for their help in preparing the manuscript for publication and constructing the index.

Abbreviations

ENPK	Eidgenössische Nationalparkkommission (Federal National Park Commission)
EKW	Engadiner Kraftwerke (Engadine Power Company)
FOK SNP	Forschungskommission des Schweizerischen Nationalparks (Research Council of the Swiss National Park)
IUCN	International Union for the Conservation of Nature
NPS	National Park Service (USA)
NZZ	*Neue Zürcher Zeitung*
SBN	Schweizerischer Bund für Naturschutz (Swiss League for Nature Protection today Pro Natura)
SNG	Schweizerische Naturforschende Gesellschaft (Swiss Natural History Society, today Swiss Academy of Sciences SCNAT)
SNK	Schweizerische Naturschutzkommission (Swiss Commission for Nature Protection)
SNP	Schweizerischer Nationalpark (Swiss National Park)
UNEP	United Nation Environmental Programme
WNPK	Wissenschaftliche Nationalparkkommission (Committee for Scientific Research in the National Park, today FOK SNP)

Introduction

In the twentieth century the national park became a global phenomenon. In the early 1900s, when the Swiss National Park was planned and set up, few national parks were in existence around the world, and Europe had none. Since then, the situation has changed dramatically. Europe now boasts several hundred national parks; globally, they number in the thousands. In the last hundred years the national park has clearly become one of the most significant spatial structures of contemporary times. At the same time, the national park is problematic. It is no accident that the total number and area of all the national parks varies depending on the source. The figures are in the order of five thousand parks and five million square kilometers, or 3 percent of the earth's surface.[1] But the numbers also depend on which facilities are actually categorized as national parks and thus included in the calculations. The term "national park" covers an astonishing diversity of entities. Individual parks differ vastly, not only in appearance but also in purpose: biodiversity, landscape conservation, or wilderness; tourism, edification, or research. The term "national park" provides a common denominator for all this global diversity, yet the denominator itself is indistinct. One might aptly summarize the paradox by saying that all national parks are not equal, yet they are still national parks, which, however, does not illuminate the phenomenon much further.

The approach I take in this book is a historical one. My aim is to understand the national park as a historical subject that arose out of a context both global and local. This in turn requires a historical approach that connects global and local levels. To meet this (substantial) challenge, in the pages that follow I will be continually altering my perspective, shifting my observation point, and fiddling with the resolution. This constant interplay will help to make local, national, and global developments comprehensible, and result in nuanced insights into the history both of the Swiss National Park and of the national park as a global phenomenon.

With its current area of 170 square kilometers, the Swiss National Park is comparatively small.[2] But its modest spatial extent belies its disproportionately larger transnational significance. This significance is primarily due not to its early emergence, but rather the weight placed on scientific research from the very beginning. The founders' core idea in pursuing total protection was not so

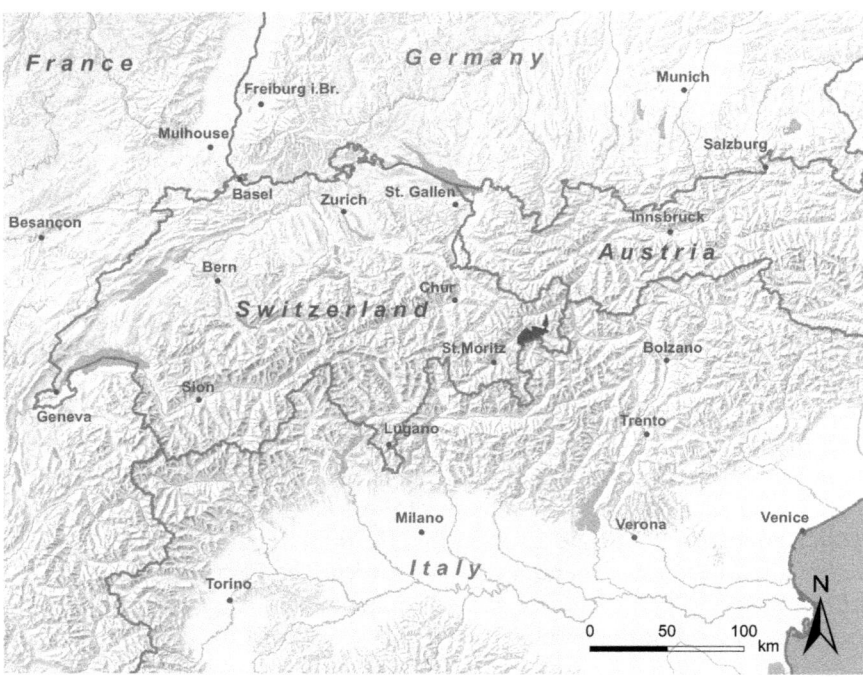

Map 1. Location of the Swiss National Park in the Rhaetian Alps and the southeastern corner of Switzerland. *Source:* GIS-SNP, Swiss National Park, Spatial Information Department.

much to preserve nature in its "original" form as it was to return such nature to modern civilization and to scientifically support and validate the process required to achieve this goal. This experimental component made the Swiss National Park into the global prototype of a science-oriented national park.

The present investigation subtends an arc of time that spans from the nineteenth century to today. One of the salient features of this period was the globalization of the nation-state model, which with the decline of empires became the predominant political system.[3] In this context, popular contemporary analyses that prophecy the end of the nation-state as a result of worldwide globalization would appear to be blind to history. A farsighted view of nation-state systems and globalization sees them neither as two phenomena following each other (and if they were, the sequence would rather be the opposite way round) nor as exclusively antagonistic forces. Rather, the process of globalization and the development of a world order based on nation-states appear to have been mutually fruitful. Accordingly, the global establishment of nation-state standards and nation-state reinforcement of global distinctions is a striking characteristic of this era, heavily influenced by European powers and the United States.[4]

The global history of the national park likewise can best be understood in the reciprocal context of globalization of the national and nationalization of the global. The term "national park" was first applied in 1872 to Yellowstone National Park in the United States.[5] The term took on global significance, however, only at the turn of the twentieth century, when the rapidly growing conservation movement began to address the worldwide loss of natural spaces and biological species, and to promote the protection of large contiguous areas as a countermeasure. Now the national park idea found adherents on every continent, and Yellowstone became a global model of nature protection discussed the world over. Contrary to standard narratives, this development should be understood neither as a simple reaction to the destruction of nature nor as a linear process of diffusion.[6] The relationship between environmental degradation and social perception and action was complex, and the worldwide system of national parks unfolded in a play of acquisition and demarcation, exploitation and rejection. The American national park jumped early into first place as a worldwide benchmark, a position it maintained throughout the twentieth century. But it was not the only one. In many places, the Swiss model—which in the years before the First World War took the form of the Swiss National Park—constituted a highly imitated alternative that was careful to differentiate itself from its American predecessor. Unlike Yellowstone Park, which was based on the close association of state-supported conservation and public recreation, the Swiss park promoted a close alliance between nature conservation and scientific research and put into place an exceptionally strict protection regime. This deliberate reinterpretation of the American national park idea was innovative and radical, and its consequences were not limited to Switzerland. In the twentieth century, the idea of national parks not only spread impressively throughout the world, but in so doing also broadened and diversified its meaning. The Swiss National Park participated in this process by introducing a distinct, scientifically oriented variant of the national park that became an internationally recognized point of reference around the world. By the same token, it was confronted itself with expectations by virtue of its standing as a national park.

The US national parks were an important basis of comparison for the Swiss National Park to which the actors returned again and again. Consequently, I will pay special attention to the differences between the two park models, as well as to their relationships and interactions. One link between the two national park movements is the idea of wilderness. As environmental historian Roderick Nash suggests in the prolog to his seminal work on the history of American wilderness, the term "wilderness" does not correspond to an actual condition.[7] Wilderness is not an objective category but a state of mind; it is a byproduct of the process of individual and social appropriation of nature. Accordingly, it is important to perennially historicize wilderness, and to situate it both in time and in space. What wilderness means—whether something to fear or to desire, to beat back or to protect—has always been the result of social communication.[8]

Ideas about wilderness circulating in American and Swiss society were not fundamentally different. They were grounded in the same traditions of European Romanticism and at core were antithetical to civilization.[9] One essential difference, which would be reflected in the design of the parks, had to do with the perception of wilderness in each country. In the United States of the late nineteenth century, the once ubiquitous wilderness was increasingly seen as endangered. It disappeared in step with the opening up of the West, and existed only in what was left of the frontier. There, national parks were established to preserve the remaining bits of American wilderness. In contrast, Swiss wilderness was no longer considered a given but rather something that had disappeared a long time ago. Consequently, before it could be preserved, it had to be (re)produced. Thus, the production of wilderness moved front and center in the Swiss interpretation of the national park idea. The park founders let their contemporaries know that they wished the national park to be a "grand experiment:" Within the national park, "alpine ur-nature should be restored and presented to the future as a sort of sanctuary for undisturbed natural life."[10] In accordance with its experimental character, this process would be approached and validated scientifically, which in turn would establish the primacy of research in the park. Moreover, the goal was assigned a priority similar to that in the United States. Because it was assumed that nature was under the growing influence of civilization and continuously moving away from its "ur-nature," every delay lessened the chances that the experiment in "creating wilderness" would ever come to pass.

The alpine primeval nature to be restored to the Swiss National Park was a wilderness "such as had adorned the Alps as a pure creation of nature before the intrusion of humans."[11] In this respect, the Swiss and American ideas were again actually very close. In both societies the prevailing idea was one of a prehistoric wilderness that was not only remote from civilization but moreover that had no people in it. Accordingly, both nations' ideas were also close to other approaches that sought to turn the respective dreams of wilderness into reality. On both sides of the Atlantic, establishing a national park went hand in hand with the exclusion of humans from the park areas, as well as prohibiting subsistence practices common in those areas at the time. People who did not come to the areas as visitors but rather made their living there were treated as disturbances to the wilderness and either expelled from the parks or kept away from them. For reasons that I will elucidate in this book, in Switzerland such measures were implemented more cautiously than in the United States or in Canada. There, Indian populations in particular were victims of government-backed policies of expulsion. That it took such policies to create the wilderness for which the parks were emblematic was a perversion that hardly reverberated at the time and that was well hidden from most of the visitors to these parks. The sometimes tragic human fates that were part and parcel of establishing the parks were successfully suppressed and then forgotten for a long time.[12] Likewise, it long remained little noticed that the seemingly pristine wilderness of America's national parks was subsequently and constantly renewed by media depictions of the parks and their exploration by millions of visitors. Automobile tourism created a new form of wilderness experience through the windshield, which had already attracted the masses in the interwar years but also provoked vehement opposition. This opposition found its echo in the wilderness movement, whose ideal of a lonely region far from civilization was in some ways comparable to the Swiss National Park idea.[13]

The urgency attached to protecting wilderness everywhere, the procedural character that marked its establishment both in the United States and in Switzerland, and the omnipresence of civilization, on whose advances the parks' destinies obviously depended, all point to the same frame of reference for the national park idea regardless of internal differences—(Western) modernity. This modernity was marked by three major movements: first, the interpretation of world history as a predetermined sequence of events; second, the comprehensive opening up of the whole world; and third, the cataloguing and classifying of the world based on a dual-category system.[14] The first movement was expressed in the idea of social progress, which drove both liberalism and socialism—the two dominant ideologies of Western modernity. It also figured prominently in scientific knowledge production, where it found what may perhaps be its most enduring expression in the theory of evolution.[15] Without these insights into the historical mutability of nature, the national park idea and especially the Swiss interpretation of it would have been unthinkable.

The second movement led to measurement and mapping of the entire earth's surface, and its appropriation and distribution into areas that in turn were assigned specific purposes. In this connection, the American historian Charles Maier speaks of territorialization, which he regarded as *the* key process in directing and driving global development since the 1860s. Not least, the emerging spatial structures provided important points of reference for national and ethnic identity.[16] The carving out of areas as national parks must be seen as part of this process.

The third, and final, major movement is the implementation of a dual-category system written directly into the global history of the national park. The national park was conceived as a natural space or wilderness separate from social space, that is, the space of culture or civilization. Carl Schröter, chair of the research commission of the Swiss National Park and a renowned botanist, recognized the significance of this dichotomy to the national park: "[The national park] is primarily a place where any human interference is prohibited for all time, and where alpine ur-nature can and will recover undisturbed and continue to evolve. It offers a refuge for plants and animals, a sanctuary, a sacred place for nature. Its borders serve as a breakfront for the waves of human culture flowing from every nation, which have destroyed the youthful countenance of Mother Earth: the park is a place apart from 'ecumenism,' from the sphere of colonization."[17] Simultaneously, in this essay in the German journal *Die Naturwissenschaften,* published shortly after the end of the First World War, Schröter emphasized the ethical value that a national park represents for "the people," insofar as it creates a space in which "everything is preserved for everyone for all time." The creation of a national park should "especially now be highly valued as a productive ferment in the hoped-for renewal of humanity, which has become too materialistic and selfish."[18]

The territory of the national park was clearly separated from the cultural space, but it also had to remain in contact with culture. In the 1960s the French philosopher and historian Michel Foucault coined the term "heterotopia" to describe such specialized modern spaces. In contrast to purely fictional utopias, heterotopias have a material counterpart in the real world, whose reality, however, is radically distinct from that of conventional places. As examples of such heterotopian spaces, Foucault lists (in his original but hardly systematic formulation) brothels, Jesuit colonies, and ships. These localized spaces produce a difference that makes them looking-glass versions of normal social spaces and creates a tension between the dominant culture and its spatial order.[19] The national park was clearly such a heterotopia. In its idealized form, it constituted civilization's "other": It was a modern sanctuary dedicated to nature for all eternity.[20] As an ahistorical wilderness or primeval nature, it eluded the development of civilization, but remained accessible to people. Thus, the national park was both an enclave and mirror of civilization. It fostered the illusion that not only could nature be maintained in its "original" state, free from human influence, but also that the difference between the park and the social space of cultural achievements could be measured and appraised. Moreover, the establishment of such an institution as a cultural achievement of its own was to be celebrated. In the neat separation of culture and nature, civilization and wildness, the national park revealed itself not only as a concept imbued with modernity but also as an active bearer and shaper of the modern dialectic order. Its history offers a privileged glimpse into changes in the social interaction with nature since the late nineteenth century.[21]

It follows that the boundaries between nature and culture are socially produced.[22] At no point is their course determined; rather, the social meaning of nature is always historically contingent. The separation between nature and culture is neither clear-cut nor disputed. It eludes a final determination and requires perpetual social processing. Nature and culture are thus bound in a permanent, ever-changing relationship. The historical approach is particular suited to elucidating this manifold and fascinating relationship because it enables critical analysis of category separation into nature and culture without overly hasty removal of this socially productive distinction.[23] Consequently, historical analysis leads to a deeper understanding of which social forces shaped the way society deals with nature, and which physical phenomena were incorporated into the perception of nature and how they were processed culturally. French sociologist Henri Lefebvre recognized this in his analysis of space: "It is never easy to get back from the object (product or work) to the activity that produced and/or created it. It is the only way, however, to illuminate the object's nature or, if you will, the object's relationship to nature, and reconstitute the process of its genesis and the development of its meaning."[24] Only in the historical reconstruction of an object can the essence of an object be elucidated. In the following pages, I will subject the Swiss National Park to precisely this sort of examination with the intention of reconstructing the historical processes in which the park was made into a place of alpine wilderness, and illuminate the consequences. Under which natural and social circumstances did the park arise and develop? Which discourses and practices were associated with the park, and how did they change over time? How did the web of spatial and temporal relationships in which the park was enmeshed develop? What consequences—intended as well as unintended—did the heterotopic design of a piece of landscape have for nature and society?[25]

These questions are addressed below in six thematic chapters. In chapter 1, I delve into the genesis of the national park on a global scale. Although in the nineteenth century the adoption of the national park idea was limited to the British settler colonies, where it specifically served the purpose of constructing national identity, by the beginning of the new century, it had spread to every continent. The national park became a globally useful label for nature protection. In the twentieth century, the national park in the United States was joined by other models. One of the most publicized was the Swiss National Park. Chapter 2 will consider how this park came into existence, how its concept changed over the course of its development, and what its link to the national park idea was, as well as how the Swiss park was perceived in international bodies. One of the most characteristic features of the Swiss National Park compared with other parks internationally is the strong political position occupied by local institutions from the very beginning. Chapter 3 will review why these initial constellations led neither to a frictionless political space nor to a well-oiled administrative machine, nor automatically to good acceptance of the park by the local population.

"Total protection" and scientific research were the two pillars on which the Swiss National Park was founded. The flora and fauna of the park would be protected from all human influence, and be allowed to develop "freely" and "naturally." Such an objective required comprehensive shielding of the corresponding areas, for which the term "total protection" was introduced. In chapter 4, I look at how the philosophy of total protection was interpreted and modified by the administration, as well as the similarities and differences between the concept of total protection and today's concept of protection of ecological processes. I will show, how, on the one hand, the park's original objective of total protection endured and never lost its importance as an ideological guide, but, on the other hand, how it was also largely responsible for the continuing fragility of the dichotomous distinction between civilization and wilderness. The park's human-free nature was intended as a research field with laboratory-like qualities for the ecological sciences, especially botany and zoology, as well as geology and geography. In chapter 5, I will explore why this admirable aim remained largely unmet. I will describe the institutional and disciplinary conditions affecting research efforts, and the attempts of scientists working in the park to establish more productive experimental arrangements. Despite only middling results, research at the Swiss National Park managed to attract significant attention, and contributed to the park's reputation as an exemplary "scientific national park." I will analyze this reception, as well as the increasing importance of park research in recent years.

Finally, in chapter 6, I will examine the fundamental conflicts over use that arose during the history of the Swiss National Park and that not coincidentally all came to a head during the boom years after the Second World War, when increased density of use of the landscape and the exploitation of natural resources accelerated. The national park came under pressure from different angles: First, the electricity industry developed an appetite for water power in the park area. As with Echo Park in the United States around the same time, the damming of the Spöl River in the 1950s raised basic questions of conservation. Second, private transport and the number of visitors both increased markedly after 1945. The Swiss National Park, which originally had not been established for but against conventional tourism, now had to withstand being an increasingly popular tourist destination. The term "national park" was an attractant for tourism, and almost inevitably there were conflicts with the park objectives of nature protection and research. But it was not only the number of human visitors that swelled dramatically. The deer that had migrated into the area at the time of the national park's founding were also multiplying. Signs of overgrazing of the vegetation in the park, periodic mass die-offs, and migratory behavior beyond the park's borders sparked no small degree of controversy from the 1950s onward, and resulted in hitherto neglected wildlife management becoming a central aspect of park administration. The interplay of these three land-use conflicts resulted in the park's guiding principle of total protection being called into question in the postwar years.

Despite the thematic structure of the chapters, the arguments also follow a chronological order. I proceed chronologically within each chapter, but in addition, I have organized the chapters such that their temporal focus moves steadily toward the present. The thematic organization allows me to show related motives unfolding over time and thus to identify longer-term trends and gradual shifts and to integrate them into the exposition. Because my perspective shifts along with the topics from chapter to chapter, I refer back to different mid-range theoretical approaches. Thus, I examine the invention and dissemination of the national park with the aid of recent concepts from the history of technology and global history. I analyze local conditions from the vantage of environmentality, animal actors through the lens of *Eigensinn,* and scientific park research through laboratory studies. I describe these approaches in more detail in the relevant chapters.

A topic that combines these approaches and that also recurs repeatedly in different guises is borders, or dividing lines: spatial and temporal, natural and social, mental and geographical; dividing lines between the park and the surrounding areas, nature and culture, animals and humans, laboratory and field, national and world. The bases for drawing these dividing lines are as interesting as the means by which they are maintained. What consequences and problems did such dividing lines cause, and when were borders questioned and renegotiated if necessary? In the final chapter, I focus on the findings that the study of these issues has produced. These findings constitute the foundation for a focused overview, but also provide a vantage point for a glimpse into the future.

An awareness of boundaries and spaces is also reflected in the choice of the descriptor "transnational." This descriptor retains the national dimension while at the same time putting it into context, which is especially appropriate for my purposes. The prefix "trans-" expresses the diverse forms of the process by which national space is transcended and borders thus made porous. In contrast to the term "international," which I reserve for official relationships at the state level, the term "transnational" encompasses various types of material and discursive movements that are not confined to national spaces. A transnational approach, such as is understood and applied here, is therefore not limited to a single narrative but rather strives to bring different narratives into the analysis and to examine the interactions between them.[26] This requires varying the spatial scale of the analysis, a method that historical anthropology already proposed several years ago. In this regard, historian Jacques Revel referred to a *jeux d'échelles,* a play on orders of magnitude.[27] Compared with the similarly (and also somewhat differently) used terms "global," "world," and "universal history," "transnational" has the advantage of not creating expectations that all times and places will be treated equally, which very rarely produces useful or satisfying results.[28]

In this book, I approach the Swiss National Park as a particular manifestation of a global narrative about conservation, shaped by local conditions. The Swiss National Park should not be taken to be a generalizable model for protecting areas worldwide, nor should developments at the international level automatically be seen as being relevant for the Swiss National Park. It follows that the interrelationship between the history of the Swiss National Park and the global history of conservation cannot simply be accepted as a given, but rather can only be discerned by source-based reconstruction. The park's historical reality and impact, its contexts, cycles, and continuities, must first be established through concrete, observable, and describable interconnections. According to this view, these interconnections are what drove the ongoing process of both the convergence and divergence of "local," "national," and "global." Dissecting this process through analysis and exposition is a central aim of my study, which in this respect is related to other works of global history that strive to systematically connect global and local developments.[29]

Such an approach is naturally fraught with practical difficulties arising from access to historical documents. Thus, global interconnections whose traces can be found in the local and national record collections pertaining to the Swiss National Park are easy to establish. These traces enable reconstruction of trajectories and linking of historical events. In contrast, where these sources reveal no traces, it is much harder to reconstruct associations, mainly because their effects were felt elsewhere. The search for such links becomes very labor intensive unless one is willing to accept a certain amount of randomness in the results. For this line of inquiry, rigorous search parameters proved largely unproductive. A heuristic search for plausible links proved to be more fruitful. Accordingly, I paid particular attention to contexts relating to world regions and to communications in which national parks or similar protected areas figured prominently, and where the sciences played a fundamental role (or were striving to).

For the present study, I was able to build on range of preliminary work dealing with various aspects of the history of the Swiss National Park.[30] I also profited from several excellent studies dealing with the history of national parks in other countries.[31] Very helpful, too, was the parallel work on an anthology titled *Civilizing Nature* that explores the development of the national park from the perspective of global history.[32] The starting point of the work presented here was a comprehensive search of sources comprising both a wide range of published documents and several unpublished archival collections.[33] I consulted the records of the institutions involved in the Swiss National Park in four archives: the archives of the Swiss National Park in Zernez; the archives of *Pro Natura* (the former *Schweizerischer Bund für Naturschutz*) in the Basel Canton archives, the archives of the Swiss Academy of Sciences (SCNAT, formerly the *Schweizerische Naturforschende Gesellschaft*) in the *Burgerbibliothek* in Bern, and in the Swiss federal archives (BAR), also in Bern. At the communal level, I researched the archives of Scuol and Zernez,[34] and the Grisons cantonal archives in Chur. For an American perspective on the history of the Swiss National Park, I examined the relevant records relating to the US National Park Service in the National Archives as well as collections in the Library of Congress, both in Washington, DC. I decided not to peruse the collections of the IUCN (International Union for Conservation of Nature) after preliminary investigations revealed that they would contain little of use.[35] I had access to media discourses through the digital archives of *Le Temps* and the *Times* (of London), as well as the archives of the *Neue Zürcher Zeitung* in Zurich. I searched the Memoriav database for audiovisual materials. Finally, in the archives and collections of the ETH Zurich library I sought out the documents of the school board and the papers of Carl Schröter. To supplement the written sources, I also conducted a dozen interviews.[36]

In closing, allow me to make two editorial comments: I have translated foreign-language quotations into English. For proper names, I use the spelling current today. So, for example, Scuol (not Schuls) and Cluozza (not Cluoza). Exceptions are quotations and titles of documents, where I have left the spelling of proper names unchanged.

Notes

1. See the UNEP-WCMC database: http://www.wdpa.org/Statistics.aspx, http://www.protectedplanet.net.
2. For current information, see http://www.nationalpark.ch.
3. See, for example, Schulze 1994; Anderson 1991, and on the relationship between nation-states and empires, see Leonhard and Hirschhausen 2009.
4. Cf. Conrad 2006.
5. See Nash 1980.
6. The approaches are discussed in chapter 1. See also Gissibl et al. 2012a.
7. Nash 1982, 1.
8. Classical accounts of wilderness are provided by Oelschlaeger 1991 and Schama 1995. Kirchhoff and Trepl 2009b explore the state of research in German-speaking countries. A record of the wilderness ideas circulating in Switzerland at the turn of the twenty-first century can be found in Stremlow and Sidler 2002 and Bauer 2005.
9. On different concepts of wilderness, see Wilderness Babel: http://www.environmentandsociety.org/exhibitions/wilderness/overview.
10. Reservationenkomitee SNK to Gemeinderat Zernez, 15 December 1908, in SNK annual report 1908–9, 52–57, quotation 54 f. Nearly the same wording is found in Schröter 1910, 18. At a later stage, less emphasis was placed on this process, as also happened in the United States.

11. Reservationenkomitee SNK to Gemeinderat Zernez, 15 December 1908, in SNK annual report 190-9, 52–57, quotation 54.
12. Spence 1999, 3–6. On Canada, see Sandlos 2005.
13. Grusin 2004; Louter 2006; Sutter 2002. On the National Park Service's active contribution to restoring park wilderness, see Reich 2001. The mid-1990s saw the relaxation of an intense historical debate over the American wilderness (see Cronon 1996b; Callicott 1998), which led to a definite shift in perspective. The anthology by Lewis 2007a provides an excellent view of the new perspective.
14. The nature of modernity has been a hotly debated topic for over a hundred years. The literature is correspondingly extensive. In place of a lengthy, yet still hardly representative list of publications, here are a few annotated suggestions: Bayly 2004 is an excellent historical source. An overview of the major theories of modernization can be found, for instance, in Knöbl 2007. The epistemological consequences of modernity are critically analyzed by Latour 1995, whereas Scott 1998 denounces the consequences of (hyper)modernist ideology. A basic critique of the use of modernity as a category of analysis is offered by Cooper 2005, who argues that the category of modernity is too blurry to do justice to the historical complexities. Sensible use of the term may, however, alleviate this problem.
15. See, for example, Koselleck 1994; Bowler 2003.
16. Maier 2000. Maier sees the impact of territoriality on the wane since 1970. On this topic, see also the edited volumes by Schröder and Höhler 2005; Geppert et al. 2005; and Geisthövel and Knoch 2005.
17. Schröter 1918, 753.
18. Schröter 1918, 765.
19. Foucault 1994 (1967).
20. For an anthology (of other) modern places, see Geisthövel and Knoch 2005.
21. See Gissibl et al. 2012a. On the term "civilization," see Fisch 1992; on its use around the world in the context of the European "civilizing mission," see Barth and Osterhammel 2005.
22. The separation of nature and society influenced not only the national park but also the sciences. In the late 1950s, C. P. Snow diagnosed a split of intellectual life into two cultures, one scientific and the other humanist (Snow 1967 [1959]). In the latter field, the guiding question was to what extent knowledge—including scientific knowledge—was socially constructed. This schism led, in the 1990s, to a protracted controversy between "constructivists" and "realists" (see Hacking 1999). One of the main points of contention was a debate over the social character and the social reality of nature, its material and constructivist quality, and their interactions (Cronon 1996a). A closely related question was whether and how social scientists could concede human agency independent of nature, a question that was also a hot topic in environmental history (see Sieferle 1999; Steinberg 2002b; and for an introduction to environmental history, see Hughes 2006; Uekötter 2007; Winiwarter and Knoll 2007). My own approach in this work is that of critical realism or limited constructivism, which predominates in political ecology (Neumann 2005). This approach treats nature and its constituent elements as having a reality independent of society and their own agency. However, knowledge possessed by all or part of society about nature is context-specific; it is mediated both by social discourse and by practices.

23. Here, I agree with Theodore Schatzki and not Bruno Latour, whose work argues for lifting the separation between nature and society (Schatzki 2003; Latour 1995; Latour 2005). Nor do I find Latour's proposal to symmetrically shape the activities of nature and society very convincing. For a brilliant critique of this concept, see Ingold 2008. For a study oriented to the social practices in the humanities, see Biernacki 2000.
24. Lefebvre 1991, 113. I will not go into Lefebvre's methodical approach here. See AnArchitektur 2002; Schmid 2005; Merrifield 2006.
25. On the current status of the humanities debate on space, see Döring and Thielmann 2008. The material and symbolic dimensions of space and nature are also discussed in landscape research: "Landscape is a natural scene mediated by culture. It is both a represented and presented space, both a signifier and a signified, both a frame and what a frame contains, both a real place and its simulacrum, both a package and the commodity inside the package." Mitchell 1994, 5. See Gugerli and Speich 2002; Kaufmann 2005; Lekan and Zeller 2005; Backhaus et al. 2007; Küster 2009.
26. White 1999. See also Bender 2001; Taylor 2008; Kupper 2014. On translational history, see Conrad and Osterhammel 2004; on transnational environmental history, see Evans 2010. More information is to be found in the Web forum geschichte.transnational (http://geschichte-transnational.clio-online.net). The question of interconnections between geographical spaces was also investigated (albeit under slightly different circumstances) in the debate over comparison and transfer (Kaelble 2003), in which a number of alternative terms were proposed, including *Beziehungsgeschichte* (Osterhammel 2001), entangled history (Conrad and Randeria 2002), and *histoire croisée* (Werner and Zimmermann 2006), none of which, however, has emerged a clear favorite (Gassert 2012). In these discussions, the prevailing question is the integration of geographically separate spaces; to date, overlapping spaces have attracted little interest. One appealing approach to the latter is Richard White's concept of "middle ground" (White 1991).
27. Revel 1996. The discussion was fueled in particular by the representatives of Italian microhistory. See Levi 1992; Ginzburg 1993. A major source of inspiration was Siegfried Kracauer's posthumously published book *History: The Last Things before the Last*, in which he advocates continually alternating perspective between "close-ups" and "long shots" (as in film). A competent introduction to the discussion is provided by Tanner 2004, 101–118.
28. On global and world history, see Manning 2003; Conrad et al. 2007; Osterhammel 2008. For a conventional universal history view, see Weber 2001. On the different research traditions behind the term, see Middell 2005. Global environmental history is still in its infancy. A pioneer in the area is Crosby 2004 (1st edition 1986). Krech et al. 2004 is helpful. Among the newer monographs, McNeill 2000, Radkau 2008, and Hughes 2009 all deserve mention. The anthology by Burke and Pomeranz 2009 attempts to bridge the gap between world and environmental history. For a synthesis of these and other works, see Marks 2010. Attempts to capture the global environmental movement include McCormick 1995, Guha 2000, and most recently Radkau 2011.
29. For example, Bayly 2004; Cooper 2005; Hopkins 2006; Conrad 2006. The mutual constitution of local and global spaces is also discussed under the term "glocalization" (Robertson 1995). The history of the US national parks was recently interpreted in this way. See Tyrrell 2012 and the contributions to the discussion therein by Astrid Swen-

son, Paul S. Sutter, and Thomas R. Dunlap. See also the project National Parks Beyond the Nation: http://nationalparksbeyondthenation.wordpress.com.
30. Relevant works include Parolini 2012a; Bachmann 1999; Fritsche 2002. A good overview of the Swiss National Park is provided by the handbook article by Haller 2006. Other references are provided in the appropriate chapters.
31. For example, Runte 1987; Carruthers 1995; Mels 1999, as well as the overviews by Adams 2004, Jones and Wills 2005, Sheail 2010. On international nature protection up to 1950, see Wöbse 2012a.
32. Gissibl et al. 2012a.
33. For a detailed listing, see the bibliography.
34. Mirta Nicolay provided invaluable help in exploring and evaluating the Romansh sources.
35. In response to my query, the IUCN stated that its archive is private. Moreover, all the manuscript collections were destroyed by fire several years ago (communication with the author). According to Holdgate, for reasons unknown, Jean Baer had already burned many IUCN records during the 1961 move from the organization's headquarters in Brussels to Switzerland. Holdgate 1999, 77.
36. The interviews are listed in the bibliography.

 CHAPTER 1

Global Parks
National Parks, Globalization, and Western Modernism

"Πολλὰ τὰ δεινὰ κ' οὐδὲν ἀνθρώπου δεινότερον πέλει" (Wonders are many, and none is more wonderful than man). These words, from Sophocles' tragedy *Antigone*, were the first to echo through the chamber of the National Council, the larger of the two houses of the Swiss Parliament, shortly after 8 o'clock on the morning on 25 March 1914.[1] Suddenly, it was clear to everyone (even those still half asleep) that the day's business would be anything but ordinary. "From the start," reported the *Neue Zürcher Zeitung*, Walter Bissegger's "presentation, which excelled in both content and form, put the parliamentary assembly in that exalted mood conducive to supporting ideational propositions."[2] At issue was a "federal law to establish a Swiss national park in the Lower Engadine" that in draft form foresaw an area to be specified for the "protection of all animal and plant life from human influence."[3]

Bissegger had chaired the parliamentary commission that prepared the item for the National Council. Now, his task was to present the proposed bill. Although the reporter of the *Neue Zürcher Zeitung* was not entirely impartial to the speaker—Bissegger was, after all, the paper's editor-in-chief—there can be no doubt that the chair's rhetorically polished delivery impressed his fellow councilors. The most vivid illustration of human greatness, said Bissegger, expanding on his opening statement, "is the fact that, once humans had become the absolute rulers of the earth and their fellow creatures, they felt compelled to protect those creatures to some degree against their own power and depravity by erecting barriers to create plant and animal sanctuaries, sacred spaces for nature."[4]

Thus, Bissegger situated the idea of a national park in the larger context of human history. Man had won the battle for existence and achieved dominion over the earth. But his omnipotence obliged him to act responsibly and to assure the well being of other living beings. According to Bissegger, these noble thoughts gave rise to the international conservation movement, and by extension to the matter at hand. Everything was in order, Bissegger told his colleagues, referring to the thorough work of his commission. The "question you must decide is ultimately a fundamental one: Do we wish to provide a sanctuary for animals and plants, protected insofar as possible from human impact, a preserve in which for 100 years all commercial use, foresting, grazing, and hunting will stop, in which no chopping or shooting will be heard ever again, and where domestic animals may not encroach?"[5]

The content of the presentation and the debate that ensued in parliament will be discussed in the next chapter. Here, I address the global issues that so occupied Bissegger. On which knowledge did Bissegger base his parliamentary address? What historical convergence enabled him to see that in 1914 humankind was at a turning point, and to call for a fundamentally new direction? And what convinced him that a "national park" was the perfect mechanism for this realignment? Answering these questions requires pulling together developmental strands from very different temporal and spatial dimensions, and understanding their mutual effects. With Fernand Braudel one could tackle the problem by applying two categories of time: *longue durée,* for gradual societal shifts, and *courte durée,* which refers to abrupt changes, most of which actually have little effect from a long-term perspective.[6] Adding a theory of social learning, such as that suggested by Hansjörg Siegenthaler for the industrial era, further helps to explain why certain short-term phases of history are marked by sudden larger changes that do have far-reaching, long-term effects.[7] Such short-term phases are characterized by deep uncertainties within society, widespread discussion of societal crises, and for these very reasons are particularly open to change. In the years preceding the First World War, the Western world was going through just such a phase, idealized as the *Belle Époque* and lamented as the *Fin de Siècle.*

In these first years of the twentieth century, not only was the idea for a Swiss national park developed and realized. As I will show, the term "national park" also acquired global meaning that, in the following decades, would be the basis of powerful, consequential conservation initiatives at the international, imperial, and national level. Focusing on this formative phase of the global significance of national parks entails a shift in the thematic as well as the spatial and temporal links. In seeking to reconstruct the conditions under which the national park idea gained form and momentum globally, the question of who invented it (a discussion that is hardly enlightening in any event) is superfluous.[8]

This shift in focus also brings into play an approach that has recently been promoted by both global history and history of technology. The previous practice of separating developments into phases of discovery and dissemination proved inadequate for historical events. First, the seemingly original invention itself builds on assumptions and thus on previous events. Second, it became clear that simple diffusion models do not suffice to explain how inventions spread. Rather, the dissemination of an invention always implies its transformation. Consequently, the history of social and technological innovation now focuses not on inventors and their inventions but rather on the communicative processes of negotiation that both support and, even more important, literally shape these developments.[9] Thus, media and forums for social negotiation move to the center of attention.

Chief among the themes to emerge from this turn is the question of the authorship of ideas. Both self-stylization and labeling processes are discursive devices conducive to constructing a master narrative that is highly persuasive and that in turn facilitates the selection and ordering of events. Thus, the idea acquires a quasi-official history that includes a distinct starting point. Through subsequent editing of the narrative, an origin myth emerges that imbues the idea with a social context and a particular identity. For over a century, advocates (and, increasingly, critics) of the national park idea have invoked such an origin myth: the founding of Yellowstone in 1872, which promoted the idea of the national park, and which became the template for countless copies around the world. The preoccupation with this origin myth, its powerful influence, and its (de)construction constitute a preface to what follows on the emergence of the national park as a global phenomenon.

The Myth of Yellowstone

"In 1872, few men had vision enough to foresee that newly established Yellowstone National Park embodied not the end, but only the beginning of the *national park idea,*" proclaimed a report on the one hundredth birthday of Yellowstone National Park in 1972.[10] Even today, for many Yellowstone represents the start not only of the global history of national parks but also (and especially) of officially designated conservation areas. This view of Yellowstone as the lodestar of a worldwide conservation movement has recently come under fire. According to social scientists Dan Brockington, Rosaleen Duffy, and Jim Igoe, international conservationists made Yellowstone into their own founding myth. Moreover, centering the movement in the Western world and especially in the United States served not least to establish and perpetuate the movement's balance of power. The authors propose three arguments why using Yellowstone in this way is a mistake. First, Yellowstone is a problematic model because it originated the practice of driving indigenous peoples from national parks. Second, choosing Yellowstone as a starting point sidelined older forms of territorial protection. For example, in earlier times throughout the world, ruling dynasties conferred special protection to religious sites and hunting grounds. Finally, the enshrining of Yellowstone represented only those activities that were undertaken at the state level and executed in writing. Local and regional protective measures by smaller social groups or illiterate societies were systematically excluded.[11] The criticism by Brockington et al. is justified, but not sufficient. A diffusion history anchored in Yellowstone is questionable not only because of the dubious moral character of its ground zero and because of what it leaves out, but also because of what it purports to depict. It suggests both historical continuity and linear and homogeneous development that, as I will show, is inconsistent with the history of protected areas.

To test this hypothesis, it is worthwhile first to cast an impartial glance at Yellowstone in 1872. In that year, the U.S. Congress declared a 3,300-square-mile-wide area as a "public park or pleasuring-ground." The term "national park" did not appear in the official decree, which would cause an uproar a hundred years later at a delicate historical moment. In 1972 the United States hosted the Second World Conference on National Parks. The international conservation community was invited to Yellowstone to celebrate the park's centennial. It was only during the preparations for the event that the term's omission in the founding documents was discovered. The US authorship of the national park idea was suddenly thrown into doubt and so was the celebration's choreography. The matter was soon cleared up to the organizer's satisfaction. The descriptor "national park" had been used for Yellowstone from its inaugural year, though legally the term "national park" only took on meaning decades later through consistent application.[12]

Two determining features made Yellowstone a model for later national parks: the magnitude of the protected area and the fact that protection was under the aegis of the highest public authority. However, in 1872 neither of these aspects was front and center; rather, both were byproducts of the park's creation. The extent of the protection was the result not of a vision of conservation but simply ignorance of the site. Contemporary debates left no doubt that the protection did not apply to integral habitats but to individual natural wonders: geysers, gorges, and waterfalls. These were to be excluded from private commerce and secured for the public. Because the wonders were still insufficiently mapped and the entire area was considered largely worthless economically, Congress drew the park boundaries generously. The second major feature, the federal solution, also stemmed from the fact that the targeted area extended over US territories—Montana and Wyoming—neither of which was yet a state. In his definitive work on the history of American national parks, Alfred Runte concluded that any resemblance of 1872 Yellowstone to modern concepts was completely unintentional. With respect to this shift in meaning, Roderick Nash notes that, for once, ideas followed actions. This finding—the absence of the later ideological structure at the founding of Yellowstone—did not prevent Nash from representing Yellowstone as the nucleus of a conventional diffusion history and celebrating the national park as an "American contribution to world culture."[13]

Without this ahistorical anticipation of eventual appreciation in value, the establishment of Yellowstone appears far less revolutionary. Moreover, continuities are visible that were obscured by the later narrative overlay. In particular, one of Runte's meticulously traced threads leads to Yosemite State Park, founded in 1864, and from there to the urban parks that appeared in large American cities around the middle of the nineteenth century. The term "public park," adopted for Yellowstone, refers to this park tradition. The American city park was inspired by the somewhat older European urban parks, which in turn built on an early modern aristocratic park tradition. In emphasizing public access, the American park concept explicitly distanced itself from this aristocratic legacy. Whether city, state, or national park, the American park would not be reserved for any exclusive stratum but rather open to all citizens regardless of who they were. This democratic impetus shaped American park history. But it did not prevent the rampant social and racial discrimination of the larger society from entering the park. The national parks long remained de facto places for the white middle class, while other groups were shut out or even expelled from park-designated areas.[14]

A second thread, similarly characterized by a dialectic of continuity and segregation, combines the early American national park with the European tradition of monuments. A goal of Yosemite and Yellowstone was to preserve natural wonders that were of both public and national interest. Monumental nature was the answer of the American cultural and traditional elite to the European nationalist cult of monuments. The natural history wonders of the American West would occupy the place that in European nations was allotted to their achievements—cultural history, ruins, castles, and cathedrals. Their wonders should fill Americans with patriotic pride and impress other nations. As Runte put it, the invention of the national park gave expression to a deeply felt lack of cultural identity, an inferiority complex vis-à-vis Europe reinforced by sharp European criticism prompted by the commercialization of Niagara Falls, the first major tourist attraction in the United States. The newly discovered natural wonders of the West would dispel all that. The aim of the inventors of the national park was to present to the (European) world a sophisticated, singular America in the form of impressive landscapes. The European framework for these efforts is evident not least in the numerous contemporary accounts in which the American natural wonders are compared with buildings and landscapes on the old continent. "Why should we go to Switzerland to see mountains or to Iceland for geysers?" the *New York Herald* asked its readers in 1872. "Thirty years ago the attraction of America to the foreign mind was Niagara Falls. Now we have attractions which diminish Niagara into an ordinary exhibition."[15]

Nature as National Symbol

In Europe, too, newspapers reported the creation of Yellowstone's national park. In 1873, under the headline "A Very National Park," the London *Times* noted the new institution and provided a detailed listing of its "curiosities": "The wonders of Yellowstone include geysers, in comparison with which the geysers of Iceland are insignificant; hot springs, vapour springs, mud springs, and mud volcanoes; falls of 350 feet in height; cañons of 5000 feet in depth; streams … ; and mountain and rock scenery." As a large part of the park was still unexplored, other marvels might be discovered, "for there seems no limit to the freaks which Nature … has played and continues to play in this wonderful region." At the time, visits to the park could be made only on horseback, over difficult bridle paths. But there were no insuperable obstacles to future construction of carriage roads and a railway. On animal or plant life the article was silent.[16]

Yellowstone was similarly received in Switzerland, where both French- and German-language newspapers reported the founding of the American national park. As did the *Times* (and also contemporary American reports), the broadsheets emphasized the marvelous world of hot springs and geysers. "A new region of thermal springs is currently attracting the attention of the geographical world," wrote the *Journal de Genève* in 1872. The *Neue Zürcher Zeitung* described the area as inhospitable and mountainous and thus ill suited to livestock or mining. "The hot springs and geysers delight the eye of the beholder not only as something wonderful to look at but also through the miraculous power of their waters to give health and new vitality to the sick. So much so that in a few years, the national park will have become a place where people in search of healing will flock from all over the world; in an area that until then had been totally uninhabited, rarely visited by Indians, and up to just a few years ago by no civilized people."[17] Nor was the *Neue Zürcher Zeitung* wrong in its prediction. In fact, Yellowstone became a public bath facility, and bathing in the hot springs was allowed until well into the twentieth century. Yellowstone's distance from civilization and seemingly unspoiled nature were a source of fascination, though the perception was false. Native American groups roamed the area seasonally, collecting plants, hunting, and fishing. Following the establishment of the national park, those activities were prevented by the military, thus bringing about the seemingly untouched-by-humans landscape that would become a hallmark of Yellowstone.[18]

In the 1870s and 1880s, national parks were founded in Canada, New Zealand, and Australia. Each of these British settler societies interpreted the American model in their own way, with the first Australian national park in Sydney more strongly oriented to the periurban parks of London's imperial metropolis than to the park far from the city in the American West. Together, these developments represent initiatives that placed the exploitation of tracts of land under state control.[19] Whether in those years similar efforts were being made somewhere in Europe is not known. The guiding principle behind the establishment of Yellowstone—to remove natural features of the landscape from the reach of commerce through state control and make them accessible as a public good—argues against such initiatives. The possession of land in Europe was usually clearly defined and was mainly in private or communal hands and, apart from state forests in certain countries, was rarely under the control of the central government. The potential for a nation-state to demonstrate ownership of disputed land by designating it a national park was exploited by Europe only in the twentieth century. Early examples include the establishment of national parks in areas of Sweden inhabited by the Sami (Lapp) people since 1909, and Stelvio National Park, created in 1935 by fascist Italy in formerly Austrian territory.[20]

Another factor was that, in European countries, nature had less national symbolic value than it did in the United States. In Europe, government promotion of national identities focused on cultural institutions and events: maintaining monuments and traditions, funding the arts, and national museums and fairs. Some measures, in particular regarding cultural heritage, involved protection of areas, for example, the Prussian government's purchase of Drachenfels at Königswinter in 1836. The preservation of the Rütli meadow by Lake Lucerne as a national memorial in Switzerland came very close to the basic plan for Yellowstone. With the successful propagation of a new national historiography that situated the origin of the nation well back into the Middle Ages, in the nineteenth century the Rütli became the birthplace of Switzerland. It was said to be the site, where, in 1291, in a conspiratorial meeting, the three "original Swiss cantons" of Schwyz, Uri, and Unterwalden swore an eternal oath of allegiance thereby giving rise to the Swiss Confederation. In the 1850s, plans for a hotel were drawn up to serve as a window on this defining setting. To prevent that from happening, the Swiss Public Welfare Society bought the land with money acquired through nationwide fundraising and in 1860 entrusted it to the federal government as an "inalienable national resource."[21]

The display of a common cultural heritage would make a nation palpable. From this vantage, nature was interesting first and foremost as a cultural landscape that reflected national characteristics. The relative importance attached to dramatization of a landscape by a nascent national iconography tended to increase in the absence of any other single objectification and thus naturalization of obvious commonalities such as language, race, or origin. In addition, in the United States, the national identification with nature following the Civil War was particularly useful because of its neutral character. American nature was there before the first settlers, and was at its finest not in the southern or northern states, but in the western territories, a place synonymous with American pioneering spirit. In a typical example of nationalistic myth making, at a time when its colonial exploration was drawing to an end, the West was becoming the cradle of America, "Nature's Nation" (Perry Miller).[22] In Western Europe, Switzerland's cultural heterogeneity and conflict-ridden recent past predisposed it to conceive national identity in a common political space. In addition to the historical myth making, in the Swiss federal state, which had only just been created in 1848 through civil war, land was a major resource in building a unified nation. Here was the chance to adopt a discourse around landscape that had its roots in the learned circles of eighteenth-century Europe. Influenced by the essays and travelogues of authors such as Albrecht von Haller, Jean-Jacques Rousseau, and Johann Wolfgang Goethe, the Alps were transformed into the Swiss landscape per se, in which the noble shepherd led a frugal but unhindered life. The aestheticization of the alpine setting and the idealizing of its inhabitants were absorbed into the national self-description of Switzerland and the Swiss. Switzerland was alpine, and the Alps were Swiss, even though only a small and ever decreasing number of people lived in the mountain regions, and statistically the Swiss portion of the Alps constituted no more than 15 percent. Throughout the nineteenth century and into the twentieth, the Swiss Alps claimed without challenge to be the most sublime landscape in Europe. They became the preferred destination of the emerging waves of middle-class cross-border tourism, which further strengthened the awesome image of the Swiss Alps and propagated it around the world along with corresponding travel literature. Also the Americans favored to measure their mountains against the Swiss Alps. In 1874, Mount Rainer, in Washington State, was characterized as "mountain scenery in quantity and quality sufficient to make half a dozen Switzerlands."[23] And several areas of the Rocky Mountains were touted as the "Switzerland of America." Samuel Bowles used the label in 1869 for his popular book describing his trip through the Colorado Rockies. Of the later national parks, the Glacier and Rocky Mountain national parks in particular styled themselves as "Swiss."[24] The omnipresent reference to the Swiss Alps, in turn, further stimulated international tourism to Switzerland. In the second half of the nineteenth century tourist entrepreneurs eagerly promoted and developed the country's alpine destinations, and tourism became an important branch of the national economy.[25]

Despite this national pride in the Alps and their importance for tourism, it would not have occurred to anybody to place the mountains under government protection. Nor did anyone raise any particular objections to commercializing the Alps. Instead, there was a rush to exploit their potential tourism through development of transportation and hotel infrastructure. The objective of government policy, both enlightened and utilitarian, was the rational exploitation of natural resources. Overexploitation was to be prevented, to which end the Swiss government was endowed with additional powers in the revised constitution of 1874. This gave the state the ultimate oversight of the mountain forests, whose uncontrolled denuding, in the opinion of forestry experts, was responsible not only for landslides and avalanches but also lowland flooding. This same period also saw the establishment of the first federally sponsored

Illustration 1. Switzerland? Promotion of Glacier National Park by NPS in 1933. Swiss-styled chalets and waitresses were part of the endeavor to create an illusion of being in the Swiss Alps. *Source:* US National Park Service, George A. Grant Collection.

hunting law, which made a significant distinction between "useful" and "dangerous" animals. The law enabled the government to temporarily set up hunting districts—known as *Freiberge*—where game populations could be replenished and then re-released for hunting. Predators, of course, were excluded from protection. The same spirit guided federal regulation of fisheries.[26]

An exception to the prevailing utilitarian ethos was the simultaneous effort to protect flora and so-called glacial erratics (boulders), and in which aesthetic and patriotic impulses converged with enthusiasm for the Alps and natural history in an urge to conserve nature. The perspective of these conservation pioneers was, however, limited. Characteristic "Swiss" alpine plants such as edelweiss and alpenrose were high on priority lists. Some cantons enacted plant-protection ordinances that, because they were mainly funded by private initiatives, ruled out smaller protected areas. The first alpine gardens were also established, motivated not least by tourism. A veritable swell of popular support drove protection of glacial erratics. Around the mid-nineteenth century, a theory positing that the stones and boulders of the central region of Switzerland had been carried there by Ice Age glaciers was widely accepted.[27] Consequently, also for interested laypeople, these objects were clearly accessible evidence of both natural history and the history of the country. The popularity of glacial erratics was instrumental to the founding of the Swiss National Park. Yet this connection also had an element of randomness. When, at the start of the twentieth century, an outstanding example of a boulder was facing destruction, the Swiss Society for Naturalists became embroiled in a turbulent rescue operation. In the wake of that episode, the society founded a commission that, as I will show in the next chapter, constituted a crucial advance not only for conservation but also for the goal of a national park.[28]

The Value of "Unspoiled" Nature

Out of the earthly struggle for existence, Bissegger told his colleagues in the National Council in 1914, man had emerged as the undisputed master. "He has cultivated the majority of the earth for his benefit, and has labored tirelessly to continue and to complete his work." In past centuries the Swiss, too, had "with unflagging zeal and little regard to cost" corrected rivers and creeks, dried up swamps and marshes, and deforested even the steepest slopes of the mountains. "But the righteous joy of achievement has recently been tinged with bitterness and something akin to remorse for the price we have paid, the dying out of animal species that were once of the pride of our land, the bear, the ibex, the vulture—and nearly the eagle—to name only the greatest and most impressive; the obliteration of our corrected waters, the diminution of our songbirds, and the extinction of noble plant species."

Bissegger was essentially describing a threefold transformation. He weighed the corralling of nature and the needs of humans with the losses that this corralling of nature entailed, and the loss of experience for society, which gave the entire progress of civilization a bitter taste. In so doing, Bissegger summed up an environmental transformation that began in the eighteenth century and that over time fundamentally altered not only society and the environment but also society's perception of the environment. Now, in addition to the threat the environment posed for people, people posed a threat to the environment. In the early 1930s, Viennese political economist Otto Neurath described this turnabout in striking terms: "In the past, when man met a swamp, the man disappeared; but now the swamp disappears."[29] And not only that: Increasingly, a swamp that had not yet disappeared was being transformed from a hostile place to a place one hankered for, from a dystopia to a heterotopia.[30]

What forces drove the rise in societal estimation of unspoiled nature? The answers, which can be found in the extensive literature on this subject, can be grouped into four strands.[31] First, in economic terms, the development resulted from the scarcity of a good—"unspoiled nature"—in the nineteenth century. In the course of industrialization and the concomitant intensification and expansion of mining, agriculture, and forestry, the amount of land not committed to production decreased. The world's population was growing, and European settlers in particular were scouting the globe for ever more contiguous settlements. New transportation technologies, in particular, the steamship and railway, not only transformed the world of markets but also increased human mobility and, not least, created the infrastructural basis for the emerging middle-class tourism industry. And tourism in turn, through a dialectical process, increased the demand for "unspoiled nature," which justified its provision. Scientific exploration and topographic surveying of the world helped to remove the last blank spots from the increasingly ubiquitous maps. At the beginning of the twentieth century, only the poles and a few mountain peaks had not yet been explored by Europeans. In the apt yet trenchant words of the French geographer Jean Brunhes, penned in 1909, "the limits of our cage" had been reached.[32]

Second, a new perception of nature had been emerging since the late eighteenth century. Romanticism ushered in an aesthetic appreciation of nature and turned it into a moral issue. Jean-Jacques Rousseau and others became pioneers of a new way of looking at nature, which sees nature as both the physical basis of life and as having an intrinsic value that liberates nature and engages with it. Outdoor experiences took on a transcendental quality and were perceived as enriching and morally uplifting. Mountain or coastal landscapes that previously had received little attention—and then, most often as barriers to traffic—became worthy travel destinations in themselves. Aside from philosophy, the natural sciences, too, were busy constructing a new perception of nature. In the 1800s, the Christian story of creation, which had shaped the image of nature in Europe for centuries, came under pressure. Scientific discoveries and findings, especially Charles Darwin's epochal *Origin of Species* in 1859, were increasingly less compatible with biblical tradition. The world was evidently not only much older than previously thought, it had also changed significantly over time. This insight increased interest in the history of nature and of places where such history could be studied. These destinations acquired the aura of shrines, and the spirituality found in nature had the power to replace the creeds and services associated with the bible and religious bodies. Nonetheless, Christian belief and the new appreciation of nature often came together and were expressed through the sacralization of the Alps in the nineteenth century, when one peak after another was adorned with a cross.[33]

Third, the new interest in nature did not spread evenly within society. Rather, natural ethics and the natural sciences flourished in a specific milieu that took shape simultaneously in the industrializing Western countries: the urban educated middle class.[34] From this stratum came the great majority of thinkers and scientists who revolutionized the image of nature and later also supported the conservation movement. In addition to its enlightened attitude, this social stratum also acquired a degree of prosperity that allowed its members to pursue ideas beyond those concerned with meeting basic needs. The educated classes that we encounter in the history of conservation did not stop at their personal studies of nature; they read Rousseau and Darwin and met up in scientific societies. They reveled in nature and developed through their scientific excursions a keen sense for changes in the landscape. Nature conservation found the objects of its desire in peripheral rural areas, whereas its elites and its base came from urban households.

The fourth and final interpretive strand is the process of establishing territories, which took on a new character with imperialism and the building of nation-states.[35] On the one hand, the existing colonial powers and countries aspiring to the global stage, such as Germany, Italy, the United States, and Japan (and, rather bizarrely, the Belgian king) not only nearly completely divided the world among themselves; they also tried, with the aid of modern science and technology, to bind their old and new colonies more strongly to the colonial center and to bring them under their rule. On the other hand, nation-states gave rise to government territories that became an important reference point for the formation of national identity. In the common space "imagined communities" became rooted.[36] Biological determinism allowed deduction of national characteristics from the living space, and the national community could be founded in natural history. The geographical unity of the country virtually guaranteed the unique character of the population.[37] As already mentioned, this model of identity had its fullest effect in nations that possessed few measurable commonalities. In the United States, the national parks were "vignettes of primitive America," whereas in Switzerland their purpose was to create spaces in which "Old Helvetia" could rise again.[38]

The Global Conservation Movement

All these processes continued to have an effect for many decades. In contrast, nature conservation as an organized movement arose within only a relatively short period of time—less than a generation. Between 1890 and 1914, in Europe, North America, and among the white populations of European colonies, associations formed and pledged themselves to the cause of preserving nature. Although at its founding in 1891, the Sierra Club stood more or less alone, by 1910 the United States boasted around twenty nature conservation organizations.[39] The United Kingdom saw the founding of the National Trust in 1895 and the Society for the Preservation of the Wild Fauna of the Empire in 1903. And at the turn of the century, on the European continent, conservation organizations emerged in quick succession. The German *Bund für Vogelschutz* and the German-Austrian *Verein Naturschutzpark*, the French *Société pour la Protection des Paysages*, the Dutch *Vereeniging tot Behoud von Natuurmonu-*

menten, the Swiss *Bund für Naturschutz,* and the Italian *Lega Nazionale per la Protezione dei Monumenti Naturali,* for example, were all founded between 1899 and 1913. This list is hardly exhaustive.[40]

These organizations shared not only the time window of their creation but also their social roots in the urban middle class, a world view influenced as much by enlightenment as by romantic tradition, and an appeal to universalist understanding of the modern natural sciences. The new movement feared the loss of nature and demanded its protection, and was clever enough to support that demand with patriotic and nationalist arguments. That momentum, built up in the nineteenth century, exploded in the twentieth, was not accidental. In double hindsight, the early conservation movement was a product of the years in which the processes of globalization were not only increasingly obvious in the movement of peoples, material, and media, but also increasingly critically viewed. It was mainly Western middle-class elites who developed an awareness that was decisive for the synchronous appearance worldwide of nature conservation as well as for its being perceived as an issue. Thus, toward the end of the nineteenth century, many people experienced the world for the first time as a single, coherent entity. The transnational stream of people and goods, information and capital reached a mass hitherto unknown, supported by new technologies—the telegraph, railway, and steamship—that revolutionized communications and transportation. Time and space seemed to shrink.[41] In European countries, rapidly expanding literacy gave rise to a new middle-class public that expressed itself in a flourishing press. As a byproduct of imperialism, the colonial powers increasingly established a European-trained middle-class elite outside Europe that shared European values and ideas about the world.[42]

The pioneers of nature conservancy came from this educated middle-class elite, which endorsed the global view of the world. At the same time, they clung to the thinking and ways of dealing with the political structures of the time, influenced by a dynamic juxtaposition of nation-states and (mainly European) empires as well as an energetic internationalism. In the latter, contemporaries optimistically saw great progress for humanity. But vision of the future that prevailed prior to 1914 was not, for instance, the establishment of supranational structures but rather international coordination and assimilation of nationally constituted units that went unchallenged as organizational building blocks.[43] The goal of a national park was perfectly compatible with this conception of global order. "Thus, if it can be integrated with broader conservation efforts that are now beginning to stir the entire world, the national park represents a fine model of advantageously adapting big international ideas at the national level," stated Swiss Federal Councilor Felix-Louis Calonder in Parliament in March 1914.[44]

Around the turn of the century, the ongoing globalization and industrialization push sparked a wave of societal uncertainty that sociologist Peter Wagner has called the "first crisis of modernity."[45] With the rapid pace of change, everyday patterns of perceiving the world and acting in it became quickly obsolete. The rescaling of spatiotemporal perceptions precipitated a feeling of loss. The way of thinking was no longer contained by geographical limits, nor was the flow of goods and people. Nervousness and rashness, overstimulation and meaninglessness figured among the much-maligned time-related phenomena. Both Europe and America fell equally prey to neurasthenia and fears of degeneration. The Expressionist movement gave oppressive, lasting expression to this unease, whereas Cubism, in particular, attempted to capture the rapid change and multiplication of perspectives, while at the same time associating them with basic forms. Wilhelm Conrad Röntgen's x-rays and Marie Curie's radioactivity, Max Planck's quanta, and Albert Einstein's relativity theory shook the edifice of Newtonian physics to its very foundations, even as Sigmund Freud's psychoanalysis explored suppressed and repressed lives and made them fodder for social debate. In no time at all, the world had become more complex, uncertain of where it stood, orientation more difficult, and the half-life of convictions shorter. The French sociologist Henri Lefebvre spoke of a "decline of the referential," a solid linguistic and social anchor for everyday life that prevailed from 1905 to 1910.[46] In view of the towering uncertainty, many contemporaries went in search of support and direction, and joined one of the numerous movements that cropped up in those years of social turbulence: one of the many new religious confraternities, one or another flavor of "life reform," a women's club, or an association for cultural heritage or nature conservancy.[47]

With their analyses of the assets and state of Western civilization, the conservationists both stimulated societal uncertainty and capitalized on the existential personal and social soul searching that it triggered. Attitudes toward nature became a basic theme of this introspection. As societal changes piled up, nature provided a salutary permanence, a still point in the turning world. "Thousands of tired, nerve-shaken, over-civilized people are beginning to find out that going to the mountain is going home," wrote John Muir, the pioneer of the American conservation movement, on the first page of *Our National Parks*, in 1901.[48] Twenty years later Carl Schröter, the co-founder of the Swiss National Park, similarly described the primary purpose of a national park as "re-creating the impression of *Heimatnatur* [native nature]; procuring for the agitated modern populace a quiet enjoyment of nature."[49] Muir, Schröter, and many others lamented the loss of an intimate relationship with nature and saw in it not only the dark side of civilized progress but a moral threat to civilization itself. By losing its connection with nature, civilization, so the subtext of the argument went, was sawing through its own branch. The rupture of the branch would cut the lifeline of civilization, separate it from its organic roots, and thus from the natural source of its renewal. Excluding areas from exploration and civilization and preserving their "authenticity" would maintain these sources and simultaneously put the stamp of civilization on them. Thus, in 1914, "the pedagogical and ethical side of the new direction" was especially close to Bissegger's heart. "The very idea fills me with joy that, one day, father, mother, and child will be able to wander for hours, refraining from plucking flowers and tossing them away, that the edelweiss on Alp Murtèr and in [Val] Cluoza may grow, bloom, and fade without any tourist ... cramming his backpack with the immaculate plants." Who, Bissegger asked his fellow councilors, could not be sufficiently moved by this beautiful vision of the future to sing, with Schiller's Spirit of the Mountain: "Earth has room for all to dwell."[50] The horrors of the First World War gave extra weight to this cultural critique. The Swiss National Park, said Schröter in 1918, "must already be seen as a productive result in the hoped-for renewal process of overly materialistic, overly egoistic humankind."[51]

The risk to mental and physical health associated with the process of civilization was not believed to affect all social classes equally. Urbanites, softened by modern city living, were especially susceptible. Confrontation with the wild forces of nature preferably at an early age and periodically repeated was an excellent way of restoring masculinity and countering the latent feminization of society, which (to make matters worse) also threatened the nation's military might.[52] This link between urban civilization and vanishing manhood was largely responsible for the fact that protection of "wild nature" became nearly exclusively a male affair. Nowhere were social opportunities for women so restricted as in nature conservation. Their field of activity was primarily limited to animal welfare, and in particular the protection of birds, where female commitment combined to advantage with motherly empathy for the magisterial creatures and criticism of consumerism, such as the contemporary woman's taste for furs and feathered hats.[53]

National Parks and Natural Monuments

At the center of modern nature conservation, as it stood at the turn of the twentieth century, were two moral issues: the preservation of unspoiled nature or wilderness sites, and the protection of plant and animal species from extinction. In this context, extensive, contiguous protected areas took on new meaning. In the United States, in the late nineteenth century, the contours of a national park were already emerging. Yellowstone was the first, and was to become a global model of nature protection and a founding myth of the international conservation movement. No longer was it merely spectacular views and quirky curiosities that merited protection but entire landscapes, including their flora and fauna. This expanded perspective drew added impetus from the rapidly growing idea of the 1890s that, with the end of the westward-oriented continental push, a chapter in American history was coming to a close. A frontier-less America would be a different America. The national parks addressed the resulting cultural insecurity by offering what seemed to be an opportunity to preserve a piece of American wilderness as the early settlers had encountered it. Protection of original landscapes would in turn preserve the cultural heritage of the already mythical figure of the frontiersman—that embodiment of typically male virtues such as energy, endurance, and resourcefulness—and enable future generations of Americans to share the frontier experience. The nascent conservation movement supported this interpretation, as did the railroads, which sensed a business opportunity in opening up outlying areas for leisure travelers. Together they developed the line of argument, soon to dominate the discourse, that in view of the expected proceeds from tourism, national parks in certain areas offered the best option from an economic standpoint, and the national economy was still attracting money that up to that point American holiday travelers had been spending in Europe. In the twentieth century, this utilitarian argument formed the basis for establishing a national park system that assigned a central role to visitors and their recuperative needs. The experimental character of the first decades eventually gave way to a firm ideological structure that bestowed on the US national parks their unique identity.[54]

In turn-of-the-century Europe and the European colonies, too, after hundreds of years of expansion, "frontiers" everywhere were disappearing, from the tropical forests to the polar regions, and from the deserts to the mountains.[55] In this context, Yellowstone underwent a process of renewed discovery both inside and outside the United States. Beginning with the 1880s, in addition to the hot springs and geysers, the parks increasingly took on a function as refuge for the last American bison and other endangered species.[56] In the colonial discourse, Yellowstone now emerged as a plausible model for the establishment of game preserves in Africa. The rapid depletion of African megafauna, especially elephants, had startled European researchers, big-game hunters, and colonial authorities. In London in 1900, the European colonial powers agreed a convention "for the preservation of wild animals, birds, and fish in Africa." Although the convention itself never came into force, it promoted the designation of wildlife preserves in several African colonies.[57]

The reception of the American national park was hindered by the negative image of America nurtured by the European elite. America stood primarily for shallow commercialism. However, this image could also work to the benefit of national parks: Contrasting the idealistic goal of the national park with materialistic Yankee capitalism gave creating the European equivalent a cultural urgency. Wilhelm Wetekamp may have been the first to use this strategy when, in 1898, in the Prussian House of Representatives, he portrayed

North America "whose materialism would otherwise be a dreadful deterrent" as a model to be emulated and called for the establishment of "state parks" in Prussia that would "serve as monuments to the developmental history of nature."[58] Wetekamp's offensive was heeded by the Prussian Ministry of Culture, albeit hesitantly.[59] The follow-up, undertaken by Hugo Conwentz, a biologist and director of the provincial museum in Danzig, did not, however, adhere to the model of the American national parks. Rather, in a memorandum that appeared in 1904, Conwentz focused on so-called natural monuments as witnesses to original nature in all its diversity. In so doing, he made reference to no other than the father of German natural history, Alexander von Humboldt, who had used the term "natural monument" in one of his travelogues. According to Conwentz, who in 1906 was appointed to head Prussia's newly created *Staatliche Stelle für Naturdenkmalpflege*, German nature was preserved best in many small, individual elements and not in a few large-scale reservations. The latter he believed to be only suited for sparsely cultivated areas. Therefore, Conwentz firmly rejected American-style national parks for his own country. When, beginning in 1909, the German-Austrian *Verein Naturschutzpark* strongly argued for the protection of "the typical German landscape" in three large parks that it envisioned situating in the Alps, the highlands, and the northern German plain, the plan found no favor with Conwentz. Nor did it help that the term "national park" was replaced by "nature conservation park" to give the matter a German flavor. Without state support, the society could not meet its own goals and had to be content with establishing a small private park on the Lüneburg heath.[60]

Conwentz fought passionately for his ideas and promoted them beyond Germany, where they met with a rapid and positive response. The natural monument became the key concept of an early European discourse on nature conservation. State and linguistic boundaries proved surprisingly easy to surmount. In Holland, the *Vereeniging tot Behoud von Natuurmonumenten* was founded in 1904; in Switzerland, the *Kommission für die Erhaltung von Naturdenkmälern und prähistorischen Stätten* in 1906; and in Italy, the *Lega Nazionale per la Protezione dei Monumenti Naturali* in 1913. Legal structures were established for the protection of *monuments de la nature* in France (1906) and *naturminnen* in Sweden (1909), whereas in Russia, around the same time, conservationists had begun to worry about the survival of their "*pamiatniki prirody*."[61] The European natural monument represented a protective strategy comprising many small areas, in contrast to the American national park, which epitomized an approach oriented to protecting large areas. The question of which of the two strategies was more successful in preserving species would be one of the great recurring environmental debates of the twentieth century.[62]

That both strategies could be pursued in combination was shown by Sweden, which in 1909 enacted two laws: one on natural monuments, and a second on national parks. The concept of the natural monument was inspired by Conwentz, whereas the national park was largely adapted from the American model. The parliamentary legislative committee spoke of the double character of the national park, which was both a natural wonder to be preserved and a tourist attraction to be exploited in patriotic fervor. Thus, along with state responsibility Sweden adopted the paradoxical goal of the American model: preservation through public use. The more scientifically oriented rationale put forward by the Royal Academy faded to the background. In 1910, the boundaries of nine national parks were fixed. Whereas the five parks located in the southern part of the country encompassed only a few square kilometers, the four parks in northern Sweden assumed American dimensions, which dovetailed with Norrland's image as Sweden's America.[63]

The concept of the natural monument also came in useful in the United States, although whether that is due to a random coincidence of time and terminology is unclear, as to date no obvious link has been found to the debate in Europe. The Antiquities Act, adopted in 1906, authorized the president to set apart so-called national monuments, which included historic and prehistoric sights. The president then in office was Theodore Roosevelt, whose connection to nature conservation was strong. But Roosevelt also used the law to bypass Congress and create national park-like entities, such as the over 3,300-square-kilometer Grand Canyon National Monument, in 1908. This and other national monuments were later transformed into national parks that, with the creation of additional categories of protection, became the crown jewels in the system of protected areas and enduring icons of American conservation.[64]

The Globalization of the National Park

In 1905, the Swiss forester Robert Glutz delivered a paper before the Solothurn nature history society titled "Natural Monuments: Threats and Preservation." Glutz regaled his listeners (and later readers) with a detailed overview of Conwentz's concept of the natural monument and the American national park. He described Yellowstone as a protective area for the American buffalo, then segued immediately to the idea of natural monuments. "This national park in the Rocky Mountains is the greatest effort to protect natural monuments ever undertaken," he said, "an idea worthy of the great American Republic, the land of 'unlimited opportunity.'" For Glutz, Yellowstone was no longer the wonderland of geysers, tumbling waterfalls, and bizarre rock formations, as it was perceived at its founding three decades earlier. No, it was a "museum of natural monuments, a botanical and zoological garden, in which all individual animals and plants threatened with extinction by North America's rapidly growing civilization could find a last refuge." In Glutz's portrayal, the national park was the best mechanism for saving nature from the damaging effects of civilization. The park was comprehensive and served ideally to unite the conservation functions of museums and gardens. But Glutz also saw that the use of this mechanism in Europe could be problematic, "because in this expanse we can no longer find any area that is unlicked [sic] by culture."[65]

Glutz bundled together a transnational discussion of the global loss of natural space and biological species with the civilizing consequences to be drawn from that. Only in this context did the national park triumph outside the United States and other British settler colonies. A Yellowstone National Park charged with additional meaning was now viewed worldwide as a model of nature conservation that Western cosmopolitan elites adopted, discussed, and reproduced locally around the world. Contrary to popular narratives, the global spread of the national park should not be understood as a linear transfer but as a complex game of takeover and appropriation, imposition and rejection, dependence and isolation, fostered by a global conservation movement that grew rapidly after 1900.[66]

As Glutz's text also exemplifies, the national park did not constitute the only model of conservation. Indeed, the US national park was newly interpreted, selectively adopted, and fused with other approaches. The most important of the competing ideas was the small-scale natural monument that targeted the protection of individual natural elements. In his address of 1914, Walter Bissegger noted that the German *Länder* and Austria had established state agencies for conservation and "small reservations for circumscribed aims, the conservation of certain animal and plant forms."[67] The natural monument remained closely associated with Germany and with Conwentz's name, and was especially recommended for countries or areas that were densely settled and highly developed. For such regions, which owing simply to the then-current definition of civilization were concentrated in Europe, national parks were mostly viewed as inappropriate and impractical.

In contrast, for less populated and exploited landscapes, the large-scale conservation area was a proven means of preserving conditions at a distance from civilization. Against the expected march of "civilization," geographic boundaries and "nature" enclaves could thus be created. For this type of nature conservation, the United States in the 1900s was the inevitable reference. The strongly associative connection between national park and North America promoted or hindered adoption, depending on whether the similarities or differences to the American landscape and society were emphasized, and whether the term "America" was meant positively or negatively. The national parks of other countries of the "New World" were hardly noticed globally. They were overshadowed by the Yellowstone "original," whose myth making was now in full swing and largely left out historical contingencies—not surprising since this is precisely the inherent function of creation myths. The legend of the birth of

Yellowstone National Park in 1872 was created in 1900 largely to mute criticism that persists up to today.

In his address, Walter Bissegger also invoked the first national park and associated its founding with the "fear of impending extinction of the bison, ... which had captured the attention of the finest Americans."[68] This portrayal was historically false, though Bissegger can hardly be expected to have known it. The Zurich politician purely and simply passed on the Yellowstone myth, whose chain of reasoning was sublimely adaptable to a Swiss national park. There might be "just one way to effectively combat the gradual destruction," asserted Bissegger, citing a pamphlet titled "*Die Naturschutzbewegung und der schweizerische Nationalpark* (The conservation movement and the Swiss National Park)" published in 1911 by Gustav Hegi, a Swiss botanist at the University of Munich: "Creating larger national parks, in which everything that was originally native is granted permanent asylum."[69] In 1914, the Swiss Parliament voted to establish such a sanctuary. Thus it happened that, shortly before the outbreak of the First World War, the national park established over the previous years in Grisons found solid federal government support. How this national park came about, and how it quickly rose to be the best-known alternative worldwide to the American park model, will be the subject of the next chapter.

Notes

1. *Amtliches Bulletin Nationalrat* 24 (1914), 156.
2. *NZZ*, "Zur Nationalpark-Debatte," 27 March 1914.
3. Schweizerischer Bundesrat 1914, 19; see also Schweizerischer Bundesrat 1912.
4. *Amtliches Bulletin Nationalrat* 24 (1914), 156. For biographical information on Bissegger, see Historisches Lexikon der Schweiz.
5. Ibid., 159 f.
6. Braudel 1958. In his work on the history of the Mediterranean world, Braudel (1976) described a third "geohistorical" time axis, the "quasi-motionless time" of natural elements such as seas, islands, and mountains, as well as climate. In the same vein, Reinhard Koselleck (2000, especially 27–77) proposed a three-tier time concept based on notions of experience.
7. Siegenthaler 1993.
8. See the essays by Nash 1970, Nash 1980. In attributing American authorship for the national park, Nash repeatedly resorts to narrative tricks. For an interpretation that emphasizes the gradual formulation of the national park idea over a longer time period (ca. 1870–1930), see Jones 2012.
9. See, for example, Gugerli 1998; Kaelble 2006.
10. Elliott 1974, 15. The report appeared at the beginning of the Proceedings of the Second World Conference on National Parks, held in 1972 at Yellowstone National Park, underscoring its significance as the springboard for the national park idea.
11. Brockington et al. 2008, 18–21.
12. See Nash 1980.

13. Nash 1970, 731. Runte 1987, 47. Cf. Miles 2009, 9–26. On the founding and the early years of Yellowstone, see also Magoc 1999. The invention of the national park is also often credited to the painter Georg Catlin, who as early as 1832 was calling for a "nation's park, containing man and beast" to protect Native Americans and wild animals. In addition, whether Yosemite (1864) or Yellowstone (1872) should be considered the birth of the national park is a matter of considerable debate. See Runte 1987, 33–47. Absent the insistence on defining the exact origin of the national park idea (as is the case here), this debate and others like it lose much of their relevance.
14. On traditional parks, see Jones and Wills 2005; Olwig 1995; Schwarz 2005. On exclusion: Warren 1997; Spence 1999; Jacoby 2001. Hot Springs, Arkansas, secured the protection of the federal government in 1832.
15. Cited in Runte 1987, 11. See also further remarks therein. However, Runte overstates his case in claiming that European countries lacked only a stimulus like the commercialization of Niagara Falls to develop the national park idea (7). Areas attractive to tourists have always been largely unrestrictedly commercialized, even in Europe.
16. *The Times*, "A Very National Park," 10 April 1873. See also *The Times*, "A National Park," 23 November 1877.
17. *Journal de Genève*, "Un parc national aux États-Unis," 28 July 1872; *NZZ*, "Der Nationalpark der Vereinigten Staten von Nordamerika," 5 August 1873.
18. See Spence 1999, 41–70; Jacoby 2001, 81–148.
19. Harper and White 2012; Sheail 2010. For a general overview, see also Dunlap 1999.
20. Mels 1999, 68 f; Graf von Hardenberg 2009, 120 f.
21. Kreis 2004. On Drachenfels, see Lekan 2004; Schmoll 2004.
22. Miller 1967. On the environmental history significance of nature for US history, see Steinberg 2002a; on the differences with Europe, see Mauch 2004.
23. Cited in Runte 1987, 19.
24. Bowles 1869. See also Shaffer 2001, 59–91 (for Glacier National Park) and Pickering 2005. On attitudes toward the Swiss Alps in the context of the American national park movement, see Kupper 2009a.
25. On the "Swissification" of the Alps, see Stremlow 1998; Gugerli and Speich 2002; Mathieu and Boscani Leoni 2005; Walter 2005; Speich 2008, and for the role of the Alps in a global history of mountains: Mathieu 2012.
26. The corresponding Swiss laws were enacted in 1875 (hunting, fisheries) and 1876 (forests). Bachmann 1999, 65–72; Schmid 2010, 105–131.
27. See Krüger 2008.
28. See chapter 2.
29. Cited in Schmoll 2004, 11.
30. Classic: Nash 1982; see also Cronon 1995; Lewis 2007a. On Switzerland, see Walter 1996.
31. However, the available literature refers mostly to individual countries. Surveys worth perusal include Walter 1996 (Switzerland), Schmoll 2004 (Germany), Steinberg 2002a (United States), Beinart and Hughes 2007 (British Empire). In contrast, a comprehensive global treatment of the nineteenth century from an environmental history perspective is still lacking. Preliminary attempts can be found in Radkau 2008; Burke and Pomeranz 2009; Uekötter 2010. Compelling syntheses of global history of the nineteenth century are those by Bayly 2004; Osterhammel 2009.
32. Brunhes 1911.

36 Creating Wilderness

33. Mathieu 2006. For an overview of the development of Western concepts of nature, see Coates 1998 and Worster 1985.
34. On Germany, see, for example, Daum 2002; on Switzerland, Bürgi and Speich 2004.
35. Maier 2000.
36. Anderson 1991.
37. This train of thought had already been well elaborated in the eighteenth century by Johann Gottfried von Herder. Kirchhoff and Trepl 2009a, 39–41.
38. The expression "vignette of primitive America" appeared in the influential Leopold Report of 1963 (Leopold et al. 1963). But primitiveness was already a feature of national parks between the world wars. See Kupper 2009a. The second expression comes from a speech by Carl Schröter during the excursion of the *Schweizerische Naturforschende Gesellschaft* to the national park in 1916: Tarnuzzer 1916, 223.
39. Runte 1987, 84 f. In 1887, and thus five years before the Sierra Club, the Boone and Crockett Club was founded by sportsmen at the urging of future US president Theodore Roosevelt. See Reiger 1986, 114–141.
40. The list can be expanded by including involvement of other countries as well as simultaneously emerging goal-related organizations for heritage protection. Such an inventory would be complicated by the poor state of research on the history of nature conservation in Europe. For a few clues, especially in relation to national parks, see Kupper 2008. Trom 1995 offers a Franco-German comparison. For a landscape and environmental history of Europe, see Delort and Walter 2001; Walter 2004.
41. Kern 1983 is still the best book on this topic.
42. See, for example, Bayly 2004; Conrad 2006.
43. See Geyer and Paulmann 2001; Herren 2000, and on the relationship of nation-states and empires, see also Leonhard and Hirschhausen 2009.
44. *Amtliches Bulletin Nationalrat* 24 (1914), 184. Paul Sarasin's concept of world nature conservation, which also dovetails with this theme, will be introduced in chapter 2.
45. Wagner 1995. An atmospherically rich evocation of these years can be found in Blom 2008. See also Hobsbawm 1987, 243–261; Drehsen and Sparn 1996; Haupt and Würffel 2008, and with reference to the history of technology in Switzerland, Humair and Jost 2008.
46. Lefebvre 1968, 209–240. On neurasthenia, see Messerli 1995, 217–228; Radkau 1998; Roelcke 1999. On physics, see Galison 2003.
47. See Bachmann 1999; Rohkrämer 1999; Graf 2000; Hall 2011.
48. Muir 1901, 1.
49. Schröter 1924, 387.
50. *Amtliches Bulletin Nationalrat* 24 (1914), 160.
51. Schröter 1918, 765.
52. See Haraway 1989, 26–58; Jarvis 2007; Isenberg 2000, 164–192. This was also the impetus behind the international scouting movement.
53. On Germany, see Wöbse 2004; Gissibl 2005; on Great Britain, Gates 1998. In the United States, the spectrum of female activity was somewhat broader; see Merchant 1984. No corresponding research exists for Switzerland.
54. On Yellowstone as an experimental landscape, see Jones 2012. The connection between national parks and tourism will be delved into more deeply in chapter 6.
55. On early modern times, see Richards 2003.

56. On the American discourse, see Reiger 1986, 93–113; Sellars 1997, 7–46; Spence 1999; 60–70; Isenberg 2000, 164–192. A testament to the new perception in German-speaking countries can be found in the corresponding entry in Brockhaus Konversationslexikon, 14th edition, 1894–1896, vol. 16, 892 f.
57. See MacKenzie 1997, 200–224; Gissibl 2006; Cioc 2009, 14–57.
58. *Stenographische Berichte über die Verhandlungen des Preussischen Hauses der Abgeordneten*, vol. 3. 1898, 1958 f. See Frohn 2006, 85–314, especially 88–93.
59. Conwentz 1904.
60. The quote comes from Floericke 1910, 13. See Kupper and Wöbse 2013, 10–37. The plans were later expanded to include a fourth park that was to be situated at the seashore. Floericke 1913, 15.
61. Kupper 2008.
62. See Lewis 2007b.
63. See Mels 1999.
64. Rothman 1989. On US attitudes toward the father of the German national monument, Alexander von Humboldt, see Sachs 2007.
65. Glutz-Graff 1905, 18 f.
66. Cf. Gissibl et al. 2012b. Tyrell 2012.
67. *Amtliches Bulletin Nationalrat* 24 (1914), 157.
68. Ibid.
69. Ibid. Hegi 1911. For biographical information on Hegi, see Historisches Lexikon der Schweiz.

CHAPTER 2

National Natures
The Swiss National Park and the Conservationist Internationale

"Homo novus Helveticus" blared an article in the 1 April 1910 issue of the Bern newspaper *Der Bund* reporting the Swiss government's attempt to mediate a dispute that had broken out in a parliamentary committee over the proposal for a Swiss national park. The committee drafting the proposal had initially favored the idea, but had gotten bogged down in the details. The Federal Council now promised to support both draft versions of the bill. By way of background for this decision, the news article recapitulated the history of the national park plan to date and reminded readers that "both the singular plant and animal (fauna) worlds of Switzerland will be left undisturbed by humans, so that, over time, these specially designated areas will come to resemble a sort of primeval forest." However, in the interim, scientific thinking had led to "expansion of the original plan to feature as faithfully as possible typical human representatives of traditional Switzerland in such reserves." The commission had enthusiastically welcomed this additional goal, but had fallen out over how to implement it. The spokesman for one side was "the excellent Zurich zoologist and ardent fan of Haeckel's recapitulation theory," Ulysses Gessner. Gessner suggested surrounding the park with a wall "so high that it would be impossible to climb over it. Then, analogous to the evolution of the human race from lower forms over a suitable period of time—which, as is well-known, plays for naturalists both a minimal and a huge role—you would have nothing more to do than to await the rise of a new primogenitary people in the area now left to the totally mysterious workings of pristine natural forces. Of course, because the existing mixed Swiss population would have no influence on the procreation of these new people, thanks to the protective wall, they would represent the pure archetype of the alpine Swiss." Gessner was opposed in the committee by Henry Debarges, a professor from Geneva. Debarges agreed to building a wall, "but I would not wish to trust the generation of new native Swiss to the anonymous power of nature, but rather to carefully selected specimens of already living Swiss of both sexes who could be placed in the park as a paradisiacal pair." A schoolmaster should ensure "that the people enclosed in the park keep up with culture, but that they should not be exposed to its harmful effects." Indeed, in Peter von Almen from Oberhasli and Louise Chalamala from Gruyère, Debarges already had an initial pair that he deemed suitable to present to the commission. Gessner saw little value in Debarges's idea. Abandoning mating pairs of humans was brutal, he said, according to the report in the *Bund,* and could not capture the natural evolution of lower to higher forms. Thus, despite the government's support of both initiatives, the substantive debate remained open. The *Bund* invited its readers to attend a lecture by Debarges that very same evening in the auditorium of the University of Bern: "Please heed the date."[1]

Anyone disregarding that bit of advice and making their way to the university on 1 April 1910 would surely not have encountered the dubious Geneva professor, but more likely the author of the newspaper article, a certain Dr. Slop, alias Josef Viktor Widmann, longtime head of the *Bund*'s cultural section. Moreover, the reader would soon have recognized the trap set by the well-known cultural and literary critic: Widmann had permitted himself an April fool's joke at the expense of the national park idea. What else to do but to laugh and to wonder at having missed the author's parodies, caricatures, and allusions?[2]

Widmann's April fool's joke was witty and probably just as entertaining then as it is today. But it is also an intriguing historical document. The text does not concern itself much with facts, which does not detract from its value as a historical source. On the contrary, Widmann's fictional report can be read as a treasure trove of history, so long as the reader is mindful of the genre. Then as now, a successful April fool's joke is a balancing act. It must present a story in such a way that the reader or listener believes it to be true. At the same time, it must be sufficiently over the top that, once it has been explained or the victim has caught on, he throws up his hands at his own credulity. Moreover, the victim must have a little prior knowledge, a superficial familiarity with the subject matter of the joke. Consequently, a public April fool's joke depends on material that is timely enough to enliven social conversation but still so new as to leave ample room for the imagination.

When considered in this light, Widmann's joke says something about the evolution of the Swiss National Park on a level rarely found in other source documents. Four points are particularly worth mentioning: First, one can infer from Widmann's report that creation of the first Swiss National Park in 1910 was a topic of public debate. The idea was both so newsworthy and so sketchy that Widmann could make it into the stuff of an April Fools' Day joke. Second, the park was political. The nation-state came off as a key player and gave a nationalistic flavor to the notion of protecting nature that simultaneously opened the way to a social Darwinist, racial interpretation. Third, scientific reasoning and expertise played a prominent role in the debate. The academic backdrop was evolutionary theory and the new discipline of ecology, which must have been familiar to the well-educated middle class. Finally, Widmann perceptively recognized that establishing a national park was not about preserving nature, but rather re-creating it in its original form. This would require freeing an area from all human influence. Yet the resurgent "primordial nature" should also be maintained in intimate contact with society, a contradiction that Widmann delighted in exploiting.

These four themes—openness, nationalism, science, and restoration of pristine nature—are integral to the description that follows of the stepwise process that led to establishing the Swiss National Park between 1909 and 1914. How these themes played out in the deciding phase of the park's history is best explained by considering five crucial issues: First, how was the site selected, which factors were integral to that decision, and what were the alternatives? Second, why was the concept of the Swiss National Park so unlike those for comparable areas of protection, and so strongly oriented to scientific research? Third, who were the players in this project? How did they shape its direction, and how were they shaped by it? As Bruno Latour would put it, how were actors, networks, and artifacts dynamically co-produced?[3] Fourth, what was the significance of the designation "national park," which was not foreseen at the outset and which proved very consequential? Finally, I will examine the close connection that existed between the founding of the Swiss National Park, the international conservation movement, and Swiss hopes of playing a leading role in this movement.[4]

"A Beautiful Vision of the Future"

The turning point in the debate on a possible Swiss national park is credited to the Swiss Association of the Natural Sciences' (*Schweizerische Naturforschende Gesellschaft*, SNG) committee on nature conservation, which had formed during the 1906 annual meeting under the chairmanship of the Basel naturalist Paul Sarasin. The committee owed its existence to plans of a quarry company to blast through a famous boulder—*Pierre des Marmettes*—near Monthey in Canton Wallis. The plans sparked a broad protest in which the SNG was also involved. Events followed thick and fast, and before the SNG knew, to avoid losing face it would have to contribute a disproportionate amount to rescuing the boulder. To prevent a repeat of such developments, the newly appointed SNG committee put together a proactive conservation strategy. Following a Prussian example, the committee called itself the Commission for the Conservation of Nature Monuments and Prehistorical Sites (*Kommission für die Erhaltung von Naturdenkmälern und prähistorischen Stätten*), which it soon abbreviated to the Swiss Commission for Nature Protection (*Schweizerische Naturschutzkommission*, SNK).[5]

In autumn 1906, as the members of the SNK met for the first time to clarify organizational issues and to put together an initial work program, Zurich botanist Carl Schröter proposed creating a national park. Schröter immediately linked the idea to a specific area, Val S-charl (S-charl valley) in the Lower Engadine. He himself had roamed there just a few years earlier with the Swiss chief forest inspector, Johann Coaz, and had described it in detail in a publication in 1905.[6] The picture Schröter painted at that meeting greatly influenced the further development of the park. "This valley would be especially ... well suited to a Swiss national park, 'where no ax or gunshot may be heard': it has rich pine, larch, and spruce forests, stands of dwarf mountain pine, beautiful alpine flora, and if you were to take a section of the Ofengebiet, extensive stocks of tall mountain pines still inhabited by bears. If a sufficiently large bit were to be fenced in, it would be a magnificent haven for the last remnants of alpine animal forms and might even be suitable for repatriating the ibex. A beautiful vision of the future took shape in the minds of the conservationists."[7] The idea of both a large, protected area ("still inhabited by bears"[8]) and of the return of the ibex were forever fixed in his listeners' heads. Schröter also decisively laid the groundwork for the later choice of area.

The SNK attacked the details of setting up protected areas at its first general assembly in summer 1907. The idea was welcomed in principle, and the cantonal committees that had been appointed in the meanwhile were asked to identify suitable locations. To designate the targeted areas, the delegates chose "reserve," a term whose closer definition, however, remained largely unresolved.[9] In the following months, the SNK's initially vague aims began to take shape in three ways. First, using a specific area—the Petersinsel—the SNK began to grapple seriously with the question of criteria for a reserve. The future of the 400 hectare (988 acre) island in Lake Biel, which belonged to the Bern city hospital, was available, so the SNK reviewed the advisability of the Petersinsel as a reserve. The group presented a number of studies on the botanical and zoological suitability of the proposal, but came to the unanimous conclusion that the island possessed little of interest from a conservation perspective. According to one of the studies, the Petersinsel harbored no "unusual formations or plant communities." It was a lovely landscape, whose conservation was desirable, but more in the order of heritage protection.[10]

Second, committee member Hermann Christ was tasked with studying the applicability of relevant US regulations to the Swiss case. He found no suitable rules in the provisions pertaining to national forests. In the US focus on preferably efficient use, Christ saw "opposites rather than analogies" to the Swiss aspirations. However, he found the second category of protection, the national park, noteworthy: "It includes valleys and mountainous regions notable for their beautiful and magnificent vegetation and landscapes that are to be preserved as monuments of nature, though with the express goal of serving as recreational areas for the public. Thus, care for the parks involves not only the upkeep of their natural character but also attention to accessibility in the form of trail systems, concessions, hotels, and so forth. The latter consideration is less well suited to our reserves, whereas the maintenance of natural objects is completely in line with our concept."[11] European approaches to nature conservation were also examined. Efforts in Sweden to set up national parks were noted, though no special attention was paid to them. On balance, the SNK came away from the international review encouraged that it was at the cutting edge. It felt itself not only a part of an emerging international conservation movement but, by virtue of its own idea, also potentially one of its pioneers.[12]

Finally, in the summer of 1908, several members of the SNK turned their gaze to the Ofengebiet proposed by Schröter. Armed with the publication by Johann Coaz and Schröter, SNK president Paul Sarasin roamed Val S-charl together with his cousin Fritz Sarasin, who was also a committee member as well as chair of the SNG. In the Hotel Ofenberg, they ran into Hermann Christ and botanist Steivan Brunies, who was from the area. In 1906, Brunies had done his doctoral work on the flora of the Ofen Pass under Schröter's supervision. Now, he pointed out to the men that nearby Val Cluozza was very close to the SNK's gradually crystallizing ideal of a nature conservation area. Val Cluozza was uninhabited, difficult to access, and little used. During the summer months, a few cattle grazed there and timber was occasionally harvested, though removing it was complicated. In a report for the SNK's forthcoming annual meeting hastily written by Brunies and edited by Christ, the valley was described as a largely untouched wilderness whose rich natural phenomena had yet to be investigated. As it had up to then escaped the reach of tourism, the area seemed almost to have been "saved for such a reserve."[13]

The narrow canyons and barren, rubble-strewn hillsides around the Ofen Pass had a wild allure. But the spectacular landscape was ill suited for contemporaries, who would have preferred that it not have prominent peaks or glaciers or rushing waterfalls. Unlike the proponents of the national park in the United States for whom, at the time, the aesthetic effect of a landscape—magnificent scenery—was the decisive criterion for designating a national park, the audience of SNK scientists and nature conservationists could care less about them.[14] Their main concern was to find a pristine area, far removed from civilization and thus conducive to the restoration of pre-human, "natural" biological communities. "The natural flora and fauna of the European alpine mountain peaks shall find their untouched home in specific, circumscribed areas," wrote the SNK in 1908 to the town council of Zernez, whose territory included Val Cluozza; "here, they shall proliferate, and adapt to one another. Over the course of years, plant and animal societies shall flourish, just as they adorned the Alps in a pure work of nature before the intrusion of humans; a natural, living society—a biocoenose, to use the scientific term—shall come into being in the heart of Europe, in the heart of the most beautiful mountainous land in the world." The scientific perspective of the authors of the initiative was obvious. At one point, they even described their project as a "great experiment to restore primordial alpine nature and, at the same time, to bequeath to the future a major refuge of pristine natural life."[15]

Preserving evidence of the past from eclipse enjoyed a boom in those years of rapid societal change that was reflected in simultaneous efforts in archeology and ethnology, in conservation of monuments and heritage, as well as in the creation and expansion of museums.[16] The SNK's intention to restore primordial nature was also in keeping with the times. Even within cultural heritage and art history, debates were raging over the extent to which restoration of all buildings and works of art could return them to their "original" condition.[17] The general popularity and familiarity of such concerns smoothed the way for the SNK. On the other hand, Paul Sarasin and his colleagues skillfully exploited the resulting opportunities to gain allies and to strengthen their own position.

Thus, the "reserve question" was not only pursued by the SNK but was also taken up, in parallel, by the Swiss Forest Association (*Schweizerischer Forstverein*) and the Swiss Heritage Society (*Schweizerische Vereinigung für Heimatschutz*). The latter organization, which had only just been founded in 1905, like the SNK first had to establish a profile that would permit it to take stands on issues and to develop positions. The former, the forest association, had begun to tackle the establishment of "primordial forest reserves at the suggestion of one of its members, Robert Glutz, in 1906. The foresters, too, were primarily interested in scientific studies of the natural development of nature—in this case, forests—in areas exempt from land use. The SNK and the forestry association subsequently exchanged ideas and plans on a regular basis, but continued to work separately on their own projects. By 1911, the forestry association had established three small "primordial forest reserves" ranging between five and forty hectares, or twelve and ninety-nine acres. After the founding of the national park in the Engadine, one-third of whose area was covered by forest, interest in individual forest reserves dwindled perceptibly, so much so that in 1919 the association shut down its own three reserves.[18]

The SNK managed very neatly to secure the support of the national government. In August 1907, the Federal Council independently approached the SNG with the request that it review a petition the council had received from the *Société de Physique et d'Histoire naturelle de Genève* for "geological and geographic reserves" modeled on the American national parks. The motivation for the petition was a controversy sparked some months earlier by the application of a license for a railway to the top of the Matterhorn. The action unleashed a storm of protest that drew attention to cultural heritage through the organization of a national petition. The SNK also seized the opportunity, but did not join the protest movement owing to internal differences of opinion.[19] The Geneva scientific society now proposed classifying the Matterhorn as a "reserve," which of course threw the railway plans into disarray. Federal Councilor Josef Zemp, who as head of the railway department had received the letter, forwarded it to his colleague Mark-Emile Ruchet in the Department of Home Affairs with the recommendation that he seriously consider the proposal: "No doubt, this idea is not new, and Switzerland could long ago have taken a page from the United States and created national reserves in different areas that would have lacked neither utility nor renown. If it was not done, it is surely because we believed that vast regions of our Alps would remain intact and would constitute natural and desirable reserves without any state intervention whatsoever. Today, we must acknowledge that such is not the case. The push of the railways is sparing no part of the land, and the 'entrapment' of our most beautiful peaks is proceeding apace."[20] Ruchet referred the matter to the SNG and its chair, Fritz Sarasin, a move that clearly reflected management practices at the time. Since the small federal administration lacked knowledge and manpower, it routinely relied on the expertise of professional societies. Sarasin accepted the job with alacrity, and in this way was able to integrate the federal councilor advantageously into his own network.[21]

The controversy surrounding the Matterhorn continued to smolder up to the First World War, when the war-related slump in the tourism sector showed that implementation of the project might be illusory. Although the SNK refrained from intervening in further developments, the public debate over Swiss mountain scenery made it easier for the SNK to convince both the authorities and the public of the urgency of conservation. In five years, if urgent steps were not taken, "the most beautiful parts of Switzerland would be criss-crossed with hotel blocks and railroad tracks," opined Hermann Christ in May 1908 in the Basel newspaper. As a countermeasure, Christ recommended establishing "Swiss national parks." As with Federal Councilor Zemp, for Christ the Matterhorn plans symbolized the omnipotence of modern technology, which even the hitherto forbidding alpine peaks were now helpless against. Their preservation had to be addressed with the utmost urgency. Christ himself wrote: "It is high time, the eleventh hour. Let us make haste to accomplish as least the essential steps before the Matterhorn vandalism is a *fait accompli*."[22]

Laying the Foundations

At the end of August 1908, the members of the SNK gathered in Glarus for their yearly meeting. The main item on the agenda was the presentation and discussion of the results of the national survey on future reserves. The proposal for the Ofengebiet clearly stood out. In addition to the report on Val Cluozza, Brunies, who had been invited to the meeting, read out a letter from the communal officials of Zernez, who welcomed the idea of a reserve. Most of the other proposals were limited to smaller areas; only the Bern committee's proposal for the Finsteraarhorn massif, from the Grimsel to the Aletsch glacier, matched Val Cluozza in size. The group came to no decision, but Paul Sarasin was entrusted with forming a subcommittee to evaluate all the proposals and to make "a preliminary selection."[23] This authorization signaled the beginning of a three-year phase dominated by the SNK chair. Sarasin brought to the task energetic leadership and creative drive. By the same token, his reluctance to relinquish control of developments led the project to veer narrowly between success and disaster. When, in autumn 1908, the forest association suggested closer cooperation on the reserve question, Sarasin confidently demurred.[24] The nature reserve was to bear the stamp of the SNK. In those early years, both mutual assistance and competition characterized relations between the forest association, heritage conservation, and nature protection. Issues continued to crop up over work boundaries, allocation of responsibility, and who should get credit for what. To see the national park only as "the result of positive and fruitful cooperation between foresters, naturalists, and conservations"—as six decades later the then federal forest inspector and park commission president did—was to see only one side.[25]

Sarasin did not abide by the guidelines of the SNK meeting. He was ready and willing to put his money where his mouth was, and with typical stubbornness set off on his own pursuit of a reserve in the Ofengebiet. To this end, he assembled a "reserves committee," a handpicked group with the necessary range of skills and contacts. His cousin, Fritz Sarasin, was not only his most trusted advisor but, in those years, also chair of the SNG. The two professors, Carl Schröter and Friedrich Zschokke, contributed their academic authority to issues involving botany and zoology. And 75-year-old Hermann Christ had the advantage of both legal expertise and the esteem he commanded both personally and among the naturalist community as an expert on Swiss flora.[26] Finally, Steivan Brunies was indispensable as a translator of German into Romansh and vice versa, as well as an intermediary between the educated world of the naturalists and the rural culture of the Lower Engadine. Johann Coaz, who had also been invited to join the group, declined because he feared it would conflict with his duties as federal forest inspector. In fact, in a later phase of the project, he contributed invaluable support as a consultant to the Federal Council.[27] The committee was very homogeneous. Its members shared an appreciation for scientific research, quiet enjoyment of nature, and the Alps as a natural landscape. Most of them belonged to the Swiss Alpine Club and, aside from Schröter, who was from Zurich, all lived in Basel. City living was their normal milieu, and excursions into the wilderness their elixir.

The men did not take long to select a site, but rather proceeded immediately to firm up plans for the Ofengebiet. By December 1908 the committee had conveyed to the communal council of Zernez their desire to turn Val Cluozza into a nature reserve. The council appeared very interested, but asked for a period of one year to study the matter. The delay suited the committee in the sense that it gave them time to arrange the financing for the scheme. It was clear to the founders that protecting a large area—for Val Cluozza would only be the beginning—would entail significant costs over time.[28] From the outset, acquiring it as real estate even for the economically marginal areas was unrealistic owing to the price of land; consequently, the idea was to lease it long term. Additional funds would have to be provided for guarding the territory and creating an infrastructure for researchers and visitors. Major costs were estimated at more than 10,000 francs annually.

The funding issue was raised at the very first meeting of the Reserves Committee in October 1908. At the suggestion of Fritz Sarasin, it was decided to found a "one franc club." In early 1909, calls were made by means of the newspapers to join the Swiss League for Nature Protection (*Schweizerischer Bund für Naturschutz*, SBN) and, through a yearly payment of one franc, "to help the noble work of the fatherland in keeping its pristine nature from harm." A lifetime membership could be had for 20 francs. The idea underlying the SBN was not new. Although the archives give no hint, one may assume that the parties involved were aware of the German Association for the Protection of Birds (*Deutscher Bund für Vogelschutz*), founded ten years earlier by Lina Hähnle, in 1899. Thanks to the initially low fee of only 50 pfennigs, the organization quickly gained members, which in addition to financial resources also brought it a mass following and a certain degree of political clout. It was precisely these objectives that the SNK, too, had sought in founding the SBN.[29]

Private fundraising was only one arm of the financing strategy. In addition, the Reserves Committee planned on obtaining federal and state support. In December 1909, the SNK incurred its first financial obligations when it signed a more than 25-year-long lease with the town of Zernez. In return for annual interest of 1,400 francs, the town released Val Cluozza to the SNK as a "nature reserve."[30] One month later, in January 1910, Paul Sarasin met with Federal Councilor Ruchet to explore the possibility of a federal subsidy. Ruchet encouraged Sarasin to submit an appropriate application to the Federal Council. Sarasin delayed taking this step for many months, however, while he was occupied with negotiations already under way with a number of Engadine communes as well as with staffing and equipping the reserve. When he finally submitted his request to the Federal Council in February 1911, the SNK had negotiated (and, in some cases, signed) yearly leases for around 25,000 francs, hired its first guard, and ordered the construction of a log cabin in Val Cluozza. The SNK reckoned that maintaining the reserve would require an additional 10,000 francs per year.[31]

In view of the facts, obtaining funds was increasingly urgent. Although recruiting members for the SBN got off to a difficult start, it made fast progress, such that in January 1912, around twenty thousand members were on the rolls. Still, the income of around 35,000 francs was not enough to cover the running costs. As processing of the SNK's grant application to the Federal Council was delayed due to changes within that body, the financial situation was becoming precarious. Paul Sarasin was now sharply criticized within the SNK for his unconventional approach, to which—as usual when opposed—he reacted with anger. If necessary, Sarasin declared dramatically, he would cover the liabilities from his private funds, but then the success of the enterprise would be his, not the SNK's. Yet a confidential letter to Johann Coaz showed Sarasin to be deeply concerned about the future of the park.[32] The SNK refrained from assuming further obligations in 1912, and made savings where possible: It rejected an offer from the town of S-chanf for Alp Trupchun (an alpine meadow), and subleased another already leased meadow—Alp Tavrü—to the former tenant (at a considerable loss). The SNK temporarily put the planned expansion of the Cluozza log cabin put on hold.[33] Some large individual donations, which for 1913 matched the regular membership dues, gave a little relief up to 1914, when the first government funds arrived and the SBN's financial situation began to look up.[34] What would have happened if the SNK request for federal support had been delayed just a few months longer than the summer of 1914 and then by the outbreak of the First World War? What if, in view of the war, the Federal Assembly had decided instead to shelve the application, or simply discarded it? Would private donors have stepped into the breach? And would Paul Sarasin actually have tapped his own resources? Naturally, the answers to these questions are a matter of speculation. But given the setbacks that the national park idea experienced in Switzerland and in Europe both during and after the First World War, it seems likely that, in such a case, the national park would at least have had to battle seriously for survival, with no certain outcome.[35]

The National Dimension

But first back to early spring 1911: Sarasin's submission of the application to the Federal Council signaled that he believed the national park plan to be entering a new phase of consolidation. The ongoing negotiations with the communes of S-chanf, Scuol, and Zernez in 1911 and 1912 resulted in further leases patterned along the lines of the earlier agreements. In public, the SNK campaigned diligently for its national park and nature conservancy, striving at the same time to ensure the financial security of its projects by way of federal subsidies. Federal councilors and parliamentarians toured the park in the following years. Paul Sarasin lobbied the Federal Council, while Schröter and

Zschokke sought to address concerns through their scientific expertise. Additional expertise was contributed by Chief Forestry Inspector Johann Coaz, to whom the Federal Council had transferred responsibility for processing the matter.[36] Given the mix of personalities and the previous history, it is hardly surprising that Coaz advocated state involvement. To the SNK's arguments, Coaz added his own: Protected from the impact of grazing livestock, the forest in the reserve would naturally regenerate and take over the pasture: "This advantage is so great that it outweighs the economic cost of maintaining the forests and anticipated losses." Thus, also from a utilitarian perspective of rational use of natural resources, establishing a national park in the area made sense.[37]

As the SNK's application made its way through the federal bureaucracy—a roughly three-year process—two major shifts occurred. First, the Federal Council stipulated that the contracts be increased from twenty-five to ninety-nine years and that the government have the right to unilaterally terminate them after twenty-five years. Whereas Zernez agreed to these terms and signed easements with the confederation, S-chanf and Scuol, along with the alpine cooperative Tavrü, rejected the demands. As a result, the federal legislation was subsequently limited to the commune of Zernez. The other areas remained contractually bound to the SNK, with the SNB shelling out the rents.[38] Second, the responsibilities relating to contractual relationships between the confederation, SNG, and SBN were redefined. The supervision of the national park was transferred from the SNK to a government-sponsored five-member Swiss National Park Commission (ENPK), to which the Federal Council and the SBN each sent two, and the SNG one representative. The SNG was responsible for the scientific exploitation of the area, while the SBN, which in this context received new articles of association and was entered into the commercial register, was to cover all the park's administrative and research costs.[39]

This complex structure made it possible to balance the interests of all the participants. It also served to sow the seeds of future conflict. In particular, as the SBN grew increasingly independent of the SNK and the national park and expanded its own field of activity, having it hold the purse strings became more problematic. The players were all aware that the actual initiator of the project, the SNK, had no function in the national park's organization. This was made all the more clear when SNK chair Paul Sarasin, whom the Federal Council had appointed to the head of the ENPK in 1914 as a matter of course, quarreled with the SBN, despite Sarasin having been chair of the SBN in 1909 and having served as its representative to the ENPK. When Sarasin resigned the chairmanship of the SBN in 1921, he also forfeited his position with the ENPK.[40]

In March 1914, the national park finally came before the federal parliament. The bill provided for transfer of the overall supervision of the national park to the Federal Council. In addition, the confederation would have the usage rights of the park spaces for ninety-nine years, for which it would pay their owners the yearly sum of up to 30,000 francs. In the National Council, which was the first of the two legislative chambers to deal with the proposal, a protracted debate ensued again but resulted in no substantial changes. Criticism came from the ranks of the council's leftist members. Whereas a few members of the socialist faction would have preferred to use the federal money for social purposes than for nature conservation, a group led by Glarner democrat David Legler fought against the project on principle. Legler considered the information on the extinction of animal and plant species to be highly exaggerated and for that reason denied the need for a large reserve. The biggest beneficiaries of the national park would be predators, whose protection Legler described not only as an "absurdity" but also a threat to visitors to the park and the surrounding areas. That no large predators inhabited the park weakened Legler's argument. In any event, the possibility of intervention was included in the case bears did return—which proponents hoped would happen—or some other undesirable development came to pass. Article 1 of the resolution was amended to state that "all flora and fauna is allowed to develop naturally and protected from any human influence *that is not consistent with the goals of the national park.*"[41] In this way, the concerns of some of the parliamentarians were addressed.

In criticizing another aspect of the project, Legler touched a sore spot: If you really want to set up a national park, he argued in the National Council, then put it right in the middle of the Swiss Alps, where it can benefit the Swiss and be properly monitored. Neither of these requirements was guaranteed at the proposed site at the Swiss-Italian border. Consequently, the park would primarily be a "rich hunting ground" for Italian poachers. In fact, in the following years, attacks from the Italian side did become a major worry for the park administration. Moreover, with the nationalization of the park, the question of national representativeness took on significant weight. A member of the Council of States confessed that he did not really understand "what was so Swiss about a high forest in the Engadine. All our neighboring states, Austria, Bavaria, Württemberg, will always have forests that are much more beautiful and rich in wildlife than we Swiss, so we will not be creating anything of specific national interest."[42] In fact, in the wake of this criticism, the criteria for selecting the area began to shift: Scientific justification began to give way to categories related to national policy. In 1910, Carl Schröter was already requesting that "the most characteristic example of each type of pristine nature worthy of preservation be delivered untouched and sacrosanct to posterity." The "alpine national park in the Lower Engadine" would be a first step.[43] When, during the interwar period, the establishment of further national parks was considered, even scientists weighed the question of location no longer on environmental grounds but on political representation. The hosts of the next two national parks should not be the Mittelland (midlands) and Jura—the other two major geographical areas of Switzerland—but French-speaking western Switzerland and Italian-speaking Ticino. Accordingly, in the 1920s plans were introduced for a "Swiss French national park" in the area of Haut de Cry in Valais and a "Swiss Italian national park" around Castagnola-Gandria. Both, however, soon foundered.[44]

Coming into effect as it did on 1 August 1914, the Swiss national day, the federal resolution decreeing a national park in the Lower Engadine was symbolically freighted. However, the coincidence was not the result of careful planning but rather the expiration in mid-July of the three-month deadline for the referendum mandating the measure. All the same, the symbolism of the date was certainly fortuitous for the participants. In its annual report, the SNK called the park "our national nature sanctuary."[45] There was no official ceremony, possibly because the park had de facto already been long established, but also perhaps because international tensions had peaked in recent weeks and the start of the war prevented the relevant preparations. When, in the following months, the First World War drove a wedge between German- and French-speaking Switzerland, and people on both sides sympathized openly with their respective linguistic community, the SNG urged national unity. In 1916, the SNG held its annual meeting in Scuol, on the edge of the national park, and the traditional excursion naturally led through it. In a speech from Alp Mingèr, Carl Schröter praised the park as "a reflection of the true cooperation of all confederates: situated at the extreme eastern limit of our country, in the area of *alt fry Rätia* [old, free Raetia] among our valiant Romansh, from Schanf to Scuol, it is enthusiastically supported by western Switzerland. … Thus, the park is a work of joint national dedication, a symbol of unity, the most idealistic form of centralization." Before the excursion continued, the national anthem was sung. During a subsequent break, Paul Sarasin gave a speech in French in which he stressed the overall character of the national park.[46] All the well-intentioned rhetoric could not, however, disguise the fact that the park was not only geographically distant from French-speaking Switzerland. In Romandy it was perceived as a Swiss-German institution. That it was located in the Romansh-speaking (and not the German-speaking) part of the country did nothing to dispel this perception since at the time the Romansh were viewed not as a distinct national minority but were counted among the Swiss-German majority. In 1920, to counteract the Germanic influence, the ENPK was expanded to include an additional French-speaking member. As in the Swiss executive, the Federal Council, henceforth two of the seven park commission members would be French speaking. In so doing, at least at the federal government level the national park conformed to the delicate realities of Swiss representation.[47]

Reserve or National Park?

The rise of the national dimension had already been anticipated in a conceptual shift around 1910. Between 1907 and 1909, SNK discussions regarding the planned protected area usually involved the term "reserve." But from 1910, the term "national park" was increasingly preferred. In the SNK's annual report covering mid-1909 to mid-1910, the terms are used interchangeably, appearing under the heading "The Scarl Quatervals Reserve or the Swiss National Park." The text that follows notes that "it was decided to call the whole of the area envisaged for this nature park the Swiss National Park."[48] Neither the annual report nor the minutes of the SNK meetings give any further clues to the motives behind the decision. The committee made no official declaration, but seems to have gradually pushed the term "national park" over the course of the first half of 1910. This notwithstanding the opinion of Hermann Christ that the participants understood that their idea was materially different from that of the American national park whose label they were borrowing.

Two considerations appear to have influenced the name change: First, the advocates quickly learned that "national park" was well suited to winning both politicians and the public to the cause. The founding of the SBN in 1909 also strengthened the SNK's publicity efforts, at which both Schröter and Sarasin excelled. All in all, the national debate on conservation, which was clearly dominated by German Switzerland, proceeded in a vein very similar to that of neighboring Germany, with which it kept up a lively exchange. However, the use of the term "national park" provided a very interesting contrast. At precisely the same time the Swiss began to use the term, German conservationists shunned it. In 1909, the proponents of large protected areas gathered together in the Austro-German *Verein Naturschutzpark,* which was modeled on the SBN and to whose "additional working committee" Sarasin had also been appointed. The protection of characteristic "German" landscapes that the society was striving for would have its own appellation—"nature protection park"—which emphasized the independence of the concept. Conservationists were forced to this step by the latent anti-Americanism of the empire's middle-class elites. Despite some ambivalence, the Swiss image of America was clearly more positive. Although the German-Swiss bourgeoisie nursed reservations about American consumer culture similar to the Germans', politically Switzerland had a longstanding association with its big American "sister republic." Moreover, the "land of opportunity" may still have had a special fascination for little Switzerland that manifested itself in the fact that the United States was one of the preferred destinations for Swiss émigrés. Whereas German conservationists saw the associative link to "America" as a burden, their Swiss colleagues saw it as an opportunity.[49]

Second, the German and French meanings of "reserve" did not entirely coincide. This was pointed out in late 1909 by the Geneva conservation pioneer, Henry Correvon, who founded the *Association pour la protection des plantes* in 1883 and in 1889 established the first alpine garden to cultivate alpine plants. In the Geneva illustrated weekly *La Patrie Suisse,* Correvon presented the "Swiss national park plan." In a footnote on his choice of words, he wryly noted that "the term *reservation,* which people use for this creation, cannot realistically survive unless its meaning is changed in French dictionaries. It is a *district franc* [protected zone], a protected or special park, a national area, whatever one wishes, only not a *reservation*."[50] "National park" presented no translation difficulties; in addition, it would be easily recognized in all languages. These rhetorical and translational qualities made the combination of "nation" and "park" attractive in many countries.

However, the SNK had to see to it that its specific interpretation of "national park" prevailed against other current uses of the term. As a result of the bourgeoning interest in heritage, nature, and land conservation, after 1900 "national park" was already being bandied about to mean different things. The term was used consistently to refer to the American national parks, but since knowledge of the American situation did not go very deep, there was considerable room for creative adaptation. Applied to the preservation of natural tourist attractions, the term retained more or less the meaning of the American model. In 1903, the Schaffhausen cantonal council proposed to increase the water rates and to use the funds thus gained "to restore the original beauty" of the famous Rhine Falls and to turn "the Rhine Falls basin into a national park accessible to anyone."[51] A few years later, as noted earlier, the suggestion was similarly made to declare the Matterhorn a national park. In contrast, a greater focus on the park idea as traditionally interpreted was evident within the SNK in 1908. "Although acquiring the Petersinsel would be an inexpensive way for the government to create a beautiful *national park,*" stated the local Bern section in rationalizing its decision not to protect the island, "it would not deliver an appropriate *reserve* to satisfy the requirements of a scientific committee."[52]

Thus, in 1908, even within the small circle of the SNK, the term "national park" failed to evoke the desired associations. In the following year, the Lower Engadine writer and publicist Peider Lansel stepped into the debate, tactfully suggesting that one might better succeed with a "national park" in Val S-charl than a "reserve" in Val Cluozza. Lansel imagined a large "alpine garden" with specimen collections and laboratories for research and vivariums, along the lines of Hagenbeck's zoo in Hamburg. "In contrast to the savagery of the reserve, the term 'park' includes the idea of care," said Lansel regarding the fundamental difference between his proposal and that of the SNK. Paul Sarasin responded quickly and over the summer months engaged in a public slugfest with Lansel in the pages of the Grisons newspaper *Der Freie*

Rätier.[53] After that, Lansel's proposal deflated. The idea of using exhibits to approximate a natural presentation of native wildlife was quickly and effectively banished from discussion. Moreover, such a presentation was, at the time, both a hallmark of Hagenbeck's zoo and common practice in the American national parks. Yellowstone's tourist attractions included bison that were kept in an enclosure near Mammoth Hot Springs.[54] Lansel's use of "national park" was consequently in no way far-fetched; and, in any event, he definitely stayed closer to the American interpretation than the SNK did. The SNK launched a media campaign to undermine the park proposals of Lansel and others, and to establish an associative link between national parks and wilderness uncommon at that time. Switzerland would create the "first comprehensive reserve, a national park," reported Christian Tarnuzzer, president of the Grisons section of the SNK, to the readers of the *Süddeutsche Monatshefte*. To that end, "an exceptionally suitable mountain region, Val Cluoza, near Zernez," had been found, "that could only be described as wilderness."[55]

Nonetheless, the idea of the park as a cultivated garden and not a wilderness far from civilization was obviously not so easily dismissed by his contemporaries. The Swiss national park advocates subsequently began to lobby actively against this common image of the park. In 1918, this is how Carl Schröter opened an article in the German magazine *Die Naturwissenschaften:* "The term 'national park,' which we adopted from North America, lends itself easily to false expectations, as though we intended to cultivate exotic plants, or were seeking to create circumstances where wild animals that once happily wagged their tails in paradise would swarm visitors and be fed by them. Quite the contrary, the aim of a 'national park' is the revival and preservation of endangered *indigenous* wild, pristine nature, as untouched by human influence as possible."[56]

The name change had far-reaching, long-term consequences. "National park" enabled the Swiss conservation pioneers to claim as their own a label that would prove enormously successful in the twentieth century. The national park became a global brand whose use was not controlled by any central authority. The worldwide use of this brand made it possible to relate, through a common terminology, different ideas and concepts that spanned great distances and boundaries of all sorts. In the 1920s, Schröter suspected that national park idea would find widespread use "precisely because of its suggestive effect."[57] Indeed, it is clear that the combination of "nation" and "park" sounded appealing to Western ears. The park was a beautiful, open space that urbanites (upon whose support the national park movement relied so heavily), in particular, sought out to relax. The modifier "national" also endowed this new park with a higher purpose and justified the commitment of the highest government authority. As in the Swiss example, the park could evoke undesirable associations with an artificially arranged landscape. It was also possible that, as we have seen, the appeal to the nation could shift the priorities toward a nationalist agenda. In imperial contexts, the term also raised the question of national identity, which is why in colonial situations it encountered opposition and occasionally was replaced with more innocuous names.[58] It is certainly not the case that the idea of the national park spread easily from one country to another around the world. Rather, complex translations of the term arose that had a retroactive effect on countries that adopted the term early, and later served as models for imitators.[59] Those with a growing interest in national parks selected from the available offerings, let their creativity run riot, combined and modified what was handed down, and enriched it with their own ideas. In turn, the designation "national park" ensured for each individual creation international connectivity and visibility, though of course not all the "parks" in the conservation market attracted the same attention and appreciation. The US national park model was inarguably the one that drew the greatest attention worldwide. It was synonymous with American society—the "American way of life"—and later also linked to American global policy, which meant that adapting it could both help and hinder, as evidenced by its uneven reception in Switzerland and Germany. After 1910, the Swiss National Park offered another outstanding model that combined stringent protective regulation and scientific research. It quickly assumed a prominent position in the rapidly emerging global discourse on national parks, and was often held up as an alternative—and sometimes a complement—to the American-type "recreational park." This pervasive influence was in the spirit of the "inventors" of the Swiss park model.

National and Global Conservation

In the public and political propaganda that the SNK had been promoting since 1910 in favor of its national park, the committee stressed not only the park's national significance but also the international implications of their idea. Here, despite the substantial conceptual differences, the SNK happily followed the American precursor: "This area would constitute the first large reserve in Europe in the style of American reserves, and thus establishing a national park, a natural open area that deserves its proud name, would put little Switzerland on the map," argued the SNK in February 1911 in an application to the Federal Council for government support. Nor did the SNK stop there. The Swiss National Park presented a unique opportunity to "create a model for Europe that, as a comprehensive reserve for all animals and plants, is as yet without peer."[60] This rhetorical appeal to national prestige, which could be won through the creation of a national park or threatened, in the case of failure, was also applied diligently elsewhere. Kurt Floericke, one of the drivers of the Austro-German parks movement, asked around the same time: "Should we really let ourselves be shamed not only by the notoriously dollar-hungry Americans but even by little Switzerland and underpopulated Sweden, which also have now created great national parks?"[61] Invoking its vision of "small country, big paragon," the SNK wooed the support of official Switzerland. In so doing, the organization was completely in line with the foreign policy orientation of the country at the time, a fact that cannot have escaped the members of the SNK. In the decades before the First World War, Switzerland actively directed its foreign policy efforts at getting new policies on the international stage, which was dominated by the European powers. Around 1910, conservation was a promising candidate for this strategy.[62]

Paul Sarasin put Switzerland's foreign policy aspirations to use in a further initiative that he launched in August 1910 at the International Zoological Congress in Graz as well as three weeks later at the annual meeting of the SNG in Basel under the slogan "World Nature Protection."[63] Sarasin's intention was to exploit the initiative to transfer his organizational concept, already proven in Switzerland, to the international level. Sarasin already had this step in mind when he set up the SNK. Only together with other countries, he announced at the end of 1906 in a welcome letter to the newly elected heads of the cantonal conservation committees, could they reach their goal. "We must strive to bring about an organization that, like the geographical latitudinal and longitudinal grid, seamlessly connects neighboring countries."[64] Sarasin's basic idea was to export his organizational structure to every land. Everywhere, national committees would be established for the purpose of coordinating and directing an international body. The Swiss National Park in turn would serve as a prototype of a worldwide network of reserves. Accordingly, beginning in 1910, Sarasin advanced his international plans and his efforts in Switzerland in a synergistic fashion.

Born in 1856 into a well-off, far-flung Basel merchant family, Paul Sarasin is deservedly recognized as a pioneer of nature conservation. As a scientist, he was a transitional figure. Sarasin studied medicine and zoology in Basel and Würzburg, and did his doctorate under the supervision of the zoologist and explorer Karl Semper. But Sarasin's interests went far beyond those of his discipline. In the tradition of the independent polymath—he never held an academic position and did not have to earn a living—he also published on geology and botany, geography and ethnology, not to mention prehistory, art history, and astronomy. Sarasin had an energetic and authoritarian personality that manifested itself in his work and his leadership style as SNK chair. In social interactions he could be very gruff, and he was known and feared for his stubbornness. His younger cousin by three years, Fritz Sarasin, who knew him as no one else did and was extremely close to him all his life, wrote of this side of Paul in a moving obituary in 1929: "He brooked no opposition, or better put, he could not endure it, although he himself hardly spared the feelings of others. Consequently, once he had made a decision, he was deaf to further advice, no matter how well-meaning."[65] Given the powerful ongoing process of disciplinary differentiation and academic specialization, Paul Sarasin clearly belonged to a dying breed. His scientific work was reminiscent of Alexander von Humboldt's in its breadth. Sarasin's long view and his keen eye for social change, which showed in his program for world conservation, put him among the cosmopolitan avant-garde who, at the turn of the twentieth century, began to grasp the world as one large, connected series of actions and reactions.

One reason for the scope of Sarasin's thinking was no doubt the experience he gained on extended research trips to South and Southeast Asia that he made with Fritz over the course of three decades. Sometimes lasting several years, these expeditions took the Sarasins to Ceylon (now Sri Lanka) and Celebes (now Sulawesi) and brought them into direct contact not only with foreign peoples and cultures and their occasionally disturbing customs and traditions, but also with the effects of European colonialism. The time between 1880 and 1914 was the heyday of imperialism, and wherever the Sarasins went, they found evidence of the growing influence of European culture on local societies. These observations strongly affected the two men and were repeatedly mentioned in their travelogues. Paul and Fritz were deeply divided over the changes they saw and the speed with which the changes were occurring.

They welcomed the spread of the achievements of European civilization; by the same token, they shuddered to think that European civilization would soon become a global civilization. "The changes wrought in the course of just 70–80 years by government and mission working together is certainly admirable; for earlier, cultural experiments were limited to the coastal areas," wrote Fritz at one point in their jointly published (1905) diary of the trip through Celebes. "Philanthropists cannot help but be happy about this. Natural scientists and ethnographers, on the other hand, will gaze into the face of civilized Minahassa not without a secret dread about a future in which the entire planet will sport the same livery!"[66] Behind the globalization of Western progress lurked the specter of global uniformity, and the unfortunate—not least from a scientific perspective—and irretrievable loss of biological and cultural diversity.

From his confrontation with the colonial world, Paul drew two conclusions for his future conservation activities. First, the suppression of nature by civilization was a global phenomenon; and second, "primitive peoples" whose very survival was threatened by the same civilizing process also had to be an integral part of global nature protection. Sarasin's first observation was shaped by the social dichotomy that pitted nature against culture and that allowed the latter to displace the former. His second observation, however, ran countercurrent to the overwhelming view of his crowd that culture was a property

Illustration 2. Paul Sarasin and Fritz Bühlmann, ENPK president and secretary, at the entry to Val Cluozza, c. 1920. *Source:* Swiss National Park.

of the human species and thus to be kept separate from protected nature. In the American national parks, indigenous inhabitants were expelled from the parks or kept at distance from them, as were whites that had settled there. Hunting and gathering were forbidden in the national parks, which criminalized the traditional means of subsistence in the area.[67] From this perspective, Sarasin's demand that primitive peoples be included in the conservation efforts was unusual, but at the same time it was imbued with the Eurocentric and patriarchal mindset typical of the times. Like most of his contemporaries, who counted themselves elite Westerners, Sarasin believed human progress to be a deterministic process that took its cue from the advances of the European West. Only Europeans simultaneously possessed and made history; the rest of the world population (perhaps with the exception of China and the Arab and Indian world) were portrayed as living in a nonhistorical continuum that they escaped only by virtue of the European expansion. "In history, the Minahassa appear only with the arrival of the Europeans," Fritz Sarasin wrote in his diary. The ethnic groups that the cousins encountered were categorized into lower and higher types, mountain people being described as "backward" and coastal people as "advanced." An essay by Fritz on "the lowest human forms of Southeast Asia" described these creatures as "real human rubble, ... in some sense living fossils."[68] As Paul Sarasin pointed out in his article "On the Tasks of the World Nature Protection Movement," this vestige of an ahistorical human form should be preserved as an "anthropological natural monument" in the same way as endangered nonhuman forms of nature. They should be isolated in reserves and thus safeguarded "in the greatest untouched purity for science, for ourselves, and for posterity."[69]

Sarasin sought to achieve a breakthrough for both causes—the worldwide coordination of nature protection and the inclusion of primitive peoples in such a conservation program—within the framework of his world nature protection initiative. At his instigation, Swiss diplomats began to test the waters for establishing an international nature protection commission. When the results of these preliminary enquiries came back positive, the Swiss Federal Council decided in September 1913 to invite selected countries to a constituent assembly in Bern the following November. Seventeen countries accepted the invitation, which given the short notice could be read as success, in particular since with Great Britain, France, Germany, Austria-Hungary, Russia, Italy, and the United States, all the important contemporary powers would be represented. A notable exception was up-and-coming Japan, which from the outset had declined to participate in such an international commission.[70]

The conference provided Sarasin a formidable stage for promulgating his ideas of world nature protection. Sarasin was neither a political revolutionary nor a social visionary. Accordingly, his design took into account the existing international state system and its established entities and mechanisms.

Although he subscribed to the belief that "just as Nature knows no political boundaries, safeguarding it is also not limited to the confines of states," he did not take that to require that political borders be lifted but rather that "each nation that achieves conservation within its own borders also does so at the global level."[71] Accordingly, his idea of an effective world conservation strategy was precisely to seek it for as yet territorially unassigned areas like the Arctic and Antarctica, as well as for the oceans, directing each country to entrust its protection to a national authority. In so doing, Sarasin exploited a mechanism born of European nationalism and imperialism, and argued for a division of the world according to the norms of European nation-states.[72]

The functions that the proposed international nature protection commission was supposed to assume were those of coordinator and catalyst. The commission should seek, on the one hand, to "internationalize wildlife laws all over the world, i.e., to bring them in line with a common perspective," and on the other, to foster creation of "comprehensive reserves everywhere around the globe, from pole to pole." The conceptual transfer of the SNK based on Swiss federalism to a world nature protection commission based on internationalism was obvious. For the second field of action Sarasin brought the Swiss National Park into play: "It is not out of national vanity, but to assert a fact, when I say that for the first time, anywhere on Earth, there is a single, comprehensive, closely guarded (in every sense of the word) large-scale reserve, and that is the Swiss National Park in the Lower Engadine; it should and can serve as a model for all others."[73]

Sarasin cannot have been fully satisfied with the outcome of the conference. Although his plans vis-à-vis an international nature protection commission were taken up, its seat in Basel awarded, and Sarasin appointed its first president, the sphere of activity granted to the commission was far below what Sarasin had hoped for. The commission was to gather material and generate conservation propaganda. The commission would have no further powers, a point made even clearer by the modifier "consultative" added to the commission's name. In particular, the German delegation under Hugo Conwentz's direction successfully blocked a broader commission mandate. Similarly, Sarasin's desire to include the protection of "primitive peoples" as a field of activity was rejected by the majority.[74]

Although Sarasin had to restrain his ambitions, the most important objective—a place to start, and to build on—appeared to have been achieved at the 1913 meeting. Invitations for a follow-up gathering had already been sent when war broke out in the summer of 1914, and all further work on the project stopped. The First World War was a turning point. It put a sustained damper on the civilizing optimism of the conservation movement and on the movement itself, which was a setback for many park projects, especially in the countries neighboring Switzerland. Most of the plans of the Austro-German

Association of Nature Parks remained on paper, as did those for a park adjacent to the Swiss National Park on the Italian side. The *parc national de la Bérarde*, established in the French Alps in 1913, faded into obscurity.[75] The guide to the Swiss National Park published in 1914 to coincide with the park's official founding read auspiciously: "In the sharing of the borders of its protected area with amicable, mighty empires, Switzerland announced its confidence in the united cooperation of all civilized nations on the issue of *global conservation* and, under the leadership of Paul Sarasin, thereby heralded that momentous international convention whose goal is 'to effectively ensure the full protection of nature from pole to pole, throughout the entire earth, land, and sea.'" In the second edition, published in 1918, after four devastating years of war, this passage was dropped without substitution.[76]

After the war, Sarasin tried unsuccessfully to revive world nature protection as part of the League of Nations. But the old networks were irreparably broken, and many conservationists had been killed in the war. Moreover, in its aftermath, conservation had fallen way down the list of priorities at both the national and international level. Despite persistent prodding, Sarasin failed to obtain the support of the Swiss authorities. The initiative migrated to other countries. Between the world wars, Paris hosted two international congresses for the protection of nature (1923 and 1931), and in 1933 Great Britain invited the ruling powers of Africa to organize conservation on that continent along imperialistic lines. Somewhat similar to the way in which Sarasin's provisional world nature protection commission was approved in 1913, in 1928 Belgian and Dutch conservationists established an International Office for the Protection of Nature in Brussels, headed by Pieter van Tienhoven of the Netherlands. The office received financial support from the United States, probably triggered by the commitment of American scientists in the establishment of the *Parc National Albert* in the Belgian Congo, but was regarded with suspicion by imperial London. It was still busy with collecting and compiling documents when Second World War's German invasion of Belgium put a stop to further work in 1940.[77]

After peace had been restored, the SBN tried to build on Sarasin's legacy and to regain the initiative in international nature conservation. In 1946, the British Wildlife Conservation Special Committee, chaired by Julian Huxley, petitioned the SBN for a guided excursion through the Swiss National Park. The committee was involved in preparing proposals for national parks and nature reserves in Great Britain that had originated in the 1930s, been delayed by the Second World War, and now were again being promoted. The head of the SBN saw a visit by the British as an opportunity to simultaneously invite conservationists from other countries to an informal meeting to discuss the revival of the international conservation movement. Thus, in July 1946 the British delegation met in Basel with representatives from France, Belgium, the

Netherlands, Norway, and Czechoslovakia. The SBN also invited the American National Park Service (NPS) to the meeting, but was turned down. The NPS welcomed the SBN initiative, wrote Acting Director Hillory A. Tolson in responding to the invitation, but the NPS was experiencing the "greatest travel season ever" and consequently could not spare the manpower.[78] The NPS also declined the SBN's invitation to a follow-up international conference at Brunnen, on the Lake of Lucerne, in 1947. The Brunnen conference paved the way for the conference in Fontainebleau in 1948 where, under the auspices of Unesco and its first director-general, Julian Huxley, the International Union for the Protection of Nature (IUPN, the later IUCN) was finally established. What had already become apparent at the meetings of 1946 and 1947 was confirmed in 1948, throwing cold water on the obvious ambition of the SBN to take over the reins of the international organization itself. Although Charles Bernard was elected the first president of the IUPN, the seat was awarded to Brussels, and Belgian Jean-Paul Harroy was entrusted with managing it. In 1958, Jean Baer, a parasitologist and chair of the scientific committee of the Swiss National Park, succeeded Frenchman Roger Heim as third president of the IUCN. Baer used the organization's financial difficulties, as well as the reputational damage Belgium had incurred owing to its colonial rule in Congo, to eventually bring the seat of the organization to Switzerland. The fact that, in the postwar years, politically neutral Switzerland had become a fulcrum in international politics may have facilitated this move.[79]

During Baer's presidency, a national park committee was created, chaired by American Harold J. Coolidge, a zoologist working at the US National Academy of Sciences, fueling discussion within the IUCN about protected areas. In 1961, the committee published the first *World List of National Parks and Equivalent Reserves*; the first World Conference on National Parks took place in Seattle in 1962. Also appearing just in time for the conference was *National Parks: A World Need*. This volume was the conference contribution of the American Committee for International Wildlife Protection, which had been co-founded by Coolidge in 1930. The volume editor was Victor H. Cahalane, vice director of the New York State Museum, a wildlife biologist who had previously worked for the NPS. In his introduction Cahalane emphasized that the national park idea was expressed differently around the world. He presented four contrasting approaches: the scientific approach realized in Switzerland, the Congo, and French West Africa; the protection of wildlife that prevailed in Africa; the stewardship of the landscape typical of North and Central America; and the national parks in Great Britain and Japan, whose purpose was to integrate humans and nature. The book was organized by continent and contained twelve reports, including one by Jean Baer on the Swiss National Park.[80] Ten years later, in 1972, at the second World Conference on National Parks, Harold J. Coolidge revisited Cahalane's work. Coolidge now addressed the assembled elite of international conservation as the president of the IUCN. Around the world, Coolidge affirmed, the term "national park" had assumed many different meanings. From among the welter of national parks that had been founded in the interim, he singled out the Swiss park as a "splendid example of a scientific national park."[81]

The diverse meanings attached to the term "national park" gave rise to international efforts at categorization, which in turn prompted a move for global standardization of conservation measures. The 1961 list of protected areas was periodically updated jointly by the IUCN and the United Nations, and a nomenclature of protected areas was also being drawn up. As an offshoot of this process, on the one hand, the national park was knocked from its pedestal (in 1997, for the first time, the term was left out of the title), and on the other hand, it was assigned as one among many internationally recognized national categories of protected areas. Beginning with the path-breaking systematization of 1978, the national park came under Category II.[82] This structure had already been drafted at the time of the tenth General Assembly of the IUCN in 1969 in New Delhi, at which the IUCN agreed a definition of "national park" for the first time: to wit, a relatively large area, first, whose ecosystems were not materially altered by human exploitation, that contained interesting natural phenomena, or that represented a landscape of great beauty; second, whose protection was assured by the highest government authority; and third, was open to visitors.[83] At the same time, governments were requested to refrain from designating as national parks protected areas that did not fit the definition. Of the four approaches enumerated by Cahalane, only the second and third—the "African wildlife park" and the "American scenic park"—accorded with the IUCN category "national park." Parks integrating traditional human land use were assigned to Category V, "Protected Landscape." Scientific parks came under Category I, "Strict Nature Reserve." Consequently, in the 1990s, the Swiss National Park was transferred from Category II to Category I. In 1994 it was subsumed under the newly introduced subdivision Ia, encompassing protected areas that are "managed mainly for science." Subdivision Ib was intended for wilderness areas, whereas Category II "National Park" was reserved for protected areas "managed mainly for ecosystem protection and recreation."[84]

Dynamics and Contingencies

The *World Database on Protected Areas* gives 1914 as the year of the Swiss National Park's founding. In some ways, however, 1914 represented less of a beginning than a conclusion. The results of the efforts that produced a national park in ten short years culminated in the transfer of the park to the long-term care of the government just before the outbreak of the First World War. At the same time, the global shocks that triggered the war ended the ambitious plans to promote worldwide conservation on the Swiss model and under Swiss leadership. Although these plans were successfully relaunched by the Swiss at the end of the Second World War, and the Swiss National Park did play an instrumental role in this, in the following phase (where the criteria for a national park were hashed out within the IUCN) the Swiss park was still present but largely irrelevant. The American model of preservation and recreation became central for the IUCN category "national park," whereas the Swiss "scientific park" model was relegated to the "Strict Nature Reserve" category.

The years prior to 1914 that were critical for the Swiss National Park can be divided into three phases: In an initial phase that lasted from 1906 to 1908, existing ideas for large protected areas were evaluated and put into concrete terms within the newly established SNK. This evolved both within the small group privy to the committee's discussions about concepts and sites as well as in the process of building a network of people, organizations, and institutions on which the SNK could subsequently rely. A second phase, lasting from 1908 to 1911, was characterized by the single-minded implementation of the specified ideas at a previously decided location under the direction of SNK chair Paul Sarasin. Now the question of how the enterprise would be financed took priority. Consequently, the project was popularized and nationalized, and then materialized in the form of a national park, which though very different in key respects from the American benchmark carried the day. The third phase began in 1911 and included the safeguarding of the national park by the intervention of the state as financial and institutional guarantor, which led to a shift of responsibility and further enhanced the nationalistic perspective on the park.

In retrospect, several of the participants perceived the founding of the Swiss National Park—from Schröter's first declaration to the enactment of the federal decree in 1914—to have been a thorny task whose solution required extraordinary muscle, whose underlying issues, however, remained stable throughout.[85] This view is contested by historical research, which suggests a much more contingent and dynamic process that entailed a constant shifting of task and solution, means and people. In this process, the solution finally settled for was not only forged but also politically and socially stabilized. Just how successful the endeavor was, was evident in the coming decades, when the Swiss National Park showed an amazing permanence in the face of change. "Total protection" and "scientific research" became solid pillars supporting the park. Before exploring these issues, it is worth a detour to examine local conditions and to analyze the factors that determined the sociogeographical relationship between the park and the Ofen Pass region.

Notes

1. *Der Bund*, 1 April 1910.
2. Ulysses Gessner was clearly a combination of Ulysses Aldrovandus and Conrad Gessner, the two founding fathers of zoology. Henry Debarges was probably thinking of Henry Correvon, founder of the "*Association pour la protection des plantes*," director of the *Jardin d'Acclimatation* in Geneva, and initiator of the first alpine garden. Peter von Almen is easily recognized as goatherd Peter from Johanna Spyri's *Heidi*, and Chalamala was the name of the legendary last court jester from the *Tales of Gruyères*, on which Louis Thurler composed an opera, first performed in 1910 (Thurler 1910). The newspaper article is in the SCNAT Archives, Box 532, and marked "Widmann," most likely in Paul Sarasin's hand.
3. Latour 2005.
4. The park's founding is described in detail by Stefan Bachmann (Bachmann 1999, 117–165). I have analyzed the archival records anew relating to the five issues mentioned (which Bachman does not go into, or only peripherally). Selected aspects of the park's creation I also re-examine in the following chapters.
5. Even in entrusting its new committee with collecting money for the *Pierre des Marmettes*, the SNG treated the boulder ambivalently: "You might want to redouble your efforts to obtain contributions for the *Bloc des Marmettes* from your canton, so we can finally have done with this rock for good," wrote Paul Sarasin in 1908 to his cantonal stewards in obvious frustration. That same year, the collection was successfully completed. SNK annual report 1907–8, 43. The founding members of the SNK were Paul Sarasin, Hermann Fischer-Sigwart, Jakob Heierli, Albert Heim, Hans Schardt, Carl Schröter, Ernest Wilczek, and Friedrich Zschokke. Hermann Christ was called in as legal advisor. On these people and on the founding of the SNK, see Bachmann 1999, 73–91.
6. Coaz and Schröter 1905.
7. Rudio and Schröter 1906, 505. The text first appeared in the *NZZ*, 2 November 1906, in a somewhat shorter version. The phrase "no chopping and no shooting" was very popular among German-speaking park supporters. Walter Bissegger used it in his speech to the National Council (*Amtliches Bulletin Nationalrat* 24 [1914], 160), as did Kurt Floericke for the German-Austrian nature reserve (1910, 15) and Carl Georg Schillings for similar parks in the German colonies, where "every ax and rifle" should be "silenced" (cited in Regensberg 1912, 55). On ibex, see chapter 4.
8. Bears no longer inhabited the Lower Engadine and roamed the area only sporadically. They had completely disappeared from the rest of Switzerland. See chapters 3 and 4.
9. SNK annual report 1907–8, 1 f., 24–29.
10. SNK annual report 1907–8, 37–43. The quote is from the botanical observations of Hermann Christ, loc. cit., 39.
11. SCNAT Archives, Box 537, Hermann Christ: Gutachten über die Gesetze der amerikanischen Reservationen, 2 May 1908. The report was presented at the annual meeting of the SNK in August 1908 and published in the SNK's annual report of 1908–9 (43–47). However, the final section of the report, in which Christ makes specific suggestions, such as how the rules for Switzerland should be established, was omitted, probably so as not to influence the assembly.
12. See Rudio and Schröter 1909.

13. SNK annual report, 1908–9, 27–33, quotation 33. Paul Sarasin's account of the meeting in the Hotel Ofenberg, although anecdotal, is credible.
14. In the interwar years, the United States began to expand the criteria for the first national parks in the east and southeast (Everglades, Shenandoah, Great Smoky Mountains). The scenery remained important, but biological aspects gradually gained in importance. See Runte 1987, 65–81, 106–137.
15. SNK Reservationenkomitee to the Zernez communal council, 15 December 1908, in SNK annual report 1908–9, 52–57, quotation 54 f.
16. This also includes the temporal concentration of monuments that Georg Kreis notes for the years 1899–1910. Kreis 2008, 182.
17. On the contemporary debates on heritage conservation regarding restoration or conservation, see Falser 2008. The environmental historian Marcus Hall also draws attention to these parallels in his history of environmental restoration (Hall 2005).
18. Of the three forest reserves, one (Thurau) was abandoned, and two (Vorderschattigen and Scattlé) were transferred to the SBN. See Escher 1994. Their mastermind, Glutz, who became district forester in the canton of Solothurn, died in 1914 at age 41. In his exposé of 1906, he also mentioned the Tamangur pine forest that he knew from the publication of Coaz and Schröter, and that Schröter in turn later that year suggested (citing Glutz) as the nucleus for a future national park. Schweizerische Zeitschrift für Forstwesen, June 1906, 184–191. Despite all efforts (see chapter 3), the forest was never made part of the national park.
19. A clear majority of the committee members wanted to speak out against the project. But a minority led by geologist Albert Heim successfully resisted the move. They argued that the railroad would do no obvious damage either to the ecology or appearance of the mountain—the final stage to the top was planned to go underground—and that by building an observatory at the summit, the railroad would also further science. The majority countered with the moralizing line of heritage protection. The construction would rob the Matterhorn of its majesty, they said, and ideals would be traded for filthy lucre. The positions were irreconcilable. Finally, peace was preserved by the members declaring themselves in favor of a strong commitment to science and thus to be unqualified to judge societal matters of nature and heritage protection. Bachmann 1999, 93–116.
20. Zemp to Department of Home Affairs, 22 July 1907. Cited in SNK annual report 1907–8, 31 f.
21. SNK annual report 1907–8, 30–34.
22. Hermann Christ, Schweizerische Nationalparke, in *Basler Nachrichten*, 8 May 1908.
23. SNK annual report 1908–9, 24–48; SCNAT Archives, Box 521, SNK, meeting of 29 August 1908, Protokollbuch, 19.
24. SCNAT Archives, Box 521, SNK Reservationenkomitee, meeting of 31 October 1908, Protokollbuch, 81.
25. Jungo 1972, 4. The aspect of competition is also given short shrift by Bachmann 1999. No contacts were established with the socialist *Nature Friends* (from 1905 in Switzerland, see Schumacher 2005).
26. The authority that Hermann Christ enjoyed within the ranks of the SNK was manifest, for instance, in Christ's amendments to the reserve recommendations of the cantonal sections. SNK annual report 1908–9, 24–43.

66 *Creating Wilderness*

27. SCNAT Archives, Box 521, SNK Reservationenkomitee, meeting of 31 August 1908, Protokollbuch, 81. Coaz, who also represented the forestry association on the Reserves Committee, was later succeeded by Grison's forest inspector Florian Enderlin. But Enderlin only attended the second and (already) last meeting of the committee on 20 November 1909. Loc. cit., 85 f.
28. Schröter invoked the financial aspect as early as 1906. Rudio and Schröter 1906, 505.
29. SCNAT Archives, Box 521, SNK Reservationenkomitee, meeting of 31 October 1908, 83. SNK annual report 1908–9, 59–64. On Hähnle and the *Bund für Vogelschutz*: Wöbse 2003.
30. Kupper 2009c. On the related negotiations, see chapter 3.
31. SNK to the Federal Council, 1 February 1911, in SNK annual report 1910–11, 49–53.
32. BAR, E 16, vol. 41, Sarasin to Coaz, 25 October 1911.
33. The community of S-chanf was "very surprised" by this turnabout. SNP Archives, 122.100, Dazzi to Brunies, 18 September 1912 (German trans. Brunies). Tavrü: SNK annual report 1911–12, 111 f. Cluozza: SCNAT Archives, Box 521, SNK, meeting of 10 September 1912, Protokollbuch, 52 f.
34. The SNK annual report praised the "generous and effective help" of Rosina Gemuseus-Riggenbach. She was the only woman among twenty-five men appointed honorary members of the SBN at the second general meeting in December 1914—further evidence of male dominance in the conservation movement. SNK annual report 1913–14, 202 f. Gemuseus-Riggenbach, a Basel native who lived in Schloss Spiez in the Bernese Oberland, had already made a name for herself as a patron in 1907 by donating 150,000 francs to found an animal sanctuary in Basel (www.basler-stadtbuch.ch/stadtbuch/chronik/detail.cfm?Id=4627, 9 September 2010). In 1914, the federal government assumed responsibility retroactively for the rent owed by the commune of Zernez for 1912 and 1913 in the amount of 18,200 francs. On the finances of the SBN, see the SBN annual report, in SNK annual report 1909–10, ff.
35. For the circumstances, see the material on the world nature protection movement later in this chapter as well as in chapter 5.
36. All three reports are in the SNK annual report 1911–12, 85–98.
37. SNK annual report 1911–12, 89. In his so-called worthless lands essay, Runte presents the view that, for a long time in the United States, only such areas could be incorporated into national parks as had no profit potential and that consequently were considered to have no value (Runte 1987, 48–64 and xii–xvi; see also the discussion in Frost and Hall 2009a). Coaz's statements show that these sorts of considerations also played a role in the founding of the Swiss National Park.
38. SNK annual report 1911–12, 85. In 1918, however, S-chanf concluded an easement with the federal government. The negotiations with the communes will be covered in the next chapter.
39. Schweizerischer Bundesrat, 1914. For details of the negotiations, see the description in Bachmann 1999, 144–156.
40. Treated in detail by Bachmann 1999, 291–310.
41. Bundesbeschluss betreffend die Errichtung eines schweizerischen Nationalparkes im Unter-Engadin, 3 April 1914, art. 1. In addition, the community leases already contained a clause to cover cases of bears or other large predators appearing in the park area.

42. States Councilor Heinrich von Roten, *Amtliches Bulletin Ständerat* 24 (1914), 157.
43. Schröter 1910, 24.
44. *NZZ*, 3 March 1922 and 4 September 1925. See Vischer 1946, 242–252. For the background of this turn of affairs, see the final chapter.
45. SNK annual report 1913–14, 198 f. In 1924, looking back over the founding of the national park, park commission secretary Bühlmann called the overlap with the national day "a good omen." Bühlmann 1924, 11.
46. Tarnuzzer 1916, quotation 223 f.
47. SBN Archives, M 3.2, ENPK, meeting of 4 March 1920. As early as 1918, the ENPK had added a representative from Grisons. On this matter and on the Romansh-speaking areas, see chapter 3. Of the seven members of the ENPK, three were appointed by the Federal Council, and two each by the SBN and the SNG.
48. SNK annual report 1909–10, 14.
49. See the portrayal of America in Glutz-Graff 1905. Moreover, the appreciation was mutual (see Hammer 1995). On the discourse about America in Europe before the First World War, see Schmidt 1997; Klautke 2003, 87–109. See also Tanner and Linke 2006. On the *Verein Naturschutzpark,* see Verein Naturschutzpark 1910; Lüer 1994 and Schmoll 2004, 113–121, 212–223.
50. Henry Correvon, "Un Parc National," *La Patrie Suisse*, no. 422, 24 November 1909, 291.
51. *NZZ*, 29 December 1903. See Barthelmess 1987, 165–170. The Blausee in Kantertal was also suggested as a national park, but the *NZZ* considered the location inadequate. *NZZ*, 7 July 1904. An earlier call to create a "Swiss national park" from an anonymous writer in the Zurich *Tages-Anzeiger* in 1895 and reprinted in the hunting magazine *Diana* found no takers (Schmidt 1976, 254 f.).
52. SNK annual report 1907–8, 56 f. Emphasis mine.
53. Lansel initially phrased his idea in Romansh in *Fögl d'Engiadina* ("Un parc naziunal svizzer in Engiadina bassa," 29 May 1909). Brunies translated the article for the SNK (SCNAT Archives, Box 532). Sarasin replied in the *Freie Rätier* of 9 July 1909. The above quotation comes from Peider Lansel's rejoinder "Reservation oder Nationalpark" (Der Freie Rätier, 28 July 1909). Regarding Lansel, see www.peiderlansel.ch.
54. Isenberg 2000, 180 f.
55. Tarnuzzer 1911, 247.
56. Schröter 1918, 761. On this subject—unfulfilled expectations—see also the description in chapter 4 of the reactions of the first park wardens.
57. Schröter 1924, 387.
58. See Gissibl et al. 2012b.
59. Roderick Nash was the first to trace the international proliferation of national parks historically. However, the transfer model he proposed was seriously flawed. In particular, in conceptualizing "nature" and "civilization" as essentialist entities he opted for an export-import relationship that is both one-dimensional and teleological.
60. SNK to the Federal Council, 1 February 1911, in SNK annual report 1910–11, 49–53. This statement was as a matter of fact inaccurate because in 1909–10 Sweden had already ruled out several national parks.
61. Floericke 1910, 14. On the (inter)national profiling of national parks, see Wöbse 2012b.

62. On international Swiss diplomacy, see Herren 2000.
63. Sarasin 1910. See also Sarasin 1911. On the following discussion, see also Wöbse 2012a, 36–53.
64. Correspondence from Sarasin to the NK chair of 31 December 1906, in SNK annual report 1906-7, 95 f.
65. Sarasin 1928-29, 22. On the work of Paul and Fritz Sarasin in their native Basel, see Simon 2009, 109–115. Simon is also working on a biography of both Sarasins to be published in 2014.
66. Sarasin and Sarasin 1905, 45 f. On the ethnographic work of the Sarasins, see Reubi 2011. The Sarasins' trip to Celebes is the focus of the forthcoming PhD thesis by Bernhard Schär.
67. Warren 1997; Spence 1999; Jacoby 2001.
68. Sarasin and Sarasin 1905, 42, 86, and passim. Sarasin 1907, 245.
69. Sarasin 1914, 55. See Wöbse 2006b. The topic will be revisited in chapter 3 in connection with the national park and the local communes.
70. Bachmann 1999, 271–274. The other conference participants were Argentina, Belgium, Denmark, Holland, Norway, Portugal, Sweden, and Spain. Austria and Hungary showed up with separate delegations. Australia and Australian Victoria were both represented but could not vote. Conférence Internationale pour la Protection de la Nature Berne 1914.
71. Sarasin 1914, 6.
72. See Maier 2000.
73. Sarasin 1914, 50. Herren's judgment (2000, 354 f.) that the national park played a secondary role in Sarasin's plans is incorrect.
74. The official name of the committee was *Commission consultative pour la protection international de la nature*. On the German delegation's conduct of negotiation, see Wöbse 2006a, 634–639.
75. On these park projects, see the discussion in chapters 4 and 5.
76. Brunies 1914, 18; and Brunies 1918.
77. See Bachmann 1999, 278 f.; Herren and Zala 2002, 82; Wöbse 2006a, 639–671; Wöbse 2012a, 54–64. On the rivalry between international and imperial efforts at categorization, see Gissibl 2009, 435–442.
78. NA, RG 79, 3.1, entry 7, Box 2920, SBN to the NPS, 4 May 1946; NPS to the SBN, 18 June 1946.
79. Holdgate 1999, 17–48, 76–78. On the British efforts, see Evans 1997, 60–78.
80. Cahalane 1962. On the American Committee for International Wildlife Protection, see Barrow 2009, 135–167.
81. Coolidge 1972, 33. Coolidge presided IUCN from 1966 to 1972. The attitude of different countries to the Swiss National Park's scientific orientation is discussed in chapter 5.
82. World Conservation Monitoring Centre 1998. See Heijnsbergen 1997, 172–196; Phillips 2004. For the legal foundations and principles of this process, see Gissibl et al. 2012b.
83. "A National Park is a relatively large area (1) where one or several ecosystems are not materially altered by human exploitation and occupation, where plant and animal species, geomorphological sites and habitats are of special scientific, educative and recre-

ative interest or which contains a natural landscape of great beauty, and (2) where the highest competent authority of the country has taken steps to prevent or to eliminate as soon as possible exploitation or occupation in the whole area and to enforce effectively the respect of ecological, geomorphological or aesthetic features which have led to its establishment, and (3) where visitors are allowed to enter, under special conditions, for inspirational, educative, cultural and recreative purposes." Cited in Harroy 1972b, 5 f. The resolution was adopted at the second World Conference on National Parks 1972. See also World Conservation Monitoring Centre 1990; Lewis 2012.

84. IUCN 1994b, 17–19. The most recent version of the categories is dated 2008 (Dudley 2008). For current data see the World Database on Protected Areas (WDPA, www.wdpa.org).

85. Brunies 1914, 1–18; Schröter 1920, 2–4; Bühlmann 1924.

CHAPTER 3

Local Landscapes
Political Spaces, Institutional Arrangements, and Subjective Attitudes

The regional focus of the Swiss National Park has given rise to no small number of problems over the last one hundred years. A telling introduction to the topic is a controversy that played out comparatively recently, at the end of the twentieth century. In the mid-1990s, the park was to be expanded. The new park would encompass an area of around 500 square kilometers spread over twenty communes rather than four. The core zone, comprising 170 square kilometers of the existing park—where, as previously, nature would be left to develop freely—was to be extended to at least 200 square kilometers. In addition, a surrounding area of around 300 square kilometers was envisioned for the sustainable, natural use and care of the traditional agricultural landscape.

In subsequent years, the idea was heatedly debated in the region and concrete steps were taken. In 1999, Lavin became the first commune to approve the park expansion plans for its territory. At the same time, Lavin's voters decided to include in the core zone the Macun Lake Plateau, situated some 2,500 meters above sea level. On 1 August 2000, the Swiss national day, the 3.6-square-kilometer parcel of land was officially transferred to the national park in an official ceremony held on the high plateau. Lavin thus became the fifth national park area, ninety years after the first contract with the commune of Zernez entered into force and eighty-two years after Valchava became the (now) second-to-last commune to be leased to the national park.

This was an encouraging sign, but the real test was still ahead, in the form of an upcoming vote in Zernez. All the parties realized that this vote would determine the direction of the entire project. Zernez was not only the first commune to have given land to the national park; it also owned two-thirds of the parklands. Moreover, the park service was headquartered in Zernez. The communal assembly that convened on 1 December 2000 drew an unusually large crowd. However, to the disappointment of both the park and the communal authorities, the turnout proved no boon to the national park. Indeed, in the final ballot, the opponents of the park expansion won a clear majority of 227 to 145 votes. The National Park Commission acknowledged defeat and called off the plans. The project had failed. The Macun Lake Plateau would be the only territorial expansion. The surrounding area was no longer an issue.

The negative decision by Zernez was not completely unexpected. Prior to the vote, the local youth section of the rightwing political party *Schweizerische Volkspartei* (SVP) had mounted a vocal opposition that effectively mobilized a large number of voters. Still, there was surprise at the clear repudiation of an initiative that would have rewarded the commune generously in return for restricting a small amount of land. But emotions, not objective arguments, ruled the final phase of the debate. The opponents of expansion accused the authorities of partisanship, of intentionally deceiving voters, of paternalism, and of a dictate imposed from outside.[1] Though the "no" campaign had no merit, it succeeded nonetheless. Key to its victory appears to have been its ability to foment distrust of the park authorities. From a historical perspective, what is disconcerting about the Zernez verdict is that, ninety-odd years after the national park transacted its first lease, a populist campaign was still able to destroy five years of preparatory work almost overnight. The voting result of December 2000 was a brutal reminder of how tenuous the relationship was between the national park and the commune even after decades of shared history. The parties had built no familiarity, trust, or ties.[2]

This lack of connection constitutes the starting point for the considerations that follow, in which I aim to elucidate the historical relationship between the national park and the region. Chronologically, the chapter focuses on the period before the Second World War, when attitudes formed. What explains the social structures that brought about the national park at the beginning of the twentieth century? How did the region respond to the national park idea, and which local attitudes and behavioral patterns emerged along with the national park? How did the park influence the region? What developments did it encourage? And what disagreements did it occasion?

The problem of how to establish a national park in a specific, local environment comes up again and again, all over the world, and must always be dealt with anew. The analysis of this process centers on what the Indian political scientist Arun Agrawal calls "environmentality." The concept derives from Michel Foucault's notion of governmentality, whose general theme is varieties of domination and subjectivation.[3] Agrawal relates governmentality specifically to the environment. Environmentality encompasses "the knowledges, politics, institutions, and subjectivities that come to be linked together with the emergence of the environment as a domain that requires regulation and protection."[4] In particular, for Agrawal it is about understanding how state-controlled environmental regulations and subjective attitudes toward the environment affect each other and are thereby changed. New approaches to international conservation, aimed at strengthening self-government, form the background of his work. According to Agrawal, the success of such community-based conservation is determined by the simultaneous implementation of three strategies: "(1) the creation of governmentalized localities that can undertake regulation in specified domains, (2) the opening of territorial and administrative spaces in which new regulatory communities can function, and (3) the production of environmental subjects whose thoughts and actions bear some reference to the environment."[5] In short, it is about the development of political spaces, instruments, and subjects that help or hinder regulation of the environment based on the interplay of these three strategies.

Especially in the context of international efforts to bring parks and people closer together, the comparatively long history of the Swiss National Park deserves particular attention. What clearly stands out in the Swiss case is the strong political position taken by local institutions from the very beginning. Without their explicit consent nothing would ever have happened. That this situation had led neither to frictionless politics, nor to a well-oiled management machine, nor to higher acceptance of the park by local residents became clear in 2000. In what follows, I will examine the localization, institutionalization, and subjectivization of the Swiss National Park, clarify the dynamics and interactions of these processes, and also consider their local specificities as well as their global attributes.

Global, Local

Around the world, precarious relations with the local population are a defining characteristic of the national park as an institution. The tension and conflict between national park advocates and local groups that at times has erupted into violence is a fixture of the history of the national park from its earliest beginnings until today. No matter where in the world, establishing a national park often profoundly affected the lives of the local communities. People were driven from their ancestral lands, traditions restricted or prohibited, and social structures shattered. Yet the parks also provided opportunities for development. The extent to which the local population—or at least some of them—was able to profit from these opportunities differed as much with time and place as did the degree of participation that people were allowed or that they were in a position to demand. For a long time, this aspect of national park history was neglected. In recent years, however, that situation has changed owing to two increasingly overlapping developments. First, the international conservation movement itself began to question whether parks could be effective without being locally anchored. Second, a sizable international human rights movement arose that served to link local groups from around the world and that proved increasingly adept at defending their ancestral rights at the international level. The culmination of this activity was the "Declaration on the Rights of Indigenous Peoples" adopted at the United Nations General Assembly of 2007.[6]

In many regions of the world, demands for nature and biodiversity protection and the restoration or assertion of indigenous rights are at odds, and relations can be tense. The historical origin of this opposition goes back to a desire that evolved in the Western world of the nineteenth century: the educated, middle-class hankering for unspoiled nature and empty wilderness. Historically, it was left to the United States to give physical form to this desire by creating large, unpopulated areas within its national parks. Yellowstone became the epitome of a landscape left untouched by humans and a model of "fortress conservation" that forbade the local population access to or use of the protected areas. As a result, not everywhere, but in many parts of the world, the label "national park" was associated with the idea of unpopulated, pristine nature. Of course, despite their often remote location, areas designated as parks were not really unpopulated, let alone "untouched." And under these conditions, disputes with locally based or traditionally nomadic peoples were inevitable. Yet attempts to deal with the problem and the preoccupation with it varied considerably from place to place and over time. The form that relations took depended largely on the prevailing social structures that shaped and restricted stakeholders' conceptual worlds and freedom to act. Moreover, the resulting, frequently very asymmetric distribution of power—to the detriment of local actors—was not only structurally determined; the establishment of national parks was also specifically exploited as an opportunity to strengthen national or imperial access.[7]

These last remarks also apply to regions and countries where "national park" was interpreted to mean the integration of local people within the designated area, manifested through two distinct approaches: In the first approach, typical especially of Latin American and European countries, national parks were intended to perpetuate not wilderness but traditional cultural landscapes. These parks comprised both settlements and land management. Conservation was a motive, but one that was strongly linked to the preservation of cultural heritage. In the 1930s, national parks in this category were established in Mexico and Holland, and after the Second World War, also in England.[8] The alternative approach consisted of taking indigenous peoples back to nature and "preserving" them as an integral part of the wilderness, away from civilization. Thus, in Sweden's national park, the Sami were able to preserve their traditionally vested rights, and in the Belgian Congo, the colonial authorities left the Twa in the area set aside in 1926 as the Albert National Park. But the concept was mainly applied in Asia.[9] Just as with fortress conservation, beginning in the 1980s this approach was heavily criticized by development and human rights organizations because it linked existence in the parks with adherence to conditions previously determined by park authorities to be consistent with life in the wild. Under threat of expulsion, affected groups were denied a stake in the developing society, tantamount to "forced primitivism."[10]

Among the well-known early conservationists, Paul Sarasin was probably the most vocal proponent of this approach, both at home and internationally. In his memoir on the occasion of the International Nature Protection Conference in 1913 in Bern, he declared the most important and also most worthwhile task of nature protection to be "to save the last of the primitive tribes, the so-called indigenous peoples, from extinction and to keep them as untouched as possible for posterity; yet we can congratulate ourselves that, up to now, fortune has favored human tribes that, based on manner of living and thinking and feeling, according to what we call ergology or learning by doing, represent a transient phase of our own culture. Indeed, in observing their lives and actions, we glimpse our own past as though looking down from a tower with flesh and blood eyes."[11]

Sarasin was a Haekelian-influenced Darwinist who had done ethnographic fieldwork in Celebes and Ceylon, and in these "primitive tribes" he saw the preservation of an early stage of human evolution achieved through spatial confinement. That put Sarasin squarely in the mainstream of contemporary anthropology, which taught a temporally linear sequence of social organizational forms, leading from hunter-gatherers through agrarian societies to the industrialized West. "The most culturally backward of human tribes are scientifically the most important," Sarasin concluded. Anyone who espouses the protection of animal species must "a fortiori also commit himself to the energetic protection of primitive man, this noblest of all wild creatures of nature."[12] This approach, which Sarasin called "anthropological nature protection," was very similar to fortress conservation. As did others, Sarasin categorically distinguished culture and nature, differing only in where he drew the line. His line was between civilization and nature, and "indigenous peoples" belonged to the side of nature. Both approaches, fortress conservation and anthropological nature protection, shared Sarasin's guiding principle "to preserve those remnants—which have miraculously survived on our planet—as *purely as possible* for science, ourselves, and posterity."[13]

In so thinking, Sarasin also proposed to bridge the interests of nature conservation and contemporaneous efforts aimed at inventorying human testimonials and preserving them in museums, spurred on by ethnology and anthropology as well as archeology and folklore. Well into the twentieth century, both non-European peoples and—certainly in conscious analogy—the people of the Alps were investigated and described as primitive societies. In his magnum opus *Ur-Ethnographie der Schweiz*, published in 1924 and dedicated to Fritz and Paul Sarasin, the Basel physician and eminent folklorist Leopold Rütimeyer tried systematically to capture the traditional material culture of the Swiss mountain people: "As in creating ethnographic collections of primitive peoples, here, too, one must collect and preserve," Rütimeyer wrote in the foreword to his book, adding immediately that, in his case, at issue was "the survival of our country's long-gone primitive cultural conditions," which thanks to the conservatism of the mountain people had been preserved.[14] Sarasin also drew a clear time line. At his instigation, the SNK was officially named *Kommission für die Erhaltung von Naturdenkmälern und prähistorischen Stätten* (Commission for the Conservation of National Monuments and Prehistoric Sites). Sarasin justified the inclusion of the latter by arguing that "our prehistoric ancestors may be included among the primitive peoples" and consequently that it was the task of nature protection to preserve "their surviving traces for us." In this matter, however, Sarasin garnered little support among the SNK, and the topic was increasingly taken up by the *Schweizerische Gesellschaft für Urgeschichte* (Swiss Society of Prehistory).[15]

In Switzerland, there was no question of having living humans as objects of a national nature protection program. To the contrary, the search for large conservation areas focused on spaces devoid of human settlement. None of the areas included in the Swiss National Park contained permanently inhabited dwellings, thereby avoiding the need for relocations. Here, the desirable was reconciled with the realizable, since any such relocation would in all likelihood not have been implemented due to local resistance. Although a few relocations did take place in twentieth-century Switzerland, to accommodate dams, these projects were backed by significantly more powerful political and financial forces. In many instances, local opponents even succeeded in resisting those forces and defeated plans for power plants.[16] That notwithstanding, while no settlements were abandoned in creating the national park, use of the land for agriculture and forestry was no longer permitted, a turn of events that met with some disapproval among the local population. In the pages that follow, the particularities of the Swiss situation will be discussed in regard to the global history of the national park.

Local Culture and Economy

The solitude and natural wildness of the landscape are what sold the members of the SNK on the area around the Ofen Pass. In fact, by Swiss standards (but also those of alpine and central Europe) the area was undeveloped. The mountainous domain occupies the southeastern corner of Switzerland. The high valley of the Engadine—crisscrossed by the Inn River and extending from 1,800-meter-high Maloja in a northeasterly direction—forms the region's central axis. A narrowing just before Zernez at Brail (1,600 meters) marks the transition between the broad expanse of the Upper Engadine, dominated by lakes, and the very differently structured Lower Engadine, with its steep declivity, narrower and smaller spaces, whose south side abuts the Ofen region. From the north, the region was accessible at 1,900 meters by way of the Julier, Albula, and Flüela passes. Two additional passes, the Bernina and Maloja, linked the Upper Engandine via the Poschiavo and Bregaglia Valleys with northern Italy, whereas the Ofen Pass led from Zernez over Val Müstair to the Austrian (and post–First World War Italian) Vinschgau Valley. After around 80 kilometers, at 1,000 meters, the (Lower) Engadine ends at the Swiss-Austrian border, beyond which it is known as the Inn Valley, stretching down to Austrian town of Innsbruck.

Politically, the Engadine was part of the large but sparsely populated canton of Grisons, which was subdivided into numerous valleys. Once a "perpetual ally" of Switzerland, Grisons joined the confederation as a consequence of the

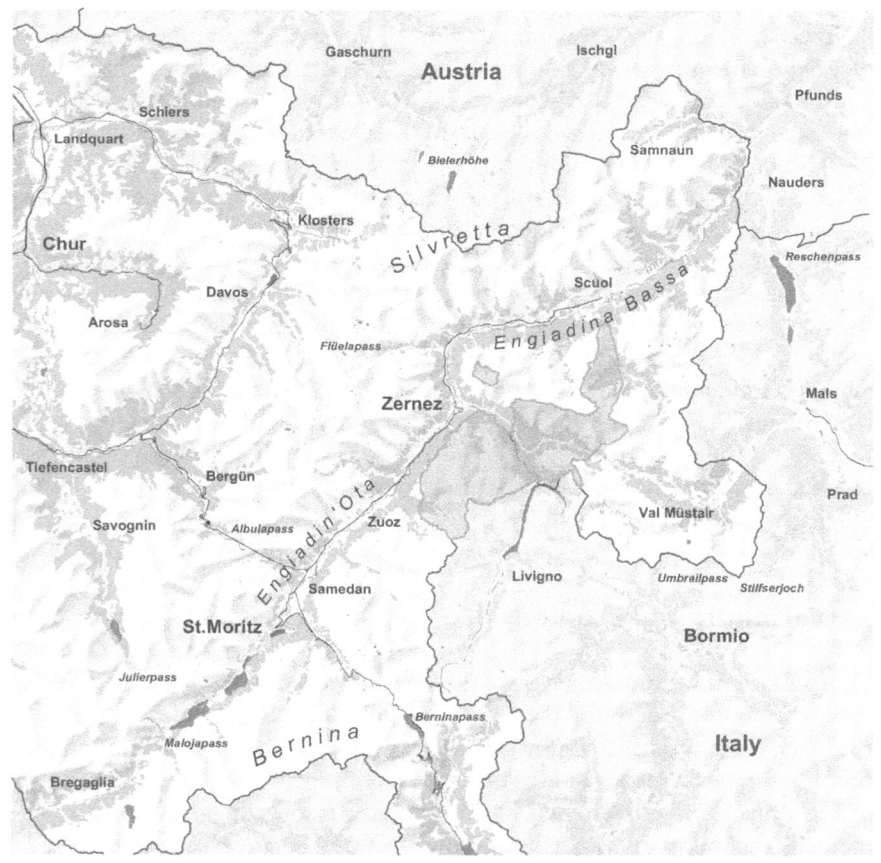

Map 2. Southeastern Switzerland. *Source*: GIS-SNP, Swiss National Park, Spatial Information Department.

Act of Mediation issued by Napoleon Bonaparte in 1803. With the exception of Tarasp, which until 1803 belonged to Austria, and the remote Samnaun Valley, the predominately rural population was Calvinist. Two Romansh dialects were spoken: Puter, in the Upper Engadine, and Vallader, in the Lower Engadine. In the Lower Engadine, which formed the park's central valley segment, the vast majority of inhabitants lived from subsistence farming well into the twentieth century, and the area was accordingly considered poor. Trade, mainly cattle and wood products, was conducted primarily with northern Italy and the Tyrol.[17] These areas were also the preferred destination of largely temporary emigration. In addition, successful emigrants—mostly notably confectioners[18]—were socially and economically significant. They chiefly settled in the cities of central Italy but maintained ties to their native villages, where they built the equivalent of feudal homes for themselves. Relations with the other parts of the canton as well as with the rest of Switzerland long remained loose, though they gradually became more important as a result of nation building, improved roads, and links to the cantonal railway network. A few families, mostly those who owned vast estates, dealt in commerce, or had made their fortune abroad, formed a narrowly circumscribed, cosmopolitan elite. In addition to the village teachers, a traditionally strong and numerous protestant clergy ensured a relatively good level of education.[19]

An upswing in the first half of the nineteenth century, suggested by growing population figures, came to a halt at mid-century. Emigration outpaced immigration, with a negative balance that the birth surplus only just managed to counterbalance. Thus, beginning in 1850, the number of inhabitants in the Lower Engadine remained constant at about 6,500, and that for Val Müstair at about 1,500. The population of the future park communities also generally stabilized to 1850 levels. Zernez counted about 600 inhabitants, S-chanf 450, and Valchava 200. Only Scuol defied the end-of-the-century population decline. Its numbers, which had stabilized to about 900, grew to over 1,100, perhaps due to the appeal of alpine tourism in those years, which in Scuol was associated with spa tourism. Overall, the Lower Engadine was little touched by the tourism of the Belle Époque, which was concentrated on the lakes of the Upper Engadine. The population there began to swell in 1880 and it also started to attract a labor force from the Lower Engadine and Val Müstair (see chart 1).

The difference between the population growth in the area around the national park and the tourist destinations of St. Moritz and the Upper Engadine was marked. The population peak in Zernez (and the Lower Engadine) in 1910 was the result of railroad construction, which brought temporary workers to the village (and the region). Population development in St. Moritz and the Upper Engadine clearly reflected the two wars and the crisis-induced collapse of

78   *Creating Wilderness*

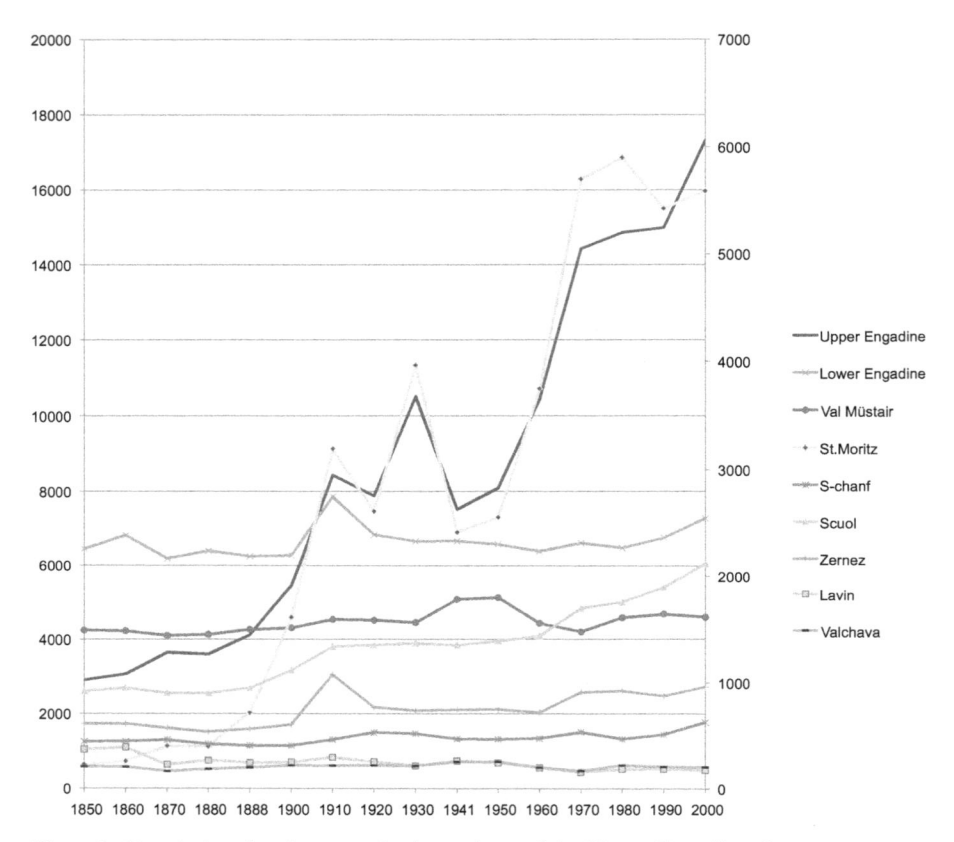

Chart 1. Population development in the regions of the Upper Engadine, Lower Engadine, Val Müstair (left axis), and in St. Moritz and the five national park communities (right axis), 1850–2000. Data: Federal Census.

the tourism sector in the 1910s, and the 1930s and 1940s, which had no significant effect on other areas and regions. The differences in social development of the Upper and Lower Engadine were also reflected in the use of language: In 2000, 13 percent of the population in the Upper Engadine indicated that Romansh was their main language, and 30 percent their everyday language; in the Lower Engadine, the figures were 63 percent (main language) and 79 percent (everyday language).[20]

Expanding transport along the north–south axis—the Gotthard tunnel was opened in 1882—had little effect on the region since the trans-alpine routes through the Engadine were only ever regionally important. However, the expansion of the railroad engendered hope. In 1903, the section between the cantonal capital Chur and St. Moritz in the Upper Engadine, was opened, and between 1909 and 1913 a link was built through the Engadine high valley connecting St. Moritz to Scuol in the Lower Engadine. Plans were also being devised to connect the railroad with the Austrian rail network through the Ofen Pass or along the Inn River. As we saw in chapter 2, this option, though it was never materialized, played a role in the negotiations over the national park.[21] In contrast, motorized traffic was not a factor until the second half of the 1920s. Up to that point, a canton-wide prohibition against automobiles dating from 1900 prevented deployment, which cut Grisons off from Swiss and European developments in road traffic.[22]

In 1900, two-thirds of the population earned their living in the primary sector, agriculture and forestry.[23] For them, the economic situation held little promise. Income from working the land and forests had long been decreasing. With the coming of the railroads and steamships, which enabled large shipments over large distances, foreign demand for wood from the forests of the Ofengebiet waned, as did the profits to be had in the timber trade. In 1904, a cantonal expert on Zernez silviculture maintained that "for years," Zernez had struggled to obtain acceptable prices for its timber. The picture for agriculture was similar. Many of the pastures, which had been reclaimed in the early modern era, were leased for decades to foreigners, mainly sheep farmers from Bergamo, but also to Valtelliners and Tyroleans.[24] Forests and pastures were largely collectively owned; they belonged to the communes or the alpine cooperatives, which also regulated their use. Not infrequently, property and use rights overlapped. Thus, in Val Trupchun, which was part of S-chanf, the Upper Engadine commune of La Punt-Chamues-ch possessed so-called *Waldsuperfizies* (forest superficies), that is, forest use rights separate from land ownership, which had to be considered in integrating the region into the national park in 1911. The local population benefited from the forests and pastures in two ways: First, they shared in their use as a source of self-sufficiency organized within family units; second, revenues from commercial timber and grazing leases flowed into the community funds.[25] In addition to local administration, the communes used the money especially to run schools and provide relief to the poor, as well as to maintain roads and trails, and for water- and earthworks.[26]

Beginning in the mid-nineteenth century, the increased regulatory power of cantonal (and later also national) authorities became apparent and consequently narrowed the scope of action of the communes. The use of forests for timber also became a matter of cantonal and federal planning and regulation, as did wooded pastures and alpine farming. For example, the maximum number of animals that could be pastured on an alp became subject to cantonal provisions. Seasonal cross-border movement of livestock (transhumance) caught the attention of the plague police, who subjected the animals to greater scrutiny. In spring of 1910, the repeated introduction of hoof-and-mouth disease finally prompted the Federal Council to ban the import of Italian livestock into the Engadine, and a longtime source of income for the local communities evaporated for good.[27] Some of the alps thus freed were immediately incorporated into the emerging national park.

Fears and Expectations

The Ofenberg region was thus little touched by the economic boom of the two decades before and after 1900. With the exception of Scuol, the region did not benefit from the tourism that flourished just a little up the valley in St. Moritz, which within thirty years was transformed from a village of four hundred people to a small town of over three thousand inhabitants (1910). On the other hand, the rise of industrialization brought competition, rather than increasing demand, to the regional economy. The longtime practice of transhumance was increasingly restricted, and in 1909 a ban seemed inevitable. There was no lack of work, but opportunities to achieve a livelihood that went much beyond subsistence were few.[28] With some exceptions, the region figured generally among the losers of its time, reflected not least in the departures of young people. Taking this regional experience into account is essential to understand the fears and expectations with which the local actors greeted the overtures of conservationists in those years.

When Steivan Brunies reached Zernez and S-chanf in later summer 1908, the news that the area was being targeted for a large nature reserve spread rapidly. When the reserves committee of the SNK met for the first time at the end of October of that year, a pile of letters from regional inhabitants was waiting for them. The basic response was positive. The mayors of the commune of Zernez and of the *Bürgergemeinde* (municipality) of S-chanf welcomed the SNK's idea. The proposal had found "universal approval," reported the latter, and "I have no doubt that our community would consent to lease Val Müschauns to a national park."[29] Two factors likely contributed to this favorable reception: First, from the very outset, the conservationists hinted that they would be willing to adequately compensate the landowners. In the official letter sent by the SNK to the commune of Zernez, the committee detailed the scientific and environmental significance of its plans. It was also careful to play to the commune's nationalist and patriotic sympathies, as well as to appeal to idealism and sacrifice for the honor of the country. However, the SNK's success in arousing the interest of the communal officials may just as well have been due to a passage at the end of the letter promising "rent, with interest."[30]

Second, it mattered that the bearer of the message was not a stranger. Steivan Brunies (1877–1953) was raised as the youngest of nine children in Cinuos-chel, a hamlet belonging to the commune of S-chanf. His father was a wealthy farmer who, it was said, had made his fortune in the North American Gold Rush. This background explains what otherwise would have been an unusual education for a peasant family. Following elementary school, Brunies senior sent his youngest son to Chur. Thereafter, Steivan continued his education in Breslau (Wrocław) and Zurich, where he studied natural sciences. In 1906, at the University of Zurich, he submitted his dissertation on the flora of the Ofengebiet. His doctoral supervisor was SNK member Carl Schröter, with whom Brunies felt a bond. Years later, he would address him as "my dear paternal friend."[31] In 1908, Brunies took up a teaching position in the *Real-Gymnasium* in Sarasin's hometown of Basel. At the same time, his unique combination of local origin and academic qualifications and socialization made Brunies much sought after by the SNK. In summer of 1908 he wrote a report on the suitability of Val Cluozza as a nature protection reserve, and was immediately appointed by Sarasin to the SNK's reserves committee. In 1909 Brunies took over the secretariat of the newly founded SBN, and served as its representative when he joined the ENPK in 1914. The ENPK made him superintendent of the Swiss National Park, a post he held from 1914 until his retirement in

Illustration 3. Carl Schröter and Steivan Brunies on Murtèr ridge in 1912. *Source:* Staatsarchiv Graubünden, Swiss National Park Photograph Collection.

1941. Every year he spent several weeks in the Engadine. In addition to the national park, Brunies was also very keen on Romansh languages and local folklore, especially folk music, which he practiced himself.[32]

The SNK involved Brunies fully in its cause. Brunies moved as easily throughout the region as a fish in water. He had informants who fed him tidbits of unofficial news, in particular his friend and brother-in-law, Curdin Grass, who was on the Zernez communal council.[33] Brunies poked around villages and towns, wove a network, and arranged meetings. He corresponded with the locals in Romansh, and translated their responses into German for the SNK. In additional, Brunies also familiarized the SNK members with regional customs and communal hierarchies, and in this way helped to bridge the cultural gap that separated the German-speaking, urban middle-class conservationists from the rural Engadine elites.

Yet to view these elites only in the narrow context of farming and remote geography would be quite wrong. The SNK's local partners were experienced businesspeople. Rudolf Bezzola, the mayor of Zernez, owned postal horses; Otto Mohr, mayor of Scuol, was a lawyer; and Gian Töndury, mayor of S-chanf, was an influential financier and politician: director of the Engadine bank, board member of many companies, and longtime member of the Grisons cantonal parliament. These men did not lack negotiating skills, however flattered they might have been by the attention paid to them by known scientists and government officials, including federal councilors Josef Anton Schobinger and Marc-Emile Ruchet, who both paid a visit to the park in 1911.[34]

In 1908, the game was new for all participants, and the configuration unfamiliar. The communes may have been used to leasing their land, but the content and extent of what the SNK was asking was singular. The restricted use of large protected areas, and especially the long contract periods, was difficult for the local actors to digest. In the face of such uncertainties, they wondered what the future would bring: How would the monetary value develop? What changes would the impending link to the railroad bring, and would the emerging electricity industry also include the remote valleys and waterworks?[35] Moreover, people who lived directly by the work of their hands knew only too well the unpredictable side of nature to hand it over lightly themselves. Of course, even here nature had been tamed through use and construction, but its misanthropic dimension remained. In contrast to the inhabitants of the midlands, for the people of Grisons, bears still meant something. The last big predator to survive in the Alps was sighted rarely in the Ofengebiet, and encounters with bears were highly unlikely. Yet they could not be ruled out. What conservationists in the midlands saw as an indicator of wilderness ("where bears still live"[36]), the locals regarded with suspicion. The last bear shooting in Val S-charl had occurred in 1904, and the proud hunters had exhibited its cadaver in Scuol. But the animal had not disappeared from the region. In subsequent years, bears were seen sporadically in the Ofengebiet crossing to and fro over the border, including in the summer of 1909, when the plans for a national park were being discussed in Zernez.[37]

Sarasin and his colleagues found themselves in an unfamiliar situation. Thus far, they had campaigned for the preservation of "nature monuments," such as old trees and erratic boulders, whose extent was limited and whose protection could usually be settled for a price. This approach was out of the question for the large reserve envisaged. Purchasing terrain in Switzerland, even as remote and unproductive as in the Ofenberg area, would be too expensive. Even to raise the money for the annual lease amount, the SNK had to find an original solution involving private and government funding. The context of communal ownership in Switzerland was completely different from other countries and regions of the world. In the United States, up the 1950s, land destined for national parks that was not already owned by the government had to be transferred to it free of charge. Comparatively low land prices combined with the high touristic value of the national park label made this requirement enforceable.[38] In Sweden, whose first national parks emerged at the same time as Switzerland's, the parklands were owned by the government, whereas in the European colonies, in particular in Africa, oftentimes colonial authorities simply established ownership by decree.[39]

Area Selection and Initial Leases

The goal of the SNK was to totally avoid human impact over a large area for a long period of time. However, how that could be done in the Ofengebiet had not yet been set in stone. Rather, efforts now sought to substantiate both the principles established by the SNK and existing geographical knowledge of the region, through field surveys and in discussions led primarily by Sarasin and Brunies with representatives of the community. Gradually, the choice of which areas to include in the national park began to be evident within the SNK. A map drawn up in early 1910 (see illustration 4) gave concrete shape to these ideas. The original planning focused on two areas: in the east Val S-charl, originally suggested by Schröter, and to the west Val Cluozza, championed by Brunies in 1908. These two areas would be connected, and the area thus formed rounded out as fully as possible along natural geographical borders with the external world. Going counterclockwise, the envisaged area bordered the Inn Valley to the north, Val Trupchun to the west, Italy and the Ofenberg Pass to the south, and Val S-charl to the east.[40] Sarasin also favored several wildlife-rich areas, but was shouted down by members of the community who feared that opposition by hunters might then threaten the entire project. Consequently, Sarasin ruled out the right flank of Val S-charl with the exception of the Tamangur Arven Forest, and agreed for the time being not to pursue a hunting ban on the right bank of the Inn at S-chanf and Zernez.[41]

84 *Creating Wilderness*

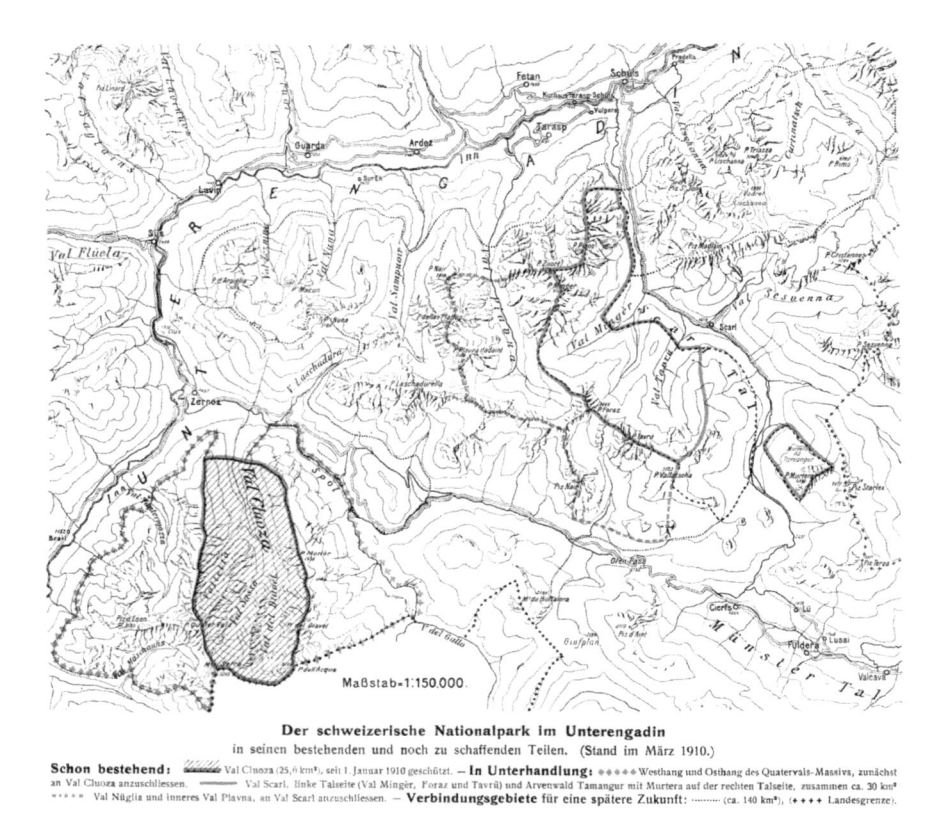

Illustration 4. Park map published in the March 1910 issue of the journal Heimatschutz, which was entirely devoted to the national park. *Source:* Heimatschutz 3/1910, annexe 2.

In the years that followed, the nature conservationists strove mightily to implement the spatial arrangement of the national park set out in the 1910 map. Because both Val Cluozza and the central plot connecting it to Val S-charl lay within Zernez, the SNK made dealings with that commune their highest priority. In December 1909, the SNK and the commune of Zernez signed an initial contract. Its ten articles governed the "transfer" of Val Cluozza to the SNK from 1 January 1910 for twenty-five years, in return for a yearly "rent and interest" of 1,400 Swiss francs—significantly more than could be had by timbering and agricultural use of the land, which the contract prohibited.[42] The SNK alone was permitted to construct trails, erect shelters, and establish markers, and to purchase wood from the forests to do so. The SNK made immediate use of this right in constructing a hut in Val Cluozza in 1910. The hut served as the first park warden's housing, and as a lodging and meal station for researchers and visitors. Two species were governed by special rules: at the request of the SNK, the possible reintroduction of ibex; and at the request of the commune, how to handle the appearance of bears. In the case of the latter, the SNK was to pay damages and, if need be, arrange for the animal to be shot. For the eventuality that area-based hunting was to succeed licensed hunting in the canton of Grisons, which was discussed time and again but never happened, additional compensation for hunting rights would be paid to the commune. Another reservation by the communal council regarding the future installation of waterworks in the valley was abandoned in the final negotiations. A last point stipulated that the SNK could cede the rights and obligations covered in the contractual agreement to the confederation.[43]

This first lease was the model for all others made between autumn 1909 and summer 1911 with the communes of Zernez, Scuol, and S-chanf, as well as the contracts concluded with the cooperative of Tavrü.[44] The result was a compromise that was not entirely to the SNK's satisfaction, in particular vis-à-vis the length of the leases. In the negotiations with Cluozza, the SNK had initially asked for fifty years, but settled for half that number.[45] From a conservationist and scientific perspective, however, twenty-five years was far too short, and without the guarantee of continuation, the meaning and goal of the enterprise was thrown into question.[46] This drawback was also voiced by the federal councilor, who extended the leases to ninety-nine years on the condition that, if the national park did not fulfill expectations, the government retained a unilateral right to terminate a lease after twenty-five years. In addition, the parliamentary commission involved also specified that the leases were to be replaced by legally binding easements. This forced the SNK to negotiate new contracts. Agreement was reached with Zernez as early as 1911, whereas S-chanf, Scuol, and Tavrü rejected extension of their contracts. In the case of S-chanf, probably for financial reasons, the SNK itself rejected an offer from the commune simultaneously proposing an extension of the contract and an expansion of the lease area.[47] Since only Zernez met the federal requirements, the federal decision on the national park was limited to its territories, whereas the rest of the contracts beyond 1914 remained in the care of the SNK.

In these dealings, the canton of Grisons assumed a very passive role, out of proportion to its legislative powers. For example, hunting and fishing bans fell under cantonal jurisdiction, as did permits for park rangers to carry weapons. The creation of the national park also overlapped with other cantonal interests in the areas of transport (railways and roads) and hydroelectric power. Nevertheless, the contribution of the cantonal bodies was essentially limited to approving the appropriate applications to the federal authorities, the SNK and ENPK, and the communes.[48] One reason for this passive stance may have been that the pressure of the debt incurred in building the railroad kept the canton from fulfilling the government's expectations that it share in the cost of the national park.[49] The cantonal authorities abandoned their reticence only after the Second World War, when they began to make their true influence felt, especially in connection with regulation of wildlife resources.[50]

Table 1. Changes in the park area, 1910–2010

Date of establishment	Area	Owners or users	Area size (km²)	Park size (km²)	Compensation (Swiss francs)	Total compensation (Swiss francs)	Remarks
1 January 1910	Val Cluozza	Zernez	21.74		1,400		
1 January 1911	Val Tantermozza	Zernez	13.75	35.49	600	2,000	
1 January 1911	Part of Val Trupchun, Val Müschauns	S-chanf, La Punt-Chamues-ch	12.85	48.34	1,600	3,600	Prior to the 1932 lease: Communal pasture and timber use rights; 500 francs to Punt Ch. for parcels of forest
1 January 1911	Val Mingèr, Val Foraz	Scuol	22.65	70.99	4,000	7,600	Communal timber use for part of the land
1 January 1911	Alp Tavrü	Tavrü cooperative	9.35	80.34	1,800	9,400	Area subleased for pasturing
1 January 1914	Praspöl, la Schera, Il Fuorn, Stabelchod	Zernez	58.96	139.3	16,200	25,600	Communal pasture and timber use (partial), right to railroad construction, Fuorn pasturing rights abdicated in 1927 for 8,000 Swiss francs
1917	Stabelchod				1,100	26,700	Abdication of pasturing rights
1 January 1918	Val Nüglia	Valchava	8.05	147.35	800	27,500	
1920	Falcun	Zernez	4.5	151.85	400	27,900	Communal rights for waterworks, and (prior to the 1932 lease) grazing and timber use

1 September 1932	Area between Ova Spin and Val Ftur	Zernez	11.0	162.85	6,000	33,900	No communal objections to no-hunting zone
1 September 1932	Rear of Val Trupchun	S-chanf	5.28	168.13	1,600	35,500	No communal objections to no-hunting zone
31 December 1935	Alp Tavrü	Tavrü cooperative	-9.35	158.78	1,800	33,700	Contract expires
31 December 1935	Val Mingèr, Val Foraz	Scuol	-22.65	136.13	4,000	29,700	Contract expires
1 January 1937	Val Mingèr, Val Foraz	Scuol	22.65	158.78	3,000	32,700	
1961	Left side of Val Trupchun	S-chanf, Zuoz and Madulain	5.22	164			Compensation newly calculated for the entire park area (see table 2)
1961	Murtaröl, Costas da Cluozza	Zernez	2.8	166.8			
1961	Brastuoch d'Ivraina	Zernez	1.9	168.7			
2000	Macun	Lavin	3.6	172.3			
2006	National Park	All park areas	-2.0	170.3			Correction following recalculation of the area using GIS (geographical information system)[51]

88   Creating Wilderness

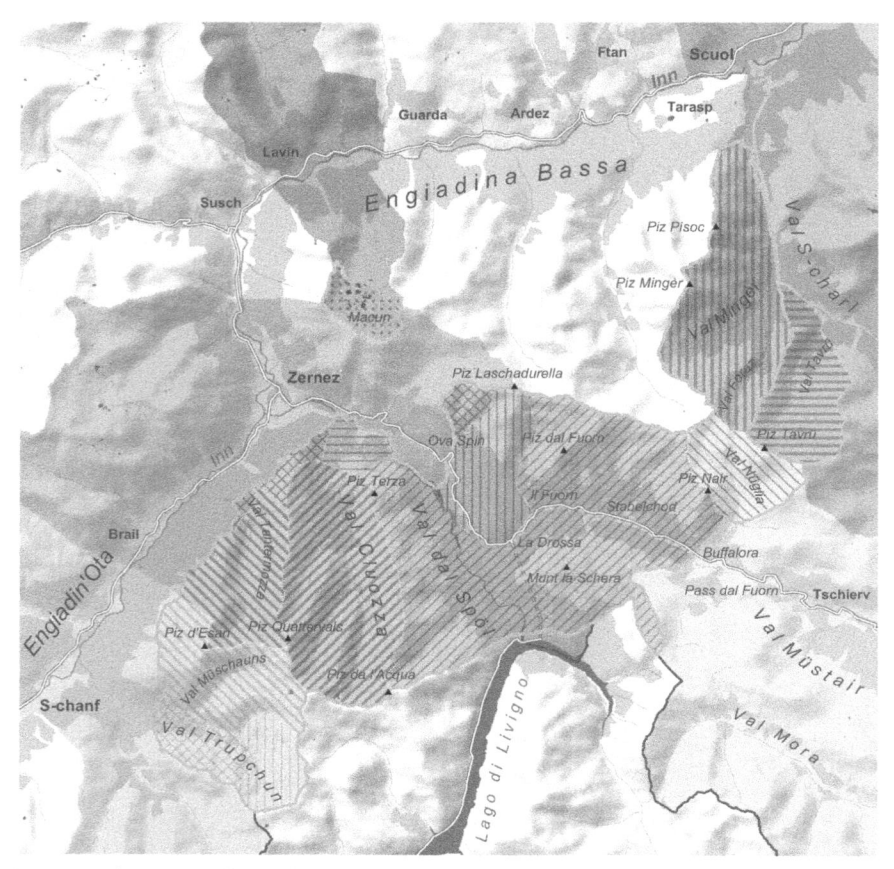

Map 3. Changes in the park area. *Source:* GIS-SNP, Swiss National Park, Spatial Information Department.

Table 2. Recalculation of annual compensation, 1959

	Old	New
Zernez	25,700	55,000
S-chanf	2,700	12,000
Scuol	3,000	10,000
Valchava	800	1,200
La Punt-Chamues-ch	500	3,800–5,800 (estimate)
Wildlife compensation		10,000–20,000 (estimate)

Source: Swiss Federal Council 1959, 1337 f.

Local Diversity

Thus, the creation of the Swiss National Park, from its earliest form in 1908 to its state (partly) under the custody of the federal government from 1914 onward, resulted from a complex interaction between the SNK, the federal authorities, and local actors. Although the conservationists and the federal authorities behaved fairly uniformly, at the local level action was dictated by context. One example is the SNK's individual dealings with the communes. These negotiations were in fact not all that individual. In the interest of a single regime the SNK was intent on transferring provisions from one lease to the next. The communes in turn knew exactly what was transpiring in the neighboring localities. The communities themselves were marked, however, by an astonishing social and political diversity. *Bürgergemeinde* and political commune, authorities and voters, farmers and traders, hunters and nonhunters, and surely also (though hard to measure from historical sources) kinship and friendship ties and antipathies divided the communities into multiple, partially overlapping camps that also were reflected in attitudes toward the national park. Consequently, the communal and regional level must be seen through a finer lens than is typically the case.

In all the communities the park idea experienced opposition from hunters and farmers, who feared the loss of their traditional usage rights. In the *Bürgergemeinde,* which comprised all the men who were citizens of that particular community and therefore shared exclusive rights to use the commons, this opposition had greater weight than in the political communes, which included any Swiss citizens who had settled there—in other words, newcomers active in trade and tourism who tended to make less individual use of the communal lands. Thus it mattered a lot which institution was responsible for negotiations with the SNK. In Zernez it was the political communes, whereas in most of the other communes—including S-chanf and Scuol—long-term leases were the jurisdiction of the skeptically minded *Bürgergemeinde*.[52]

A further rift at the communal level was that between the elected officials, who led the negotiations with the SNK, and the communal assemblies, whose duty it was to approve or reject the results. This rift was evident in the very first communal vote in August 1909 in Zernez. In response to a suggestion by the communal council, the SNK had proposed an immediate hunting ban for Cluozza and Tantermozza preceding the lease of these valleys by the SNK. In the communal assembly, however, the proposal had no chance. Following the meeting, an obviously crushed Mayor Bezzola was forced to tell Paul Sarasin that the SNK petition had failed against the "nays" of the "nimrods." In 1910 in Scuol, on the other hand, the *Bürgerrat* (citizens' council) voted unanimously to lease Val S-charl, although the vote passed in the *Bürgerversammlung* (citizens' assembly) by the slimmest of margins (35 to 29 votes).[53] Assessing the balance of power before the meetings proved to be extremely difficult. At the invitation of the mayor of Scuol, in 1910 Sarasin and Carl Schröter reported personally on the SNK's plans for the reserve. A crowd turned up, and the main hall of the Hotel Post was standing room only. In the ensuing discussion, only the proponents spoke, while the opponents (assumed to be present) kept their silence "despite repeated encouragement." As the correspondent for the *Freie Rätier* wrote: "An eerie unity and excitement hovered over the meeting."[54] As the close outcome of the vote in the *Bürgerversammlung* showed later that same year, the correspondent was right in doubting the apparent harmony among the villagers.

Ultimately, each community built its own case. The commune of Tarasp, which has not been mentioned yet, took an extreme position: It was the only commune to categorically reject the park idea from the start. Upper Val Plavna, which the conservationists had been eyeing, contained the commune's only alpine pasture, the SNK was told in 1911, and thus was unavailable.[55] Scuol, in contrast, stood out by reason of its social structure: As a result of tourism, the nonfarmers among the village population were more numerous than, for instance, in Zernez or S-chanf.[56] The traders may have been favorably disposed to the project because they hoped to benefit from the effect of tourism advertising. However, this was not conducive to general support for the national park. Quite the contrary: The unequal distribution of benefits and costs within the community probably had a negative influence on the overall acceptance of the park. In the communal assemblies, traders were easily overruled by the majority of citizens.[57] S-chanf, finally, modeled itself on Zernez. But because the S-chanf contribution was only of peripheral importance, the SNK accorded it far less attention than it did Zernez.

The electoral defeat at the Zernez communal assembly in August 1909 caught the SNK and the Zernez communal council by surprise. The hunters obviously posed a greater obstacle than anticipated. But Curdin Grass, the initiator of the failed bid, diffused the worst fears. As he wrote his friend Brunies, the Zernez hunters were not against the reserve in principle. Their spokesmen—whose favor Brunies would soon try to curry—had merely worried that an uncontrolled area would be a "haven for foreign hunters" and leave law-abiding locals at a disadvantage. Mentioning his name in the proposal, Grass lamented, had hit a wrong note: "You know how easily the people in our community are made jealous."[58] Grass would prove correct in his estimation that the opposition to the national park plans was not fundamental in Zernez. Just two months later, on 25 October 1909, the same communal assembly authorized the communal council to lease Val Cluozza to the SNK by an overwhelming majority. This high level of approval continued through the following years. Up until the end of 1913, the communal assembly voted five more times on the national park:

on territorial expansion, extension of the lease period, and finally the conversion of the lease to an easement. All of the proposals were very clear, and were for the most part passed nearly unanimously.[59]

The high level of acceptance in Zernez was also due to the fact that its communal council had negotiated very advantageously with the SNK. The basic principle was that, as with other communes, Zernez would be compensated for the loss of revenue. To this end, the communal forester was given the job of estimating the annual income from forests and pastures. On the basis of his estimate, the annual rents for 1911 for the Zernez areas of Cluozza, Tantermozza, Praspöl, Schera, Fuorn, and Stabelchod totaled 18,200 Swiss francs.[60] The federal appraiser and forestry inspector Johann Coaz found this estimate to be "rather on the high side" and an audit requested by the preparatory parliamentary commission corrected the forester's estimate to two-thirds of the original amount (i.e., 11,990 francs). The Federal Council nonetheless left the basis for the interest calculation at 18,200 francs. The council expressed the view that the "extraordinarily long duration of the contract and the high probability that the values under consideration would rise" justified higher compensation. Among the potential added values envisaged were the planned Ofenberg railway and the possible change of hunting regulation from licensed hunting to leased hunting in canton Grisons. This argument was not very convincing. Both possibilities (which never did occur) could also have been introduced as options, which was the tack taken in the Cluozza lease. In fact, the retention of interest primarily served to secure the approval of Zernez; an attempt to lower the sum would inevitably have threatened the commune's support, and the entire project along with it. The amount of compensation was criticized in parliament but ultimately accepted as a fait accompli.[61]

In the decades that followed, the interest from the national park covered a substantial part of Zernez's public burden. Up until the construction of the Engadine hydroelectric plants, the interest amounted to roughly 10 percent of the commune's revenues. And since, unlike other revenue items, the park cost little, it contributed significantly to covering loss-making activities.[62] Indeed, all of the SNK's lease partners achieved their financial aims; however, the amount of budgetary surplus varied from commune to commune. When, in 1959, the Federal Council had the compensation recalculated, it evened out these differences (see table 2).[63] The long term of the agreements also contributed to the favorable financial balance as it relieved the communes of having to constantly renegotiate lease and use terms, thus lowering administrative costs. The interest from the park resulted in a long-term, secure, and reliable source of revenue for communal financing. From this perspective, the ninety-nine-year extension was of no additional benefit to the communes; rather, it limited their freedom to act to a time frame that left nothing more to expect politically. In 1911, the Scuol *Bürgergemeinderat* rejected the extension on the grounds that "the future population will be better able to assess the advantages of an extension after twenty-five years of leasing than could today's."[64] In refusing to limit the scope of the next generation, the commune pursued a genuinely sustainable policy. For the conservationists, who invoked abstract "future generations" and eternal values, and whose goal was irreversible, unlimited protection, orienting policy to the lifespan of a human generation was a major problem. Fixing this shortcoming was one of the priority tasks that the Federal Council's National Park Commission set for itself for the period following 1914.

Rounding Out and Expanding

In 1915 the newly formed ENPK began to round out the territory according to the 1910 plan, and to bring it under the jurisdiction of the federal government. The commission proposed that S-chanf, Scuol, Ardez, Lavin, Tarasp, and Valchava sign easements with the confederation for ninety-nine years. An annual amount of 11,800 francs was available to cover these leases, the difference between the interest payout to Zernez and the ceiling of 30,000 francs stipulated by federal law. The interest on the outstanding leases with S-chanf, Scuol, and the cooperative of Tavrü, which was covered by the SBN, came to 7,400 francs. Financially, a coherent solution seemed feasible.

But the response from the region was disappointing. In the eyes of the ENPK, the requests for compensation filtering through the grapevine were excessively high. As had happened five years previously with the Cluozza contract, now the Zernez easement set the tone for all the other communes. In S-chanf and Scuol, people felt wronged and were holding out for improvements to the existing contracts.[65] In a letter to Carl Schröter in 1916, Paul Sarasin conceded that "at the time, in assessing the Zernez region, I—and the confederation along with me—were hoodwinked." The amount had been 6,000 francs too much (that is, the difference determined by the government experts), and now they were all "in the hands of the communes."[66] Sarasin's reflections were prompted by efforts to protect the Aletsch Forest. Here, lessons learned from the national park should have been applied, and from the outset a more comprehensive easement should have been drawn up. This was easier said than done. The national councilor and ENPK secretary Fritz Bühlmann struggled for years on behalf of the SNK and the SBN to obtain the agreement of the local communities. In the early 1920s, negotiations finally broke off.[67]

With the national park, Bühlmann and the ENPK had combatted an enormous number of simultaneous startup problems. With Zernez and S-chanf, tedious disputes droned on over how certain passages of the contracts should be interpreted, which uses they granted the communes, and which misuses were to be treated criminally. At the peak of the stalemate, in 1917, the ENKP withheld interest payments from both communes. At the same time, the commission had cause to worry about the military troops that, since the outbreak of the war in 1914, had been stationed in the park as part of the "border watch" and cared little about its regulations.[68] The situation improved with the end of the war in 1918. Not only did the troops leave, but that same year the dispute with Zernez and S-chanf was resolved. S-chanf did sign another easement with the federal government, and the misunderstandings with Zernez were settled through a supplementary contract. Moreover, the Val Müstair commune of Valchava ceded its grazing rights in Val Nüglia to the national park, and thus at least on the south side of the park, the rounding out of the area went according to plan.[69]

The situation in the Lower Engadine portion of the park, however, continued to be unsatisfactory. On two occasions, in 1919 and in 1922, the citizens of Scuol rejected the conversion of their leases into easements—the second time contrary to the recommendation of the *Bürgerrat* and despite an increase in compensation from 5,800 to 7,900 francs, which represented the remainder of the federal allotment and consequently the highest possible offer. At that time, the park commission had strong reason to believe a government takeover to be of the utmost urgency. In 1921, a dispute smoldering for years between Steivan Brunies and Paul Sarasin had escalated. As a direct consequence, Sarasin withdrew from the chairmanship of both the SNK and the SBN, and thereafter had to resign also from the ENPK. In the meantime the business of the SBN was stalled, resulting in a payment crisis. To pay the running bills of the park ENPK secretary Fritz Bühlmann had to advance money out of his own pocket.[70] In 1920, yet another attempt failed, this time involving Tarasp and Val Plavna. The expansion of the national park in the same year to include the Falcun area, where ibex had just been reintroduced, entailed extremely difficult negotiations with Zernez, which managed to wring several concessions from the ENPK.[71] Among them, the option to construct a hydroelectric plant on the Spöl River would soon be fodder for much debate. In contrast, the reintroduction of the ibex occasioned a public celebration enjoyed by all, leading the ENPK to hope "that this event has *restored*, once and for all, the good understanding between the park authorities and the commune of Zernez."[72]

But the euphoria was fleeting. Soon, the parties were at loggerheads over grazing rights in Fuorn, and the ENPK's intention to establish a no-hunting zone along the Inn River met with stubborn resistance in Zernez and S-chanf. The ENPK was increasingly irritated by the attitude of the communes and took to publicly scolding them in the commission's annual reports. In its report of 1923, the ENPK noted that the uncooperative conduct of Scuol was "not to be believed," and three years later found "especially disturbing how little understanding and responsiveness there is vis-à-vis the national park among the Engadine community." The following year, the ENPK was convinced that "further efforts toward the completion and extension of the reserve area are totally useless, and thus we are abandoning them for the time being."[73] The Zernez communal council, in turn, complained about the ENPK's manner of dealing. The commission had poisoned the atmosphere with condescension and insults. Now, as the council wrote to the ENPK chair in 1927 regarding the imminent withdrawal of grazing rights in the Fuorn area, it had to bear the consequences: "Direct contact with the commune in this matter would most certainly have resulted in a less expensive solution for you." Two years later, a ban on skiing in the national park that the ENPK issued without consulting the communes renewed the bad feelings. The communes felt ignored and reacted angrily.[74] At the end of the 1920s, fifteen years after the park's founding, relations were perceived all around as badly broken.

The 1930s brought some movement to the entrenched positions. A change in personnel within the ENPK may have played some role: Fritz Bühlmann, who as secretary had dominated the commission from the beginning, stepped down in 1930. On his withdrawal, "an apparent relaxation ensued," read a note presumably written by Steivan Brunies. Over the years, the relationship between Brunies and Bühlmann, who was close to Paul Sarasin, had been tense, bordering on hostile.[75] Another important factor was the effect of the global economic crisis on the Engadine region communal budgets. In particular, timber prices plummeted, which made a change in the use of forests doubly attractive to the communes.[76] In 1932, both Zernez and S-chanf reversed their opposition of six years' before and signaled their readiness to expand the park and to ban hunting in the park areas adjacent to the Inn River.[77] Further ideas for expansion came a cropper due to the ENPK's limited funds, an increase in which "could not be considered ... at the present time."[78] By 1933, the ENPK's expansion activities consumed all the available funds from the government. Zernez received an additional 6,000 francs and S-chanf 1,600 francs, which increased the government's annual payment to the communes to a total of 29,700 francs, thus almost drawing down the maximum amount set in the 1914 federal park bill of 30,000 francs.

The economic crisis was also an important factor with respect to the future of the portion of the national park situated in the S-charl Valley. The twenty-five-year leases ran out at the end of 1935. In autumn 1934 the ENPK and the SBN entered into negotiations with Scuol and Tavrü. It soon became clear that their ideas were diametrically opposed. Scuol was looking to substantially increase its interest by half again as much. The terms obtained by Zernez, whose records had been scrutinized for purposes of comparison, served as a model and a basis for discussion. The national park's representatives, on the contrary, considered the interest paid previously to be excessive. Accordingly, they proposed reducing the interest for Alp Tavrü from 1,800 to 1,400 francs, which corresponded to the interest they had incurred in 1935 for subleasing the alp, a proposal that the Tavrü cooperative rejected. Negotiations then collapsed and were never resumed, and on 1 January 1936, Alp Tavrü was withdrawn from the national park. For the ENPK this was no great loss; it had in any event only treated the area as partially protected, and had regularly leased it for grazing. Moreover, the federal government had declared Alp Tavrü a nohunting zone, which guaranteed the protection of wild animals even without a renewed lease.[79]

The SBN offered the commune of Scuol a continuation of interest in the amount of 4,000 francs (provided the *Bürgergemeinde* agreed to a ninety-nineyear easement) and, as a gesture of good faith, additional compensation of 500 francs for the government-mandated no-hunting zone. When the *Bürgerrat* realized that no better offer would be forthcoming from the SBN, they gave in. However, a well-attended *Bürgerversammlung* in December 1935 revealed strong opposition to the terms. Following an emotional debate, the proposal was rejected by a vote of 2 to 1. "The hunters and the farmers who wish to gather mugo pines have been agitating against our cause for a long time. We have done our best, but it has all been for naught. At the *Bürgerversammlung*, the hoteliers were just outnumbered by the farmers," wrote Otto Rauch, actuary for the *Bürgergemeinde*, lawyer, and champion of the proposal, to the chair of the ENPK.[80] The opposition equated the long term of the lease with selling out native land, which they either objected to in principle or were prepared to agree to only for a much higher sum. "If they do not want to pay, let them go to hell!" went one verdict to applause. In addition, the shortage of wood, the hunting restrictions, and the rising game damage argued against the leases, whereas the proponents emphasized the direct and indirect advantages: the secure revenue, especially in times when declining timber prices were driving communes to ruin; and the promotion of the hospitality industry, and its associated suppliers.[81]

It was all in vain. At the end of 1935, the rest of the Scuol area dropped out of the national park. However, as early as February 1936, the *Bürgerrat* and the communal council decided to leave the forest and pastures of the former national park area unused, and to seek another contract with the SBN.[82] Now, and very quickly, a new contract was negotiated that, like the old one, ran to twenty-five years, but that carried annual interest of 3,000 francs—1,000 francs less than the expired lease and 1,500 francs less than the rejected easement. Nonetheless, in January 1937 the *Bürgerversammlung* overwhelmingly approved the new lease by a vote of 10 to 1, which enabled the area to be added to the national park retroactive to the beginning of 1937. The shorter duration of the lease facilitated approval. However, many really only became aware of the consequences of the rejection on withdrawal of the SBN payments, and when it was clear that people were not lining up to exploit the forest and pasturage. Prominent opponents of the earlier proposal—such as the mayor and cantonal parliamentarian Men Rauch, *Bürgerrat* and agriculturist Joannes Bischoff, and the head of Tavrü cooperation and former Scuol mayor Otto Mohr—now argued for adoption.[83]

The 1930s economic crisis had an effect similar to that of the 1910 ban on cross-border transhumance. Both were events over which the actors had no control and that shook the regional economy, one result of which was to increase the corresponding economic incentives for the park. With the next major regional economic change in the 1950s, the incentives changed again, this time to the detriment of the park. The impetus was plans for a large hydropower plant that threatened to damage the park but that promised high water rates to the communes. The fierce and protracted negotiations generated by the plans will be discussed in chapter 6.

Dealing with Conflicts

A fundamental issue regarding the conflict between the ENPK and the local communities was that no tools existed at the institutional level for resolving conflicts over the national park. No park regulatory bodies had been installed at the local level, nor was there any scope for new management structures. In 1914, when the ENPK was established as the political body responsible for the park, the confederation and the SBN were each allowed two seats on it, and the SNG one. In 1918, at its own request, the ENPK was expanded to include as its sixth commissioner a representative from Grisons who was expected to exert a positive influence on the communities affected by the park. The Federal Council selected Jon Vonmoos, a cantonal councilor from the Lower Engadine. In 1920, the commission was expanded yet again with the addition of a French-speaking member, chosen from the *Naturforschende Gesellschaft*. This appointment fulfilled the needs of national representation, and proved all the more significant when the proposal for a second national park in French-speaking Switzerland evaporated. The communes, in contrast, were not offered representation on the park's governing body. In the 1920s, and again in the 1960s, Zernez tried in vain to procure a seat on the ENPK. Only with the passing of the National Park Act of 1980 were the "park communities" granted government representation.[84]

As contractual partners of the national parks, the communes had defined rights and responsibilities. Their continuing or active participation in the park was not part of the deal. "To find the best way forward with the Engadine communities," the ENPK expressed its desire for a Grisons member with "some influence."[85] Despite occasional verbal stroking, the communes were viewed not as potential allies but primarily as counterparties. Consequently, the relationship that developed between the park and the region was not one of partnership but of antagonism. The leases almost enabled the park to be bought out of the local context, which made the park's boundaries at once geographic, political, and social. Traditional local ties to the landscape were cut, and incentives to build new, subjective connections to the park were rarely offered. The national park promoted no pro-park change in mentality; rather, for the locals it became a sort of foreign body. It was not the sacred place that some conservationists and patriots (often both) took it to be, but just the opposite: a secular place sold off to far-away Bern or Basel for cold cash. The renunciation of the land brought interest, attracted tourists, and created a few jobs for park rangers and support staff. But for many the park was like a soulless money machine. It had its uses, but at best the machine did not evoke any emotions, and at worst, it was perceived as evil. Its vicinity was to be avoided, and contact with it even more. In 1935, when the Scuol town doctor exhorted the *Bürgerversammlung* not to think of the park as a source of profit but to be proud "to have the national park within our borders," one imagines his listeners would have been a small minority.[86]

Interestingly, the enhanced status enjoyed by Romansh in the 1930s and its recognition as the fourth national language in 1938 did nothing to change this alienation. In contrast to German, French, and Italian, Romansh belonged to no outside major language group. But as a reflection of the *Geistige Landesverteidigung*—an ideology of Swiss national defense emerging in the 1930s and stressing spiritual and intellectual nationhood—it was declared to be an indigenous national language and Romansh culture to be unspoiled Swiss culture. The national park, which stood for primordial Swiss nature, thus was transformed from a culturally and geographically peripheral site to the cultural heart of Switzerland. In 1937, Paul B. Riis—a Swiss-born American landscape architect who had designed the infrastructure of many US parks, including Yellowstone—described this connection as fortuitous: "Thus, the location of the Swiss National Park in these valleys is nearer a sincere expression of pure Swiss cultures than could be found anywhere else within its limited domain."[87] The ENPK, too, embraced the symbolic elevation of Romansh: When new cast bronze panels were being installed at the park entrances, in connection with the park expansion of 1932, the inscription they bore was no longer French, but Romansh—*Parc naziunal svizzer*—"in a proper nod to Latin folklore," the SBN's annual report noted.[88] Also in a departure from previous practice, the text of the lease signed by the SBN and Scuol five years later, in 1937, was no longer in German but in Romansh. Nevertheless, the association of the park and Romansh culture remained an external conceit that was hardly shared locally. Generations of primary school students may have learned about the flora and fauna of their surroundings from blackboards decorated in Romansh by park supervisor Steivan Brunies, but they did not develop an emotional bond to the park. Moreover, Brunies's Romansh park publications were less likely to instill a self-confident Romansh identity than those of the poet Peider Lansel, the man who in 1909 had attacked the SNK's plans for a reserve. His rallying cry, "*Ni Talians, ni Tudais-chs, Rumantschs vulains restar!*" ("Neither Italians nor Germans, but Romansh forever!"), captured the Romansh self-image of the 1930s in a simple slogan.[89]

After Steivan Brunies stepped down from both the ENPK and the duty of park supervisor in 1941, the presence of the park authorities in the region declined. This change was especially noticeable in the 1940s and 1950s in the conflicts brewing over the construction of the Engadine hydropower plants and the regulation of the growing wild animal populations. This state of affairs may well have contributed to the 1960s trend toward a stronger anchoring of the park in the region. In 1960, Jachen Könz, the forester for the commune of Zernez, temporarily took over as park supervisor. In a letter seeking the consent of the commune of Zernez to assume this duty, Könz indicated that the post would be better filled by someone from the commune rather than "any odd official from the federal administration in Bern." In this way, the commune would also "have a say in future," as the park supervisor took part in the ENPK meetings.[90] The function of park supervisor was abolished, however, four years later in 1964, with the creation of a full-time position of national park director. The first appointee was not someone from the region, but wildlife biologist Robert Schloeth, from Basel. Since the 1960s, the local park administration had expanded, resulting in the creation of an increasing number of local jobs. In 1966, the *Pro Nationalpark* foundation was established for the purpose of constructing a national park center in Zernez. In addition to members of the ENPK, the foundation's board of trustees included the commune's mayor. From then on, the mayor was periodically invited to ENPK meetings, until the national park communities were awarded a seat on the commission in 1980, which the communes then held on a rotating basis.[91] Regionalization finally reached the top of the ENPK in the 1990s. In 1991, departing from the custom of having the federal forest inspector head the ENPK, the Federal Council appointed Grisons national councilor Martin Bundi, a Romansh. His successor, Andrea Hämmerle (2001), was likewise a national councilor from Grisons. Finally, in 2008, Robert Giacometti from Lavin became the first person from the national park communities to lead the commission.

Institutionalization and Subjectivation

Local perceptions of the Swiss National Park in the Ofenberg region were very similar to those of local populations in Africa and Asia. Parks were seen as impositions of foreign authorities. Africans and Asians experienced the parks established in their homelands as institutions of European imperialism, which after decolonization often fell into the hands of equally foreign central governments. In many respects, however, the Swiss National Park region and colonial territories in Africa or Asia could hardly have been more different: In Switzerland, ownership was sacrosanct; the communes enjoyed substantial political autonomy, and processes at all levels followed democratic rules and were guaranteed by a functioning constitutional state. As landowners and local political bodies, the communes were in a good position; nothing could move forward without their consent. In their view, unsurprisingly, the financial possibilities of the park were what interested them, whereas conservationists and park authorities used money to achieve their goals. Indeed, relations between the park and the region were based almost exclusively on money: cash in exchange for exploitation rights. The emotional overtones, such as expressed at the Scuol *Bürgerversammlung* of December 1935 or in the 1927 letter from the commune of Zernez regarding the amount of compensation, were largely ignored. Consequently, the local population developed no positive emotional ties to the park with rare exceptions, such as the photographers Johann and Domenic Feuerstein, who devoted much time to photographing the park land and thereby shaped the park's imagery. The park region may well have been the one part in all of Switzerland where the words "our national park" were the least uttered. The national park was the park of others, of the German-speaking midlanders, the authorities in Bern, and the conservationists in Basel. Although the physical presence of the park could not be denied, it was marginalized in everyday life. Locals seldom visited the park, and it remained as alien to most of them as the midlanders who administered and explored it. Under these circumstances, it was impossible to develop either a real feeling for the park or trust in its administration.

Indeed, for a long time, locals were hardly involved in administrating the park. Whereas rangers increasingly came from the region, the governing bodies of the park remained closed to communal officials. Only in the 1960s were tentative attempts made at regionalizing the park administration. That building an administrative center did not automatically ensure greater support among the local population was made emphatically clear to all parties when the vote to expand the park in Zernez was defeated in 2000. In fact, the developments regarding the Swiss National Park appear to confirm Arun Agrawal's environmentality thesis, which emerged out of a case study in India. Sustainable, local protection of nature requires changes in the political sphere, regulatory environment, and subjective attitudes.[92] Only in this way can long-term local acceptance of environmental protection measures be achieved. In addition to obvious approaches to communication and building identity with the park, creating an institution is critical as a means of permanently representing local interests and allowing local actors access to legitimate planning opportunities.

This seems to have been recognized at the federal level following the failed expansion of the national park. In the meanwhile, in late 1999, *Pro Natura* (the former SBN) had called for "a new generation of protected areas" in which humans would be much more directly involved. In accordance with international programs and categories, new large-scale protected areas in Switzerland should encompass not only wilderness but also cultural landscapes, "whose upkeep [requires] certain human use." Among other things, the conservancy wished to see eight new national parks set up, ranging in size from 100 to 1,000 square kilometers. Three of these parks were to emphasize the protection of natural processes, whereas the remaining five were to combine ecosystem protection and recreation opportunities, as foreseen by the IUCN "national park" category. *Pro Natura* expected the federal government to take a leading role at the national level and to provide public funds. On the other hand, the organization viewed the participation of locals in the projects to be "an important prerequisite for their success."[93]

The federal policy addressed *Pro Natura*'s concerns in a partial revision of the Ordinance on the Protection of Nature and Cultural Heritage (NCHO), which went into effect in 2007. The law included a new chapter on "Parks of National Importance," that defined three national park categories: "National Parks," "Regional Nature Parks," and "Nature Discovery Parks." In its dispatch on the revision, the Federal Council stressed that the initiative had to begin with the regions and be supported at both the communal and cantonal level. "In accordance with the principle of voluntary transfer, the federal government promotes only parks that arise from regional initiatives, are supported by the local population (bottom-up), and are associated with a cantonal program."[94] A range of park projects was already being created in parallel with the legislative process. Under the revised NCHO, from 2008 such plans were free to seek federal funding and apply for one of the three national park-categories. Up until January 2013, the government assigned the label "Park of National Importance" to sixteen parks.[95]

The Swiss National Park was explicitly excluded from the reorganization of the federal government's reserve policy. The National Park Act of 1980 remained untouched by the NCHO revision.[96] Nevertheless, relations concerning the national park were shifting. Regional interactions strengthened after 2000, despite or perhaps precisely because of the failure of the expansion plans. As with the controversy over the Spöl River in the 1950s, the debate over expanding the national park had increased contacts between park authorities and regional exponents. In Zernez, these contacts continued as part of the discussion on building a visitor center. After a disagreement about where to locate the new building had been resolved, construction began in 2006. The building, designed by the renowned architect Velerio Olgiati, opened in 2008. In this same year, the commune and the park administration traded buildings. The communal administration moved to the national park building erected in the 1960s, and the national park administration took over the grand Wildenberg Castle. At the same time, the national park worked together with the communities of Val Müstair to develop a common biosphere. It was approved by Unesco in summer 2010, with the proviso that a continuous buffer zone would be created identical to the national park's core zone.[97]

Notes

1. See Müller 2001; Müller and Kollmair 2004.
2. On the meaning of trust in social interactions, see Luhmann 1989.
3. The term "governmentality" (*gouvernementalité* in French), which juxtaposes government and mentality, was introduced by Michel Foucault in the late 1970s during a lecture at the Collège de France (Foucault 2004). On the reaction to it and its further elaboration, see Bröckling et al. 2000; Bratich et al. 2003; Krasmann and Volkmer 2007.
4. Agrawal 2005, 226.
5. Ibid., 14.
6. See Brockington et al. 2008; Dowie 2009; and *Conservation and Society* no. 1 (2009), in particular the introductory paper by Agrawal and Redford 2009.
7. See Gissibl et al. 2012a. This complex material can only be elucidated by in-depth historical case studies. Such studies have been done for Africa and North America, among others: Carruthers 1995; Catton 1997; Warren 1997; Neumann 1998; Ranger 1999; Spence 1999; Jacoby 2001; Brockington 2002; Sandlos 2007.
8. Wakild 2012; van der Windt 2012; Evans 1997, 60–78.
9. Mels 1999, 93–95; Van Schuylenbergh 2009; Kathirithamby-Wells 2005; Kathirithamby-Wells 2012.
10. The term comes from Goodland 1982, 21. See also Colchester 2003.
11. Sarasin 1914, 54 f.
12. Ibid., 55. For more, see Wöbse 2006b. On the construction of primitive society in ethnology, see Kuper 2005. On the evolutionary background, see Sarasin and Sommer 2010.
13. According to the statement of purpose for anthropological conservation in Sarasin 1914, 55. Emphasis mine.
14. Rütimeyer 1924, x. On the topic, see Egli 2011.
15. SNK annual report 1909–10, 52. See Bachmann 1999, 258–260.
16. See Haag 2004.
17. By the nineteenth century, mining, which gave the Ofen Pass its name and was also done in Val S-charl, had lost its influence. See Schläpfer 1960; Parolini 1995, 48–63; Schreiber 2004.
18. See Kaiser 1985.
19. For remarks on economic development in the region in the nineteenth and twentieth centuries, see Rohner 1972 and Parolini 2012a. For a description prior to 1800, see Mathieu 1994. A regional historical overview of the more recent times is lacking, as is a local history of the national park communities. The one exception, Paul Grimm's

history of Scuol (Grimm 2012), appeared too late to be incorporated. Current information on the region is available from Pro Engiadina Bassa, a regional association founded in 1970.
20. Clavuot 2008. For additional statistical analyses, see Fritzsche et al. 2001.
21. On the construction of the railroad, see Catrina 1972, 107–121. On the plans for the Ofenberg railway, see also Gottschalk 1994, 24–48.
22. See Merki 2002, 147–167; Hollinger 2008. See also the remarks on tourism in Chapter 6.
23. In the 1900 census, 65 percent of the population in the Inn region (Lower Engadine) was engaged in agriculture. In Val Müstair, the figure was 71 percent. In contrast, at 32 percent, the Maloja region (Upper Engadine) was a little under the Swiss average of 33 percent. Statistisches Bureau 1907, map 1. The 1920 census data, which are broken down to the communal level, show that the national park communities of Scuol, Zernez, and S-chanf were less engaged in agriculture than the Lower Engadine as a whole (39 to 45 percent compared with 60 percent). In contrast, 77 percent of the Val Müstair commune of Valchava was given over to a rural economy. Eidgenössisches Statistisches Amt 1923. The numbers for 1910 are not representative on account of the railroad construction, which brought temporary workers to the Lower Engadine.
24. Parolini 2012a, 133. On alpine economy, see also Schorta 1988; Mathieu 1994, 54–77.
25. See Parolini 2012a.
26. Sprecher 1942. A random examination of the account books of the commune of Zernez confirms this impression. GA Zernez, C 4. Cudeschs da quint.
27. Due to the 1910 ban, Zernez experienced a revenue shortfall of 1,525 francs. Seventy percent of that was compensated by the federal government and the canton. Parolini 2012a, 135.
28. There appear at least to have been seasonal labor shortages. See BAR 9500.25, vol. 37, Bezzola to Sarasin, 23 August 1909.
29. SCNAT Archives, box 533, Töndury to Brunies, 26 September 1908; BAR 9500.25, vol. 37, commune of Zernez to Brunies, 24 August 1908. There were five letters altogether. SCNAT Archives, box 521, Reservationenkomitee, meeting of 31 October 1901, Protokollbuch, 81.
30. See the exchange of correspondence (SNK annual report 1908/09, 52–59) as well as the extracts from the meeting minutes of the commune of Zernez in GA Zernez, B 21.
31. Brunies 1906. ETH Library, manuscript collections, Hs 399, Schröter-Brunies correspondence.
32. Bachmann 1999, 355 f.
33. Curdin Grass was the brother of the Ofenberg landlord J. Gian Grass, who was married to one of Brunies's sisters. Oral communication from Manuela Rodigari.
34. About this visit, see Bachmann 1999, 146 f.
35. See the SNP Archive, 121.100, Scuol communal executive board to Sarasin, 20 June 1910; GA Zernez, B 21 a, Cussagl comünal e soprastanza, meeting of 5 November 1910; Redunanza d'abitants of 21 August 1911.
36. Rudio and Schröter 1906, 505. Hermann Christ, Schweizerische Nationalparke, in Basler Nachrichten, 8 May 1908.
37. See BAR 9500.25, vol. 37, Curdin Grass to Brunies, 8 June 1909; Brunies to Sarasin, 21 September 1909. On the 1904 shooting, see Metz 1990, 177–182. The antagonism

between urban conservationists and rural populations was not unique to Switzerland. On the United States, see Johnson 2007. It has also featured in contemporary debates over predators in Switzerland. For a fundamental treatment of the relationship between work and nature, see White 1995.
38. Runte 1987, 225 f.
39. On Sweden, see Mels 1999. For an overview of the British Empire, see Beinart and Hughes 2007, 289–309. On German colonial policy, see Gissibl 2009; Gissibl 2012.
40. In the SNK annual report of 1909–10, Paul Sarasin mentioned the "Scarl Quattervals reserve," a reference to the highest point in the area, the 3,000-meter-high Piz Quattervals at the western edge of Val Cluozza.
41. SCNAT Archives, Box 521, Reservationenkomitee, meeting of 20 November 1909, Protokollbuch, 86; Box 533, correspondence, SNK to commune of S-chanf.
42. Parolini estimated the annual revenue shortfall due to lost grazing leases to be around 500 to 800 francs (Parolini 1995, 177) the value of the forests was modest. See Botschaft 1912, 418.
43. BAR 9500.25, vol. 37, Bezzola to Sarasin, 15 November 1909. An original of the lease, dated 1 December 1909, can be found in GA Zernez, B 21 a.
44. The leases were printed in the SNK annual reports for 1909–10, 16 f., and 1910–11, 42–48.
45. GA Zernez, B 21 b, Cussagl comünal e soprastanza, meeting of 22 October 1909. The lease stipulated that, at the end of twenty-five years, "a new agreement will be made." Two Zernez communal councilors wanted to replace "will" with "may." But a majority of six communal councilors decided to sign the contract on the spot *"tale e quale"* (such as it was). GA Zernez, B 21, Cussagl comünal e soprastanza, meeting of 21 April 1909.
46. SCNAT Archives, Box 521, SNK, meeting of 6 September 1909, Protokollbuch, 26 f.
47. The actuary of the Bürgergemeinde of S-chanf was "very surprised" at Brunies's announcement that his "federal government was at the moment not in the position to lease our Alp Trupchum for 99 years." SNP Archives, 122.100, Dazzi to Brunies, 18 September 1912. The motivation for the rejection is not entirely clear, but may have been financial considerations combined with the fact that Alp Trupchun lay outside the 1910 border line. In 1932, the area eventually became part of the national park. On the lease negotiations, see SCNAT Archives, Box 521, SNK, meeting of 14 January 1912, Protokollbuch, 41 f. SNK annual report 1911–12, 104–110 as well as the Federal Council's dispatch of 1912.
48. This passive role assumed by the cantonal bodies is consistent with the sparseness of the national park file in the cantonal archives. The petition to carry weapons was rejected in one case by the lower chamber (the executive) because the person involved had a criminal record. StaGB, X 23 f 3 a, decision of the lower chamber of 19 December 1911.
49. Federal forest inspector Johann Coaz had expressed this expectation in his park report. SNK annual report 1911–12, 92.
50. See chapters 4 and 6.
51. Cratschla, 1/2006, 29. The areas of the five park areas were newly redefined, as follows (the former size is in parentheses): Zernez 112.6 (114.7), S-chanf 23.0 (23.3), Scuol 22.8 (22.7), Valchava 8.3 (8.1), Lavin 3.6 (3.6) km².

52. In the case of Scuol, the limit was fifteen years. In the case of rejection by the Bürgergemeinde, a shorter lease might possibly be negotiated with the political commune, Mayor Mohr wrote to Sarasin. SNP Archives, 121.100, Scuol executive council to Sarasin, correspondence dated 20 June 1910.
53. GA Scuol, Bürgerrat, meeting of 18 November 1910; Bürgerversammlung of 20 November 1910.
54. Der Freie Rätier, no. 52, 1910.
55. BAR 9500.25, vol. 37, correspondence between Sarasin and commune of Tarasp, 28 May 1911 and 211911. Relations between Tarasp and the national park remained strained. Negotiations subsequent to 1914 failed several times. At the end of the century, the commune was decidedly against the expansion of the national park. Meier 2010.
56. See the results of the federal census.
57. For instance, in the 1935 vote (see next paragraph). BAR 9500.25, vol. 10, Rauch to Petitmermet, 16 December 1935. It is therefore questionable whether the ENPK's strategy to further the interests of the hoteliers was successful. BAR 9500.25, vol. 37, ENPK to Dir. Pinösch, Vulpera, 24 July 1918. Bühlmann to Könz, Hotelier Schuls, 25 October 1918.
58. SCNAT Archives, Box 521, SNK, meeting of 6 September 1909, Bezzola to Sarasin, 23 August 1909, Brunies to Sarasin, 21 September 1909. It was also Grass who recommended to Sarasin that he court the leaders of the opposition, especially Christel Serrardi.
59. 25 October 1909: Cluozza lease: 49 yes votes out of 52. 3 September 1910: Tantermozza lease: 41 yes votes out of 44. 21 November 1910: Expansion to include Praspöl, Schera, Fuorn, Stabelchod: 52 yes votes out of 54. 26 October 1911: Preliminary vote to extend the contract for seventy-five years, 44 yes votes out of 46. 26 October 1911: Definitive contract renewal: 58 yes votes out of 68. 9 September 1913: Switch to easement: 43 yes votes out of 47. (This issue was also voted on in the Bürgergemeinde and unanimously passed on 29 November 1913.) All the data from the communal meeting registers (GA Zernez, B 21 a, Redunanzas d'abitants). Some of the vote counts reported in the literature are erroneous.
60. BAR 9500.25, vol. 37, Bericht zur Ertragsschätzung einzelner Waldgebiete im Ofenberg, Gemeinde Zernez, 26 October 1910, Ch. Buchli, district forester. Estimates were also made for Falcun (2,700 francs) and Grimmels (6,600), which both later became national park areas.
61. Coaz report of 14 November 1911, in SNK annual report 1911–1912, 85–93, here 92. Supplementary dispatch by the Federal Council of 1913. For critiques, see the minutes of the debates in the National Council and States' Council for 1914. On the development of hunting in the cantons, see Jenny and Müller 2002; on the Ofenberg railroad Catrina 1972, 119–121; Gottschalk 1994, 24–48.
62. Estimate based on random checks of the account books for the commune of Zernez. GA Zernez, C 4. Cudeschs da quint.
63. The increases involved Zernez (214 percent), S-chanf (444 percent), Scuol (333 percent), Valchava (150 percent). Basis of calculation: Swiss Federal Council 1959. Note that Zernez and S-chanf transferred additional land areas to the park (see tables 1 and 2 and map 3).

64. GA Scuol, Bürgerrat, meeting of 18 September 1911. On 28 March 1912 the Bürgerversammlung approved an extension of the lease from twenty-five to sixty years with an increase in interest from 4,000 to 6,000 francs. But the proposal did not meet the government's guidelines, and the SNK refused to go along with it.
65. SBN Archives, M 3.2, ENPK, meetings of 18 July 1915, 18 June 1916.
66. ETH Library, manuscript collections, HS 399, Sarasin to Schröter, 24 May 1916.
67. Vischer 1946, 246–251. In 1934, the SBN did manage to secure a lease for the Aletsch Forest. Some saw in this move the nucleus of a national park in French-speaking Switzerland. The economic crisis of the 1930s appears to have made the communes more enthusiastic about the income-generating potential of conservation.
68. See the persistent complaints in the ENPK meeting minutes for this year.
69. In tandem with S-chanf, La Punt-Chamues-ch revised its lease for the same area.
70. ENPK annual report 1921, 13 f. The quarrels within the SNK and SBN are detailed in Bachmann 1999, 291–316.
71. ENPK annual report 1920, 5.
72. ENPK annual report 1920, 8. Emphasis mine. On the reintroduction of the ibex, see chapter 4; on the Spöl conflict, see chapter 6.
73. ENPK annual report 1923, 13; ENPK annual report 1926, 7; ENPK annual report 1927, 6.
74. GA Zernez, B 21 a, commune of Zernez to ENPK, 23 July 1927, 2; Lower Engadine section of the SAC to the commune of Zernez, 3 January 1929.
75. SBN Archives, M 3.2, ENPK, remarks on the meeting of 4 June 1930.
76. In 1935, the average net income for a cubic meter of wood in the canton of Grisons was precisely half the amount fetched in 1925 and 1930 (4.90 versus 9.80 francs). The net receipts from the Scuol forests for 1933–34 amounted to 6,000 francs compared with 13,238 francs for the period 1925/26 to 1930/31. SNP Archives, 121.100, Bürgergemeinde Scuol to SBN, 20 October 1936.
77. BAR 9500.25, vol. 9, ENPK, meeting of 12 August 1932, 1 f. Based on the recollections of Eduard Campell, forester for the commune of Zernez at the time, it took a lot of convincing. Schloeth 1989, 194 f. The approval of the Zernez communal assembly eventually was clear, with 73 votes out of 90. The voting results from S-chanf are unknown.
78. BAR 9500.25, vol. 9, ENPK, meeting of 15 February 1932, 4.
79. GA Scuol, Protokollbuch Bürgergemeinde, entries beginning with 8 December 1934, in particular 6 June 1935 and 13 June 1935.
80. BAR 9500.25, vol. 10, Rauch to Petitmermet, 16 December 1935. Rauch had also supervised the negotiations.
81. Ibid., 15 December 1935. Rauch attached detailed minutes of the assembly to the correspondence, in which he did not hide his anger at the opposition. The official minutes are to be found in GA Scuol, Protokollbuch Bürgergemeinde, Bürgerversammlung of 13 December 1935.
82. GA Scuol, Bürgerrat, meetings of 10, 17, and 29 February 1936; communal council, meeting of 18 February 1936. Initially, Alp Mingèr was intended for sheep breeding, but the idea was dropped during the negotiations. Perhaps it was clear that revenues generated from the sheep pasture would be disappointing.
83. GA Scuol, Bürgerversammlung of 20 January 1937. The vote was 50 to 2. The negotiations are well documented. See GA Scuol, Protokollbücher Bürgergemeinde und

Politische Gemeinde, 1936–37. BAR 9500.25, vol. 11; SNP Archives, 121.100. In 1937, substantial differences in the proposed compensation led once again to a breakdown of negotiations with the commune of Tarasp. BAR 9500.25, vol. 11, ENPK, meeting of 27 February 1937, 2. One year later, the ENKP considered invoking the twenty-five-year clause in Zernez's contract, to force concessions from the commune. Following initial talks with the communal council, the commission abandoned the idea. SNP Archives, ENPK, meeting of 25 March 1939, 2 f.

84. GA Zernez, B 21 b, EDI to the commune of Zernez, 30 June 1926. SNP Archives, ENPK, meeting of 1 March 1966, 3 f. See also GA Zernez, B 21 a, Lower Engadine section of the SAC to commune of Zernez, 3 January 1929. Nationalparkgesetz 1980. The term "park communities" is used in the act (Art. 4).
85. SBN Archives, M 3.2, ENPK, meeting of 23 September 1918. However, the Grisons government rejected an extension of the no-hunting zone, citing the food shortage.
86. BA 9500.25, vol. 10, Rauch to Petitmermet, 14 December 1935.
87. Paul B. Riis, Switzerland's National Park, 1937. The article may originally have appeared in "Parks and Recreation Magazine," which Riis published. NARA, RG 79 Records of the National Park Service, 3.1. General Records, entry 7: Central Classif. Files 1907–49, 1933–1949, Foreign Parks 0-30.
88. SBN annual report 1932, 6 f.
89. Lansel 1936. Brunies 1919a; 1919b; 1930. On Romansh identity formation, see Catrina 1983; Kraas 1992. On Lansel's polemic against establishing the park, see chapter 2.
90. GA Zernez, B 21 b, Könz to Suprastanza Zernez, 3 December 1960. On the selection of Könz, see SNP Archives, ENPK, meeting of 8 November 1960, 2.
91. ENPK annual report 1966, 3. SNP Archives, ENPK, meeting of 1 March 1966, 3 f. Nationalparkgesetz 1980.
92. Agrawal uses the terms "governmentalized localities," "regulatory communities," and "environmental subjects." Agrawal 2005, especially 6 f. and 23 f.
93. Pro Natura 1999. See also Fehr et al. 2006.
94. Schweizerischer Bundesrat 2005, 2155.
95. www.paerke.ch/en/schweizerpaerke/uebersicht.php, accessed 5 April 2013. See also www.bafu.admin.ch/paerke.
96. NHG 2008, Art. 23m. This failure to bring the NCHO and the National Park Act fully in line with each other leaves much open for discussion in the future. See the remarks in the conclusion to this book.
97. Unesco had already declared the national park a biosphere reserve in 1979, but the criteria of the so-called Sevilla strategy no longer sufficed in and of themselves. Medienmitteilung des Bundesamts für Umwelt, 2 June 2010. The attitudes of local people toward the national park in 2010 have been investigated by Meier 2010.

CHAPTER 4

Total Protection
Philosophy and Practice of Freely Developing Nature

In summer 1935 the *Société nationale d'acclimatation de France* organized a tour through several Central European national parks. The program included the Swiss National Park, the Karwendel and Gross Glockner Parks in Austria, the Triglav in (then) Yugoslavia, and finally, Tatra and Pieniny, two parks situated in the border area of Czechoslovakia and Poland that were emerging as transboundary protected areas. One of the participants put together a detailed, illustrated travel report that was published in the magazines *Des Eaux et Fôrets* and *La Terre et la Vie*. At the very beginning of his report, the author divided the parks into two categories: those with total protection and those with only partial protection. The first category contained only the Swiss National Park, whereas all the other protected areas fell into the second category.[1] Neither the division into two categories nor the allocation of the Swiss national Park to the first category was surprising. Not only had the Swiss National Park's strict protection rules gained it an impressive reputation up to the 1930s; the separation into total and partial nature reserves evolved directly out of the Swiss model.

It was the stated intention of the founders of the Swiss National Park to give full reign to nature within its borders. At the October 1908 meeting where the Reserves Committee of the SNK discussed the principles to be applied to the desired protected area, a division into different categories was suggested: "1. Total reserves (e.g., as with Cluoza and Müschauns), 2. Reserves only for game and other wild animal species, 3. Reserves for flora above the treeline."[2] There were practical grounds for such a division: The committee members anticipated that it would not be possible to leave vast areas completely to nature. Consequently, they foresaw further categories for areas to be placed under only partial protection. The committee chose the term "total" to designate the comprehensive type of protection, whereas "partial" described the less comprehensive form of protection. Ultimately, the Swiss National Park did include partially protected areas. For example, Alp Tavrü, which was leased to the park by the alpine cooperative in Scuol, was continually stocked with cattle during its twenty-five-year (1911–36) affiliation with the park. Partially protected park areas also included the no-hunting areas created in the Lower Engadine in the 1930s, which were abolished again in 1962.[3] Most of the park areas, however, were subject to stringent rules intended to ensure that they complied with the federal decree of 1914. The decree required that "all animal and plant life be left to their freely developing nature." The concept of "total protection" became a trademark of the Swiss National Park.

In the SNK's annual report for 1909–10, Paul Sarasin envisioned the successful transformation of Val Cluozza "into *a total reserve,* as I like to call it, ... in which all life forms, all animals and plants will enjoy utter protection." A decision was also made "to designate the whole of this area envisaged as a nature park as a Swiss national park." The use of the descriptor "total" and the designation "national park" was no coincidence. In adopting the term "national park," the founders were also mindful of the need for distinction. "National park" was commonly associated with America, but the staging of nature for the benefit of visitors that was typical of American parks did not fit the vision of the Swiss park founders. Consequently, they urgently wished to find a new term more reflective of their own goals. The cast-iron plaques that the commission put up at the borders of its protected areas beginning in 1910 were inscribed as follows: "Swiss National Park. Total protection of animals and plants. The Commission." The plaque was written in French, which the SNK believed could be "understood by all concerned nations."[4]

The park founders advocated very effectively. Their lively publications and the many lectures they gave both home and abroad helped them to rapidly make this (at the time) unusual and radical concept more widely known. Total, or absolute, protection became an international trademark and served to set the Swiss National Park model apart. As early as 1912, only two years after the first area had been placed under protection, the British science journal *Nature* not only proclaimed the park the most important nature reserve in Europe, "but in some respects [it] excels the celebrated American Reservations, which are only partially reserved, and do not form one unbroken block."[5] The Swiss park founders also took every opportunity to distinguish their concept from that of the Americans. They might not have created the first national park in the world, but it was the first of its kind: the "first total, fully protected large reserve on Earth."[6]

The concept of stringent protection coupled with promotion, awareness, and the effective transnational networking of people like Paul Sarasin and Carl Schröter assured the Swiss National Park of enduring worldwide attention. The idea of a park geared toward total protection became a model of conservation practiced around the globe. A 1928 report by a League of Nations commission on the state of international nature protection also contained a list of national parks, identified by their different concepts, and ranked. The Swiss National Park not only occupied a prominent position, but even claimed the top spot, followed by the Spanish national parks, which served as a model for developing nature through tourism.[7] A similar distinction was made nearly twenty years later in *Nature* by an English scientist and conservationist who addressed the question of how national parks might be created in crowded Great Britain. He, too, divided the parks on the basis of their purpose into the same two types. Whereas he saw the American national park as the embodiment of a "public pleasure ground," the Swiss National Park concept of total protection of natural processes represented an alternative that was irreconcilable with the American model.[8]

The Swiss National Park's reputation was probably at its highest around that time. Based on an initiative of the *Schweizerische Naturschutzbund* (SBN), the World Conservation Union (IUCN) was founded in Fontainebleau in 1948. The two-year preparatory phase, led by the SBN, guaranteed the Swiss National Park high visibility. During the summers of 1946 and 1947, a large and illustrious international group of conservationists made pilgrimages to the Lower Engadine. In the national park publications that appeared in the following decades under the auspices of the IUCN, the Swiss National Park was always well represented. Yet it did not set the standard. In the late 1950s, in collaboration with the United Nations, the IUCN began developing a classification system for all nationally protected areas. The category "national park" was reserved for protected areas that (according to the 1994 definition) were "managed mainly for ecosystem protection and recreation." Thus, for its Category II: National Park, the IUCN adopted the US interpretation assigning to the parks the dual mission of preservation and recreation. The Swiss National Park now fit uncomfortably into this category, and in the 1990s, it was reassigned to Category Ia: Strict Nature Reserve. At the international level, however, this reclassification had no effect on the reputation and orientation of the Swiss National Park. The tradition it began of the national park as "total reserve" remained a defining feature.[9]

The abiding image of the concept of total protection may well have been that of dead trees that were not cleared away, as in a neatly managed forest. Rather, the idea was to leave them where they fell to decay gradually. This point was carefully made over and again. For instance, the British scientist reporting in *Nature* saw it as the epitome of the Swiss National Park: "Even fallen trees are also allowed to decay in peace."[10] These trees, and remains of trees, were also a popular object of photography that was mass-produced and published, and that consequently also influenced the visual image of the Swiss National Park.

Other events, however, had a less salubrious effect on this carefully cultivated image of total protection. To take one well-known example, how was the reintroduction of the ibex to be reconciled with the policy of total protection? The first such release, which occurred on 20 June 1920 at Falcun, was described by the correspondent for the regional newspaper *Freier Rätier* as follows: "A curious image, this long parade, headed up by park warden Langen, who set the pace, followed by the bearers with their boxes—seven in all—and

Illustration 5. Fallen trees decaying "in peace," Munt la Schera, c. 1920. *Source:* Swiss National Park, Collection Hermann Langen.

behind them the entire company of some 150 people, large and small." The seven boxes each contained a one- to two-year-old ibex, three bucks, and four nanny goats. After a half-hour march, the bearers set down their heavy loads, the tops of the boxes were opened, and the animals "freed." At first the young ibex seemed wary of the wide openness; gradually, however, they began cautiously to explore their new home. Meanwhile, the human population retreated to a nearby meadow to celebrate the event with a sumptuous picnic and a round of speeches. Representatives of the national park, the commune of Zernez, and the cantonal government, as well as a hunting lobbyist praised the national park and its new residents to the mutual enjoyment of all.[11]

The seven released animals came from two herds at the Peter and Paul Wildlife Park in St. Gallen, and the Harder Wildlife Park in Interlaken, which had been rearing ibex within their enclosures since 1906 and 1915, respectively. All of the animals were originally to have been taken from the Peter and Paul Wildlife Park. But after the local breed suffered a series of unexpected setbacks, the number of available animals was insufficient. Consequently, the release was first put off for a year. Then the Interlaken wildlife park sprang into action and suspended an initial release planned for the same year in its own region in favor of that of the national park. In addition to symbolic profit gained by the enterprise through this "patriotic concession," the combination of the

St. Gallen ibex with the "magnificent pure-bloods" from Interlaken appeared beneficial from the vantage of breeding.[12] Fresh blood promised more robust offspring. But pure-bloodedness (as it was then called, no one spoke of genes) did not score as well. The stocks of both zoos were very closely related. Not only did the two wildlife parks exchange offspring to refresh their "bloodlines," but both breeds were the product of fawns from the same colony in Gran Paradiso, the hunting ground of the Italian king, and the only spot in the Alps where the ibex had escaped extermination. For twenty years, from 1906 to 1937, the two wildlife parks procured around a hundred fawns from two local hunters in Val d'Aosta who specialized in (illegally) trading ibex. The poachers would catch a fawn in the royal hunting ground, tie it up, and smuggle it across the border to Switzerland, where it was delivered to representatives of the wildlife parks.[13]

The ibex survived their first winter in the national park, which was a promising sign for their establishment there. However, with the spring came challenges. Hermann Langen, the park warden entrusted with monitoring the young ibex colony, announced to the national park secretary that, attracted by nearby salt licks, the ibex had left the park area. Two ibex never returned. They were sighted in the summer on Piz Albris in the Upper Engadine, where together with other newly released ibex, they produced the fastest-growing and to date largest ibex colony in the Swiss Alps. Years later, Emil Bächler, the Peter and Paul Wildlife Park's ibex expert, accused two Italian poachers from the neighboring Livigno Valley of having chased the two ibex from the park and also having shot two bucks on the same occasion. Owing to the time elapsed since the event, it is unclear how trustworthy this account is. Yet most contemporaries would probably have believed Bächler. Not only were worries about cross-border poaching in the national park widespread in those years, but park and border authorities routinely skirmished with poachers who crossed into the park through the borders it shared with Italy. In 1923, one such case ended fatally for a man from Livigno.[14] To encourage the ibex to stay closer to home, in 1921, on Bächler's advice, the ENPK gave Langen the task of creating artificial salt licks. That made it possible to maintain the ibex colony in the national park, though not without difficulty. The first kid born in the park was sighted in 1922. With the introduction of additional young animals in 1923, 1924, and 1926, the stock was secured.

"Total Protection" and Intervening in Natural Processes

The successful reintroduction of the ibex would remain a high point in the history of the national park. But to return to the question posed previously: How can the release of the ibex and the use of artificial salt licks to retain animals be reconciled with the idea of total protection? Don't such measures fundamentally contradict the philosophy? Did the founders preach one thing and do another? In actual fact, the park's original statute did leave some room for intervening in natural events. According to the Federal Council's first draft, animal and plant life were to be "protected *from any human influence.*" This categorical formulation encountered opposition in the parliamentary debate, however, and the provision was watered down to merely preserve flora and fauna "from any human influence *not in the interest of the national park.*" The legislative assembly saw this caveat as a "valve" that would countenance action against unpopular developments in the park if needed. What the parliament feared most about abandoning nature to its own devices was the proliferation of predators and the spread of epidemics with devastating consequences for both the park and the surrounding area. As a precautionary measure, the political process thus equipped the naturalists' experiment with a safety mechanism.[15]

However, neither the release of the ibex nor the creation of artificial salt licks was driven by such fears. These measures were not intended as a defense against nature. Rather, the aim was to voluntarily add elements from outside into the natural environment of the park. This was such an obvious violation of the cherished mantra of "freely developing nature" that the park authorities found themselves forced to explain. Looking back on the twenty-five-year anniversary of the national park in 1939, Natanael Georg Zimmerli, secretary of the ENPK, justified the reintroduction of the ibex and the installation of the salt licks for these animals as "exceptions provided for from the outset," just like the construction of roads and huts and the collection of material for scientific research.[16]

As far as the reintroduction of the ibex went, Zimmerli's statement was certainly correct. In launching the national park idea within the SNK in 1906, Carl Schröter had considered their resettlement as one of the promising prospects of such a reserve. The lease agreements that the commission concluded with Zernez and Scuol in the following years retained the right to do so in writing. The reintroduction of the ibex, which had last been seen in Switzerland in the sixteenth century, was an age-old desire that predated the birth of the modern conservation movement. As enthusiasm for the Alps swelled in the Romantic era, so did interest in alpine fauna, as evidenced by the success of Niklaus Friedrich von Tschudi's *Das Thierleben der Alpen* (Animal Life in the Alps), which first appeared in 1853 and went through eleven reprintings. Natural scientists and charitable organizations alike campaigned for the reestablishment of the ibex. But repeated attempts at breeding and settlement failed. When in 1876 the federal government passed a Swiss game law under the expanded powers granted by the constitutional revision of 1874, the confederation committed itself to "colonizing the *Freiberge* [the no-hunting areas] with ibex." This was the legal basis on which the federal authorities later generously supported the costly breeding of ibex. They also subsidized the above-mentioned twentieth-century Swiss wildlife park practice of procuring fawns from Gran Paradiso, which was viewed as highly questionable from the standpoint of both legal and animal welfare.[17]

After several years of breeding in enclosures, the Peter and Paul Wildlife Park effected its first release of ibex in the Wiesstannental in the canton of St. Gallen. A second colony was established in 1915 on Piz Ela in Grisons. Unlike previous attempts, these reintroductions were successful, which encouraged Fritz Bühlmann, Bern national councilor and secretary of the ENPK, to proceed similarly with regard to the national park. But his optimism was premature. As with the population in the national park, the two colonies in the Weisstannental and on Piz Ela suffered from high attrition and had to be constantly restocked with breeding animals. The Piz Ela colony nevertheless faded toward the end of the 1920s. The stocks were small and accordingly fragile. In addition, the areas where the animals were released proved in retrospect to be a poor choice of habitat. Little was known about the life of ibex in the wild. Moreover, from the vantage of cultural criticism, the received wisdom that the animals preferred barren mountainous regions was interpreted by the wildlife park ibex experts not as natural behavior but the result of displacement by humans. In their 1920 report to the ENPK, the experts explained that it was "an old, fundamentally distorted view that ibex preferred to live around glaciers, snow, and rocky deserts. No! It was humans, with their culture (alpine commerce and hunting), who drove the ibex higher and brought about their extinction due to more precarious living conditions. Ibex need food to live, not snow and ice." The release of the ibex, said the experts, should not take place on the alpine terrain within the park, but rather in Falcun, a sub-alpine plot on the north slope of Piz Terza that was forested with pines and bordered the park, but was not part of it.[18]

The ENPK heeded the experts' recommendations and in subsequent tough negotiations with the commune of Zernez made a strong case for the "unmistakably propitious conditions" presented by Falcun. In a contract concluded just prior to the scheduled release, Zernez eventually agreed to assign Falcun to the national park but in return got ENPK's concession that it would not be opposed if the commune wanted to use the Spöl River for hydropower in the future. In the following decades, in which the hydropower exploitation was repeatedly planned (it was finally realized after the Second World War), this clause was the source of no small amount of indigestion for the park bodies. In this regard, it was ironic that the released ibex had so little appreciation for the efforts of the commission and rapidly abandoned Falcun in the direction of Val Cluozza, whose barren slopes they apparently found more pleasing. Ibex experts and the park commission proved teachable, however. For future releases, they chose Val Cluozza, which had belonged to the park since the early days.[19]

114 *Creating Wilderness*

Illustration 6. Introduction of ibex at Murtèr above Val Cluozza in the 1920s. The front bearer of the first box is park warden Langen. *Source*: Swiss National Park, Collection Hermann Langen.

Zimmerli was right that the release of the ibex was an exception envisioned by the park's founding fathers from the start. The creation of the salt licks, however, was another matter entirely. At the time, artificial salt licks were widely used by hunters to lure wildlife to certain areas. This hunting practice was taken over by the national park wardens, a move that caused unease among the ENPK. In 1917, ENPK secretary Bühlmann stated that artificial salt licks were incompatible with the principles of the park. In a landmark decision, the ENPK nevertheless decided to allow the use of artificial salt licks to continue at their current level. At the same time, the commission banned another common tool of wildlife management: feeding stations. Nor did they backtrack even when, in the same year, the president of a Swiss hunting association condemned the decision, saying that the deer in the park area would starve due to lack of food.[20] Half a year later, in autumn 1917, the ENPK also declined a petition from the Scuol-based Lischana section of the Grisons hunters' association about extracting hay from the park valley of Val Mingèr for the purpose of winter feeding in the nearby hamlet of Scarl because such an "intervention would run counter to the character of total protection. We have learned from experience that healthy wildlife can perfectly well help themselves."[21] In contrast, the salt licks became weapons in a running battle between hunters and the park authorities, and already in 1918 the ENPK was laying up further arms in the park's arsenal. After it was learned that Grisons hunters had been installing salt licks along the park borders, the commission officially instructed the park wardens "to discretely put salt licks at appropriate spots to neutralize the actions of the hunters."[22]

Humans and Animals

As the events surrounding the ibex and the salt licks show, the nature in the park was not left so untouched as the ostensible commitment to the elimination of all human factors would lead one to believe. Instead, humans intervened in various ways, and over time these interventions became common practice. Before taking a closer look at these practices and their development, it is worth considering two conceptual aspects. The first has to do with the question of which categories of actors are historically relevant and how they can be understood scientifically. The second involves the intrinsic meaning of the (park) borders in structuring reality.

Human interventions in the park involved an ever-changing cast of characters. For example, the actors in the matter of the ibex and salt licks included breeders and hunters, national park managers and wardens, community leaders and citizens, federal officials and journalists, as well as Italian poachers (both as suppliers of wild animals and as a threat to them). Yet the story would be strangely incomplete if it were limited merely to human actors. As already shown, animals were not only the objects of human action. Their own willful behavior helped to shape events irrevocably. The migration of the ibex in the park constituted a thumb in the eye of the professionals' expertise. And the animals' taste for salt served not only to deeply embarrass the park leaders; it also caused them to back away from their noble principles and to use "artificial" salt licks to persuade the animals to accept an "unhindered, natural" life in the national park.

Describing the animals' behavior as willful is an allusion to the historical anthropology concept of *Eigensinn* introduced by the social historian Alf Lüdtke. By *Eigensinn*, Lüdtke meant "the particular reasoning that people concede to themselves or to others." Lüdtke did not see the behavior of industrial workers that he studied primarily in terms of power relations, as was customary. Rather, he looked for a logic of its own in the workers' behavior to make sense of it. In conceding that workers had their own agenda and in taking it seriously, Lüdtke simultaneously raised them from objects defined by domination to independent actors.[23] The same concern is relevant here with respect to wildlife insofar as their behavior should not be understood only as a reaction to human actions. That is not, however, to say that the categorical distinction between humans and animals should be dismissed, for instance, equating ibex with factory workers. This would be epistemologically impossible: The tools available to history and science for understanding the agendas of animals are limited compared with humans. Unlike people animals leave no written personal testimonies, of course. Interpretation of their past behavior is thus necessarily based on human descriptions, whether contemporary accounts or subsequent analyses based on material remains, genetic investigations, and biological models.[24] Yet here there is another, if not complete, analogy, that is, to the historical study of lower-class strata. The often poorly educated underclasses left behind not zero, but comparatively few personal accounts. Consequently, the description of their behavior, too, relies on the testimony of outsiders and on alternative sources. In either case, the perspective of the researcher influences the interpretation of the behavior. The environmental historian Andrew Isenberg points out the striking parallel between the "moral economy," which the eminent British historian E. P. Thompson attributed to the English lower classes in the eighteenth century, and a moral ecology, which the American Aldo Leopold—one of the founders of academic wildlife biology—ascribed to nature. Isenberg speaks of a moral ecology of wildlife that sees the natural order as a higher, morally and scientifically incorruptible order and humans as a disruptive influence. This perspective tends to automatically attribute to wildlife a stabilizing role in the ecosystem.[25] The expectation of early ecologists that untrammeled nature would evolve toward equilibrium was also fueled by the cultural conceptualization of harmonious nature, disturbed only by the actions of humans. The proponents of the Swiss National Park hewed to this line of thinking for a long time. To cite just one example among many, in the mid-1920s, the park commission expressed its hope "that in the not-too-distant future, a certain equilibrium will reign not only in the stocks of individual animal species but also in the interactions between domestic prey and predators."[26] Note that the historian must at once critically scrutinize such historical moral beliefs, and be aware of his own moral beliefs and how they affect his research.

In addition to the human-animal relationship, a second social aspect deserves special attention: borders. The boundaries of the park serve as a razor-sharp delineation between inside and outside. At the same time, they form a buffer where inside and outside come into contact. This dialectic of inside and outside gives the boundary both meaning and explosive force. It is no coincidence that most conflicts center on this dividing line: whether the issue was crossing it in one or another direction, for example, by ibex sensing salt or by Italian poachers—where often even the threat of encroachment was provocation enough—or whether the issue was tweaking the boundary to provoke or hinder transgression. Here, examples include hunters and national park wardens who set up salt licks along the border but on the other side, or national park administrators who attempted to shift borders in order to expand park areas.[27]

Previous chapters have commented on the social function of the national park as a heterotopia, as a counter to modern civilization, by being simultaneously part of it and yet apart. The idea of total protection was a reaction to modernity; it provided an answer to the modern desire for unlimited territorial access. On the one hand, modernity's all-encompassing goal made the totally protected national park seem a necessity; on the other hand, it was modern thinking that initially made such a concept conceivable. The intellectual and physical separation of the landscape into a sphere of civilization driven by cultural history and a sphere of nature driven by natural history was nothing if not a modern paradigm. Thus, the Swiss National Park and its claim to total protection must be fairly considered to be a typically modern institution.

The Role of Park Wardens

A section of the border came to have a double meaning. Here, the border separated the park area not only from the surrounding areas, but also the territories of Switzerland and Italy. This shared border with Italy was a problem for the park from the very beginning. The park's wildlife, as was already being argued in 1910, was at the mercy of Italian poachers. The SNK shared these fears. Consequently, they made use of their Italian contacts and in 1910 managed to interest the Italian minister of the interior in the idea of setting up a reserve on the Italian side that would directly border on the Swiss park. But the plan made little headway in the following years. While the Swiss National Park stabilized up to mid-1914, the outbreak of the First World War that summer meant the end of the Italian plans and consequently the idea of a large protected area across the national borders. It was one of the many initiatives arising from a vision of progressive, peaceful cooperation between nations that were launched with great optimism before 1914 only to be forgotten amid the horrors of war. The idea of the park was revived during fascism and led, in 1935, to the establishment of Stelvio National Park in Trentino. But now the focus of the park was on boosting tourism, and even the areas in Livigno adjacent to the Swiss National Park were no longer within the park perimeter. They were brought into Stelvio only as a byproduct of the expansion of the 1970s.[28]

The collapse of the Italian plans complicated protection for the Swiss National Park, but required no fundamental alteration of the overall concept. Beginning with the leasing of Val Cluozza in 1910, the NSK was fully "aware that the first condition for safeguarding total protection is attentive monitoring, for which the employment of a park warden for the specified area has already been foreseen."[29] However, finding a suitable park warden was surprisingly difficult. The first hire, a Grisons native from the Upper Rhine Valley, proved a mistake. In June 1910, less than ten days after the man had signed a contract, Brunies received a telegram in Basel from the Grisons capital of Chur that contained the following message: "Took a close look at the area. illusions dispelled instead of alpine idyll hellish valleys devoid of green. possible to cancel wife desperately ill household transport suspended I'm ruined may I request a train subscription answer—Tscharner." The contract was annulled several days later.[30]

So drastic a case was never repeated. But candidates' conception of the work of a national park warden and the realities of the job were often worlds apart. The life of a park warden was lonely and austere, the daily routine monotonous and not free of danger. In a contract signed by Hermann Langen, who in August 1910 succeeded the unfortunate Tscharner, the duties of the park warden were laid out as follows: "From 1 June until the first snowfall he is to reside in the guardhouse we are to erect in the Cluoza valley, and to monitor the entire area of the Zernez sector all year long. During the summer months he is to regularly inspect the same area, to prohibit any interference with plant- or wildlife, to reprimand poachers and persons causing damage, and if necessary to expel guilty parties or prosecute them."[31] On the field inspections, which (as was detailed in separate instructions) in summer were to be made daily and generally had to be started before dawn, park wardens were to keep a diary in which they were also to note their special observations of wildlife and plants. They were armed with carbines and pistols for keeping order. The wardens were to take from transgressors any material collected in the park, confiscate hunting and fishing gear, as well as botanizing boxes and plant presses, and if necessary shoot down hunting dogs. Bonuses were awarded for successful prosecutions. In the winter, wardens were to inspect the protected area "as often as possible" on skis, which meant that Langen, who weathered those months in Zernez, received not only a pair of skis and some furs, but also a sleeping bag, coat, cooker, and binoculars. Besides monitoring, the duties of a warden included constructing and maintaining park infrastructure, in particular trails and huts. Finally, the wardens were increasingly solicited by scientists to provide ancillary services, and for most visitors to the park, the wardens were the point of contact. In 1912, the ENPK established the position of national park supervisor (held for the first thirty years by Steivan Brunies), with responsibility for the park wardens. Thenceforth, the wardens could leave the area and residence to which they were assigned only with permission.[32]

As the park enlarged, so did the number of wardens. For the period up to 1914, the warden for Val Cluozza was joined by three others for the S-charl and S-chanf sectors, as well as for the Ofen Pass area. The latter was stationed at Alp Buffalora. The wardens were allowed to employ helpers to a limited extent. Hermann Langen and Romedi Reinalter both ended up serving extended periods as wardens: 1910 to 1936 and 1917 to 1950, respectively. However, many of their colleagues were relieved of their jobs after very short tenures. The remoteness of the position—the supervisor and the members of the park commission lived far away, in the midlands, and were only rarely seen—apparently led wardens to take their duties less than seriously or to interpret them willy-nilly. But unfavorable reports from researchers, visitors, and locals as well as haphazard diary entries quickly revealed misconduct and negligence.[33] As law enforcement officers and as those who, along with the members of the ENPK, were the only ones entitled to leave the marked trails, wardens became the object of local resentment and envy. Moreover, the ENPK was not always surehanded in its choice of employees. Good references and recommendations were insufficient to assess the suitability of candidates. One hire that fell into the category of "curiosities" was Basel Africa traveler, big game hunter, and animal catcher Adam David. His movements restricted by the First World War, David presumably drew on his Basel network to obtain a job at the park. A year later, he was charged with poaching and let go.[34]

The park commission's requirements and selection criteria are apparent from a report written by Brunies in 1917, when once again the warden position at S-chanf was vacant. Five applications were received, one of which Brunies tossed out for inadequate qualifications and a second for reasons of age (too old). Of the remaining three candidates, Brunies shortlisted two: "Both have good credentials and impeccable reputations. Both are married, but still young, strong, and active; both enjoy nature and are undoubtedly well suited to the job of park warden." One candidate was from a Catholic area of St. Gallen, which made Brunies a bit skeptical. Would the person be at ease in protestant S-chanf? Moreover, he had a "secure position," which could be at risk were he to fail as his predecessors had. Brunies strongly favored the other candidate, Romedi Reinalter, whom he knew personally. He "grew up next door to the park and is at one both with its nature and the idiosyncracies of the Engadine folk. As a teacher, he has the respect & trust of the local population."[35]

In filling the park warden posts, locals from the neighboring regions were increasingly given preference. Following a major changeover in 1916–17, in addition to Langen, the staff included two Engadiners and one warden from Val Müstair. For the next few years, the personnel remained stable. Relations between park wardens and Supervisor Brunies were strained, however, and the wardens sometimes found themselves victims of the disputes and turf wars that divided the ENPK in those years. The protagonists were Chairman Sarasin and Secretary Bühlmann on the one side, and Supervisor Brunies on the other. With the outbreak of hostilities in the First World War, Langen found himself ostracized because of his German ancestry. When, in 1915, the French Swiss press published an article attacking the national park management, Sarasin publicly condemned the accusations and stood behind his wardens. All the guards were "Swiss citizens," wrote Sarasin in the SNK annual report, mentioning the nationality of the park wardens for the first time.[36] Langen had shortly before acquired Swiss citizenship, but that was not enough to protect him from further insults. He was alleged to have repeatedly behaved toward visitors in a patronizing manner, and to suffer from pathological egotism. Not only were such traits incompatible with the Swiss national value of modesty; they also fit the stereotype of the arrogant and vainglorious Germans. "Langen does not belong in this environment," a student from Zurich complained to the supervisor in 1926. "His character traits tarnish the lofty image of our national shrine. I am not a chauvinist. But Langen should be more careful about advertising his native roots, and be more modest in the exercise of his office."[37] The park commission admonished Langen several times about his behavior, and Brunies, whose relationship with Langen was troubled, even once requested that he be dismissed. To what extent Langen really was arrogant, and how much of his perceived demeanor was simply a projection of chauvinistic attitudes, is impossible to resolve today.[38] In any event, the hostility does betray a strengthening association between nationality and park. In 1915, Sarasin explained that the SNK had chosen Langen "without knowing at the time, nor having any concern, that he was German by birth." In contrast, in selecting Reinalter in 1917, Brunies dropped a competing candidate named Luchetta because he had only obtained citizenship three years earlier, at the start of the war. It would thus be unsuitable, Brunies believed, to prefer Luchetta over other, equally well qualified applicants.

The annual salary of a park warden was an initially modest sum of 1,800 francs. In subsequent years, that sum was doubled. In the early 1920s four park wardens had a yearly salary (including expenses and other costs) in excess of 15,000 francs. According to the park contracts, the SBN was responsible for these posts, which threatened to throw its budget and, consequently, the national park out of balance. As a result, ways were sought to ease the financial burden of the SBN. One attempt was to free the SBN from the interest payments for the Scuol park sections by transferring them to the federal government. Scuol's citizen's assembly, however, repeatedly rejected such proposals.

Relief came directly from the federal government when it agreed to delegate the task of monitoring the park to its national border patrol. In 1923 the park warden for the S-charl sector was relieved, and in the following year the park commission also said farewell to the warden at Buffalora. Their duties were taken over by the border patrols at S-charl and La Drossa, joined by S-chanf in 1933. Consequently, following Hermann Langen's resignation in 1936, for several years, Romedi Reinalter served as sole park warden.

Further changes to the park brought about by the construction of the Engadiner Kraftwerke (hydropower plant) in the 1960s also entailed a fundamental revision of park operation and monitoring. Park wardens were now federal officials, given uniforms, and put on equal footing with the border patrol.[39] Their numbers were increased to half a dozen, and later ten with the introduction of summer park wardens. In the 1990s the new park director, Klaus Robin, profoundly reorganized park surveillance. He abolished the fixed assignment of supervisory districts to park wardens and let them rotate.

Surprisingly, no women figure on the list of park wardens, which surely makes the occupation one of the last all-male bastions in Switzerland. The physical demands of the job do not explain the phenomenon. Rather, the traditional expectations of women may well have discouraged them from applying or being accepted within the ranks of wardens. At any rate, the lack does show that women and wilderness were a combination that male nature pioneers abominated. Wilderness was a male domain where the presence of women could only be a distraction. The wilderness was the making of men, but what would it do to the gentle female spirit? When park warden Langen moved into the log cabin in Val Cluozza with his wife and two children, the NSK was alarmed. With her nervous nature, she would be a bad influence on her husband, the commission reasoned, and decided therefore to replace Langen's wife "with a stouthearted male employee."[40]

Managing Nature

By 1939, the first twenty-five years of park supervision were deemed a success. The number of park violations remained "extremely small," and the feared invasion of miscreants from Livigno proved limited to a few cases.[41] The wardens had managed not only to keep poachers and timber thieves, trappers and gatherers away from the park, but also livestock and domestic animals. In the early years, the park authorities were especially worried about herds of sheep encroaching on the park. Thus, the expansion of the park in 1918 to take in the barren Val Nüglia—"death valley"—served primarily to protect the lower boundary of the area from grazing sheep.[42] Many years later, in 1951, an escaped house goat was the occasion of some excitement. The escapee joined the groups of chamois and ibex in the park, and for three months it was impossible to capture or to expel him. Finally, with the permission of both the owner and the authorities, a park guard put an abrupt end to the "free-ranging" goat's life with a bullet. As the ENPK wrote in its annual report, with obvious relief, the antics of the vagabond had no broader implications for the integrity of the park wildlife because "(as a eunuch) it was, fortunately, in no position to foster unwanted offspring."[43]

Strict separation of the park and surrounding areas, of wilderness and civilization, was a high priority. However, because this separation was not physically possible—a permanent fence around the entire area was discussed but quickly dropped for reasons of feasibility—it was always precarious. Fears that the separation would be breached and the wilderness and civilization would mix preoccupied park affairs over the years.

The concern was not only the intrusion of civilization into the park, as described above, but also the emergence of uncontrolled park wilderness and its incursion into the civilized surroundings. The park's founders had to confront these fears from the outset, and they—and their successors—took them seriously. In marking the twenty-fifth anniversary of the park in 1939, Eduard Handschin, chair of the park's science committee, wrote: "Because ... anything uncontrolled poses an inherent danger to the controlled surroundings, here, too, it must be a priority to put into place monitoring mechanisms to detect these changes and to study their impact on the environment."[44]

Effectively containing such fears was critical to the legitimacy of the park and the concept of total protection. And in the early years, the park authorities managed the containment well, as they successfully nipped several circulating concerns in the bud. For example, when the Zernez community expressed worry that leaving fallen wood in the national park would invite bark beetles and thus could threaten the surrounding forests, a forestry report published in 1918 considered the fears but dismissed them as unfounded. The following year, hoof-and-mouth disease returned to the Engadine with a vengeance, and the public health authorities in the S-charl area shot ill-looking deer. The carcasses were transferred to the federal veterinary office for further analysis. When the veterinarians failed to confirm the suspected cases, the park commission showed its superiority. Free-ranging wildlife could not possibly spread the disease, the commission asserted in a statement. Indeed, large-scale trials by the British in Africa had determined this long ago.[45]

Later qualms that epidemics would spread unchecked in the national park were similarly dispelled.[46] Yet a vague apprehension about the uncontrolled enclave remained. In the 1960s, when the cantonal authorities ordered the fox population to be reduced as a prophylaxis against the spread of rabies, the ENPK gave in and participated in the measures.[47] Every year beginning in 1967, as a precaution, wardens killed foxes in the park. For many years this proved to be unnecessary as rabies stayed away from the region. Only in the 1980s did the first cases appear in the Lower Engadine, but the national park remained largely unscathed. Shortly thereafter rabies subsided. In 1985, it was pronounced eliminated for the entire canton.[48] This course of events puts the reasonableness of the fight against rabies in the national park in a bad light, and the question arises whether things might have been different if a more popular animal had been involved or whether—despite the official position that all forms of life in the park are equal—a bias against the predator fox, which has been variously blamed for the decline of fowl in the park, influenced the park commission's decision. Support for this line of thinking is the fact that when a few years later (at the end of 1988) infectious keratoconjunctivitis began to strike the chamois in the park, a different approach was taken. This time, only affected animals were done away with. In addition to the social morals that preferred the edible chamoix over the predator fox, two other factors may have contributed to the differing behavior of the authorities. First, unlike rabies, infectious keratoconjunctivitis cannot be transmitted to humans, and thus it is perceived as less threatening. Second, the more measured response toward infectious keratoconjunctivitis also reflects changes in the park's policy on intervening over the years, which by the end of the 1980s were detailed in "guidelines," that the park commission issued for "handling interventions."[49]

The question of the legal basis for intervening in park events also came into play with respect to fire. That raging fires have far-reaching consequences not only for the park but also for the surrounding area is hard to argue with. So what should be the response to fires? Illustrative cases were provided in 1951 and 1962, when large areas of the national park in Il Fuorn and Ova Spin caught fire. Both fires were caused by humans and were promptly combated by firefighters.[50] However, the delicate question arose whether the reaction should be the same if a fire was not caused by humans but rather occurred naturally, for example, as the result of a lightning strike. Should the natural process be allowed to run, as required by a consistently applied policy of total protection, or should one intervene to protect park flora and fauna from these forces of nature? Monitoring the development of fires between 1951 and 1962 showed that a significant amount of vegetation regrew only very slowly, over a period of many decades.[51] Thus, large fires threatened to transform the nature of the park in the long term, a transformation that very few would have welcomed. But should that be taken into account? Should not nature in the national park be permitted to run free, even if it took a direction contrary to human interests or values? In addressing these questions, the surrounding region once more played an important role. Since the forests of the national park were no longer cultivated, deadwood and underbrush were accumulating. Accordingly, conflagrations could occur that would be bigger than any known forest fires. As soon as they reached a certain size, they would be uncontrollable and no longer limited to the area of the park. Such fires had occurred in the United States, where the Forest Service and the National Park Service had long advocated suppressing forest fires. When, following the 1970s trend of closer-to-nature park management, the park service allowed naturally occurring fires to burn, it provoked a backlash. In the meantime, the combustible material in the forests had increased to such an extent that a small fire could unleash a much bigger one that was even more difficult to put out. This awareness was suddenly made palpable in 1988, when several small fires in Yellowstone Park became a large conflagration, eventually consuming over a third of the park area. The park was closed to visitors while thousands of firefighters battled the blaze. The event sparked fierce controversy, but did not immediately result in a return to the old strategy of promptly suppressing fires. Rather, monitoring and prevention were strengthened to curb fires early on.[52] The American debates were followed in Switzerland, but the much smaller Swiss National Park decided differently in the 1990s. At the time, the park authorities decided to suppress even natural fires to keep wildfires from breaking out. But the question was left open as to whether in the future it might be possible to allow natural fires to burn temporarily or even whether a fire regime oriented toward natural processes could be established through planned fires. There were two central issues: First, the obvious accumulation of combustible material increased the risk of a devastating forest fire in the Swiss National Park. Second, fire management and total protection were in no way to be equated but rather to be brought into coexistence.[53] However, by the end of 2010, what shape this relationship would take was still largely unanswered.

Introducing Animals

In addition to measures taken in reaction to external events, another category of practices involved measures deliberately taken to actively promote return of the national park to its envisaged state of "pristine nature." These proactive strategies were a fortiori not easily reconcilable with the philosophy of total protection. However, that tension was actually built into the Swiss National Park idea from the very beginning with the plans for reintroducing ibex. If now it was permitted to settle animals in the park, what were the limits of permissibility? If human influence was not absolutely out of the question, what criteria would decide the legitimacy of exceptions? The original presence of a species was obviously a determining factor. But what constituted "Swiss ur-nature"? From a geohistorical perspective, species composition is never stable or immobile, but instead constantly moving. This made the binary distinction between native (or original) and alien species completely arbitrary and especially dependent on the chosen temporal and spatial context. As recent studies show, the choice of context is not only based on scientific criteria but also informed by contemporary social categories of self and other.[54] How the Swiss National Park dealt with these questions can be elucidated by the debates over the release of species in the park.

In American national parks of the early twentieth century, it was common practice to supplement existing nature in specific ways. To improve the aesthetic appeal of a landscape, plants were imbedded, including alien species; and to facilitate activities like fishing or wildlife watching, or even to enable them for the first time, animals were introduced to the park and maintained for spectators. This kind of park management, oriented to the needs of visitors, was abhorrent to the founders of the Swiss National Park. In Crater Lake National Park, reported Carl Schröter disapprovingly, a park ranger had asked that Schröter "send him seeds from Swiss alpine plants, to 'enrich' (i.e. to distort!) the flora of the park."[55]

A key consideration for the settlement policy in the Swiss National Park was whether there was evidence that the species to be settled had actually existed there in earlier times. If that could be shown, it was possible to argue that nature be given back what it had already once owned. Through the intervention, nature was not "distorted" but instead "corrected." Behind this reasoning was the assumption that the true nature was an "ur-nature" that had existed prior to the influence of humans once upon a time in the area of the national park and that could be restored by erasing human influence. Introducing the missing elements of that primeval nature would support the restoration process.

In this respect, it was very convenient for the ENPK that the earlier presence of the ibex in the park area could be unequivocally demonstrated. In contrast, an offer from the spa association of St. Moritz in 1916 to release roe deer and red deer in the national park was politely declined. Red deer were happily immigrating on their own, the response stated, and fallow deer were not local wildlife. Consequently, "it cannot be the goal of the park to artificially cultivate wildlife stocks; that must be left to nature, and nature alone."[56]

In the case of the rare ibex, however, the park authorities helped nature out fairly extensively over decades. After the initial stock in Val Cluozza stabilized, a second colony was established in Val Tantermozza in the 1930s. This valley had actually been an option for the initial release, but had been dropped owing to its orientation toward the Engadine main valley and the hunting area there. Unlike Falcun, the first release area, Tantermozza proved a suitable terrain. The local ibex colony developed well and later populated adjacent Val Trupchun on their own.[57] Less fortunate, however, was the 1968 founding of a third national park colony in the region of Il Fuorn. Interestingly, tourism in the park, which had expanded greatly in the interim, now played an important role in these settlements. The release was inspired by the owner of the local hotel. As with Falcun a half-century before, the released animals showed their willful side and wandered off away from the settlement area. Only after repeated attempts did a loyal local colony form in the 1980s.[58] For reasons that were unclear, at the end of the 1960s the Cluozza River was stocked with young trout. But apart from a cryptic statement in the ENPK's annual report for 1969, nothing more was documented regarding this apparently unique action.[59] It was likely quickly forgotten (or suppressed).

The ibex were not the only animals to be offered "resettlement." There was also strong evidence for the presence of bears, lynx, and wolves, as well as bearded vultures. In fact, the release of these species was considered several times. Of the four species, the bear was still present in the park at the time of its establishment. In 1904 hunters killed a bear near the future park area of Val S-charl. In the following year, there were no more shootings. But the animals were still seen or tracked in the Lower Engadine. In nearby Trentino, which at the time still belonged to Austria-Hungary, large populations of bears lived, and some wandered through the Engadine Valley on their migrations. The park founders hoped the bears would settle in the park. In so doing, they also stood expressly against the then prevailing division of the animal kingdom into useful and harmful animals. The first logo of the SBN of 1909, which had been used to advertise the park, showed a bear in front of a mountain range (see illustration 7). The representation did not trivialize the animal, but to the contrary rather emphasized its imposing stature, and its paws and claws. The logo enabled the park and SBN founders to express their general attitude toward the animal as well as their firm hope for a sustainable return of bears to the park. However, their vision was not shared by everyone. The local population, for instance, had no affection for bears. At their instigation, the bear clauses in the park contracts provided for compensation for damage outside the park and countermeasures that went as far as permission to shoot perpetrators. Park opponents in the federal parliament were also horrified by the possible appearance of bears and thought it senseless, if not dangerous, to create a park for bears.[60]

Bears were detected in the park up until a few years after the outbreak of the First World War, a fact that caused the ENPK to announce joyfully in its annual report for 1915 that it was "highly likely that the bear would definitely settle as wildlife." But the commission's joy was premature. In the following years, trace of the bears was lost, and alleged sightings reported from time to

Illustration 7. SBN membership promotion of 1909. *Source:* Pro Natura.

time could not be confirmed. In a first look back from 1925, the park commission stated with resignation: "Today, in the Engadine and in the national park, bears are probably a thing of the past."[61]

The timing of the disappearance of the bears suggests that their migration route into Switzerland was interrupted by the hostilities of the First World War (between 1915 and 1918, the Trentino Valley was one of the scenes of the fighting between Austria and Italy). The ENPK's 1925 assertion held until 2005, when a bear paid a visit to the park for the first time in ninety years.[62] In the intervening decades, the release of bears in the national park had been considered aloud several times. However, owing to the animals' tendency to roam, which led few to believe they would remain in the area of the national park once released, and foreseeable problems of acceptance by the local population, the proposals were coolly received.[63]

An important change occurred in 1962 with the revision of the federal hunting act. Bears and lynx were added to the list of protected animals. This action removed the distinction between useful and harmful wild animals that was introduced into the federal act on hunting in the 1870s. The original law had been favorable to ungulates such as roe deer, red deer, chamoix, and ibex. Now, the new law established the legal conditions for the survival of the two predators whose conservation had been of little interest under the old law, and which in the meanwhile had disappeared from Switzerland.[64] Indeed, efforts were made promptly to ensure that the Swiss National Park topped the list of release areas. In 1963, an Appenzeller businessman, Gottfried Suhner-Müller, launched an initiative to reintroduce bears that was received by the park commission with skepticism reinforced by the park's scientists. The ENPK questioned the suitability of the park for bears, pointing to the lack of basic food, the disturbance caused by tourism, the livestock in adjacent areas, and the negative attitude of the farmers. In addition, the ENPK worried about the consequences that an attack on a human by a bear released by the commission might have for the park.[65] In subsequent years, further release areas were suggested, such as Val Mora, a valley to the south of the national park, and Misox, in Ticino. The Zurich Zoo actively supported the project and pronounced itself ready to provide bears for release, which were raised in the zoo with as little interference by animal keepers and visitors as possible. These conditions should allow the young to preserve their natural fear of people. When the Swiss provisos could not be met, the promoters turned to Italian Trentino, where a small and endangered population of bears still lived. In spring 1969 a pair of young bears from the Zurich Zoo was released. However, the bears immediately began searching out the vicinity of the settlement, and the trial was stopped after only a few weeks. The animals were anesthetized and transported to an Italian zoo. The following year, in the newspaper *Bündner Wald*, national park director Robert Schloeth clearly rejected the idea of releasing bears in the national park. Because of the park's altitude and barrenness, the bears would not remain in the park but would expand their foraging to lower-lying, densely populated areas.[66]

In the same article, Schloeth described the lynx as the only large predator that might plausibly be reintroduced. He dismissed the wolf from consideration because no area of the country seemed to satisfy its needs. This conclusion had already been reached by the hunting law of 1962, which did not equate wolves with bears and lynx but rather—also new!—as huntable.[67] Releasing wolves was never an issue. Reintroduction of the lynx, however, was enthusiastically encouraged both by the federal authorities and by the park commission. In an international resettlement program for the Alps, Switzerland took a leading role. In 1971 an initial pair was released in the central Swiss canton of Obwalden. The ENPK readily involved the national park in the program. Not only was the resettlement of the lynx in the park favorably received, but it was even hoped that the big cats might help to control the rapidly growing deer population. Journalists who visited the park in 1969 on the occasion of the so-called *Taleraktion*—the traditional annual fundraising event for natural and cultural heritage protection, which that year was targeted to the Convent of St. Johann at nearby Müstair—were told that natural life in the park was still influenced by earlier human use: "Even the wildlife stocks are not 'natural.' Wolves, bears, and lynx are missing, which previously checked the deer population growth within natural limits."[68] The ENPK's request to release lynx was rebuffed by the cantonal authorities in 1970, however, on the grounds that the human population was not ready for it and that the release of predators was inconsistent with current rabies control.[69] Two years later, that is, exactly one hundred years after the last documented shooting of a lynx in the Lower Engadine, two cats appeared in the national park. A regional section of the WWF, which in 1969 had proposed the release of lynx in the park, had unilaterally released a pair without official authorization. The two animals lived quietly in the region for a few years, but did not reproduce. The ENPK, seeing its own efforts torpedoed by the WWF, put its release plans on hold. In 1980 a further illegal lynx release occurred that was even less successful than the first. The following year the animals were tracked one last time before disappearing. That was the end of the releases. However, in winter 2007–8 a lynx roamed the national park, having migrated in from the lower Alps in eastern Switzerland—a first.[70]

In the late 1960s and early 1970s the re-establishment of vanished animal species was all the rage. At the same time, the experimental release of bears and lynx spurred proposals for releasing otters. The otter, whose imminent extinction Paul Sarasin had lamented in writing in 1917, disappeared from Switzerland entirely until the 1960s. At the start of the twentieth century, it was still extant in the Spöl valley and river, but neither the efforts of the park nor the protected status granted it by the federal government in 1953 were enough to halt the decline in the otter population. Nonetheless, the idea of releasing otters in Spöl was soon dropped. New studies had shown the varied demands of the species on its environment. The relatively monotonous landscape of the park and its environs could not guarantee otter survival in the 1970s.[71]

These developments showed that total protection did not imply conservation of biodiversity; indeed, the two concerns might be entirely contradictory. This notion had been mooted early on. When zoologists regretted in the national park's annual report for 1923 that "the fauna of the protected area was 'relatively lacking in species and monotonous," they were simultaneously voicing the suspicion that the lack of humans and grazing livestock would be impoverishing.[72] When national park director Schloeth personally took stock in 1980, he noted that since the early years of the park, bears, otters, and hazel grouse had disappeared, red deer and alpine wallcreepers had dwindled, and only red deer and ibex had increased.[73] In the eyes of the ENPK and the WNPK (the science commission), these losses were acceptable. "The conservation of endangered species is not a declared goal," wrote both park commissions in 1989 in a jointly developed set of guidelines to ensure the park's objectives. These guidelines would serve the park's institutions from then on in assessing changes to the park area and the legitimacy of making (or not making) interventions.[74]

The second species to be introduced to the park after the ibex was the bearded vulture, in 1991. As with the lynx, the release of the bearded vulture had the support of an international resettlement program that wished to reestablish the largest European bird of prey in the Alps. Since 1986, following preliminary breeding in zoos, animals had been released in several locations across the Alps.[75] An initial proposal to release bearded vultures in the Swiss National Park had been made to the ENPK decades earlier. In the 1920s, a furrier named Carl Stemmler, who was committed to the protection and study of the eagle, had written to the ENPK with just such an idea. The commission rejected it. As long as the bird was not protected, its chances of survival were nil.[76] Like Stemmler, the SBN also supported the protection of endangered birds of prey. However, the removal of the eagle from the list of huntable species occurred only in 1953, along with the otter.

For the bearded vulture, purely protective measures would already have been too late in the 1920s. At the turn of the twentieth century, the bird had disappeared completely from the Alps. The bearded vulture's very bad image doomed it. It was denounced as a "lamb vulture," and was said to attack and carry off not only young sheep but also small children. Its name conjured up gruesome events in lonely mountain pastures that were dramatically portrayed by contemporary landscape painters. As with other birds of prey, rewards were paid for shooting bearded vultures.[77] In the 1990s, these unfounded fears—the bearded vulture is not a hunter but a scavenger—evaporated. As with the release of the ibex seventy years earlier, the resettlement of bearded vultures was widely welcomed and aroused keen public sympathy. The infrastructure of the national park provided ideal conditions for effective observation of nests and monitoring of the birds. The well-prepared and widely supported project has (to date) enjoyed substantial success: At the end of the 1990s, the first chicks were born in the wild, and since 2007, the bearded vultures within the Swiss National Park also regularly produce young.[78]

Seeking a New Equilibrium

An examination of the interventions of the park authorities in park events over time reveals that these interventions began with the founding of the park and persisted throughout its existence. These measures took on a life of their own, and sometimes continued even when the original reason for them was gone. Such was the case with the artificial salt licks, which were still in operation long after the threat of hunters had dissipated. Although in the 1950s the ENPK declared that the salt licks should gradually be decommissioned, the change was slow to take effect. It was only three decades later in 1987 that for the first time no salt was put out in the park.[79] Now it was also accepted that the population of chamoix would decrease with the elimination of the salt licks. "It should not be our job to maintain or to increase animal stocks in the park area by means of artificial attractors, according to old and outdated practices, and certainly not *to inflate numbers of animals* or even to present them for show," read the annual report for 1980. "The old image of paradise, which even Stephan Brunies once envisaged and—as evidenced in the old diaries of park wardens—was vigorously promoted by countless salt licks, must give way to a new image of populations adapted to nature. To the point that one may in the future have to admit that certain stocks have declined on account of it."[80] Even the repeated luring of ibex from the national park—this time "resourceful types from Livigno" were accused not of poaching but of using the ibex to boost tourism—did not lead to a revision of the salt policy.[81]

On the one hand, park authorities questioned interventions over the decades. On the other hand, the intensity of controls and the depth of interventions increased from the second half of the 1960s onward. Examples include the years-long reduction of foxes and—as will be shown separately in a later chapter—the deer population in the park, but also the repeated releases of ibex, the stocking of trout in Cluozza, and various other unrealized but seriously debated resettlement projects.

The significant weakening of the concept of total protection in those years is the result of several factors. First, the idea that the national park would be allowed to develop into a natural state of equilibrium became less compelling with time. Carl Schröter was doubly wrong in broaching the topic in 1918: "The large extent of the area guarantees that, with time, a fully naturally balanced community will form, which will find its own harmonious equilibrium."[82] On the one hand, the park area was far too small for thriving species, especially deer. They chose their habitats as they pleased, and not always in conformity with the park's borders. On the other hand, the idea of a harmonious equilibrium under the direction of nature was really the expression of a moralizing ecology. It was no match for the discourse of scientific ecology, and in the final quarter of the twentieth century it gave way to a paradigm of imbalance. New theoretical approaches emphasized the openness of ecological processes and built into their models concepts such as contingency and chaos.[83] Second, the expansion and professionalization of the park management and the cantonal administration was accompanied by an increase in the capacity for intervention. The programmatic "let nature prevail" method was also a practical one. It was consistent with the very modest means available to the park management during the early decades. In this respect, the 1960s marked a clear departure. Third, post–Second World War decades saw the failure of the illusion that the national park could function almost as an island, surrounded by the flow of modernity without being caught up in it. The reasons for the reality check were the emergence at that time of debates over the damming of the Spöl River and the overpopulation of deer in the park, the increase in traffic, and the burgeoning number of tourists. These debates, which I will highlight in chapter 6, became a major political challenge for the park.

A preference for useful animals over predators was continually rejected: "All wild things are equal in the national park," read the annual report for 1939.[84] But popular species appeared to be more equal than others. Would the cantonal push for prophylactic shooting have been so readily indulged if the animal in question had not been the fox, but the ibex? Would it even have been requested? And might the reason the ENPK was so slow to release the lynx have been the animal's lack of fans in the canton? The national park had its own, sometimes quite distinctive take on the relationship between animals and humans. By the same token, it could not break all ties to its social surroundings, nor could the physical nature of the park be insulated from the seamless continuum of the elements. As in other social realms, the pursuit of totality proved to be a utopia in the national park. Yet it was a productive utopia, whose far-reaching significance for the development of the park should not be underestimated. The claim of total protection was present at all times, and every attempt to undermine it had to be justified. It served as a bulwark against interference in the park, and ensured not only that actions were taken in context and with great restraint compared with other large protected areas, but also that, for more than a hundred years, the approach to the park was remarkably consistent. The objective of the federal decree of 1914 that in the park "all plant and animal life be left to their freely developing nature" may have been scarified time and again and its absoluteness made relative. But as an ideological guide, it stood the test.[85]

For some years now, the talk has been not of "total protection" but "process protection."[86] The goals have remained the same, but the association space has shifted with the change in terminology. Just as total protection can be applied to the partial protection of other nature reserves, process protection draws on static biotope or species protection and on the conservation of pre-existing conditions. "The focus is on allowing natural processes to take place and not interference to preserve individual species or communities," reads the *Leitbild Nationalpark* of 2007.[87] The subtext is the now familiar idea that nature left to itself, removed from the influence of humans, will not inevitably revert to a state of equilibrium but stay in motion. *Process protection* clearly corresponds better to the current, indeterminate ecological perspective than does *total protection*.

Notes

1. Pardé 1935, 486. On Triglav, see Roeder 2012; Biance Hoenig is currently writing a dissertation on Tatra.
2. SCNAT Archives, Box 521, Reservationenkomitee SNK, meeting of 31 October 1908, Protokollbuch, 82.
3. On these sectors of the park, see chapter 3.
4. SNK annual report 1909–10, 14, 22. On Carl Schröter's concept, see chapter 5.
5. *Nature* 90/2243 (24 October 1912), 224. On the international reception see the discussion in chapter 5.
6. Sarasin 1914, 40. Fifteen years later, Brunies affirmed the primacy of the Swiss National Park based on a comparison of large protected areas in the Alps.
7. Wöbse 2012b. On Spain, which established two national parks during the First World War, see Voth 2007.
8. Smith 1947, 457.
9. IUCN 1994b, 19. The Swiss National Park figures largely, for example, in Cahalane 1962 and Harroy 1972a. On the founding of the IUCN, see chapter 2.
10. Smith 1947, 457.
11. *Freier Rätier* no. 154 (3 July 1920). ENPK annual report 1920, 7 f.
12. ENPK annual report 1920, 6.
13. See Giacometti 2006.
14. ENPK annual report 1923, 5 f.
15. *Amtliches Bulletin Nationalrat* 24 (1914), 155–220. See especially the detailed consultation on Art. 1, 195–210. Emphasis mine. On the debate, see chapter 2.
16. ENPK annual report 1939, 12.
17. See Giacometti 2006, especially the contributions of Blankenhorn 2006 and Bundi 2006.

18. SNP Archives, 201.300, Mader, Bächler, Schmidt, Bernhard. Gutachten über die Eignung des Terza-Gebiets bei Zernez als Steinwild-Reservation im Schweizerischen Nationalpark zu Handen der Schw. NPK, June 1920. See also Schneider 2006.
19. On the releases see Bachmann 1999, 227–236. The hydropower plans will be discussed in chapter 6.
20. Bühlmann to Sarasin, 8 January 1917; SBN Archives, M 3.2, ENPK, meeting of 29 April 1917. On the death of deer in 1917, see chapter 6.
21. ENPK to the Lischana Section, 4 October 1917.
22. SBN Archives, M 3.2, ENPK, meeting of 2 February 1918, 3. BAR 9500.25, vol. 1, Bühlmann to Sarasin, 8 January 1917; vol. 37, Brunies to Schröter, 13 February 1918.
23. Lüdtke 1993, Lüdtke 2002.
24. See Marvin 2009. This sort of analysis avoids having to draw an essential distinction between humans and animals. For an introduction to the relevant philosophical debates, see Wild 2008.
25. Isenberg 2002. For alternative theoretical perspectives, see Eitler and Möhring 2008. Historical overviews on human-animal relationships can be found in Dinzelbacher 2000; Kalof et al. 2007.
26. ENPK annual report 1925, 10.
27. See Kupper 2010.
28. Pedrotti 2005. On the Swiss influence on the Italian conservation movement, see Sievert 2000, 101–130.
29. SNK annual report 1909–10, 31 f.
30. BAR 9500.25, vol. 37, telegram from Blasius Tscharner to Brunies, 8 July 1910. Also available are Tscharner's employment contract, dated 29 June 1910, and his written request to be discharged, dated 18 July 1910. A telling detail in the margin: One of the high valleys behind Val Cluozza bore the name "Devil's Valley."
31. BAR 9500.25, vol. 37, contract with the park warden for the Zernez division, signed by Sarasin and Langen, Basel 10 August 1910.
32. BAR 9500.25, vol. 37, contract with the park warden for the Zernez division, signed by Sarasin and Langen, Basel 10 August 1910. A guide for park wardens was established in 1914 and later revised several times. At first, the wardens shared in the money from fines; beginning in 1918, they received a premium of 10 francs for every successful prosecution. SBN Archives, M 3.2, ENPK, meeting of 23 September 1918, 3. The diaries of the park wardens are to be found in the SNP Archives.
33. Giving rise to an extensive correspondence from Brunies as well as with the park wardens and members of the park commission. It is strewn about the SCNAT Archives, Box 533; BAR 9500.25, vol. 1; and the SNP Archives, 510.100 ff. and 631.100 ff.
34. SBN Archives, M 3.2, ENPK, meeting of 25 September 1916 and 1 December 1916. David denied the charge: SNP Archives, 933.100, David to Brunies, 25 September 1916. The outcome of the affair could not be discovered. In David 1945, 50–69, David himself describes his experiences as national park warden.
35. BAR 9500.25, vol. 1, Brunies, Bericht des Oberaufsehers über die Bewerber um die Parkwächterstelle der Abteilung Scanfs, 29 November 1914. His reservations regarding Catholic origin were expressed by Brunies in an earlier letter; ibid., Brunies to Bühlmann, 12 November 1917.
36. SNP Archives, 510.100, P. Sarasin, chair, ENPK, press communiqué, June 1915. SNK annual report 1913–14, 198.

Total Protection   135

37. SNP Archives, 510.100, A. Stierlin, stud. Phil. from Zurich, to Brunies, 25 January 1926. Brunies answered approvingly on 28 January 1926.
38. SNP Archives, 510.100, P. Sarasin, chair, ENPK, press communiqué, June 1915. BAR 9500.25, vol. 1, Brunies, Bericht des Oberaufsehers über die Bewerber um die Parkwächterstelle der Abteilung Scanfs, 29 November 1917. The disagreements between Brunies and Langen are documented in the SNP Archives, 510.200.
39. ENPK annual report 1963, 3 f. SNP Archives, 900.100, Dienstreglement der Parkwächter von 1963.
40. SCNAT Archives, Box 521, SNK, meeting of 10 September 1912, Protokollbuch, 52–54.
41. ENPK annual report 1939, 12 f.
42. ENPK annual report 1916, 2.
43. ENPK annual report 1951, 8.
44. Handschin 1939, 56.
45. ENPK annual report 1918, 22, and 1919, 6 f. Barbey 1919. Fifteen years later, in the early 1930s, Ernst Gäumann investigated fungal diseases of pines. Gäumann and Campell 1932.
46. See Schmidt 1976, 255–257.
47. The ENPK's decision was five votes to one. Captured animals were delivered to Bernhard Nievergelt, the future chair of the WNPK, who was experimenting with vaccinations against rabies. SNP Archives, ENPK, meeting of 6 July 1967, 104.
48. ENPK annual reports 1967–85.
49. ENPK annual report 1989, 11, and 1990, 7–9. Eidgenössische Nationalparkkommission (ENPK) und Wissenschaftliche Nationalparkkommission (WNPK), 1989. In 1996 the disease appeared in the park again briefly. ENPK annual report 1996, 22 f. In a 2007 nationwide sampling of ibex (which are also susceptible to infectious keratoconjunctivitis) that was part of a research project, no affected animals were found in the national park. Ryser-Degiorgis et al. 2009, which also contains current information on the disease.
50. ENPK annual report 1951, 5, and 1962, 9 f.
51. The local climate and soil-related conditions, as well as grazing ungulates, also contribute to very slow growth of vegetation. See Geissler and Hartmann 2000.
52. Franke 2000 and, in general, Pyne 2004.
53. Wissenschaftliche Nationalparkkommission und Nationalparkdirektion 1991; Schweizerischer Nationalpark 2001; Allgöwer et al. 2005. See also Haller 2006, 9 f.
54. Eser 1999; Coates 2006.
55. Schröter 1918, 764.
56. ENPK annual report 1919, 7 f. (skull findings), and 1916, 3 (fallow deer). On "ur-nature" see the SNK annual report 1908–9, 55–64; Schröter 1918.
57. Nievergelt 1966, 15–17.
58. ENPK annual reports 1968 ff. In a one-off move in 1947, two ibex were released in the Fuorn region. ENPK annual report 1947, 8.
59. According to the ENPK annual report 1969, 9, 230 specimens were released.
60. See the discussion on bears in chapters 2 and 3. On bears in Grisons, see Metz 1990.
61. ENPK annual report 1925, 10. First quote: ENPK annual report 1915, 7. Further reports, ibid. 1916, 6, and 1919, 11. A bear sighting in 1932 remained unconfirmed. ENPK annual report 1932, 6.
62. In the following years a few more bears temporarily stayed in the park region.

63. For instance, according to Brunies 1951. In 1929 readers of the newspaper *Der Bund* had greeted a release with references to Yellowstone and bears seeking human food. *Der Bund*, no. 8 and no. 16, 11 January 1929.
64. Schmidt 1976, 101 f.
65. SNP 202.101, ENPK to Suhner-Müller, 20 November 1963. FOK Archives, WNPK, meeting of 8 February 1964, 2. See also Meyer-Holzapfel 1963.
66. Schloeth 1970. Schweizerischer Nationalpark 1998, 23 f.
67. Schmidt 1976, 102. On the extermination of the wolf, see Etter 1992.
68. SBN Archives, M1, Pressefahrt Taleraktion 1969, 26–27/81969, 3. The Taleraktion of 1964 was paid for by the national park (on its fiftieth anniversary). Schweizerischer Bund für Naturschutz und Schweizer Heimatschutz 1964.
69. SNP Archives, ENPK, meeting of 19 June 1970, 4–7; ENPK annual report 1970, 14.
70. SNP Archives, ENPK, meeting of 17 December 1969, 12 f. Breitenmoser und Breitenmoser-Würsten 2008, 90–129, 210–217; Haller 2009.
71. ENPK annual report 1971, 12, and 1974, 15. Sarasin 1917. SNP Archives, 202.500, Manni Müller: Fischotter-Beobachtungen in Graubünden, 2002 (draft). On otter extinction and release in Switzerland, see Weber 1990. Since 2000, growth of the otter population has been observed in the eastern Alps, from where it could one day also venture into the area of the Swiss National Park. Kranz 2009.
72. ENPK annual report 1923, 12 f.
73. SNP Archives, Tourenbuch Hermann Langen, 1 August 1910–15 November 1912, handwritten. Notice at the very end of the book. See also Schmidt 1976, 259–262.
74. Eidgenössische Nationalparkkommission (ENPK) und Wissenschaftliche Nationalparkkommission (WNPK) 1989, 3.
75. Robin et al. 2004.
76. Stemmler 1932, 233–237.
77. See Bachmann 1999, 211–220. On Adler, see also Haller 1996.
78. www.wild.uzh.ch/bg, accessed 1 April 2013.
79. SNP Archives, ENPK, meeting of 22 March 1956, 2. ENPK annual report 1986, 16.
80. ENPK annual report 1980, 14 f. Emphasis mine.
81. ENPK annual report 1984, 14. This accusation was first made in the annual report for 1971 (10). After 1980, it appeared regularly.
82. Schröter 1918, 763. This conviction is also represented in the park regulations of 1914. In § 11 on scientific observations, these were to show how flora and fauna "search and find their equilibrium."
83. See Potthast 2004; see also Reichholf 2008. Ideas about (dis)equilibrium in ecology are discussed further in chapter 5.
84. ENPK annual report 1939, 12.
85. In the National Park Act, in force today, the relevant passage reads, "all flora and fauna is allowed to develop naturally" (National Park Act 1980, Art. 1).
86. Haller 2006. The term "process protection" entered the German conservation discourse in the 1990s (see Ziegler 2002; Potthast 2004). The terminology is also reflected in the IUCN guidelines of 1994 for Category Ia, "Strict Nature Reserves," which was also associated with the SNP. One of the management objectives described in the guidelines is "to maintain established ecological processes." IUCN 1994b, 17.
87. ENPK, Leitbild Nationalpark, 14. 12/2007.

CHAPTER 5

Ecological Field Laboratory
The Park as a Scientific Experiment

In spring 1980 Bernhard Nievergelt, a wildlife biologist at the University of Zurich's Zoological Institute and chairman of protected areas for the Swiss League for Nature Protection (SBN), submitted a working paper to the national park's research commission (WNPK) laying out a fundamental plan of research for the Swiss National Park. In analyzing the current situation, Nievergelt concluded that the Swiss National Park figured among "the most researched areas on Earth." However, the abundance of individual contributions "added up to *no overall understanding,* as one might have hoped. This raises the question of how to direct research efforts toward new and important aspects, as well as how to produce reports that make a coherent whole."[1] In particular, Nievergelt took issue with the lack of a common reference frame for the individual researchers and disciplines working in the national park. The statements in the paper were carefully phrased, but the members of the WNPK understood very well that the critique was aimed squarely at them. Their main task was precisely to direct and coordinate research in the national park. It would be false to say that Nievergelt's overture to the WNPK broke down doors. Nevertheless, the committee decided to appoint a working group under committee chair Willy Matthey and Nievergelt himself to further consider the issues raised.[2] No one could have suspected that they were setting in motion a ten-year process during which the commission would essentially be reinvented. In 1985 Nievergelt replaced Matthey as chair of the WNPK, intensified activity, and moved the joint working group to the center. These efforts bore fruit: In the early 1990s, following several reports, the WNPK adopted a comprehensive "research design for the national park" that put research on a new footing and that would continue to evolve in subsequent years. By expanding the research infrastructure, the framework enabled work on deeper problems. In 1985, the WNPK was given its first (part-time) scientific secretary in the person of Thomas Scheurer.[3]

In the second half of the 1990s, the research committee was examined by an international group of experts, whose judgment was highly favorable. In their evaluation report, the experts reached the unanimous conclusion that "the committee operates well, is basically on track, and works smoothly."[4] This positive evaluation was undoubtedly due to the continued efforts at the level of research design and coordination, which had begun to produce dividends. Presumably, an evaluation in the 1970s would have come to a totally different conclusion than the one conducted under Nievergelt's watch. In his 1980 report, looking ahead, he asked: What conditions need to be met to focus national park research toward a common goal? In enumerating the missing prerequisites, he also simultaneously diagnosed (without explicitly saying so) the failures of the past. By 1980 the national park had been operating for sixty-five years under the aegis of the WNPK. One of the main motivations for founding the park had been to make a large protected area available to science. For that reason, Article 1 of the federal decree on the park of 1914 not only stipulated that "all flora and fauna [be] left to freely developing nature," but also that "the park shall be placed under scientific observation."[5]

How could it then be that, decades later, basic conditions for fruitful research activity were still deemed not to be achieved? Were these conditions never created, or had they been lost in the interim? In the 1920s quantum mechanics made clear that observation and measurement could not help but disturb the object being studied. Could it be that the credo of "freely developing nature" and "total protection" was incommensurable with the concerns of research? In this chapter I will first review the initial ideas about scientific observation as conceived by the park's founders. I will then explore how these ideas were transmitted to a research organization in the early years of the park, and the challenges that entailed. I will show, among other things, that the research program and the means of realizing it were inconsistent. But lack of means was only one problem. A fundamental tension resulted from the poor relationship between laboratory and field research. As an ecological "field laboratory," the national park should have bridged this gap and united the two research practices to their mutual benefit, yet it largely failed to do so. The difficulties faced by the researchers in the "natural laboratory" of the national park will be presented in the context of the division of university biology into field and laboratory sciences.[6] Despite mixed (to say the least) results, park research was responsible for the considerable international recognition of the Swiss National Park as a "scientific national park." This external perception will be the focus of my attention before I proceed to the park itself to illuminate the research practices applied there and their evolution. As I will show, these practices were influenced in ways so varied that they defy simple schematization. One standout development is the growing trend toward experimental research. I will describe the difficulty in reconciling academic careers and national park research through the example of long-term botanical monitoring. Its varying fate leads directly to a concluding discussion of why research in the national park has recently enjoyed a resurgence.

A New Field within Ecology

For the members of the *Schweizerische Naturschutzkommission* (SNK), themselves all scientists, that the national park should serve scientific research was a foregone conclusion requiring no explanation. A firm grounding in the natural sciences was instrumental in shaping the park. Although (as shown in chapter 2) a number of contingent factors and favorable opportunities drew attention to the Ofen Pass, its specific suitability for a protected area as well as the dimensions of the park were discussed within the commission mainly with reference to ecological criteria. Here, the views of the botanist Carl Schröter and the zoologist Friedrich Zschokke were decisive.[7] The first detailed line of argument dates from 1911, when the two professors each prepared a report for the Federal Council on the significance of the national park for botanical and zoological research. The reports agreed on the scientific value of a national park based on three conditions: that the protected area be large; that it possess a diverse ecology; and that it show minimal influence of previous human use. As a botanist, Schröter in particular emphasized the richness of the vegetation in the Ofen Pass area, which he attributed to the varying calcium content of the rock surface, the geographical position on the border between the flora of the eastern and western Alps, as well as the vertical reach of the park area, which encompassed both sub-alpine and alpine regions. Zschokke, the zoologist, insisted that "the reserve be as large as possible" to meet "the vital needs of the most varied forms of animals and animal communities." Both professors promised a variety of benefits for scientific research: from the conservation of endangered plant species and "plant communities" to the study of the undisturbed development of vegetation (Schröter); and from the repopulation in Switzerland of extinct animal species to the systematic investigation of alpine fauna by means of "meticulous exploration [Durchforschung] of a high mountain area" (Zschokke). Owing not least to the political audience, Zschokke emphasized the particularly Swiss dimension of this animal mapping: "Our science, which otherwise knows no borders, does in this case have a national responsibility to fulfill."[8]

Of the two professors, Carl Schröter (1855–1939)—known and respected in academic circles far beyond Switzerland—undoubtedly had the greatest influence over the shaping of the research agenda. Schröter was the son of a German engineer who in 1865 was appointed professor of mechanical engineering and machine construction at the federal polytechnic in Zurich. Shortly afterward, however, he died. The family stayed on in Zurich, and Schröter began his own, very successful career at the polytechnic. After completing his studies in the natural sciences, he became an assistant to Carl Cramer, professor of botany. In 1878 Schröter qualified as a lecturer, and in 1880 he received his PhD at the University of Zurich under the supervision of the renowned paleobotanist Oswald Heer for work on fossil woods. Heer died in 1883. In December of that same year, Schröter became professor for special botany at the polytechnic, a post Heer had also held since the polytechnic's founding in 1855. Schröter's main work became alpine flora. Between 1904 and 1908, he published his monumental, 800-page opus *Das Pflanzenleben der Alpen* (alpine plant life). His thoughts on plant ecology aroused enormous international interest. At the turn of the twentieth century the new discipline was booming, fueled by the Dane Eugenius Warming's groundbreaking textbook, which was translated into German in 1896 and after 1900 into Russian and English, among other languages.[9] In a much-read article that appeared in 1902 Schröter suggested the term "synecology" as a common denominator for the crystallizing discipline. Schröter meant synecology to describe those newer approaches to science that comprised not only the investigation of relationships between individual organisms and their environment—Schröter called this kind of research, modeled on the ecological studies of Ernst Haeckel, "autecological"—but also the interplay of "cohabiting communities" with their surroundings. To describe these communities, Schröter borrowed Karl August Möbius's term "biocenosis."[10] Schröter's proposals were well received by the international scientific community, and the terms "synecology" and "biocenosis" were common up until the 1950s, when "ecosystem" became established as a central scientific theme, and essentially turned scientific thinking upside down. Now the knowledge focus of interest of the ecological sciences was no longer the description of cohabiting communities but the explanation of the systematic conditions of their existence.[11]

In academic circles, talk ran to the Zurich school of plant ecology as well as the Zurich-Montpellier school—by reason of Schröter's collaboration with Frenchman Charles Flahault from Montpellier—or to the Continental school, thereby highlighting the contrast to the Anglo-American schools of ecology. Schröter's methods were expanded by his students to include both large-scale geobotanical space—particularly by Eduard Rübel's institute in Zurich—as well as small-scale flora-based studies in "plant sociology," which later were associated with the work of Josias Braun-Blanquet.[12] Schröter was also one of the central figures in the so-called International Phytogeographic Excursions (IPEs) that were launched in 1908 following an international conference of geographers in Geneva. For decades, the IPEs gathered leading European and American plant ecologists together for more-or-less regularly occurring multiweek excursions. The first of these excursions was to the British Isles in 1911, organized by Arthur Tansley; the second, in 1913, led by Henry C. Coles, crossed the United States from the east coast to California. The third excursion, planned for Switzerland in 1915, was canceled because of the war. After the war ended, the idea was revived among Schröter's circle. Both the highlight and concluding event of the Swiss tour of 1923 was the group visit to the Swiss National Park.[13]

Schröter lost no time in transferring his scientific interests to the design of the national park as a research field. Post-1900, the major topic of the new biocenosis research-oriented ecology (avidly followed internationally) was succession research. "Succession" was understood by ecologically minded biologists to be the gradual transformation of cohabiting communities, or biocenoses, from one state to another, on the assumption that biocenoses that were not disturbed by the outside would eventually reach a stable state of equilibrium. The American botanist Frederic Clements coined the term "climax state" to denote the point at which a biocenosis reached its ecological optimum.[14]

For Schröter, the Swiss National Park concept of completely barring human influence from a formerly agricultural area posed an exceptionally interesting experimental problem for succession research. He expected that, in a first phase, the traces of human use in the area would blur, and that the area would revert to a quasi-natural initial state. This first phase, which was paradoxical insofar as it represented an evolution toward a state achieved in the past, was described by Schröter as "retrograde succession." In an essay completed in early 1919, the first of the national park research series of publications, he wrote: "For science, the national park is a priceless field of observation, quite unique owing to the absolute elimination of interference by humans in the natural balance. All previous changes to the ur-state lasting centuries through the effects of hunters, fishers, foresters, farmers, herdsmen, and haymakers, through fertilizer, plowing, mowing, and grazing will disappear again with time, and the old, primeval biocenosis will be restored. A great 'rewilding experiment' will be carried out there."[15]

Schröter's mention of "rewilding" was a reference to his German colleague Robert Gradmann, who had enriched the ecology literature with an early monograph on plant life in the Swabian Alps (1898) and as a result had become interested in the rewilding of the European cultural landscape since Roman times.[16] In this respect, the Swiss National Park offered unique test conditions. In his contribution to the *Handbuch der biologischen Arbeitsmethoden*, ultimately a nearly 100,000-page comprehensive reference work published in Germany between 1920 and 1939, Schröter listed four "invaluable benefits" that the "national park as a fully, constantly monitored reserve" could offer research: "1. Absolute protection from human interference. 2. Unlimited duration of this protection. 3. Unlimited duration of scientific observation. 4. Constant monitoring and observation by park wardens. Thus is the field of biology giving rise to a rich, important, new area of endeavor that will favor the further development of biology into a genuine 'field biology.'"[17]

The new field site should enable biologists no less than new epistemic access to their object of study. "Herbaria, gardens, and laboratories must be joined with the protected area," wrote Schröter, citing his Berlin colleague Ludwig Diels.[18] In his report of 1911 Friedrich Zschokke compared the national park favorably with the laboratory, and used an uncustomary superlative in announcing that the "it would offer the opportunity to study 'biocenoses'—the undisturbed interplay between animals and plants and between animals and animals—in the most natural conditions, without having to resort to deceptive observations in the laboratory."[19] For his part, Schröter emphasized that long-term scientific observation over a large research terrain free of human interference could liberate the discipline from unproved ideas that relied too much on theoretical assumptions. "This is especially true of 'dynamic' plant geography, which by following the development of plant communities can gather valuable factual material to correct its often purely hypothetical schemas." Here Schröter must have been thinking not least of Frederic Clements's deterministic model of succession and his concept of plant communities as a superorganism. There is evidence for this in the identical critique that Schröter's student Braun-Blanquet lobbed at Clements in his textbook on plant sociology a few years later.[20]

The demands and expectations vis-à-vis research at the national park were enormous. To fulfill them would require establishing an equally huge and comprehensive scientific agenda. To be able to track change meant accurately recording the initial state of the park as well as ensuring the systematic repetition of surveys over long periods. The park regulations adopted by the *Eidgenössische Nationalparkkommission* (ENPK) in 1914 cloaked this agenda as follows, simultaneously expressing what the scientists around Schröter expected: "The *Schweizerische Naturforschende Gesellschaft* will carry out a comprehensive monographic survey of all the nature in the park that will represent the condition of the national park at that time. Photographs shall be taken of a range of typical locations and must be supported by extensive follow-up surveys, which will determine the changes and shifts in the qualitative and quantitative composition of the plant and animal worlds and in their way of coexisting, and will also discover how they seek and find equilibrium."[21]

In its report two years later, the newly established WNPK adopted regulations that formalized the ENPK's recommendations as six research guidelines:

1. The main thrust of the research work in the national park shall be the study of living things in the park, their life style, and their development in the absence of human influence.

2. The extent of the area to be studied shall reach beyond the current and projected borders of the national park in the west and north as far as the Inn River.

3. The total area shall be partitioned into naturally delineated sections to be investigated in succession.

4. The monographic work shall encompass the following points: topographical, hydrological, geological, and climatological conditions, and a complete

location catalog of all living beings, especially microflora and microfauna. Depictions of typical plants and animal communities (biocenoses). Special depictions of anthropogenic influences, in particular studies of the colonization and forest history of the area.

5. Special emphasis shall be placed on obtaining the richest possible, biologically relevant meteorological and soil data, explicitly including very small scale study of climate and soil (microclimate).

6. The following work shall also be permitted as long as it fits into the main program: study of small plant and animal groups throughout the area. Study of special geological, topographical, meteorological, and other questions.[22]

No doubt, the WNPK's research program was carefully thought out and logical, but at the same time, the burden it put on the scientists was titanic. Of particular note were two of the principles enshrined in the research guidelines: first, the expansion of the research area beyond the park boundaries to enable developments within the national park to be systematically compared with those in adjacent regions; and second, in the same vein, the requirement that anthropogenic influences in the park and their historicity should receive special attention—in other words, performing not just spatial but also temporal comparisons. The coming decades, however, saw very little progress on either front. As in other respects, the efforts of the WNPK to implement its ambitious research program fell far behind its own plans.

Organizing and Financing Research

What caused the WNPK's failure to realize its own ambitions? One simple reason is that the WNPK had simply set the bar too high. But a whole raft of additional causes can be identified as well. First, the organization and financing of the scientific research program were inadequate to the task. Second, the research interests quickly came into conflict with the park's other purposes, especially the requirement for total protection. Third, the chosen area proved not particularly useful for many of the investigations. And finally, there was limited demand from the academic sciences for use of the park as a research laboratory. These four causes, which I will examine in more detail below, were mutually interconnected and reinforcing. Thus, the lack of research infrastructure, the stipulated narrowing of research activities by park regulation, and the limited ecological variety of the area surely hindered scientists to start their own research activities in the park as well as to lend their support to park research. The academic science enterprise itself relied on evaluation criteria that did not favor park research as a way of advancing academic careers. Neither did the disciplinary developments in twentieth-century biology, the key science for the park, have a positive effect on park research.

The organization and funding of research activities was agreed prior to the federal decree of 1914. In December 1913 the confederation, the *Schweizerische Naturforschende Gesellschaft* (SNG), and the SBN signed a contract setting out the rights and responsibilities of the three parties with respect to the park. The SNG was committed to ensuring "the scientific observation of the reserve area and its scientific exploitation," and the SBN "to provide the funds necessary to do so."[23] This was a momentous decision. The SNG was issued a binding order to explore the park with funding to be provided by another institution. In addition, the research was left entirely to the two nongovernment organizations, which meant that the amount of the funds available depended on private donations. Complicating matters, the contract required the SBN not only to assume the costs of park research but also all the expenses of administering the park. Finally, for decades the SBN was also responsible for paying the rent on the Scuol section of the park because the confederation and the local landowners could not agree on a lease.[24] The rent and a good part of the administrative costs were fixed. Covering them took precedence over research, which had to be content with modest grants.

This problem was recognized as early as 1914 in devising the park regulations. The organization of scientific observation would be "the most challenging question in the near term," wrote the future secretary of the ENPK, Fritz Bühlmann, to the future chair of the commission, Paul Sarasin, in July 1914. Zschokke and Schröter had insisted on a comprehensive treatment of park nature, but to Bühlmann, "this massive monograph went far beyond the actual task and goal of the national park." The requisite funds were lacking, and SNB could not support the costs.[25] An attempt to get the SNG to finance park research failed. Then SNG president, Eduard Sarasin, removed the corresponding clause from the draft regulations edited by Bühlmann, arguing that the handing over of financial responsibility for park research to the SNG had never been mentioned.[26]

"As far as costs of scientific observation are concerned, you will have to stretch the ceiling," wrote Bühlmann to Sarasin. There was no question of the SBN putting in more than a thousand francs a year.[27] This then was the amount it took to run park research in the early years. In the 1920s the amount rose to 3,000 francs and remained at that level until 1960. One source of costs was researchers, who were reimbursed for travel and paid a daily allowance. This was capped at 15 francs, but could also be cut by half if resources were scarce, which was often the case in the first years. Another significant cost driver was publishing research results. The printing costs of Ernst Bütikofer's 130-page monograph on mollusk life in the park, the first volume of the WNPK's series on results of scientific investigations in the Swiss National Park published in

1920, ran to over 4,000 francs.[28] The SBN's funds covered little of it, and the lion's share of the WNPK's research funds came from private donations, cash collections, and legacies. In addition, the Federal Council was persuaded to subsidize the costs of printing. Only after the Second World War did the situation improve perceptibly. Charles and Mathilde Kiefer-Hablitzel made the national park a beneficiary of the charitable trust they founded in 1946. A third of the annual contributions to the national park from the foundation flowed into research. In addition, with the founding of the Swiss National Science Foundation in 1952, a new funding pool at the federal level was made available and was subsequently well used by the national park researchers.[29]

In 1915 the SNG transferred the management and coordination of park research to the new WNPK. This commission was divided into four subcommissions along disciplinary lines—geography-geology, meteorology, botany, and geology—which each decided their own research programs. The commission's work was voluntary. Positions were filled according to academic qualifications as well as a balanced representation of the universities. This "check" was intended to ensure that the national park was viewed as a *"truly national, universal field of activity."* In additional to the usual federal practices regarding apportionment, this distribution formula also reflected the domestically tense atmosphere of the war year 1916.[30]

Four aspects of this particular organizational approach to research are noteworthy. First, working in an honorary capacity severely limited the commission's workload. The members were usually busy professors who had little time or willingness to administer park research. Long-term research planning and the advancement of comprehensive cross-programmatic research questions in particular fell by the wayside. The annual meetings of the commission frequently amounted to little more than keeping a record of the work achieved in the year just ended and the plans announced for the next. Second, the careful composing of the commission according to federal criteria meant that nearly all Swiss universities were involved, but it also prevented park research from becoming the specialty of any one institution. Consequently, nowhere did park research build critical mass, and it was only marginally important at any of the universities.[31] Third, the division of the commission based on disciplines was undoubtedly useful. In view of the low workload of the commission itself, however, cross-disciplinary research questions that were critical to the overall program were largely ignored in practice. When interdisciplinary work did occur, it was limited to the disciplines represented in an individual subcommission. Thus, for example, within the botany subcommission a close collaboration motivated by Josias Braun-Blanquet joined botanists and soil scientists. Finally, the collection of disciplines represented within the WNPK was limited to those practiced by the SNG. Conspicuously for the study of an area, a third of whose surface was covered by forest, was the lack of forest sciences. Foresters were organized in the Swiss Forestry Association, which was not a member of the SNG, and consequently did not figure in the WNPK. A call by the forestry association in 1908 for closer cooperation on issues regarding protected areas was rebuffed by the SNK, which at the time was preparing the founding of national parks. The SNG wanted no interlopers in its project. The consequences of this decision were that forestry research only entered the WNPK ten years after its establishment, when in 1926 the *Eidgenössische Anstalt für das forstliche Versuchswesen* (Federal Institute for Experimental Forestry) set aside five areas for long-term observation within the national park. The project was the idea of a forestry engineer, Auguste Barbey, who in 1918 had written a report for the ENPK on the effects of forest pests.[32] But forestry sciences were still not represented within the WNPK. This was partly compensated by the Federal Council dispatching the federal superintendent of forests to the ENPK. Following Paul Sarasin's departure in 1921, the respective forest superintendent held the commission chair. As a result, foresters now had an important advocate in the national park bodies. In contrast, the absence of humanities in the WNPK had additional, longer-term consequences. For decades their contribution had consisted merely in the auxiliary collecting of Romansh place and field names initiated by Steivan Brunies.[33] From this survey the botanists hoped to gain insights into the history of vegetation. The special depiction of human influence, as directed by the WNPK, was never done. Appreciation of the park as an economic and social phenomenon, as well as a cultural and historical one, began to emerge only after the 1980s.[34]

As a consequence of all these factors, national park research was loosely coordinated, only minimally interdisciplinary, and mainly oriented to biology. Meteorology took an ancillary role. With the aid of the *Meteorologische Zentralanstalt* (National Meteorological Institute), whose director was appointed chair of the relevant subcommission in 1917, two stations were installed at the periphery of the park: in the hamlet of S-charl and the *Wegerhaus* (the hut for trail maintenance workers) at Buffalora. In 1920 two totalizers (gauges) were added to measure rainfall in Val Cluozza and at Alp Murtèr. Two trail maintenance workers and park warden Langen were entrusted with operating the equipment, which transmitted weather data to the *Zentralanstalt*.[35] The geography-geology subcommission was able to build on a geological survey of the area published in 1914. In the early years of park research a father-and-son pair of geologists from Geneva, Émile and André Chaix, focused on investigations of geomorphology, and managed to get the Val Sassa and Val da l'Acqua block glaciers into the textbooks. It was the first description of the phenomenon in Europe. The Chaix completed their research in 1921, and thereafter geology came to a standstill. In the 1920s and 1930s only a few geological mappings were done. Like the weather observation of the block glaciers was transferred to the park wardens. Only after 1945 did geological research begin to be carried out again to any measurable degree.[36]

The zoology subcommission was the most active. Each summer, an impressive number of researchers flocked to the Lower Engadine to observe the fauna in the park. The zoologists concentrated mainly on invertebrate species that they inventoried largely without regard to overarching ecological or evolutionary theory frameworks. A rich mosaic of invertebrate residents of the park emerged. But because of the varying methods, accuracy, and quality of the surveys, the efforts could not be integrated or used to study the composition of species over time, nor were they amenable to interdisciplinary access. The zoologists were devoted to their respective species but failed to consider their results in the broader research context. On the other hand, the zoology subcommission was the only one to adhere to the WNPK requirements that the terrain of investigation extend not just beyond the national park but also to several districts. This spatial structure subsequently formed the basis of all the zoological work.[37]

In 1922 the chair of the subcommission, Friedrich Zschokke, was compelled to publicly defend the zoological research in the park. The research, he maintained, was proceeding "in a confident and goal-conscious manner. ... The broader plan and the methods adopted can stand up to any genuinely objective criticism." To which "non-objective" criticism Zschokke was responding, and whether it had to do with the inconsistencies in classification and the failure to integrate the work into context of the park, or the neglect of mammals, especially deer—a criticism made by the ENPK—is not, unfortunately, revealed in the text.[38]

The botany subcommission's idea of research was actually closer to that of the park than that of zoology. In 1917 Steivan Brunies and Josias Braun-Blanquet designed a series of permanent observation plots whose floristic composition was subsequently periodically inventoried under Braun-Blanquet's leadership. Later, a moss specialist (Charles Meylan) and a lichen expert (Eduard Frey) took part in the inventories, and from the mid-1920s soil scientists (first Hans Jenny and later Hans Pallmann) were consulted. As I will show, foundations were laid early in botany that would go on to be systematically developed.[39]

"Nature's Laboratory" and Its Discontents

Before broaching enduring achievements and challenges of the botanical permanent observation, however, it is worth jumping back in time to trace a creeping disillusionment following the initial euphoria. An indicator of this disillusionment is the decline in the number of workdays spent in field research in the park beginning in the mid-1920s (see chart 2). Various statements made by advocates of the park evidenced the same trend. "The advancing zoological research in the national park shows ever more clearly that the fauna of the protected area unfortunately represent *few and a monotonous* selection of species," noted a co-worker of the zoology subcommission (Walter Knopfli) in 1923. "Typical forms are rare or missing, and the influx from the east and south is unexpectedly weak. That is true for most invertebrate groups, but also for birds, reptiles, amphibians, and fish." Significantly, Knopfli also rued the monotony due to the "absence of people and grazing animals." The story was the same with ants, according to another co-worker (Adolf Nadig).[40] For zoologists focusing on individual species, the national park area had little to offer.

National park research also found little appreciation among academics. In 1914, on publication of research results from the national park in its series, the SNG expressed a certain skepticism. As the society's resources were "extremely limited", the SNG president admonished Paul Sarasin to make sure that "the works were of real scientific value."[41] The fear was that national park research could not—at least in part—meet scientific standards. Carl Schröter proved to be wrong in his estimation of where biology was heading, and this weighed heavily on the longer-term perspective. The discipline did not become a "true field biology" in the interwar years, nor did the reserve come to equal the herbarium or the garden, let alone the laboratory.

An ironical fate awaited Schröter's own professorship at the ETH Zurich. In the mid-1920s, when Schröter reached the mandatory retirement age of seventy, an advertisement went out for a successor. Five candidates responded to the notice ("botany, preferably systematic botany"), all of whom were associates of Schröter: Martin Rikli, Albert Thellung, Josias Braun-Blanquet, Walter Rytz, and Heinrich Brockmann. The president of the ETH, Robert Gnehm, who traditionally led the appointment process, found none of the applicants particularly convincing. At his request, the ETH Board, the university's governing body, postponed the decision.[42] A year later, Gnehm's successor, Albert Rohn, put the still pending professorship to a debate: "As the president noted, Schröter represented so-called special or systematic botany, which is largely a descriptive science; he possessed deep knowledge of flora, and in particular alpine flora. The Zurich candidates hail from this school of enquiry, which is not characterized by further-reaching scientific research." That none of the applicants was younger than forty years old—Braun-Blanquet, born in 1884, was the youngest—Rohn interpreted as being due to the fact that "knowledge of flora in and of itself can hardly serve as a basis for new scientific research. The question is whether this might not be the time to downplay plant description in order to investigate other important problems in systematic botany, for example, plant pathology or genetics." For a professorship oriented in this way, Rohn could immediately suggest a viable candidate: Ernst Gäumann, a plant pathologist who was working as an assistant at the *Landwirtschaftliche Versuchsanstalt* (Institute for Experimental Agriculture) in Zurich-Oerlikon.[43] After a survey of botany professors at other Swiss universities seconded the president's plans, he entered into negotiations with Gäumann without further "consulting the Zurich botanists, who were known to plump for the Schröter school." On 1 October 1927 Gäumann was appointed professor for systematic botany.[44]

Thus, the break with Schröter's plant ecology was complete. Although up to the mid-1930s Gäumann spent several seasons working on fungal diseases in the national park,[45] his main area of focus remained the pathology of forage plants, which he pursued experimentally in the laboratory.[46] His research group was similarly oriented, which meant little emphasis was placed on national park research. Disappointed in his quest for the academic position, Braun-Blanquet left Zurich in 1926. He went to work for his doctoral mentor, Schröter's former colleague Charles Flahault, in Montpellier, where in 1930 he founded the *Station Internationale de Géobotanique Mediterranéenne et Alpine*. Braun-Blanquet remained committed to the national park, but it clearly lost importance as a place for his own research. He continued to study the plant sociology of the park's flora, but he abandoned the handling and care of the permanent plots at the end of the 1930s.[47]

Why was future of the Schröter school of plant ecology at the ETH Zurich viewed as so scientifically unpromising? What stood in the way of the reserve becoming an equally respected source of scientific knowledge? What explains the failure of the concept of establishing the Swiss National Park as a place to do first-class research? In his book *Landscapes and Labscapes,* the American science historian Robert Kohler examines how the division into laboratory and field research affected the development of American ecology. In the course of the nineteenth century and into the twentieth century, the laboratory became ever more entrenched as the locus of research, where reliable scientific knowledge was generated. In contrast, the traditional locus of biological investigation—the field—lost academic prestige. By the interwar years, laboratory experiment threatened to relegate gathering and classifying to the background.

Systematic description was displaced by experimental findings, materials-based induction by theory- and method-based deduction, and the understanding of natural classifications by the explanation of order-based mechanisms. The laboratory became the dominant instrument of modern scientific knowledge production, not despite but precisely because of its artificiality and constructed quality. With its generic settings, its reproducible experiments, and consequently its intersubjectively verifiable results, it fulfilled the maxim of universal validity of scientific knowledge, and its temporal and spatial independence. "It is precisely the stripped down simplicity and invariability of labs—their placelessness—that gives them their credibility."[48]

According to Kohler, biologists who believed in the usefulness of field research basically had two ways of competing against the superiority of laboratory researchers. One way was to incorporate elements of laboratory practice in their field research; the other was to use the very particularity of natural conditions that could not be reproduced in the laboratory to reach independent, universal insights. The research orientation of the Swiss National Park reflected both strategies. By designating the park as a "natural sciences laboratory" or a "natural laboratory," Schröter resorted to laboratory semantics. His followers spoke similarly of an "outdoor laboratory" (Eduard Handschin) or an "open air laboratory" (Braun-Blanquet, Adolf Nadig).[49] The idea was compelling: As an outdoor laboratory, the national park would combine the advantages of the laboratory with those of the field. Like the laboratory, and unlike the field, access to the national park was open only to accredited researchers; and as in the laboratory, on-site conditions were systematized into a protocol and monitored, and protected from unwanted influences. The national park offered the authentic scale and conditions of the field, both of which were inevitably lost in the laboratory. Ideally, the national park would serve as a field that equally fulfilled the standards of the laboratory sciences. In the outdoor laboratory, nature itself was the experimenter. Consequently, scientists could concentrate on collecting and analyzing self-contained processes as profitably as possible. What ecologist would not be in rapture at such a prospect? Did it not represent a key to the door of scientific recognition for the young field-based discipline?

However, the road to academic recognition led through the creation of convincing actual research settings, and that posed a sharp contrast to the idealized notions of the natural laboratory. The research setup established in the national park failed to produce the expected fortuitous hybrid of field and laboratory. Rather, it combined not only the advantages but also the typical disadvantages of both research environments. First, the national park was a "laboratory" in which the researchers themselves could not perform experiments in the sense of laboratory experiments. Owing to the protection provisions, researchers could not manipulate conditions through research activities. Research was thus mainly limited to observation. Nor did the safeguards leave any room to maneuver in the ordering of experiments: Tests were neither varied nor repeated; all that could be changed was the observer's position. In this respect, the opportunities the park offered to natural scientists remained far behind those of modern biological laboratories, which came to dominate the field in the twentieth century.[50]

Second, the environment in the national park's outdoor laboratory was neither straightforward nor sterile. In contrast to a university laboratory, research questions could not be pursued in isolation; they were embedded in the complexity typical of conditions in the field. Even the wardens' monitoring of the area did not make a basic difference. Of course, monitoring prevented disruptive events and encroachments by humans—or at least minimized them—but natural processes and events were allowed their full measure of interference, which made causality difficult to determine. Which factors were responsible for which phenomena could often only be guessed at, which was hardly compatible with the epistemological claims of the natural scientists, who were increasingly aligning themselves with the exact scientists.[51]

Third, in the national park, "nature" proved a poor experimenter. Processes in the park evolved extremely slowly. In many places, systematic observations registered few changes even after many years. The early environmental case studies, which attracted international attention and made their authors pioneers in the field, all described investigations conducted in dynamic settings. Henry Cowles' pathbreaking work examined changes in dune landscapes. This habitat was also used by Victor Shelford for his studies of beetles, and later of floodplains. William Cooper worked in glacier forelands and Charles Flahault in river deltas.[52] In the Swiss National Park, too, botanists deliberately chose sites for their permanent plots where they expected the most visible changes in vegetation. "Since the most rapid changes were to be expected in camps, pastures, and forest meadows, those were the areas initially envisaged as sites."[53] However, the botanists were surprised at how slowly succession proceeded at the sites. "The natural forestation in the woodland grassy areas occurs generally much more slowly than we originally anticipated," wrote botanist Werner Lüdi in 1947 after three decades of observation.[54] Regarding the forests themselves, Alfred Kurth noted in 1960: "It may even take centuries for the forests to return to a state of composition and structure that approximates their original natural equilibrium."[55] This slow pace of change tested the patience of the botanists. Scientific standards for interpreting slight variations required prolonged data series. Inventories repeatedly taken at intervals of a few years at the same site only ever showed provisional results. This led the researchers to keep postponing evaluation of the data, and relatively little was published from these studies. Most of the time, it required an external stimulus, such as threats from the botany subcommission wishing to see the achievements in their field documented, to goad the scientists to publish preliminary results. Because the earliest publications on the national park were all by zoologists, the botany subcommission was under increasing pressure to remedy the imbalance with their own contributions.[56] Long-term research demanded enormous stamina; and the lack of results worthy of publishing was not conducive to an academic career.

Fourth, researchers began to struggle with the ENPK's strong adherence to the maxim of total protection. "The entire apparatus of the scientific research appears somewhat large to the national park commission," the commission informed Schröter, the WNPK's chair, in summer 1918. "As of 1918 no fewer than 21 scientific observers were registered. It would be more expedient to distribute the inventory of the park over several years. While the size of the work program and its implementation deserves respect, care must be taken that the large number of researchers, who naturally cannot keep to the paths but must prowl the entire park, do not constitute an unacceptable disturbance to the wildlife and thus throw the acknowledged success of total protection into question."[57] A set of rules drawn up in 1917 on scientific observation in the national park stated that the collection of plants and the capture or killing of animals "must be limited to the smallest size acceptable for the purpose of the work."[58]

Finally, the logistics of national park research were expensive. The park was far removed from the research centers, and thus at least a day just for travel had to be reckoned. In addition, the climate was harsh, so that the researchers focused on the summer season. But that meant that they lost track of the full seasonal course of development. Consequently, the WNPK repeatedly requested that work be extended beyond the summer months, but the practical hurdles to doing so were substantial. Including the wardens in the research enterprise helped somewhat. They were in the park area the year round, performed certain long-term measurements, and were encouraged to note their natural history observations in their diaries. The seasonal gap in surveying could thus be partially bridged, but not closed.

The national park also entailed certain advantages compared with both traditional field and the laboratory. The federal decree of 1914 not only placed the park under permanent protection; it also imposed a duty on the *Naturforschende Gesellschaft* to conduct research in it. Consequently, the national park constituted an institutionally guaranteed space for the foreseeable future. Thanks to this institutionalization, the park became a scientific meeting place for exchange and cooperation. On the one hand, the institutional support for the national park lowered the relative cost of research collaborations. Because collaborations could be carried out long term, it was worthwhile paying for their traditionally high initial expenses. Moreover, researchers from different disciplines and institutions met both in the field and in meeting rooms, which promoted further cooperation. A successful early example of such an interdisciplinary endeavor that proved a model for later collaboration was that between plant sociologists and soil scientists, which I will return to below.[59]

On the other hand, scientists were able to use the national park to maintain relations with the non-academic world. The national park fostered exchanges between academic scientists and lay researchers and conservationists, as well the public and politicians. From the perspective of sociology of knowledge, the park can be seen as a "boundary object," as defined by sociologist Susan Leigh

Star and philosopher James Griesemer in their work on the building of a natural history museum. "Boundary objects are both plastic enough to adapt to local needs and constraints of the several parties employing them, yet robust enough to maintain a common identity across sites. They are weakly structured in common use, and become strongly structured in individual-site use. ... They have different meanings in different social worlds but their structure is common enough to more than one world to make them recognizable means of translation."[60] As a public institution for conservation and natural science research, the national park brought these different social and academic worlds together. It served both as a place of mutual translation as well as a search for collective identity. That this potential was never fully exploited has to do with the effect of the already cited limited means on the development of national park research.

A particularly far-reaching consequence of this lack of resources was that the WNPK never managed to create an institutional center for park research. Everyone involved understood the urgency of an entity beyond the WNPK that could tie together research activities. In its regulations of 1916, the WNPK envisaged the creation of a national park museum: "A complete collection of all the scientific studies shall be gathered into a 'Museum of the Swiss National Park,' together with objects (photographs, maps, etc.) depicting conditions in the national park."[61] The museum materialized only at the end of the 1920s, when the Rhaetian Railway in Chur financed the construction of a cantonal natural history museum.[62] But it fell short of the goal. Inaugurated in 1929, the museum was unable to realize the comprehensive collection foreseen by the WNPK. The documents, field notes, and photographs, as well as maps, tables, and lists continued to migrate away with the researchers who produced them, ending up in a variety of institutions, and sometimes in private hands.

The sociologist Bruno Latour has drawn attention to the role played by such artifacts in the process of scientific knowledge production. Latour calls them inscriptions, or "immutable mobiles"—invariable mobile elements that arise continually from field surveys all the way up to publication in a scientific journal and that form chains of reference and evidence. Latour also points out the importance of institutional control and central administration of these inscriptions. Their concentration in one place enables both their efficient retrieval and their recombination.[63] Latour aptly calls the institutions that collect, manage, and process inscriptions "centers of calculation." The national park was never given a powerful center of the sort that could have accumulated the inscriptions made available in the park. As a result, research lacked the means of drawing on a common pool of data. In many instances inscriptions were spread about, and their access similarly was differently regulated and not always guaranteed. The limitations this practice imposed on research lasted a long time. More recently, this problem has not only been recognized but also seriously addressed. Since the 1990s, the research commission and the national park administration have gone to great lengths to locate inscriptions produced in the national park wherever possible, and to secure them. To facilitate access, they should be centralized in only a few locations. In parallel, the park management in Zernez built up a Swiss National Park Data Center, a web-based platform, which is intended to serve researchers as a "meta-metadata system."[64]

"A Scientific National Park": International Reception

Despite the obvious difficulties, its scientific orientation together with its commitment to "total protection" became a trademark of the Swiss National Park. When Paul Harroy, chair of the International Commission on National Parks of the IUCN, opened the Second World Congress on National Parks in Yellowstone in 1972 with a look back on a century of national park history, he specifically invoked the Swiss National Park. The national park's goal of enabling scientific studies in intact natural areas, he said, was first formulated by Paul Sarasin "in particularly happy and forceful terms." Harold J. Coolidge, president of the IUCN and former chair of the IUCN's national parks commission, echoed Harroy's remarks. He stressed the "diversity of meanings" that had accrued to the national park, and praised the Swiss National Park as a "splendid example of a scientific national park."[65]

In fact, the position of Switzerland was equaled only by the Russian and Soviet parks, called *Zapovedniki*. Around the same time that the SNK was pursuing the creation of large reserves in Switzerland, the Russian zoologist Grigori Aleksandrovich Kozhevnikov was promoting the preservation of "pristine nature" in the Russian Empire. Kozhevnikov, a professor at Moscow University and director of the Moscow Zoological Museum, argued along the same lines as the SNK. For Kozhevnikov, too, the goal was primarily to enable scientific study of areas free of civilizing influences. In 1913 he was one of two Russian representatives to the World Nature Protection Conference in Bern, where he met Paul Sarasin. Kozhevnikov was deeply impressed by Sarasin and his ideas. He strongly supported Sarasin's concerns about taking indigenous peoples into account in conservation; and in an account he wrote at the end of the conference, he copiously cited Sarasin's writings. The conference report was translated into Russian.[66] The extent of the exchange between the two zoologists on conservation issues is unknown. Fifteen years later, in 1928, Kozhevnikov emphasized the pioneering role of the Soviet *Zapovedniki*. He stressed that neither in the American parks nor at the Bern conference of 1913 was much mention made of the fact that nature reserves could and should be used for research. Nonetheless, Kozhevnikov's ties to Sarasin, on whose death the following year he wrote an obituary, suggest that Kozhevnikov was very well aware of the fact that the Soviet *Zapovedniki* and the Swiss National Park were conceptually very similar. An exchange or even a collaboration must have been an obvious option, but it did not take place, at least officially.[67]

Ignorance was mutual. In Carl Schröter's 1924 manual for research in the national park, he makes no mention of the *Zapovedniki*. There is no question of his confusing the name, either, as he cites the 167-hectare Plagfenn at Chorin in Germany as one of only three areas known to him that "were being thoroughly investigated or were part of such an effort according to a coherent plan." The second area was "Sarek in Swedish Lapland," where scientific study had been systematically going on since 1895 and that in 1910 became part of the eponymous Swedish national park. As in Switzerland, the academy of sciences played a major role in establishing national parks in Sweden. Unlike Switzerland, however, Sweden formed an alliance with the tourism industry, whose interests subsequently decided the agenda of the Swedish national parks and pushed research to the periphery.[68] The third entity Schröter named was, naturally, the Swiss National Park, which he gave pride of place. That Schröter was unfamiliar with the *Zapovedniki* is highly unlikely. In fact, at the time, Russian biology was very well considered in German-speaking countries, and especially in Schröter's field of botany.[69] Thus, the omission may have been a function not least of the political circumstances, that is, the interruption in scientific communication resulting from the Communist takeover in Russia. Significantly, the term *"Zapovednik"* was translated neither into German nor English. Even today, *Zapovednik* is described most often as one of the strictly protected nature reserves devoted to science, a description that also applies to the Swiss National Park.[70]

The emphasis on science secured the Swiss National Park substantial international attention from the very beginning. For many decades, in many parts of the world, it was held up as a model of what a science-related national park should be. Among the groups that used the park as a reference, two major categories can be distinguished. First were individuals and groups that wished to establish a national park in their country or region and who saw an ally in science. The second category comprised people—mainly scientists, but also sometimes administrators of national parks—who wished to make research either the main goal of their park or to help this aspect of their park to gain greater attention.

In the former case, allusion to the Swiss National Park strengthened the park coalition and enhanced the legitimacy of their concerns. If the motion was successful, scientific considerations usually found their way into the design of a park, even though rarely to the extent of the Swiss National Park. Typical examples are the national park movements among Switzerland's neighbors, all of which invoked the Helvetic example and exchanged information with Swiss advocates. The German-Austrian association *Verein Naturschutzpark* initially held high the banner of science and planned to establish scientific monitoring stations in its future parks. As a "characteristically German" landscape the park foreseen in the Alps would offer cultural identity, but it would also be a biological complement to the Swiss National Park.[71] The association acquired a considerable piece of land in the Hohe Tauern region of the Austrian Alps. But the plans for the park never really went anywhere. The First World War and the political and social upheaval it brought posed a challenge—in Austria and elsewhere—for conservation schemes devised prior to 1914.[72]

In Italy those years saw the disappearance of the plans for a protected area directly adjacent to the Swiss National Park. In contrast to other countries, however, in Italy a single event—the decision of Victor Emmanuel III to donate his hunting grounds to the state as a park—led to rapid revival of the national park idea and the creation in 1922 of the first Italian national park in Gran Paradiso. The park was subject to an independent scientific commission that emphasized research on and protection of ibex. In the Fascist period, paramilitary forces assumed administration of the park, and in Gran Paradiso, as in other parks—for example, Stelvio, which was founded in 1935 in the vicinity of the Swiss National Park—development of tourism took precedence.[73]

In France, in 1913, supported by the national forest administration (*Direction des Eaux et Fôrets*), representatives of the Alpine Club and the Touring Club finally founded the *Association des parcs nationaux de France et des colonies*. At the association's request, the next year the state purchased a good four thousand hectares of land in the department of Isère with the intention of establishing a national park there. The conceptual plans for the Parc de La Bérarde drew explicitly on the model of the Swiss National Park. Nature would be left to develop completely freely, and protected from all human influence. Scientific monitoring of the area was a central feature. One of the main proponents of the park idea, Henry Defert, vice president of the Touring Club and chair of the committee on picturesque sites and monuments, saw in the park "a natural laboratory in which human hands would play nary a role." However, the plans went little beyond a declaration of intent. Park regulations were never really worked out, nor were scientific investigations ever seriously undertaken. Moreover, the First World War left France with little enthusiasm or sense of urgency regarding conservation. In the early 1920s the *Association des parcs nationaux* disbanded, and the park—now known as *du Pelvoux*—was placed under the care of the national forest service. This service, however, brought about neither sufficient interest nor the means to turn the territory into a specific place, and the *Parc national de La Bérarde/du Pelvoux* rapidly faded into oblivion.[74] The nature protection organizations, in particular that for protection of birds, and the *Société nationale d'acclimatisation*, set their sights on smaller reserves. Created in 1927, the 100-square-kilometer nature reserve in the Camargue was an exception. Efforts to establish larger reserves were shifted to the African colonies, as did other European colonial powers, especially Britain and Belgium. The conceptual orientations of the national parks and reserves created in French Africa differed more or less from region to region depending on the stakeholders. Targeted explicitly to the needs of science were the ten *reserves naturelles intégrales* (complete nature reserves) decreed in Madagascar at the end of 1947, and placed under the scientific control of the prestigious *Muséum national d'histoire naturelle* in Paris.[75]

The second category of response to the Swiss National Park is exemplified by the country that had always believed itself to be the originator of the national park concept: the United States. For the national parks there, the sciences had long been of little significance. The National Park Service (NPS), set up in 1916 as the central administrative unit, successfully positioned the parks in the booming "outdoor recreation" sector and opened them up to fast-growing automobile traffic.[76] This development drew increasing criticism from conservationists and scientists. These groups saw the popularization and commercialization of the parks as a danger not only to park nature but also to the national park idea. They insisted that national parks should continue to be maintained as aesthetically superb specimens of American wilderness. At the same time, however, these very heterogeneous movements were attempting to enrich the national park idea with new elements. They wished to open the parks for research and education, and to make scientific principles the basis of park management.[77]

A central figure in these efforts was John C. Merriam, president of the Carnegie Institution. In the early 1920s he had become involved in various capacities not only for nature protection and the national parks in the United States, but also in the establishment of the first African national park in the region of Kivu in the Belgian Congo, which was founded in 1925 by royal decree of King Albert of Belgium. Kivu had achieved sudden world renown in previous years for its mountain gorillas, after the American taxidermist Carl Akeley brought back to New York animals he had killed there. Akeley prepared the gorilla carcasses and staged them to public acclaim in the New York Museum of Natural History in his famous African dioramas. He reported his travel experiences in his book *In Brightest Africa*, which became a bestseller.[78] Together with other American experts Merriam advised the Belgians on setting up Albert National Park. Eventually, the park was dedicated first and foremost to scientific research, and the Belgian colonial authorities issued strict access rules.[79]

Merriam was convinced by this approach and consequently tried to persuade the US NPS to pay greater attention to scientific questions in its parks. He now took every opportunity to remind the park service of scientific issues. In 1929, in his capacity as chair of an official commission on the educational and inspirational use of national parks, he wrote to NPS director Horace M.

Albright, "We have recently received an extremely interesting publication," the *Diplopodenfauna des Schweizerischen Nationalparks* (Swiss National Park's diplopoda fauna). Whether Albright, a learned jurist, had studied the book in depth is doubtful. He passed it on to his chief park naturalist, the forester Ansel F. Hall, who in the following years became a driving force behind the small group within the NPS that campaigned for greater consideration of research issues.[80]

On Merriam's behalf, in 1928 the botanist Harvey M. Hall traveled to Europe to study park concepts on the Continent. Hall had made a name for himself with his work on flora in Yosemite National Park. Several California plants and a nature reserve at the periphery of Yosemite National Park are named after him. Hall researched and taught for several years at the University of California, Berkeley, before also taking up a second position at the Carnegie Institution of Washington.[81] Hall found the situation in Great Britain and France worthy of only a brief note. He devoted his attention chiefly to the national parks in Switzerland, Italy, and Poland, a binational project on border of Czechoslovakia and Poland, and the nature reserves in Holland. Hall was particularly impressed by the Swiss National Park, which he visited in summer 1928 in the company of Carl Schröter. In his report, he ranked the Swiss National Park above all others and emphasized its orientation to scientific research.[82] When Schröter wrote to Hall praising the idealism of the Americans in creating the national parks, Hall responded, "I hope that this compliment is justified, but it is interesting that I came back from Europe with the feeling that the Swiss were the idealists from whom the rest of us should learn! Certainly no one has gone so far as you in the matter of safeguarding reserves for scientific purposes. We are using this as an argument for the establishment of complete reserves here, and both Dr. Adams and I have quoted from your vigorous statements in this connection."[83]

In his report on the European national parks, which initially went only to Merriam but was published shortly thereafter, Hall stressed the importance both of research and of science. He called on the American scientific community to follow the European example posthaste: "Our warning as to danger of delay comes from the experience in Europe. The problem there is much more difficult than with us, for they no longer have extensive natural areas to protect. They must first re-create natural conditions through long periods of protection, sometimes accompanied by replanting and by reintroduction of the indigenous fauna. There, leaders speak of a 'grandiose experiment to create a wilderness,' whereas we need only to protect the wilderness that we already possess. Our task is to preserve what such people as the Swiss and the Italians strive to re-create."[84]

Hall's appeal met with no lasting success despite the support by leading American ecologists such as zoologist Charles C. Adams, mentioned above.

Rather, in the following decades the focus of the American national parks on recreation intensified. Although visitors increasingly benefited from educational opportunities, efforts to anchor academic research to the national park agenda over the long term and to put park management on a scientific basis both failed. Following a short, productive episode in the early 1930s, during which in particular innovative wildlife research took place in the national parks, scientific concerns and approaches disappeared for two decades.[85] Only around 1960 was there a renaissance in interest in the national parks as research sites. As a perusal of the journal *Ecology* shows, during this time the Swiss National Park once again drew the attention of American ecologists. The ENPK publication series was favorably reviewed in the journal, and reviewers let pass no chance to denounce the backwardness of the American national parks in the area of ecological research. "In the U. S. we pride ourselves on our splendid National Park system, and we customarily say that one of its principal values is to provide natural areas for scientific study. In all the U. S. we have nothing to compare with the studies of their national park that the Swiss have made," wrote a reviewer in 1959. Another concurred a few years later: "This reviewer must admit that he is amazed at the exactness of the taxonomical and geographical treatment.... Compared to Switzerland our knowledge of the botany of the many American and Canadian National Parks is nil, an unflattering but necessary comparison." This second review discussed Heinrich Zoller's book *Flora des Schweizerischen Nationalparks und seiner Umgebung* (Flora of the Swiss National Park and its surroundings). The article was titled: "Switzerland: An Example for Our National Parks?"[86]

Over the course of the twentieth century "scientific national parks" became a recognized genus of the family of national parks that was flourishing worldwide, and the Swiss National Park its most popular species. As such, it gained global significance and broadened the range of meaning that could be attributed to any national park. But how significant was the actual research done in the Swiss National Park? Was it actually as exemplary in practice as suggested by the reviews in *Ecology*? Earlier I voiced doubts when searching for explanations of why the high expectations of the park founders were not fully realized. The remaining sections of this chapter will focus on the conduct of research in the Swiss National Park since then, and the factors that brought about change.

Changing Research Methods and Practices

Over the decades, shifts became apparent in the way research methods and practices were applied in the Swiss National Park, though the development was hardly linear. This observation itself is meaningful: The higgledy-piggledy evolution reflects, on the one hand, a weakness at the level of leadership and coordination, and on the other, the variety of factors that influenced the practice of research. Chief among these were individual motivation and combination of personnel, followed by—as I have shown—disciplinary trends and developments in science, research policy, and local developments in the park region.

A closer look at the external factors reveals that the 1950s were a turning point for park research in two respects. First, the creation of the Swiss National Science Foundation enabled entirely new forms of research. Up to then, scientists did their fieldwork during semester breaks or the summer months, when school was out. Now, longer-term projects could be taken on and data gathering in the park extended throughout the year. The expansion of the park's research infrastructure also contributed to these developments. In 1947 a small laboratory was established near Il Fuorn that was also used by researchers as accommodation. In 1964 Robert Schloeth, a wildlife biologist, was appointed the first full-time park director. In 1968 he inaugurated the National Park Center in Zernez. These years also saw the mapping of the park's vegetation that would prove essential to later research.[87] Second, debates over the growing deer population and the construction of a hydropower plant in the park area disrupted the tranquility in which park research had proceeded in the initial decades. The two final years of the Second World War, 1944 and 1945, marked a watershed. The hydropower plant on the Spöl River was announced in 1944; 1945 brought the first major winter die-off of deer. Both topics preoccupied the WNPK in the coming decades, and influenced both the research agenda and how scientists saw themselves.

These events were not, however, the first to disrupt the park's laboratory operations. Even before the construction of the power plant and the problem of the deer, park visitors had been a distraction to scientists. Already during the First World War, the WNPK complained about the excessive number of visitors: "Too many visitors are undesirable. They contradict the objectives of the park. The negative effects of tourism are especially evident in Val Cluoza," noted the WNPK at its meeting of spring 1918 and asked the park commission to investigate whether measures could be taken to avoid the madding crowd and also to restrict the expansion of hotels in the park.[88] However, the ENPK deemed the visits to be within reason, and backed up its contention with figures. According to one statistic provided by Secretary Bühlmann based on logs at the Cluozza hut, in 1917 only 298 people had visited Val Cluozza. Other parts of the park received yet fewer or even no visitors. "It is unthinkable to reduce the number of visits to the park," Bühlmann wrote WNPK chair Schröter. In deference to the goal of protection, only a narrow, arduous footpath led from Zernez to Val Cluozza and over the Murtèrgrat to the Ofenberg road. "Less is hardly possible, because ultimately according to the federal government decree each and every Swiss nature lover has a right to come and see the park."[89] At any rate, in those years of the Great War a greater burden than a few tourists was posed by the military personnel stationed in and around the park.

The debates over tourism and its effects on the park cropped up periodically. In 1960 Alfred Kurth turned the perspective around and asked "whether the national park should not be made an object of demonstration and discussion to a far greater extent than previously."[90] So doing would have meant much more active promotion of the national park and in particular by scientists. Kurth's suggestion was made against the backdrop not only of increasing numbers of visitors but especially the decision made in the interim to build a hydropower plant on the Spöl River and the palpable concern that the growing deer population had unleashed among national park stakeholders. In view of these changes, the goal of the federal decree of 1914 to leave "the entire fauna and flora [to] their freely developing nature" now seemed an untenable illusion. The scientists would have to come to terms with the continuing anthropogenic influence on the nature in the park. In some cases these human influences were specifically used for research. Thus, many observation plots were set up in the areas devastated by fires in 1952 and 1961, as well as along the Ofenberg road, whose slopes were regreened in connection with the road expansion of 1969.[91] However, such programs remained the exception. Specifically, the changes brought about by the damming of the Spöl were long neglected. Relevant investigations were undertaken only in the 1990s. In 2000 flooding experiments began in collaboration with the Engadiner Kraftwerke. Varying the amount of (excess) water released from the reservoir to the Spöl, instead of keeping it constant, resulted in small floods.[92] These experiments were inspired by experimental flooding of the Grand Canyon by the Colorado River in 1996.[93]

For a long time most scientists were uninterested in studying human effects, preferring undisturbed natural conditions in which they could conduct basic scientific research.[94] The idea of a laboratory shielded from external influences turned out to be poorly suited to investigation of such influences, not least because the image of the national park as a locus for scientific research was based precisely on its reputation for keeping them out. Hence, going to the national park to study the impact of human activities was not a very rewarding proposition. An exception was a series of ecological studies in the Lower Engadine, motivated by the construction of the Engadiner Kraftwerke. The goal of this research was to document natural conditions before hydropower-plant construction began. The study areas, however, were outside the park.[95]

Over time, the spectrum of research practices that could be applied in the park gradually expanded. The revision of the federal decree on the national park of 1959 took these changes into account: The term "scientific observation" was replaced with "scientific research."[96] Up until the Second World War,

162   Creating Wilderness

study in the park had been restricted to observing and gathering, most of which was intended for the traditional practice of classifying collected species. A few researchers deviated from this regime and subjected their findings to laboratory tests. Hans Jenny and Hans Pallmann analyzed soil samples from the park in the laboratories of ETH Zurich, and Ernst Gäumann did the same with fungi that he collected. Similarly, Arnold Pictet, from Geneva, investigated the factors affecting larvae of large butterflies and conducted breeding experiments.[97]

The first steps toward experimentalization of practices in the park itself occurred in the 1930s. In contrast to the early years, these efforts no longer met with resistance from the ENPK. In 1926 the commission still forbade forestry scientists to mark trees in their newly installed observation plots. Twenty years later, in 1946, the forestry scientists were given a green light not only to number trees but also to remove around thirty of them as test samples.[98] This change of heart may have been facilitated by the departure of the first generation of park founders, in particular Paul Sarasin and Fritz Bühlmann. At the end of the 1930s the growing deer population inspired botanists to look at the effects on their grazing grounds. In God del Fuorn and at Alp Grimmel permanent plots were set up to keep deer away from the vegetation. In 1947 Werner Lüdi, chair of the botany subcommission, described this step as a "small initiative of the simplest kind" to be followed by others: "It is planned to expand the investigations of the permanent observation plots over time to include experiments."[99] However, this expansion did not happen until long after Lüdi's time. In the 1990s a system of permanent fences was established that was subsequently expanded and refined under the direction of Martin Schütz.[100]

After the Second World War the zoologists, too, began to experiment. In wildlife research, which—after a few botched attempts between the wars—first began seriously in the 1950s, later national park director Robert Schloeth identified deer using collars and ear tags. This practice, instituted at the end of the 1950s, required capturing and tranquilizing the animals, which in turn entailed experimenting with traps and dart injection. Dart injection was a technique tested in the United States, where animals were sedated with injections administered by a special gun to minimize human-animal contact. Several decades earlier, such an intervention would have been unthinkable in the Swiss National Park. The fieldwork regulations of 1917 expressly forbade the killing and catching of "warm-blooded vertebrates," with the exception of small rodents, insectivores, and birds for specified purposes.[101] At the time, in addition to violating the integrity of the park, administrators feared the opposition of hunters. The postwar research project also provoked resistance from this same group, whereas nature protection circles did not object to those relatively invasive research methods. The hunters felt challenged by the academically trained wildlife biologists, who threatened their monopoly on know-how and consequently also their hunting authority.[102] In the 1960s several hundred deer in the national park were tagged. Three decades later, in the 1990s, the tagging practice was extended to ibex and chamois and it became electronic. Wildlife were equipped with GPS collars, which allowed both more numerous and accurate localizations. And the use of a GIS made it possible to track and analyze their movements by computer.[103] The leader in developing this method, so-called radio tracking, was once more the United States, where the technology had first been used in the 1960s with grizzly bears in Yellowstone National Park, among others.[104]

The exploding deer population had a twofold effect on the orientation of research as evidenced by wildlife research. First, the deer helped to promote the experimentalization of park research. Second, park research became application oriented. It was no longer purely basic research, but rather increasingly served the purposes of the park management. This was particularly true for ungulate research, which it was hoped would determine the appropriate size of stocks for the national park and how a stock could be brought to that level and then be stabilized. These issues were explicitly the main research objective of a large deer project in the 1970s and again of an ibex project begun in 1992.[105]

Asynchronous Rhythms: Long-Term Observation and University Research

The development of botanical research in the park nicely illustrates the mutual effect of individual and academic interactions. Botanical park research was shaped in the early years by Josias Braun-Blanquet. In 1917 Braun-Blanquet together with Steivan Brunies established in the park a network of twenty-three permanent plots, fifteen at the sub-alpine level and eight at the alpine level. In the following years Braun-Blanquet tracked the changes in vegetation of these plots by periodically determining the composition of the flora. In addition, he developed his own system of classification, which he first described fully in 1921 in a paper titled "Prinzipien einer Systematik der Pflanzengesellschaften auf floristischer Grundlage" (Principles of a Systematic Flora-Based Classification of Plant Communities). Subsequently, he worked on a detailed textbook that appeared in 1928 under the title *Pflanzensoziologie: Grundzüge der Vegetationskunde*, by virtue of which Braun-Blanquet's approach was disseminated rapidly. In 1932, the book appeared in English (*Plant Sociology: The Study of Plant Communities*) and later in Japanese. It became a standard reference in botany. Until the present day, thousands of students and scientists have applied the Braun-Blanquet method in mapping vegetation worldwide. Simultaneously, his plant sociology became synonymous with the Zurich-Montpellier school of plant ecology.[106]

Braun-Blanquet's key criterion for the classification—or perhaps better, typifying—of any vegetation was its combination of flora. The basic unit of his system of plant communities was the "association," which contained a typical combination of species. So-called character species identified a specific association and also gave it their name. Thus, Braun-Blanquet named the plant community *Androsacetum helveticae* "after the true character species *Androsacetum helveticae*, whose cushions best reflect the extreme living conditions of the association."[107] Just as, since Linnaeus, individuals have been organized into a system of species based on their biology, Braun-Blanquet's system enabled any vegetation that was encountered in the field and recorded in tabellar form to be classified according to specific associations. Thus, infinite local diversity was transformed into a manageable set of universal plant communities. Here, Braun-Blanquet emphasized that the association was an abstraction of the actual conditions encountered: "Pieces of vegetation with similar combinations of species are united into abstract types," Braun-Blanquet explained in his 1928 textbook.[108] Whereas the simultaneously emerging plant ecology of Frederic Clements looked to large-scale organization and placed great weight on climate factors, Braun-Blanquet was more interested in small-scale delineation of species communities and their interactions. As many authors had already noted, these divergent foci corresponded remarkably well with both the geobotanical and social conditions in which both botanists worked. Clements's extended "American" communities were bound together through shared climatic conditions; Braun-Blanquet's "European" communities were highly differentiated and neatly separated from one another.[109]

Braun-Blanquet acknowledged that there was "no close parallelism between plant sociology and the sociology of Auguste Comte. The two have one important point of contact: They are concerned not with the life expression of the individual organism as such but with groups or communities of organisms having more or less equivalent reactions, bound together in mutual dependence. The communal values resulting from the mutual relations of the organisms are the social phenomena; the cooperation of organisms is the social process. The community has an existence altogether independent of the individual."[110] Braun-Blanquet's association also had similarities to Max Weber's ideal type. Both were abstractions derived from concrete sociological observations to provide an interpretive schema for the classification of further social phenomena.[111] In terms of research practice, Braun-Blanquet's method was based on careful surveying of vegetation in the field, which in turn required comprehensive knowledge of flora. In establishing the permanent plots in the national park Braun-Blanquet called on other specialists for identification of mosses and lichens, analysis of the soil, and the measurement of sample areas. A working community emerged that would endure over several decades and into the 1950s.[112]

Early 1939, however, marked a turning point in botanical exploration of the national park. The chair of the botany subcommission, Werner Lüdi, petitioned the WNPK to expand monitoring of vegetation changes. At the same time, Lüdi nominated his assistant at the *Geobotanische Institut Rübel*, Balthasar Stüssi, as a future researcher for the permanent plots. Braun-Blanquet, who was not present at the WNPK meeting, rejected the proposal in writing and put forth two opposing candidates. In the debate that ensued at the meeting it soon became clear that for Lüdi the issue was not simply to promote his own protégé; by expanding the monitoring, he also wished to implement a systematic change in direction. "Lüdi agrees with Braun's method of investigation for larger plots, but he does not consider it appropriate for smaller ones," noted the taker of minutes. Stüssi not only had more knowledge about major species than did Braun-Blanquet's candidates, pursued Lüdi, but in the choice of methods he was also "freer" than they were. The commission was divided in its loyalties, but when it came to the vote, Lüdi prevailed.[113]

That same year the monitoring system was extended by about eighty plots. The difference between the old and the new observation plots was striking. Braun-Blanquet's plots were all different sizes and shapes: triangles, squares, and other polygons. In contrast, Lüdi and Stüssi's new plots were generally one- to four-meter squares precisely marked with stakes anchored in the ground—"pegged out" in botanical jargon.[114] Lüdi was only slightly younger than Braun-Blanquet, but he was taking ecology in a new direction that placed greater value on the statistical utility of the data, which in turn meant standardizing data collection.[115] In addition to the new observation plots, in 1939 Lüdi used a slope near Alp la Schera that had been devastated by an avalanche in 1917 to install a 100-meter-long "transect." The transect, while being new to the park, was by then a well-established ecological method that was used in documenting gradual vegetation changes along a section. Ten years later, in 1949, Lüdi repeated his inventory, and fifty years after that the transect was the subject of a diploma thesis.[116]

For Balthasar Stüssi, monitoring the permanent plots of the national park became a life's mission that he would serve for over half a century. Over time he doubled the observation plots to around 160. However, he failed to maintain the network of park researchers that had characterized the work in Braun-Blanquet's era. Consequently, the interdisciplinarity gradually disappeared from the botanists' monitoring program, and no successor was found to continue the monitoring of Frey's lichen plots.[117] Long-term monitoring in the national park was not a career-enhancing activity. Stüssi managed only to get a senior assistant from the University of Zurich. He did his fieldwork in the park during his holidays, and published very little of the results. For statistical reasons, Stüssi deemed fivefold samplings necessary, and because the data recordings were made at five- to six-year intervals, he reached the end point in the mid-1960s, when he was already well over fifty years old. His only major monograph on succession in the national park appeared in 1970, three years before his retirement. He carried on with his observation activity even as a retiree, seeming to consider the plots and the data they provided more and more as his own private property with the passage of time. Following his death in 1992 it was only with great difficulty that the data he collected were retrieved from his estate, and his cryptic notes decoded and made available for follow-up studies.[118]

The course of long-term monitoring revealed both the weaknesses of the key institutions of national park research and the academic lack of appreciation for the arc of time represented by the fieldwork. Apart from a few publications, Stüssi kept the inscriptions he produced under lock and key. The administrative and coordinating bodies found themselves helpless to obtain their release, and to make them accessible through dissemination. They remained, to use Latour's term, immobile, and thus scientifically unproductive. On the other hand, Stüssi's career also showed that the clock of nature in the national park ticked differently from that of university research. Schröter's enthusiastically welcomed research opportunity, which thanks to the unlimited duration of monitoring "could extend over several generations of observers," turned out to be largely impractical from the single researcher's point of view. After an initial phase focusing on the development of appropriate methods, academics lost interest in monitoring plots that might deliver useful results only in the distant future. Braun-Blanquet recognized as much at the end of the 1930s, when he suggested to the WNPK that "a mature researcher would not wish to sacrifice his time" for such work. Experimental work promised straightforward and, above all, much quicker results.

In the 1990s, only the possibility of combining the long series from the national park with experimental ordering and computer-supported simulations could turn Stüssi's collected materials into a scientifically attractive data source.[119] The similarity of developmental trends in different permanent plots remarked by Stüssi prompted Martin Schütz and co-workers to assume "that the different composition of the vegetation on the various permanent plots represent different stages in a single successional process."[120] In other words, proceeding from the simultaneity of unsimultaneous processes, they concluded that different plots represented different time points in a uniform process of succession throughout the entire park. To describe this overarching process, in a first step they standardized the observation data of selected plots and, in a second step, laid these over one another (see illustration 8). These overlays made it possible to combine data series from various plots with even longer hypothetical data series and thus to extend the actual monitoring period of decades to a centuries-long hypothetical one. The result was a succession model that reconstructed the development of vegetation in the park over a period of 585 years.[121] Their methods enabled Schütz and his colleagues to

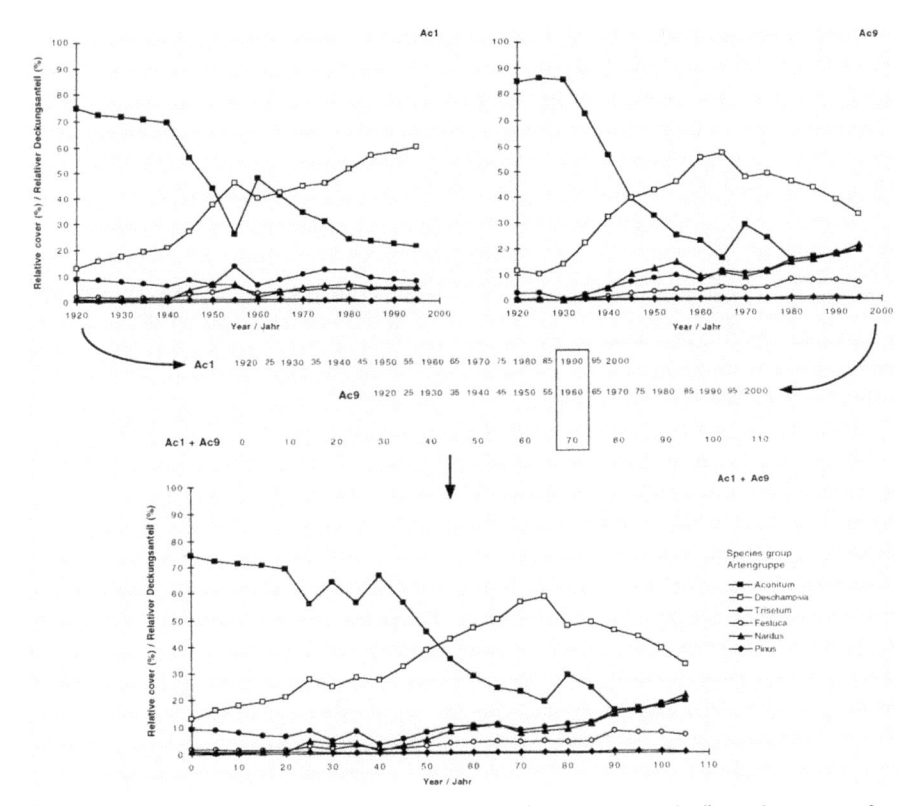

Illustration 8. Figure from Schütz et al. 2000a. The caption reads: "Combination of the two time-series, Ac1 and Ac 9, to form the time-series Ac1 + Ac9. Each relevé consists of 6 attributes (species groups). Since relevé 1990 of Ac1 resembles most to relevé 1960 of Ac9 they define the connection point (framed) between the two time series" (219).

find a creative solution to a problem that had long plagued researchers in the park: the slow, decades-long process of change in the landscape. By blending standardized observation series they were able to fit time into space, and space into time. No doubt this approach was original, but it was hardly new. In fact, the pioneers of American ecology, Henry Cowles and Victor Shelford, had already used such a method in the early 1900s in working on the ecology of dunes and pond fish.[122]

Growing Importance of the National Park as a Field Laboratory?

To recap: Following a euphoric start, for a long time research in the national park did not fulfill the expectations placed on it. In the national park, the field and the laboratory did not realize the fortunate union envisaged by the parks founders. Short-clocked academic research and long-term park monitoring were similarly incompatible. In addition, although the federal designation as a national park ensured institutional security over the long term, at the same time research was tied to specific terrains, which turned out not to be the best way to solve certain problems. The park was not particularly rich in species, and many processes evolved frustratingly slowly from the point of view of researchers. Research had to adapt to the given terrain, and not the other way around, as is far more common in science.[123] The experimentalization of research and the increasing length of data series enlarged the spectrum of possibility, but the lack of basic facilities, which was also responsible for inadequate central data management, continued to be a problem.

Despite the interpretative caution imposed by the temporal proximity of events, a recent uptick in the recognition of national park research is noticeable, of which the resurgence of scientific long-term monitoring is only one aspect. This increase in importance is positively related to Bernhard Nievergelt's initiatives of the 1980s, and was encouraged by the change in the park directorate at the end of that decade, but was also the result of deeper and more far-reaching motives. Two developments appear to have been particularly significant: First, following a temporary decline, interest in biological species diversity began to rise again. One of the main consequences of the 1992 UN Conference in Rio de Janeiro was the adoption of a Convention on Biological Diversity, or biodiversity. In this new concept, species diversity plays a central role.

In Article 2 of the Rio convention, biological diversity was comprehensively defined as "diversity within species, between species and of ecosystems," thus relating traditional species diversity with genetic variability and the ecosystem approach, which in turn represented a shift in perspective from living organisms to the (eco)systemic context of their existence. Biodiversity became a key aspect of any ecosystem. Accordingly, biodiversity rose in the hierarchy of study objects of ecosystem research, which in the postwar decades had achieved a dominant position in ecology. Species extinction morphed into loss of biodiversity, which made it possible to document, quantify, and model it using computer technology.[124] In this connection, natural spaces took on new meaning as reference areas. In places like the Swiss National Park the natural dynamics of ecosystems could be studied and compared with those in cultivated spaces. Consequently, comparative research of areas inside and outside the national park, which was already included within the research framework of 1916, gained new legitimacy and urgency. This point was stressed by the Scientific Park Commission in its new research program for the period 2008 to 2018, which addressed research in both the national park and the newly established biosphere reserve Val Müstair.[125]

Second, it became clear that the manifold external influences that the national park was increasingly exposed to since the 1950s—in particular the introduction of hydropower, burgeoning traffic and tourism, and problems with growing numbers of ungulates—required a scientific approach and that the management of the park had to be expanded and made scientifically credible. Beginning in the early 1990s these considerations were taken into account. Under the new park directors Klaus Robin and Heinrich Haller the research infrastructure available to the park administration was greatly expanded, and permanent positions for scientists were established. Wildlife research, which previously had been run by former park director Schloeth part-time, so to speak, was professionalized. The administration and processing of research data, including the operation and expansion of the GIS developed for the national park, were taken over by the park administration. This move facilitated both the transfer of research results to the park management and strengthened interactions between park research and management. Moreover, after decades of operation, the foundation was laid to provide national park research with a "center of calculation," a central research archive that would serve to accumulate all the data collected.

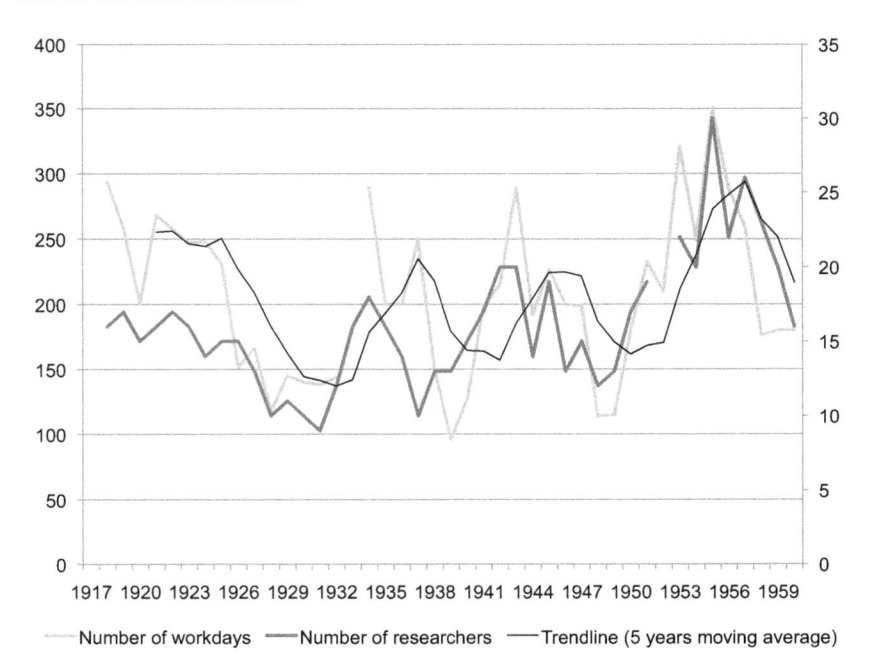

Chart 2. Yearly number of researchers (right axis) and the number of workdays spent in the park (left axis), 1918–60. For later years only partial data are available, and those data are not comparable. *Source*: ENPK and WNPK annual reports; data missing for 1933, 1952.

Notes

1. Nievergelt 1980, 3 f.
2. FOK Archives, WNPK, meeting of 6 December 1980, 4.
3. Wissenschaftliche Nationalparkkommission 1990. In addition, in the 1990s the park directors managed to considerably increase the research capacities at their headquarters in Zernez. I will come back to this point in this chapter.
4. Evaluation Group for the Scientific Committee of the Swiss National Park, Report to the Swiss Academy of Sciences, 25 August 1997, 3.
5. Bundesbeschluss 1914, Art. 1.
6. On this division, see Kohler 2002.
7. On Zschokke, see Simon 2009, 49–69; on Schröter, see more below.
8. Both reports can be found in the SNK annual report 1911–12, 93–98. See in addition the discussion in the Reserves Committee at the meeting of 31 October 1908: SCANT Archives, Box 521, Protokollbuch, 82.
9. Warming 1896.
10. Schröter 1902. Schröter considered further terms with Charles Flahault. At the International Congress of Botanists in Brussels in 1910 they suggested a "phytogeographical nomenclature." Flahault and Schröter 1910.
11. On Schröter's life, see Rübel 1940. The literature on the history of ecology is extensive. See McIntosh 1985; Worster 1985; Trepl 1987; Golley 1993; Bowler 1992; Lewis 2003; Kingsland 2005; Voigt 2009.
12. Becking 1957.
13. See the account of Dachnowski 1914, who took part in the IPE; Tansley 1939; Rübel 1940, 41 f. See also the historical account of Schulte Fischedick and Shinn 1993; Cameron and Matless 2010.
14. Clements 1916.
15. Schröter 1920, 5.
16. Gradmann 1898.
17. Schröter 1924, 389.
18. Ibid., 389.
19. SNK annual report 1911–12, 95.
20. Schröter 1920, 5 f. Braun-Blanquet 1928, 310.
21. SNP Archives, 106.100, ENPK, Reglement für den Schweizerischen Nationalpark im Unterengadin vom 16 March 1916, § 11.
22. SNP Archives, 150.100, SNG, Reglement der WNPK vom 10 July 1916, § 9.
23. Vertrag betreffend den schweizerischen Nationalpark, Art. 3 and 4, in Schweizerischer Bundesrat 1914, Appendix 2.
24. See chapter 3.
25. SCNAT Archives, Box 532, Bühlmann to P. Sarasin, 1 July 1914.
26. SCNAT Archives, Box 532, Ed. Sarasin to P. Sarasin, 14 November 1914.
27. SCNAT Archives, Box 532, Bühlmann to P. Sarasin, 23 November 1914.
28. Bütikofer 1920. For financial reasons, publication was postponed for a year. See WNPK annual reports 1918–20. SNP Archives, 150.100, Reglement für die Entschädigungen bei der wissenschaftlichen Erforschung des Nationalparks von 1916. Schröter 1926, 89 f.

29. See WNPK annual reports; www.kieferhablitzel.ch (accessed 10 October 2010), and on the founding of the National Science Foundation, Fleury and Joye 2002.
30. WNPK annual report 1916, 158. The WNPK regulations and the research program of its subcommission are in the SNP Archives, 150.100. On the influence of the First World War and on the contrasts between the French- and German-speaking parts of the country, see chapter 2.
31. On biology in Swiss universities, see Stettler 2002. No one has yet done a comprehensive overview of the topic.
32. ENPK annual report 1926, 10. On the development, see Burger 1950, 583–585. On the competition between the SNK and the *Forstverein,* see chapter 2.
33. Schröter 1926, 97.
34. Of the research prior to 1990, only the work on mining is worthy of mention: Schläpfer 1960; past 1990 the studies on forest history and tourism: Parolini 2012a; Küpfer 2000.
35. WNKP annual reports. Schröter 1926, 93 f.
36. See Wissenschaftliche Nationalparkkommission 1987, Erdwissenschaftliche Subkommission. The mapping was partly done outside the WNPK's work program. Transfer to the wardens: SBN Archives, M 3.2, ENPK, meeting of 2 February 1918, 3.
37. SNP Archives, 150.100, Programm zur zoologischen Erforschung des schweizerischen Nationalparkes im Unterengadin von 1917, 3. For a research overview, see Gonseth et al. 2007.
38. WNPK annual report 1921–22, 8. On the critique of the ENPK, see BAR 9500.25, vol. 37, Bühlmann to Schröter, 25 February 1918.
39. Braun-Blanquet 1931, 3–5. The first results were published in Braun-Blanquet and Jenny 1926.
40. ENPK annual report 1923, 12 f. On the development of biodiversity in the national park, see chapter 4.
41. SCNAT Archives, Box 532, Ed. Sarasin to P. Sarasin, 14 November 1914.
42. ETH Library, Archives, SR2: Schulratsprotokolle 1927, meeting no. 9 of 28 November 1925. As a bridge, it gave Martin Rickli a temporary lectureship.
43. ETH Library, Archives, SR2: Schulratsprotokolle 1927, meeting no. 1 of 28 January 1927.
44. Ibid., meeting no. 2 of 26 March 1927 and meeting no. 3 of 6 May 1927. Rohn consulted Ernest Wilczek (Lausanne), Gustav Senn (Basel), Eduard Fischer (Bern), and Robert Chodat (Geneva). Chodat did not answer because he was abroad. On the research debates at ETH Zurich between the wars, see Gugerli et al. 2010, 149–177.
45. See WNPK annual reports 1931–1935; Gäumann und Campell 1932.
46. See Grob et al. 1980, 394.
47. Braun-Blanquet et al. 1954. See also Zoller 1964.
48. Kohler 2002, 7.
49. WNPK annual report 1916, 158; Schröter 1920, 5; Handschin 1939, 56; Braun-Blanquet 1939, 60; Nadig 1940, 80.
50. See Rheinberger and Hagner 1993; Rheinberger 2001.
51. On the corresponding developments in ecology, see Trepl 1987, 177–204; Kohler 2002, 252–289.
52. Kohler 2002, 218–222. On Cooper, see Catton 1995, Ch. 3.

53. Braun-Blanquet 1931, 4.
54. SNP Archives, 290.101, Werner Lüdi: Auswirkungen der Vegetationsforschung im Nationalpark auf die praktische Wirtschaft, manuscript dated 2 December 1947, 4.
55. Kurth et al. 1960, 351. This estimation was confirmed by more recent research: Schütz et al. 2000b.
56. See Braun-Blanquet and Jenny 1926 and Braun-Blanquet 1931.
57. BAR 9500.25, vol. 37, ENPK to WNPK, 23 July 1918.
58. SNP Archives, 150.100, ENPK, Vorschriften für die wissenschaftlichen Beobachter des Nationalparkes, 9 June 1917. The rules are also listed in Schröter 1924, 393.
59. For the second half of the twentieth century, the interdisciplinary projects "Ecological Investigations in the Lower Engadine," "Munt la Schera," and "Stabelchod" are worthy of mention. See Nadig et al. 1999; Matthey 2007; Schütz et al. 2000a.
60. Star and Griesemer 1989, 393. A similar concept is based on Peter Galison's trading zone, which he developed in a laboratory study to explain how physicists and engineers are able to collaborate despite substantial differences in self-understanding and approach. Galison 1997. In its institutional anchoring, the Swiss National Park is more like a natural history museum than a research laboratory, which is why the concept of Star and Griesemer seems appropriate.
61. SNP Archives, 150.100, Reglement der WNPK, 10 July 1916, § 17.
62. Müller-Schneider and Müller 1981.
63. Latour 1987.
64. www.parcs.ch/mmds/about.php (accessed 1 October 2010). An inventory of the collections is currently under the leadership of the director of the Bündner Naturmuseum, Jürg P. Müller.
65. Harroy 1972a, 16. Coolidge 1972, 33.
66. Conférence Internationale pour la Protection de la Nature Berne 1914, 138 f., 181 f. Weiner 1988, 7–18, 66–70.
67. Weiner 1988, 66–70.
68. Mels 1999.
69. Schröter 1924, 391–394. In the *Handbuch der biologischen Arbeitsmethoden*, in which this essay appeared, Russian botanists are well represented. See Abderhalden 1939, 5–12.
70. Weiner 1988, ix. The World Database on Protected Areas (www.wdpa.org) includes both designations under Category Ia, Strict Nature Reserve.
71. See Floericke 1910; Guenther 1919, 231 f.
72. See Kupper and Wöbse 2013. Further parks were to have been established in the low mountain ranges, in the northern German lowlands, and along the beach. Floericke 1913, 15.
73. See Sievert 2000; Graf von Hardenberg 2009; Graf von Hardenberg 2010.
74. See Zuanon 1995. The quotation from Henry Defert is in ibid., 47.
75. See Selmi 2009; Ford 2012.
76. See Carr 1998; Sutter 2002. Work on the history of parks in the French colonial empire is just beginning. Here it is worth connecting the relocation of park research to Madagascar with (post)colonial studies that investigate colonies as "modern laboratories." See van Laak 2004. On the link between colonialism and national parks, see Gissibl et al. 2012b.

77. Kupper 2009a.
78. Akeley 1923. See Haraway 1989, 26–58; Jones 2010.
79. Harroy 1993; Van Schuylenbergh 2009. Merriam referred directly to his experience with Albert National Park in a letter from 1929, in which he suggested the creation of complete reservations within the American national parks: LoC, Papers of John C. Merriam, Box 132, Merriam to the Members of the Committee on Study of Educational Problems in National Parks, 26 December 1929.
80. NA, Record Group 79, 3.1, Entry 7, Box 632, Merriam to Albright, 4 June 1929, Demaray to Merriam, 11 June 1929. For a biography of Merriam, see Mark 2005.
81. Babcock 1934.
82. Hall 1929, 683.
83. ETH Library, Collections, HS 399, Hall to Schröter, 7 April 1930.
84. Hall 1929, 684.
85. Wright et al. 1933. For the full debate, see Kupper 2009a.
86. The first review referred to Braun-Blanquet et al. 1954. *Ecology* 40, no. 2 (1959), 330 f., *Ecology* 47, no. 4 (1966), 685 f.
87. Zoller 1964; Campell and Trepp 1968. On the inauguration of the laboratory: WNPK annual report 1947, 258. On the turnabout in the 1950s, see Baer 1962.
88. SNP Archives, 152.100, WNPK, meeting of 11 April 1918, 19.
89. Bühlmann to Schröter, 25 February 1918.
90. Kurth et al. 1960, 352.
91. See Giessler and Hartmann 2000; Klötzli 1991.
92. Scheurer 2000b. In spring 2013 the efforts to revive the Spöl river's dynamic environments took a dramatic turn. Following an incident at Punt dal Gall dam on 30 March 2013 an uncontrollable quantity of sludge was discharged into the Spöl River bed, with devasting consequences for the flora and fauna, causing among other things the deaths of thousands of fish. Engadiner Kraftwerke, Schweizerischer Nationalpark, Amt für Jagd und Fischerei Graubünden, Gemeinsame Medienmitteilung, 31 March 2013.
93. Personal communication, T. Scheurer. On the flooding of the Grand Canyon, see Andrews and Pizzi 2000.
94. See Wissenschaftliche Nationalparkkommission 1990, 7–11.
95. See Baer et al. 1968; Nadig et al. 1999.
96. The wording in the 1914 decree read: "The national park shall be placed under scientific observation." The 1959 revision read: "The national park is available for scientific research." And the federal act of 1980 states: "The Park shall be the subject of continuous scientific research."
97. Schröter 1926, 104. WNPK annual reports.
98. Burger 1960, 626.
99. SNP Archives, 290.101. Werner Lüdi: Auswirkungen der Vegetationsforschung im Nationalpark auf die praktische Wirtschaft, manuscript dated 2 December 1947, 6. On the establishment of the fenced plots: WNPK annual report 1939, 3.
100. Camenisch and Schütz 2000.
101. Archiv SNP, 150.100, ENPK, Vorschriften für die wissenschaftlichen Beobachter des Nationalparkes, 9 June 1917. The regulations are also listed in Schröter 1924, 393.
102. Schloeth 1961. For criticism of the project, see 223 f. On the conflict with the hunters, see the next chapter.

103. Allgöwer et al. 1992; Allgöwer 1996; Abderhalden 2005; Filli 2006.
104. See Benson 2010, 2012.
105. Blankenhorn et al. 1979; ENPK annual report 1992, 6 f.
106. Braun-Blanquet 1921; 1928; 1932. Cf. McIntosh 1985, 44 f.
107. Braun-Blanquet and Jenny 1926, 188.
108. Braun-Blanquet 1928, 20.
109. Trepl 1987, 157. Nicolson 1989; Eser 1999, 87–99. See also McIntosh 1985, 39–49; Worster 1985, 205–220.
110. Braun-Blanquet 1928, 1. In treating plant communities as social units, Braun-Blanquet—like Clements—took an organismic point of view. This essentialism is opposed by an individualistic concept of plant communities, whose best-known proponent was the American botanist Henry Gleason. Gleason reviewed the English edition of Braun-Blanquet's *Plant Sociology* favorably in the journal *Ecology*, though he made sure to emphasize Braun-Blanquet's criticism of Clements's ideas (they were too hypothetical, Braun-Blanquet 1928, 310) (Gleason 1933). On the conflict between organismic and individualistic concepts in ecology, see Trepl 1987, 139–158.
111. Weber 1922 (1904). Whether Braun-Blanquet was familiar with Weber's sociology or whether the alignment was unconscious is unknown. *Plant Sociology* makes no direct reference to Max Weber.
112. Braun-Blanquet et al. 1954. On the interdisciplinary work on plans for the experimental plot Plan dala Posa, see Pallmann and Frei 1943.
113. FOK Archives, WNPK, meeting of 15 January 1939, 9–12.
114. Wissenschaftliche Nationalparkkommission 1986, 4. Cf. Scheurer 2000a.
115. See Kohler 2002, 252–292; Trepl 1987, 177–204; Bowler 1992, 370–378.
116. Lüdi 1954; Riederer 1996.
117. Frey 1952 and 1959.
118. Grämiger and Krüsi 2000.
119. Interview Schütz. See also Schütz et al. 2000b. The same holds for the data series on the development of the forests. See Risch 2004.
120. Schütz et al. 2000a, 209.
121. Schütz et al. 2000a.
122. See Kohler 2002, 230–238.
123. This also constitutes a major difference between the ecological research practices that Kohler investigated (2002).
124. On the cycles of research in species diversity or biodiversity, see Kohler 2006; on the introduction of "biodiversity" to the scientific and political discourse, see Takacs 1996; Eser 2003; Potthast 2007; and for a biological introduction to biodiversity, see Baur 2010.
125. Forschungskommission des Schweizerischen Nationalparks 2008. The proof in the form of research results has yet to be demonstrated. The idea of reference plots outside the park was proposed several times after 1916 but no suitably designed research projects materialized. See Baer 1962, 59 f; Wissenschaftliche Nationalparkkommission 1990, 7.

CHAPTER 6

Wilderness Limits
Natural Dynamics and Social Equilibrium

In December 1958 Josias Braun-Blanquet, the dean of national park research who was now seventy-five years old, wrote for the *Neue Zürcher Zeitung* a widely publicized essay on biological balance in the national park. Braun-Blanquet told the newspaper's readers that the extensive mountain pine woods that blanketed large parts of the park and impressed everyone who saw them were "essentially second-growth and obscured the formerly far more valuable Swiss stone pines." In the eighteenth century stone pines fell victim to massive clear cutting when the salt flats from Hall in Tyrol were being supplied with wood from the Lower Engadine. The light-loving, fine-seeded mountain pine then invaded the cleared, chalky soil. In-depth studies had now shown that the "natural vegetation process" was once again proceeding in favor of the stone pine. "The course of development marked out by nature had no small obstacles to surmount, however," continued Braun-Blanquet, related not least to the national park's policy of total protection. Because predators were largely exterminated, big game had no more natural enemies and were multiplying to excess. The "deer surplus" in turn had an impact on the development of vegetation in the park and especially the forests, which were seriously inhibited by deer grazing on young trees. Under these circumstances, even in a large reserve like the national park, it was "impossible to restore the original *natural equilibrium*," unless—and this was the point Braun-Blanquet wished to make—humans intervened: "Under certain circumstances, *human intervention* in the nature in the park is absolutely essential."[1]

Braun-Blanquet's article appeared a week after a clear majority of Swiss voters had approved a treaty with Italy. This paved the way for the construction of a gigantic hydropower plant that not only included damming the Spöl River, which flowed through the national park, but also placed a small area of the park under water. For these reasons, conservationists had opposed the project. However, a carrot-and-stick approach involving a carefully measured mix of power play, concessions, and compensation had broken the opposition. The Swiss people had made the right decision, Braun-Blanquet assured readers at the end of his article. Given the problems that had beset the Swiss National Park owing to the uncontrolled deer population, "the Spöl question appeared differently, even to park lovers." The obviously admirable efforts to achieve complete protection and reserves should "not necessarily always be followed to their ultimate conclusion."

The legitimate competition for hydropower and the unrestricted growth of large game revealed to Braun-Blanquet the "limits of absolute nature protection," as his essay was subtitled. The concept of the national park as a totally protected reserve had never been entirely undisputed. In the decades after the Second World War, however, the criticism became louder. Apart from the disputes over hydropower and the exploding deer numbers, increasing motorized traffic and the growing number of visitors also contributed to the park's insularity more frequently being called into question. All these problems festered for decades. Nevertheless, they can also be distinguished by the decade in which they dominated the national park agenda: hydropower in the 1950s, traffic and tourism in the 1960s, and the deer issue in the 1970s. I will discuss the topics in this order, all the while considering them in the longer-term context of the twentieth century.

A Faustian Bargain with Water Power

At the end of the First World War the Swiss National Park territory was examined for its suitability for two very different, mutually detrimental purposes as the result of an additional agreement concluded in 1920 between the confederation and the commune of Zernez. Both purposes involved deliberately intervening in nature: The first was the resettlement of ibex, which as described in chapter 4 occurred in 1920. The other issue was the hydraulic use of local waters. Power plant technology had made great strides in the preceding decades, and after the turn of the century, the first large hydroelectric power stations were erected in Grisons. At the same time, plans emerged for the use of the waters of the Engadine and the adjacent valleys. The greatest interest was generated by studies recommending the damming of the Sils Lake in the Upper Engadine. The young heritage protection and conservation movement, with the active support of the *Naturschutzkommission* (SNK), vigorously opposed these plans. The proceedings dragged on for four decades, until in 1944 the communes of Sils and Stampa relinquished their water rights in return for a lump-sum compensation payment from the conservation and heritage protection organizations.[2]

An earlier draft of a plan for a Sils Lake power plant had been introduced in 1918. One of the engineers involved was Adolf von Salis, whom the commune of Zernez had also approached to make a study of hydropower within their municipality. In March 1919 von Salis presented a project for a power plant near Zernez that envisaged hydroelectric exploitation of the Inn and

Spöl Rivers. The project would require damming the Spöl over a distance of some seven kilometers within the national park, which would have created a lake with a maximum width of 330 meters.[3] The commune, which stood to receive a handsome income from the water fees, approved the project, whereas to no one's surprise, the *Eidgenössische Nationalparkkommission* (ENPK) rejected it. But Zernez held the trump card, which it now chose to play. The ENPK wished to expand the national park around the Falcun area to create optimal conditions for the release of ibex. However, the commune refused unless the ENPK would agree to the power plant project. After initial qualms, the ENPK entered into a Faustian bargain, not least because it believed the Salis project would never come to pass. In the supplement to the 1920 service contract with Zernez incorporating the Falcun area into the park, the confederation stipulated that an eventual "damming of the Spöl within the park" would not be opposed.[4]

The ENPK soon regretted this concession. Although nothing did come of the Salis project, the option for hydraulic use of the Spöl remained in effect. In subsequent decades it hung over the ENPK like the sword of Damocles. It bubbled up regularly in the context of potential alterations to the Zernez contract. In 1926 the Zernez communal assembly decided against negotiating an expansion of the park with the ENPK because that same year the SBN had opposed a new plan for a power plant. Six years later, at the time of the 1932 expansion, the commune was keen to see the Spöl option retained. And another six years later, in 1938, as the ENPK was pondering the expiration of the twenty-five-year deadline for amending the 1913 contract, getting rid of the hydropower clause was at the top of its list. When it became clear that so doing would require an entirely new contract, the ENPK decided not to persist and thus lost its last chance to eliminate the clause.[5]

The economic crisis of the 1930s had slowed electricity consumption, and with it the construction of new power plants. Then the Second World War brought an electricity shortage that exposed Switzerland's dependence on foreign resources. A quest for self-sufficiency made expansion of the domestic supply of water power a high economic priority. The electricity industry responded quickly to the changed situation, and in the 1940s began planning for a number of large power plants in the Alps, some of which were remakes of older plans from the 1920s.[6] This was the case in the Lower Engadine: In the 1940s, two rival consortia drew up schemes for the hydraulic exploitation of the area and thus largely thwarted each other until 1954, when they merged into the Engadiner Kraftwerke (EKW). The planning work was further complicated by the cross-border water bodies involved, including the Spöl, which necessitated negotiations at the state level between Switzerland and Italy.[7]

In the 1940s and 1950s several different plans for power plants were proposed. For our purposes, however, the planning history is irrelevant because it does not bear significantly on the representatives of the national park. "We oppose all projects!" declared the *Wissenschaftliche Nationalparkkommission* (WNPK) in 1952. Until the mid-1950s, this was true of all the national park bodies.[8] In 1944, when the power plant plans were taken up again, the ENPK made clear to the Federal Council that exploitation of hydropower in the park was unacceptable: "There can be no coexistence between a large power plant and the national park, only either/or." Building and operating a large power plant would put the survival of the national park at risk, the ENPK wrote to the Federal Council. Withdrawing water from the Spöl would not only impoverish the landscape but also disrupt the natural water balance in the park, which in turn would literally uproot park research. The "value gained from the inventory of park nature (initial condition), which reflects the work of many years and which provides the baseline for assessing the changes and shifts that occur as a result of total protection," would be lost.[9] Plans by the consortia to preserve the landscape by constructing parts of the power plants underground were received as skeptically as was evidence purporting to show that direct removal of water from the Spöl would increase evaporation in the new reservoirs, which would make the dry area more fertile. "Basically, it does not matter whether the climate is improved or impaired," replied Eduard Handschin, chair of the WNPK. "*Any* change, positive or negative, implies substantial intervention in natural processes, which would make the research results obtained thus far and, in any case, the essence of the park an illusion."[10]

The WNPK, the *Naturforschende Gesellschaft* (SNG), and the *Naturschutzbund* (SBN) were unanimous in their support of the ENPK. In 1947 these organizations published a 200-page treatise whose title, "*Nationalpark* oder *internationales Spölkraftwerk*" (National Park or International Spöl Power Plant), pithily encapsulated their uncompromising position.[11] The parties involved insisted on the total protection of the park over human intervention, as stipulated in the federal decree of 1914, and in the following years showed no willingness to give even an inch. This brought them into opposition with the Lower Engadine communes and the canton of Grisons, both of which had strong financial interest in going forward with the plans for a power plant. They were staring at annual water fees of around 500,000 Swiss francs, compared to which the 30,000 francs in rent that the confederation and, to a limited extent, the SBN were paying at the time for the national park seemed like charity. These figures also reflected the disproportionately greater power of the electrical industry.[12]

The legal reference for power plant designers and licensing authorities was the Spöl clause in the supplementary contract of 1920. But didn't the clause contradict the governing federal decree? Supporters and opponents demanded legal opinions that reached opposite conclusions, and thus the legal situation remained in limbo. Consequently, the debates focused on politics, where the lines that separated supporters and opponents seemed immovable and unforgiving—until 1956 when an agreement between the Engadine park communities and the ENPK was reached very quickly. The effort culminating in this "compromise solution" was led personally by the Federal Council, which was both the highest park authority and supreme licensing authority for international hydropower plants. In a commission comprising equal numbers of representatives from the ENPK and the communes, the rigid fronts caved in short order.[13]

What had happened? At the end of 1954 a popular initiative was put to the vote that the nature conservation and heritage protection groups in uniting forces had hoped would bring down plans for a run-of-river plant by Rheinau because of risk to the local rapids. The conservation and heritage groups were soundly trounced. A second water-rights initiative—frequently referred to as Rheinau II—fared no better and was rejected in May 1956. Shortly thereafter the chair of the ENPK submitted an analysis of the events to the commission and estimated the chances of being able to keep a power plant out of the national park as slim. He also pointed out that the park defenders were in opposition to the local population, who "regarded [them] as foreign invaders."[14]

The balance of power had been brutally exposed, and the ENPK used the negotiations initiated by the Federal Council to move quickly from uncompromising resistance to pragmatic mitigation. First, in addition to reaching some concessions regarding the construction process and the assurance of residual water for the Spöl, they achieved a substantial reduction in the size of the Ova Spin compensation reservoir within the park from a net capacity of 28 million cubic meters to 6.5 million cubic meters. At the same time, the park communes agreed to more than compensate the damage from land losses due to the dam through apportioning new park areas. Finally, new park contracts between the confederation and the communes would dispel the persisting legal uncertainties.[15]

Gambling with the National Park

In 1956 the WNPK reversed its position. Reviewing the situation its president had come to see "that we have much more to lose than to win by continuing along a path whose terminus is uncertain."[16] The governing bodies of the SBN seconded the decision. Thus, just as the conflict over the Spöl power plant and the struggle for the integrity of the national park became symbols of conservation up to 1956, now almost overnight the compromise solution was seen as the vehicle of a recommitment to nature protection. In addition to the two devastating votes, two other factors may have favored this change in thinking. First, in five short years, the membership of the SBN had shrunk from around fifty thousand to forty thousand in 1956. It was feared that the old slogans would attract no new adherents. Second, the radicalization of the conservationist positions in the fight against hydropower had brought a huge number of members to turn their back on the SBN. In 1953 to 1955 alone the organization suffered fifteen thousand defections.[17] Finally, scientists, whose support had always been critical to the SBN, increasingly kept their distance and warned against ideologically rigid conservation.[18]

How the fight against the power plant made the national park into a symbol of typically Swiss conservation, and how this symbol was radically reinterpreted after 1956, is revealed by a close reading of two texts by Hans Zbinden: *Das Spiel um den Spöl* (Gambling With the Spöl), published in 1953, and *Der Schweizer Naturschutz vor erweiterten Aufgaben* (Expanding the Role of Swiss Conservation), which appeared in 1957.[19] Zbinden was a cultural sociologist, publisher, and president of the *Schweizerischer Schriftstellerverband* (Swiss Writers' Association), and one of the most wildly read cultural critics of the postwar decades. In the 1950s he joined the board of the SBN, serving as its representative to the ENPK from 1954, and also in the committee, which drafted the "compromise solution" for the Spöl in 1956. In a letter written in 1953 Zbinden underscored the uncompromising position of the ENPK and SBN in blunt terms. The "dishonest and shameful game that is being played with the Spöl" had to stop. There was no interim solution, no compromise that would not betray the heart of the matter. If a power plant were approved, the founders' idea of a park, as enshrined in the federal decree of 1914, "would not only be altered; it would be annihilated."[20] Zbinden deliberately upped the stakes. At issue for the national park was not only one of the last bits of largely intact nature in the country, but its entire raison d'être. Accordingly, through the medium of Zbinden's words the national park became a symbol of the Swiss *Willensnation* (a nation forged by common will) and, according to the concluding sentence of his book, a "monument to the spirit" that "in critical decisions has always and forever elevated our land above petty desires and purely material interests. It is the spirit that our country possesses and honors and that deep down also sustains and nourishes it."[21] In invoking the *Landesgeist* (national spirit), Zbinden was alluding obviously to the *Geistige Landesverteidigung,* which during the 1930s had been conceived as a bulwark against cultural assimilation within Switzerland of Nazi ideas and that was intended to continue to strengthen Swiss autonomy through a government-sponsored cultural policy. According to a key passage in the so-called cultural dispatch produced by the Federal Council in 1938, Switzerland was a product not of race or flesh but of a common spirit.[22] In the following years the notion of spirit was linked to military defense. In this compound form, it survived the end of the Second World War and enjoyed a revival during the Cold War in the defense against "communist activities." In his foreword to Zbinden's book, Urs

Dietschi also drew on the *Geistige Landesverteidigung* and its central construct of a centuries-old tradition of national self-assertion and self-determination. For the renowned conservationist, federal councilor, and chair of the *Eidgenössische Natur- und Heimatschutzkommission* (Federal Commission for Nature and Heritage Protection), "suddenly the fight over our forefathers' soil [had turned] inward. Let us beware that we do not squander the heritage of our fathers in a few short decades, nor that the confederate's humane willingness to make sacrifices is not lost in the anonymous destiny of the utility-oriented masses." After grappling first with the federal state and then with "social questions," a further, very important task remained: to protect indigenous nature from rampant technology. "The debate over the national park has come to symbolize this new *Kulturkampf*."[23]

Four years later, the rhetoric had altered. Although Zbinden was still trying to tame the tide of technology, he had substituted his frontal tactics with a call for cooperation. "Conservation and technology must liberate themselves from their claims to primacy and join together to find solutions that will help to shape the domestic landscape and settlement in an organic fashion." This was "not in any way a concession," Zbinden claimed in defending his change of heart. Rather, it was a "broader struggle" for a richer and more beautiful human existence that depended on both conservation and technology.[24] Balance and an overall view, far-sighted planning and landscaping were the concepts key to a fundamental reorientation of nature conservation. Conservation would have to set aside its emphatically museum-like approach, stop being defensive, and accept the task "of reshaping broad-ranging, creative interventions." The national parks, too, were cultural achievements and therefore "in reality themselves ... part of the modern cultural landscape, as reserves set apart for scientific, ethical, and aesthetic goals."[25] Ultimately, Zbinden was seeking the full integration of nature conservation into the capitalist economy, as his exemplary discussion of road construction showed. "In calculating costs," wrote Zbinden, "the claims of landscape preservation and landscape shaping should be considered as important as road surface and land acquisition."[26] The future of conservation lay not in looking back but in planning forward; not in knee-jerk confrontation but in meaningful collaboration. In this light, reaching agreement about the national park suddenly became a model that could be built on, and that subsequently would be built on.

In the late 1950s the SBN made a significant course correction. On the one hand, conservation had relaxed its fixation on reserves and, on the other hand, was increasingly aiming to achieve its goals through collaboration. This had two consequences: First, social criticism gave way to political pragmatism; second, amid a widening field, the national park lost its previously central position. When, a decade-and-a-half later, the environmental movement set out to revolutionize conservation, the national park was scarcely an issue.[27]

Its turnabout on the national park initially cost the SBN serious internal turmoil. In autumn 1956 three board members quit, including the chair, Arthur Uehlinger, who opposed the compromise solution. To effectively continue the fight, the dissidents founded their own national park committee. A local resistance movement called the *Lia Naira* (Black League) was also forming around the same time, but it found little support among the population.[28] In 1957 these two groups together organized a national park initiative and a referendum opposing the treaty with Italy that was part of the compromise solution to pave the way for the power plant. The SBN half-heartedly supported both initiative and referendum after a majority of the members overturned the opposing position of the governing body. But the referendum had no chance with the voters. In December 1958 it was shot down in a popular vote by a clear majority of three to one. The opponents of the power plant now realized the futility of further resistance and withdrew the previously submitted national park initiative.[29]

The cessation of hostilities opened the way for a new federal resolution on the national park and new contracts between the government and the communes, which also now included the commune of Scuol. In 1961 Zernez and S-chanf contributed three new areas to the park for a total area of around ten square kilometers (see chapter 3, table 1 and map 3). In 1962, after the last legal problems with Italy had been resolved, the Engadiner Kraftwerke decided to start construction. In the next seven years the national park near Ova Spin—including the area by Punt dal Gall, where a large arch dam was erected along the border—was turned into a construction site. To gain access to the site from Switzerland, a road tunnel was built under the park area, which after completion of the construction was opened for private transport and shortly thereafter became a busy link into Livigno in Italy.[30]

Switzerland was not the only country where, during the postwar period, the interests of conservation clashed with those of hydropower. In all industrialized countries, rapid economic growth was accompanied by a rapidly growing demand for electricity. While every new power plant lessened the number of hydraulically exploitable rivers, the value of still-to-be-exploited ones increased. "White coal" was developed at the cost of the remaining stocks of "wilderness," and the conflicts that arose from this tradeoff were the most acute and symbolically weighted when they involved one of the showpieces of conservation—the national parks. One region rich in conflict zones was the American West. After the Second World War the US National Park Service came under increased pressure from the Bureau of Reclamation, which was planning the all-encompassing exploitation of western water power, even including areas within the jurisdiction of the park service. At the end of 1950, when the tension between these two government agencies (both part of the Department of the Interior) reached a peak, the directorate of the NPS received a memorandum from the regional bureau in Omaha, Nebraska. The

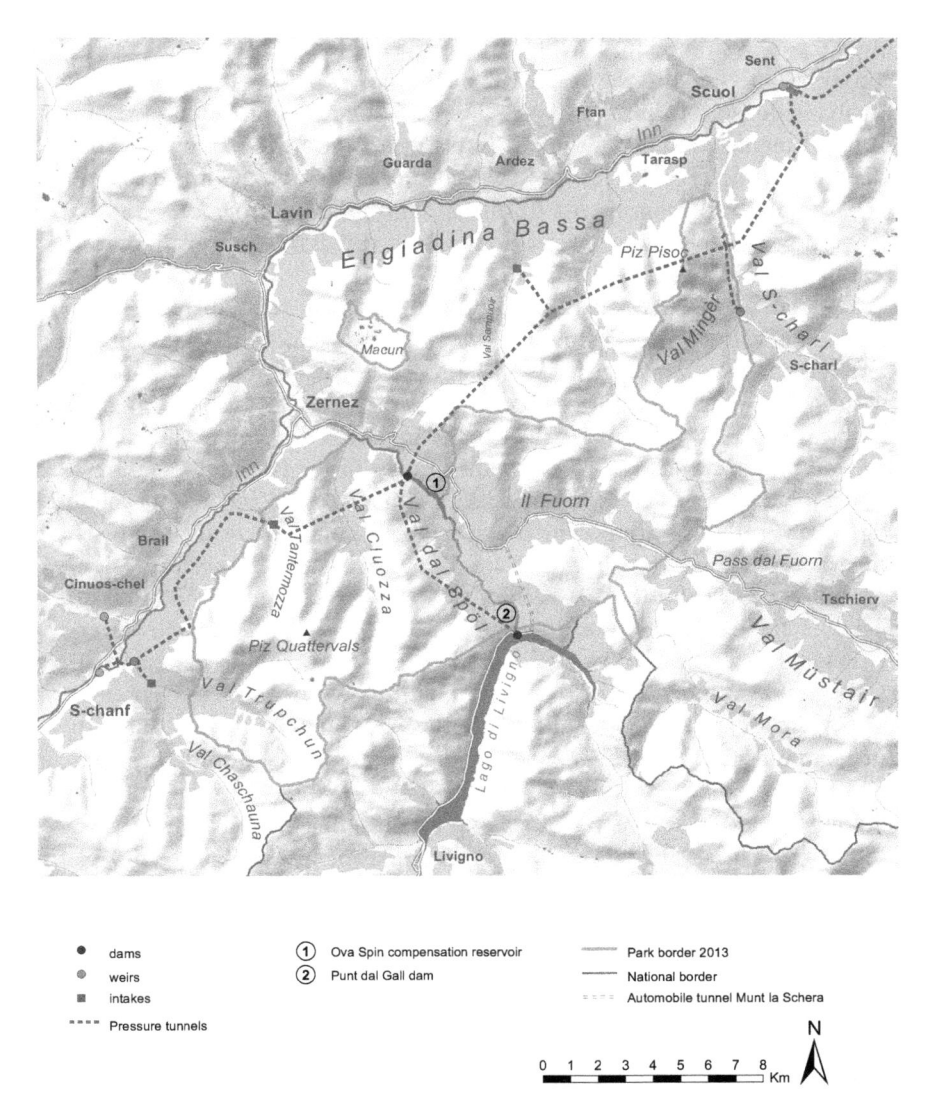

Map 4. Hydraulic installations. *Source:* GIS-SNP, Swiss National Park, Spatial Information Department.

memorandum concerned the Swiss National Park. The situation there, wrote the NPS employee, "closely parallel[s] some in our own areas."[31] Attached to the correspondence was a transcript of a piece that Swiss radio had aired on the Spöl question as well as a memorandum from Rocky Mountain National Park Superintendent David Canfield, who played an active role in organizing the resistance to a dam project at Echo Park in Dinosaur National Monument.

Over the 1950s the Echo Park Dam became the focal point of the American conservation vs. hydropower debate. In an unprecedented national campaign involving dozens of conservationist and recreational organizations, the protestors had managed to block the power plant project. In 1956 Congress passed a law excepting areas along the Colorado River that lay within the national parks or national monuments from the dam-building project. For an entire generation of American conservationists, the successful fight over Echo Park represented a transformative experience.[32]

The clashes in Switzerland and the United States ran substantially along similar lines, but with varying degrees of success. One important difference between the two campaigns was that the American opposition was broader based and included both the tourism and recreational sector. This opposition was more comparable with the one in Switzerland that had prevented the damming of the Sils Lake at the beginning of the twentieth century than with the contemporary Spöl opposition, which wished to save the national park. The Spöl opposition, which was largely limited to conservationists, on the other hand, was more reminiscent of the well-known American preservation movement from the 1910s that tried in vain to stop the flooding of the Hetch Hetchy Valley in Yosemite National Park. In two respects, however, the two contemporaneous movements of the 1950s did tread the same path: Both controversies influenced the respective alignment of national movements and both won for conservation hitherto unheard of publicity. This publicity in turn had unintended consequences: "One of the supreme ironies in American wilderness history was the appearance of a new problem (loving the Grand Canyon to death) as a result of solving an old one (the dam threat)," writes Roderick Nash regarding the long-term consequences of the victory of the conservationists on the issue of Echo Park. The debates taught Americans not only what wonderful sanctuaries they possessed, but also that they existed to be visited.[33] The same irony is also a feature of Swiss National Park history (though here the dam threat was not averted). For 1958, the year of the Spöl vote, the ENPK reported a new visitor record: "There is no doubt that the lively controversy over the Spöl referendum and the national park initiative in the press, radio, and lectures increased interest in our national reserve and moved many to visit it."[34] It would not be the last record.

Calling All Nature Lovers

In the war year of 1942 the tourist office in Grisons published a "little guide through the national park." A foreword by the president of the SBN opened and authorized the slim, photo-illustrated booklet, whose perforated last page was an application form for SBN membership. A brief introduction advised readers how they should prepare themselves for a visit to the park. Then followed a short outline of the history of the national park, and a few pages on flora and fauna. In addition, the guide offered eighteen walks through the park and its environs, topped off by an excerpt from the park regulations. The guide, which came with a bird's-eye view of the area, filled a need that would multiply in the coming years. By 1968 it had gone through eight print runs, five alone in the 1960s.[35]

In the section on wildlife in the national park, the guide first told readers that bears, lynx, wolves, and vultures had unfortunately been eradicated before the park was founded, and then listed the species to be found in the park: First and foremost, the (re)settled ibex, then the other ungulates, chamois, deer and roe deer, and finally the rest of the mammals and birds (invertebrates were not mentioned). "Now," began the final paragraph, "the main question of visitors about the home of all these park residents—a question that is reasonable and that also has already disappointed many. Wildlife in the park is not domesticated or tame; it will not approach strangers like the bears in Yellowstone Park in America. He who wishes to see wildlife must get up early, walk the trails quietly and calmly, and not believe that animals can be won over by yodeling and noise. However, he who knows how to use his eyes, treads softly, and if possible possesses good binoculars will find that the mountains in the park will readily reveal their hidden secrets."[36]

The emphasis on quiet enjoyment of nature was as typical of the description of the Swiss National Park experience as was the comparison with Yellowstone and the United States. The guide also employed language that sought both to imitate and differentiate and that can be traced back to the founding years of the Swiss National Park. In 1908, when Hermann Christ assessed the American national park regulations for their potential as a model, he found them worth copying but also pointed out salient differences: Not only was the magnitude of the parks in the United States very different, wrote Christ; "the goal [too] is very different. In America, everything is designed above all to cater to the relaxation and pleasure of the public, which results in the pursuit of the greatest openness and accessibility. The state also seems content to define protection broadly: Camping by large groups who gather wood to make fires is permitted, as is fishing, and naturally botanizing, picking bouquets etc.; even uprooting plants seems to be allowed." For Switzerland's own protected areas, other points of view would pertain. "Naturally, some of our reserves too cannot do without paths open to visitors. But the question does arise what sorts of visitors will be tolerated in our reserves. For sure tourist groups and camps with bonfires are out of the question." In ending, Christ wrote, "The conclusion is that we can accept most of the measures used by the American parks for our reserves, but we must ensure to largely eliminate from them those provisions designed for the delectation of the public, and devise more and stronger rules for protection, up to and including a ban on any interference with nature, which may even be extended to prohibiting access to certain assets."[37] Which, as I showed in chapter 2, was subsequently implemented.

A few days after completing this report, which was aimed at the NSK, Christ shared his ideas with a wider public. In the newspaper *Basler Nachrichten* he called on readers to follow the American example and to create national parks in Switzerland. He spoke of the great care Americans took of their natural beauty, leaving out the tiny matter of targeted marketing. And for good reason: Switzerland's natural beauty should be protected from precisely that kind of packaging: "When a world power like the United States lavishes such care on its natural beauty, which it truly possesses in greater abundance and expanse, let us protect our relatively smaller natural miracles—so long as they shall exist—with strong, national measures and shield them from any further exploitation by greedy speculators!" Christ blamed the speculation and its attendant "vulgarization of the noblest alpine mountains" on the ruthlessly expanding tourism industry.[38] In fact, in 1908 Swiss alpine tourism had been enjoying a twenty-year boom that had started in the wake of the economic crisis of the 1880s and that saw middle-class mass tourism added to the former luxury tourism. In those two decades, the tourist infrastructure expanded massively. New railroads eased and shortened travel to mountainous regions, where a rapidly growing number of hotels and cog railways awaited both domestic and foreign tourists.[39]

After the turn of the century, tourist development of the Alps encountered increasing opposition. In 1906 the license application for a railway up the Matterhorn sparked a veritable mass protest that in subsequent years was taken up by nature conservation and heritage protection.[40] In his newspaper article Christ referred to "Matterhorn vandalism," which for him underscored the urgency of establishing national parks before the last alpine areas fell victim to tourism. As Christ rightly stated in his SNK report, in the United States tourism and nature protection had a very different relationship to one another. When Yellowstone National Park was launched, the railroad companies were already involved, which enthusiastically welcomed additional destinations on their East–West routes. The impact of tourism and the influence of transportation companies, and later automobile associations, increased in the early decades of the twentieth century. Utilitarian ideology, which conceived nature as natural resources, shaped the national park idea. The loss of Hetch Hetchy Valley, which despite violent protest led by John Muir was carved out of Yosemite National Park prior to the First World War and dammed to supply water to San Francisco, led to a rethink of the conservation movement among idealistic groups. To obtain broader political support for their concerns, after heated debate the activists rephrased their arguments in utilitarian terms. The result was a broad consensus that the national parks should offer the greatest number of Americans not just national pride but also outdoor recreation.[41]

In addition, profits from tourism that had previously leaked abroad should now flow into the domestic economy. "See America First" was the slogan of a national campaign from the 1910s whose standard-bearers were the national parks. One of the many ironies of the global history of national parks is that, in the creation of the Swiss National Park, alpine tourism became the bogeyman, whereas it served as a shining example for tourist development in the American national parks. Both the existing and new national parks were to be established and developed along the lines of Swiss alpine tourism. America earned practically nothing from its landscape, asserted a congressman in 1915 in the debate over the bill to establish Rocky Mountains National Park, "while Switzerland derives from $10,000 to $40,000 per square mile per year from scenery that is not equal to ours. But Switzerland knows that the public is ready and willing to pay for scenery, and they have developed it for selling purposes."[42] Moreover, Swiss alpine tourism was not only a model to envy but also the competition to beat. The outbreak of the war in 1914, which essentially brought transatlantic tourism to a standstill, created favorable conditions for the latter. In 1915 Mark Daniels, general superintendent of the national parks, declared bellicosely, "War with Switzerland!"[43]

In a widely read article in *The Nation's Business* in June 1916 titled "Making a Business of Scenery," the influential writer and conservationist Robert Sterling Yard advocated creating a national park administration and also provided an extensive wish list:

> We want our national parks developed. We want roads and trails like Switzerland's. We want hotels of all prices from lowest to highest. We want comfortable public camps in sufficient abundance to meet all demands. We want lodges and chalets at convenient intervals commanding the scenic possibilities of all our parks. We want the best and cheapest accommodations for pedestrians and motorists. We want sufficient and convenient transportation at reasonable rates. We want adequate facilities and supplies for camping out at lowest prices. We want good fishing. We want our wild animal life conserved and developed. We want special facilities for nature study.[44]

The lobbying was effective, and in the very same year the National Park Service was established. The new federal agency was trusted with the delicate task of guiding the parks toward sustainable tourism, to use today's parlance, or, according to the wording in the so-called Organic Act, the 1916 founding bill of the National Park Service, "as will leave them unimpaired for the enjoyment of future generations."[45]

In Switzerland the *Bündner Verkehrsverein* advertised the future park as an excursion destination, and the Rhaetian railway supported it now and again with infusions of funds or in-kind contributions, such as transporting ibex or building the national park museum in Chur. But a symbiotic collaboration between the national park movement and transportation and tourist industries like that in the United States would have been unthinkable in Switzerland. Because of the park founders' stance against commercial exploitation of the Alps, the park began with a deeply ambivalent attitude toward tourism, to say the least. The consensus among park supporters was that mass tourism to the park was to be avoided at all costs. At the same time, it was agreed that the park could not be closed to the general public. For two reasons, it seemed opportune to allow park visits in some ways. First, the ability of the SNK to achieve its objectives depended on public and political support at both the national and local level. Federal support for an area restricted to science only would have been much more difficult to obtain. In turn, leasing of the communes' lands could be made palatable not only with the nonmaterial gratitude of the fatherland and the payment of rent but also with additional income from tourism generated by the park.[46] For the ailing region, whose main industries—agriculture and forestry—had long been in crisis, and compared with the Upper Engadine had benefited only marginally from tourism so far, this was an interesting perspective. Moreover, the founders had envisaged the park as having an educational in addition to a scientific purpose. The park should constitute an ethical example of a place that was open to everyone and where "everything for everyone" would be sustained.[47] Those who answered the call of the park would be richly rewarded. "Through this breath of original nature in the rich flora and fauna, the park will be a place of edification for every nature lover. Its doors will be open wide to all," wrote Carl Schröter in one of his innumerable writings that helped spread word about the park both at home and abroad. In lofty terms he urged people to visit the park, but cautioned them to behave with the reverence as befits a visit to a (natural) sanctuary: "Though seized with a feeling of awe, the visitor should direct his steps quietly through the sanctuary so as not to interfere with the wildlife. No loud hotel hustle and bustle to greet him, no automobiles chugging along: trails and footbridges, accommodation and meals will be of a simple, alpine character."[48] The ordinary tourist would do well to satisfy his profane needs elsewhere.

For park visits, which were concentrated in the summer—in the winter, most of the snow-covered park region was inaccessible—a rudimentary infrastructure was put in place and styled– as Schröter wished: with an "alpine simplicity" that at the same time was very well suited to the perpetual shortage of funds. In 1911 the SNK built a hut in Val Cluozza that provided meals and overnight dormitory accommodation for up to twenty visitors.[49] The hut, which also served as lodging for the first park warden, Hermann Langen, and his family, could only be reached after a several-hours-long trek on foot. For his self-sufficiency and the provisioning of visitors, Langen maintained a small farm in the park. In addition to a milk cow and a pony for transportation, he also initially kept goats, pigs, and chickens, which was forbidden by the ENPK in 1916.[50] Langen's business became the subject of repeated complaints, especially from Zernez, whose hotels and restaurants saw it as competition.[51] An existing hotel on the Ofenpass road also ended up being within the perimeter of the park, and further on formed an enclave within. Its owner Jon Pitschen Grass-Brunies, who was married to a sister of ENPK member and park supervisor Steivan Brunies, started right away to use the national park in advertising his hotel.[52] To traverse the park, the administration established a network of trails that visitors were forbidden to leave. Finally, in the 1910s the park's first maps and trail descriptions appeared.[53]

At first the park attracted only a few visitors, due in part to the outbreak of the First World War in 1914. The war in the Austrian-Italian Alps was fought in the vicinity of the park, and going through it was only possible with a permit from the army, which had stationed troops in the park region to secure the national borders. In any event, the researchers working in the park were quite happy to see fewer visitors in those years. After the war more people came to the park, to which the ENPK responded with mixed feelings.[54] "As pleasing as we are to have this display of interest in our national undertaking, the increasing visits do have a downside," remarked the commission in its annual report of 1927.[55] The commission was being pushed from various sides to regulate park visits differently, but it stuck to the existing rules. It resisted, for example, the demands of both those who wished to close the Cluozza hut and those who wanted easier access to it. Unlike in the United States, the ENPK emphasized in its annual report of 1925, the Swiss National Park was not intended to "serve as a pleasure destination" but rather "was established for more serious purposes, the pure and uplifting pleasure of enjoyment in undisturbed nature."[56] Hans Bachmann, who in those years represented the SNG within the ENPK, hewed the same line: "You would not believe the parade of characters that come to Cluoza," wrote the biologist mockingly in a report on his trip to the park in summer 1928. The physical fitness and equipment required for a visit worked as a selection mechanism. One should, Bachmann admonished, "not wish for more convenient access. In summer, Val Cluoza would experience a veritable influx, and of a public that is not desired in the national park. Control would be impossible, and the quiet, which the animals currently enjoy in the depths of the valley, would vanish."[57]

The increased attendance was also due in part to shifts in transportation. Contrary to Carl Schröter's hopes, mass motorization did not stop at the borders of the national park. In 1925 Grisons lifted its ban on automobiles, thus bringing to an end a 25-year-long exception within Switzerland and Europe.[58]

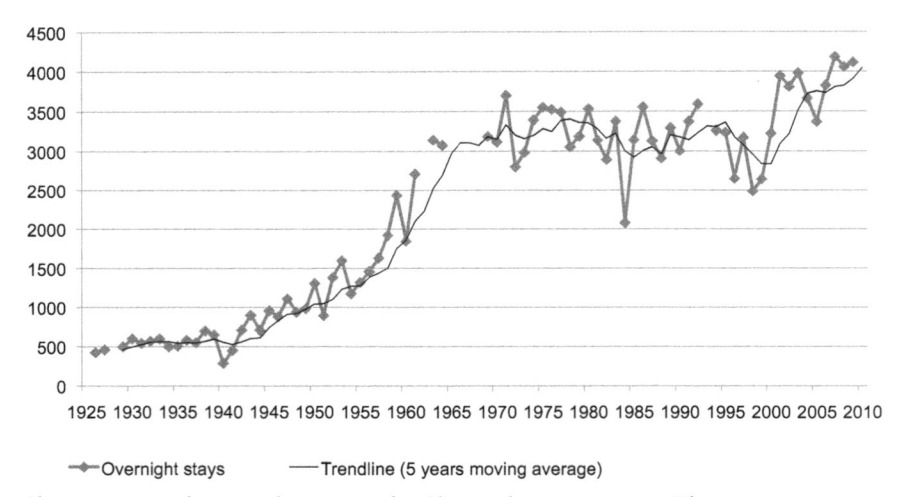

Chart 3. Annual overnight stays in the Cluozza hut, 1926–2008. The strong annual fluctuations are due, among other things, to the weather. Because the hut had only a limited number of beds, it could be booked out. Indeed, from 1970 onward the stagnating number of overnight stays may well have been due to the capacity limit. *Source:* ENPK annual reports (missing data: 1928, 1962, 1965–68; in 1993 the Cluozza hut was closed due to renovation).

Thereafter, the cantonal development of private automobile traffic rapidly caught up with the general trend. The road over the Ofen Pass, which linked Val Müstair to the Engadine across the national park, was expanded for motorized through traffic. In the 1960s, in connection with the power plant construction, the road was further extended to the Livigno Valley in Italy. Now, on peak days, thousands of cars traversed the park. In 1973, for the first time, more than 100,000 cars crossed through Munt la Schera tunnel, which had been opened to traffic three years previously, leading from the Ofenpass road to the Punt dal Gall dam. The road then went right over the dam to Livigno). In 1987 the 200,000 mark was reached, and in 2009—the record year—it hit 300,000.[59] Already in 1979, when the numbers of cars was still in the neighborhood of 150,000 per year, the Federal Council pronounced traffic in the national park as a "greater disruption than the power plant."[60]

The effect on the park of the canton's opening to automobile traffic was made clear in a document prepared in 1933 by Eduard Handschin, chair of the WNPK, for the SBN and ENPK. In it Handschin compared his experience in the summer of 1933 with the period between 1917 and 1926 in which he had regularly visited the park in connection with work on springtails and beetles. Following brief remarks on the evolution of the park flora and fauna, Handschin turned to traffic and visits. "The entire Ofenberg road has changed tremendously. The daily, greatly increased traffic over the Ofen Pass makes it nearly unnavigable on foot. For most of the day, a thick cloud hangs over the road area, and the dust that settles on the roadside out to ca. 10 m has considerably altered the variety of the fauna there." The "constant beeping," which was audible far away, could only be disturbing to the wildlife. The situation was hard to compare with that of car traffic in the American national parks because the animals in the much smaller Swiss park had no refuge. Moreover, "visits to the park had grown substantially, which from the vantage of the *Bund* [here it is unclear whether Handschin means the federal government or the SBN] was very much welcomed. But I have the feeling that a genie has been let loose that will not easily be contained." In addition, some visitors would not obey the park rules. "Sunbathing and nudism have no place in Sur il Foss, much less cooking over an open fire on the upper Mingèr meadow." Nor was the "mass deployment of tent camps and lavish fireworks on 1 August [Swiss national holiday] likely to ensure the necessary quiet." In the interest of the park, opined Handschin, appropriate measures for calming the atmosphere should be considered, including stronger rules for visitors as well as a moderate reduction in visits and means of reducing automobile traffic.[61]

"People who do not respect the park rules should be dealt with more severely," asserted the ENPK later in its annual report.[62] The following year (1934), new park regulations were released along with a little map showing the paths on which visitors were permitted to walk. Entry to the rest of the park area was strictly prohibited. Exceptions were granted for research purposes, but these could no longer be obtained from park wardens on site but had to be applied for from the ENPK beforehand. In 1938 the network of trails and the park rules were also posted at the main entrance to the park as well as at the train station in Zernez and on bulletin boards in the Cluozza hut.[63] In 1939, in celebrating the twenty-fifth anniversary of the federal decree on the park, the ENPK looked back. Despite the remote location of the area and the correspondingly long and expensive trip, visits had continually increased, asserted the commission before reiterating its ambivalence toward this development: "As pleased as we are by the interest shown by the large number of guests, we must ensure that it does not compromise the very purpose of the reserve."[64]

This statement should not obscure the fact that the national park was still only a small niche product in the overall offering of Swiss tourism. Few tourists took any notice of the park. American visitors were particularly struck by its minor importance as a tourist destination compared with their own national parks. For many American tourists, and even those back home, all of Switzerland was a national park: "Many people who have completed one of the usual tours of Switzerland depart with the impression of a small country which seems to be but one large national park containing some of the most wonderful beauties of nature," stated a staff member of the American consulate in Zurich in a piece written for the Smithsonian Institution's annual report of 1926, then clarified for her compatriots: "However, away toward the eastern frontier, rather off the beaten track of the tourist, lies a small inclosed region which is Switzerland's real or official national park."[65]

And the Tourists Came

The notion of what constituted high park attendance in the 1930s was put paid in the 1950s. The Second World War caused visitor numbers to plummet initially, but by the mid-1950s the park commission reported record attendance nearly every year. On the one hand, in those years the park was benefiting from tourism that accompanied rapidly increasing national and international prosperity; on the other hand, the Spöl controversy had both increased publicity for the park and raised concern about it. In its annual report of 1959, the ENPK announced a need for action: "Increasing the accommodation options for visitors, guided tours of the park, an information center, etc. Note, however, that the purpose of the Swiss National Park is first and foremost scientific research, and only secondarily for tourism."[66] However, the possibilities for controlling visits were limited because the park's marked trails were freely accessible. Increased monitoring, better information, and cautious expansion of infrastructure were the cornerstones of the strategy put in place to come to grips with the swelling crowds of visitors. At the same time, the resolution of the power plant dispute and the corresponding revision of the federal law helped to boost the park's budget. In the 1960s the new funds enabled hiring of additional park wardens and the first full-time park director, the choice of which understandably fell to a scientist, wildlife biologist Robert Schloeth. In 1968 a visitor center created in Zernez that also served as an administrative building went into operation, solving the perceived lack of an on-site information center. The ENPK had already taken the increased traffic into account in 1956 by erecting parking spots along the Ofenpass road from which the park could be explored on foot.

Compared with the more than 100 million visitors to the American parks, the 100,000 visitors reported for 1965 by the Swiss National Park's new park directorate was modest. Moreover, these estimates, like those for the following year, were probably much too high (see chart 4). In those years, however, the numbers held up and formed the statistical basis for discussions. In particular, the growth rate seemed dramatic. In an internal report from 1967 based on developments in America, park director Schloeth projected 400,000 visitors for 1976 and 1,000,000 for 1986. An article by Schloeth published in the SBN magazine the following year (1968) in connection with the opening of the national park house in Zernez was titled "500,000 Visitors to the National Park

Illustration 9. Cover of the 1942 guide to the Swiss National Park. *Source:* Verkehrsverein Graubünden 1942.

in 1978?!" The emphatic punctuation tellingly expressed dismay, disapproval, and helplessness in the face of seemingly unstoppable growth in tourism.[67] Actual developments surpassed prophecy: At the start of the 1970s the annual visitor count was estimated at just under 300,000. The park director sounded the alarm: In the 1971 annual report he referred to "oversaturation" of certain areas and thought it highly unlikely "that the Swiss National Park would be able to meet the ever-increasing demand for recreation over the long term."[68] In 1973 the visitor count broke its prior record without triggering specific control measures. The following year the number stabilized at an estimated 250,000 visitors, in line with a general trend in industrialized countries (in developing countries, the trend continued upward). The figures for the American national parks, for instance, told a similar story.[69] In the 1980s the number of visitors to the Swiss National Park then declined slightly. When the local tourism industry complained of empty beds, the park administration was sympathetic but "from the perspective of the park there is no cause for concern due to lack of tourists."[70] Despite the slippage, the numbers were still viewed by the park administration as exceeding capacity.

The postwar decade brought forth to the national park the genie foretold by Eduard Handschin in 1933. The proximal causes were two: First, despite misgivings, in 1910 the decision was made to name the protected area after the American national park, thus committing itself to a designation that would become a national brand for nature tourism and would also shape visitor expectations for the Swiss National Park. Second, no park system had been established such as had been done in the United States and in other countries. Fifty years after the founding of the Swiss National Park, it was still the only one in the country. The existing national park thus was exposed to the full force of tourism-related greed. In an internal report written in 1967 Schloeth fairly judged Switzerland as having "omitted to take into account, in a timely fashion, the massive development of tourism, nature protection, and the need for recreational areas."[71] Schloeth produced this clear-sighted report, titled "The SNP today—and tomorrow," in connection with a study trip to the United States, that is, a country that was peerless in its determination to position national parks as magnets for tourists and that was also a trendsetter in modern leisure. Schloeth was visibly impressed by what he had seen of the American Park Service during the four-week continuing education course. Switzerland was lagging, Schloeth wrote, and this deficit had to be remedied. Accordingly, he proposed a number of measures that partly applied to the park but that were especially targeted at national policy. He suggested that other national parks be established, as well as "national recreational areas" and "nature parks," that "as a second category of national parks" could serve the "simpler needs of tourists for experiences relating to nature and above all

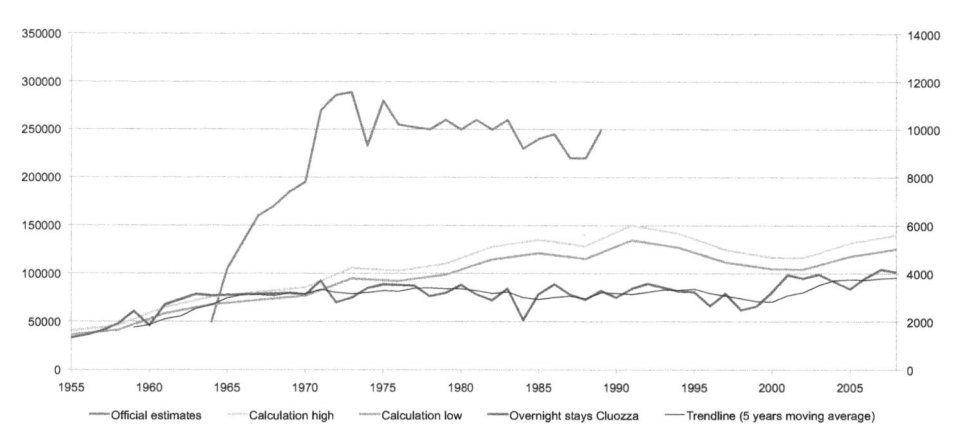

Chart 4. Number of visitors to the Swiss National Park, 1955–2008. Official annual estimates and subsequent calculations (left axis) and overnight stays at the Cluozza hut (right axis). Until the 1960s, no statistics on visitors were collected. Under national park director Schloeth (1964–89) visitor figures were estimated annually as part of general observations and surveys. In 2007 and 2008 reliable attendance figures were determined for the first time by counting mats on the floor (see Wernli 2009). A retrospective calculation based on these figures, shows that previous estimates in most cases were too high.

To arrive at the visitor numbers from 1955 to 2008, first the ratio of overnight stays in Zernez to visitors to the national park for 2007 and 2008 was calculated. Next, using Grisons tourism statistics that provided comparative figures for Zernez from 1955, the park visitor numbers for that year were reconstructed. Accordingly, the calculation was based on the assumption that the ratio of overnight stays in Zernez to national park visitors remained stable over the years. The plausibility of this assumption rests on two grounds: Over the entire period considered Zernez was by far the favored starting point for excursions into the national park, and the park was always clearly the main tourist attraction of the region (see Küpfer 2000). The calculation was run with data for both 2007 and 2008. For 2007, the ratio of overnight stays to park visits was 2.14, and for 2008 it was 1.92. The lower value for 2008 can be explained by the significantly poor weather that year, which may have deterred holiday makers in Zernez from going to the park. In contrast, in 2007 the summer season was ideal for park visits: warmer than average, with little snow or rain (see Wernli 2009, part 2). The ratio calculated for 2007 could therefore be taken to be representative of years with good weather conditions, and 2008 representative of years with bad weather conditions. The calculated values are not precise but offer a good approximation of the actual number of visitors.

Source: SNP official visitor numbers: ENPK annual reports. Overnight stays in Zernez: Federal Statistical Office, Economic Development and Tourism Agency of the Canton Grisons. My calculations.

wildlife." Coordination would ensure a "Swiss National Park service" along the lines of the US model. Schloeth's recommendations were clearly motivated by the hope of relieving the existing tourism burden on the national park by building a national structure. Nature protection and nature tourism should be decoupled: "The people want to consume nature. Thus, you must prepare one portion of it, make it tasty, and preserve the other part."[72] Schloeth found support for this view five years later, in 1972, at the Second World Conference on National Parks. The "burning question" of how the national parks could stem the tide of visitors dominated the conference in Yellowstone, wrote Schloeth in his report. The formal recommendations made at the end of the conference included a "general determination to stop mixing tourism and nature protection in national parks and similar areas."[73] However, Schloeth's repeated urgings to create a national park system found little support within the ENPK. The issue was beyond the scope of the commission, it was said, and the SBN feared that Schloeth's plans would get in the way of an inventory of "landscapes and natural monuments of national importance" that at the time the SBN was trying to establish together with other organizations pursuing similar goals. The creation of a national park in French-speaking Switzerland—a project that had been proposed once previously during the interwar period—was briefly discussed, then rapidly faded from the picture along with the larger idea.[74]

"Recreational Instruction"

Schloeth had more success with his recommendations for the national park itself. "Recreational Instruction" was the motto that he devised for dealing with tourists and that he stuck to for his entire twenty-five years as park director.[75] In this spirit, attempts were immediately made to educate visitors, which more often was analogous to tilting at windmills. In any event, the annual reports were full of complaints about violations of rules and perpetually new forms of unseemly behavior. "The mindless tossing or deliberate hiding of waste has again been increasing at an almost alarming rate," read the annual report of 1981. "As a result, our park wardens are reduced to garbage collectors, whereas they were actually trained to expound on protected nature. Unfortunately, with the increase in essentially disinterested and superficial speedy visitors, these unnecessary activities and peacekeeping duties claim much too much time. With the rise of 'modern' mass tourism, as the original vision of our national park becomes a mere object for tourists, the job of a park warden will accordingly inevitably and inexorably be devalued."[76] Schloeth believed his informational concept to be at risk, and the following spring returned to the United States to draw inspiration from the nature interpretation as pursued in the American national parks since the 1920s.[77]

Over the decades, national park officials were clearly consistent in their handling of tourism. When people were there, they made efforts to instruct them and to maintain proper park behavior. However, they would have preferred that most of these people not come in the first place, since by the 1920s they already felt there were too many of them. The common tourist was perceived as an invasive species who posed a danger to the nature in the park and whose damage potential had to be contained. In the second half of the 1970s, when discussions began on whether to create a "Lower Engadine nature park" with the national park as its core zone, Schloeth reacted negatively to the idea because he anticipated no lessening of the visitor pressure on the national park but rather even an increase due to the resulting publicity.[78] This defensive posture went hand in hand with a practice of publicly profiling the park as little as possible. In the 1930s, when travel agencies and local hotels began to host the first organized group trips to the national park, the ENPK was concerned. Emil Abderhalden, a Swiss biologist who was teaching in Halle in Germany, complained to the commission that former park warden Hermann Langen, who had opened a tourist pension in Zernez while he was still a warden, had in so doing "commercially exploited the Swiss national shrine," bringing up old aspersions against Langen's German origins. Park wardens had been prohibited from taking on private guide services since 1917. Inevitably Langen's establishment gave rise to tensions involving both the ENPK and the local authorities and hoteliers and eventually led to his retirement as park warden in 1935.[79] When discussing Abderhalden's complaints the ENPK also condemned the "blatant advertising" of the group-trip promoters but saw no legal recourse for addressing it. Consequently, in 1939 the commission and the SNB decided forthwith only to ban advertising and participation in promotions.[80]

Their passivity deprived the park authorities of the opportunity to shape the image of the park as a travel destination. Occasionally, it was criticized for it. "People come to the park whether the park commission 'publicizes' the park or not," wrote later SBN central secretary Dieter Burckhardt in the mid-1950s, during a two-year sojourn in the park area in connection with a wildlife biology research project, and urged the commission to play a more active role in public relations.[81] But the park authorities continued to avoid dealing with tourism until the 1990s, after Schloeth retired. The new park director, Klaus Robin, and his successor, Heinrich Haller, tried hard to strengthen the appeal of tourism as an opportunity and to manage it actively. Informational efforts were intensified and, through the restructuring of the administration, were put on equal footing with research and operations. At the same time, national park tourism became a research focus. It quickly became clear that in many issues park administration was groping in the dark because little reliable data existed on park visits. Beside the rough estimations of annual park visits, the basis remained a visitor survey and visitor concept from 1973 and 1974, respectively.[82] Now, new visitor surveys were organized, and a large research project worked out the importance of the national park for the local economy, which turned out to be surprisingly high.[83] Thus, the park visitor became an object of research and management, and as such fared the same as another collective actor that since the creation of the park had descended on it in ever greater numbers: deer.

Managing Wildlife

In late summer of 1917, shortly before the opening of the hunting season, an article published in the *Schweizerische Jagdzeitung* provoked a brief but fierce exchange in the hunting press. An editorial signed "O. M." (for Otto Meyer, president of the *Schweizerischer Jagdschutzverein,* the hunting association representing the practitioners of leased hunting and publisher of the *Jagdzeitung*) was headlined "Starvation in the National Park" and reminded readers of press reports that had appeared in spring of that year. Following the harsh and snowy winter of 1917, come April, many roe deer perished. Warden Langen reported having found eleven dead roe deer within a short distance in a single day. Military personnel stationed in the area had taken still alive but weakened animals to Zernez, where despite the care given them by the park warden, they expired. Langen, and the press, concluded that the roe deer were sick, and lungworm disease was blamed for the die-off. Meyer now doubted this explanation in the *Jagdzeitung* and surmised that a grazing shortage, not a disease, had led the animals to "die of starvation." This, in turn, he attributed to poor organization on the part of the national park and a lack of "critical insight into how to ensure the survival of artificially boosted game numbers over the harsh winter in rough mountain regions." For it "would be shameful to intentionally and fully consciously acknowledge a willingness to let game starve to death in an effort to copy a 'primal state of nature.' Such an attempt would outrage any nature or animal lover." Artificially boosted game should either be hunted "back to a sustainable number" or fed through the winter. Leaving the animals to fend for themselves was inhumane and, especially in wartime, also uneconomical.[84]

Meyer's statements were a frontal attack on the national park, the idea behind it, and its leaders. ENPK chair Paul Sarasin responded immediately with a sharp counterattack in another hunting magazine, the *Schweizer Jäger,* which addressed those who hunted under a hunting license system. Sarasin rejected the accusations, defended the "exercise of nature" as a core principle of the national park, and objected to any "artificial intervention."[85] Many hunters disliked Sarasin. For several years he had been championing a revision of the federal hunting regulations of 1904, which like previous versions distinguished between "useful" and "harmful" animals and in so doing supported the cantonal practice of offering cash rewards for killing predators. Sarasin demanded a radical realignment: In a complete reversal of the then current legal position, protection of wildlife should no longer be the exception but the rule. Sarasin was not one to mince words. In his lectures and writings, he disparaged the hunter's guilds in corpore as "meat shooters and carrion hunters."[86]

Counterattacking again in the *Jagdzeitung*, Meyer called Sarasin "hunting's most zealous and obstinate enemy." Meyer reaffirmed his stance and labeled the hands-off approach of the national park as "cruelly toying with living creatures." He also objected to the "anti-hunting excesses of the conservation movement." Both nature and game reserves would considerably limit hunting. "A rational hunting operation, that is the leasing system, would make such reserves completely unnecessary."[87] As will become evident, in addition to the antagonism between hunters and conservationists, a further point of opposition divided the hunters themselves: those who supported the lease-based system and those who supported the license system. Licensed hunting was introduced into most cantons in the nineteenth century. Anyone who qualified for a hunting license could hunt anywhere in the canton. Grisons adopted such a system in 1877. In contrast, under the leasing scheme, a certain area could be rented for the exclusive use of a hunting association. This form of hunting, which had about it an air of high society, initially existed only in the canton of Aargau. In the first half of the twentieth century, most of the German-speaking midland cantons shifted to the lease-based system. This process was accompanied by decades of sometimes toxic disputes between proponents of licensed hunting and renting, with the former mostly on the defensive, accused by the latter of not being able to sustainably manage their stocks as expressed above by Meyer.[88]

In addition to the two aspects of total protection or wildlife management, and licensed hunting or renting, the controversy over the roe deer die-off of 1917 involved a third element: Who possessed the right knowledge? Did the animals die of lungworm disease, as the park authorities insisted, or was the cause in fact malnutrition, as hunter Otto Meyer claimed? The results of investigations into winter die-offs of deer happening later in the century suggest in retrospect that Meyer was right. In a further report in the *Jagdzeitung* in 1917, a letter to the editor signed "J. J. M" maintained that it would be a fatal mistake to rule out lack of food as the cause of the late incidence of deaths in April. "The transition period in April is especially dangerous if animals previously deprived of food return to full grazing." Here, the author was proved only too right by later events.[89]

The debate over starvation was left unresolved and quickly forgotten. It is primarily interesting because it already contained all the components that would appear in the later debates over the so-called deer problem. How should a wildlife population be controlled in a totally protected area? Is intervention ever justified? Was the license system partly to blame for the disaster? And who had the responsibility and the competence to judge matters relating to wildlife?

In the years subsequent to 1917, wildlife issues initially rarely gave rise to serious debate apart from the skirmishes described in chapter 4 between hunters and park authorities over the use of artificial salt licks either to keep animals in the park or to lure them out. The national park commission was satisfied with the apparently ever-growing wildlife stocks as well as with the fact that animals were gradually losing their fear of people because they were no longer chased by hunters. Based on the "experiences in the great American reserves" no less was to be expected, the ENPK announced in 1921.[90] But over the years it gradually dawned on the commission that their knowledge of the wildlife in the park was very shaky. In 1918, possibly as a consequence of the debate over the roe deer deaths, the commission for the first time instructed the park wardens to count the game in the park. These counts, which thereafter were repeated annually, and the observations the wardens made in their diaries, were the main sources of information. In summer 1924, also for the first time, a scientist (and hunter), the veterinarian Karl R. Hoffmann, made a study of the game animals in the park. Hoffmann's report was very critical. He found "the area of the national park too small and too inadequately rounded, on the one hand, and the neighboring areas too barren, on the other, to allow for a significant enhancement of the chamois stocks, and the preservation of a significant roe deer population given the condition of absolute protection, even for predators." As countermeasures he proposed "eliminating" old predator foxes, a suggestion that the ENPK subsequently took into consideration, though it did not implement it.[91] Four years later, in 1928, in his inspection report, Supervisor Steivan Brunies noted the "striking relative paucity of game in the area."[92]

Beginning in 1917, Brunies regularly conducted inspections of the national park lasting several days and also evaluated the reports of the park wardens. Of all commission members, he had the keenest sense of the park and the evolution of the flora and fauna since the initiation of protection, and had his own opinions and observations to rely on as well as those of the park wardens. In a report written in 1929 he noted a growing discrepancy between his observations and those of the wardens. The wildlife estimates, Brunies explained to the ENPK and WNPK, were "executed in a very amateurish manner." In addition, "so as not to be suspected of poor management, every year [the wardens] put more emphasis on maximum average numbers." The chamois population in particular was actually declining at an alarming rate. Other figures, for instance, those on roe deer and red deer, were guesses, since the animals lived mainly in the forest and defied counting. "Consequently, in informed circles the NPK ends up looking ridiculous."[93]

As a result, in its report of 1929 the commission neutrally noted that opinions about the direction in which the wildlife stocks were developing were "significantly at odds." Simmering conflicts between Supervisor Brunies, on the one hand, and ENPK secretary Bühlmann and the park wardens, on the other, made constructive debate difficult. Accordingly, the ENPK requested scientific support: The WNPK should study the wildlife. However, the zoology subcommission responsible for research on fauna showed little interest, and not for the first time. Jean Carl, the chair of the subcommission, flatly rejected the suggestion. "It would also be necessary to assign several qualified people to make observations throughout the year, and similarly to take into account all parts of the park and all aspects of the game animals and to extend this to series covering years." Such an investigation would be "alien to the program and work methods of the zoology subcommission," and the funds to do it would be in short supply.[94]

The year of 1932 brought a new start. At the request of Eduard Tenger, president of the SBN, the ENPK convened a commission to examine the question of scientific study of higher animal species in the Swiss National Park, in the context of which Ulrich Duerst, another veterinarian, developed a comprehensive research program.[95] However, implementing it proved a challenge. In 1938 Eduard Handschin, chair of the WNPK, complained to the ENPK that the work on the higher vertebrates was "to date too amateurish and scientifically unsatisfactorily done" and wished to give it his "undivided attention."[96] But nothing changed. Duerst poured twenty years into researching wildlife on his own without ever publishing any results. One reason for that may have been that his methods were unorthodox and did not meet scientific standards.[97] Here another interesting contrast with the United States arises. In America it was wildlife biologists who around 1930 made the national parks into locations for scientific research. The zoologists in the WNPK, on the other hand, kept the wildlife at arm's length. At the time, in contrast to the United States, the universities were devoid of wildlife biology. The national park zoologists preferred to continue working with invertebrate species and were only too happy to leave vertebrates to veterinary medicine and hunters. In so doing, the WNPK abdicated responsibility for wildlife research, which subsequently and quasi perforce became the domain of the ENPK.[98]

The ENPK also took charge of wildlife statistics. In 1930 it transferred organization of the annual counts to Supervisor Brunies, who focused on improving the counts methodically and completing them within a few days of the year with the help of the park wardens and the border patrol and other support staff. Brunies hoped that the figures thus obtained would more reliably describe the development of the wildlife population, even though he had to acknowledge that the densely wooded area would permit no precise counts, and that varying weather conditions could influence the stock taking. Moreover, interpreting the figures posed a challenge. The numbers for red deer showed a clear upward trend, and the released ibex appeared to be maintaining well. But the figures for chamois and roe deer showed no clear trend.[99]

Ulrich Duerst associated the supposed "paucity of wildlife" in the park with the increased disturbance from traffic and tourism. Given these developments, he raised the seemingly heretical question whether the reserve idea perhaps should be abandoned and the national park redeveloped more along the lines of a zoological garden. In this way, the attractiveness of the park would increase, and the overwhelming desire of visitors—to see animals—would be gratified. Duerst's proposal was unanimously rejected by the WNPK; nor would the ENPK hear of moving away from the original purpose of the park. Duerst's idea did appeal somewhat to two ENPK representatives from the ranks of the federal government and the SBN, although they would hardly have approved presenting the animals in enclosures, as was common in the American national parks at the time.[100]

Of Hunters and Deer

Since the 1930s the deer had begun to draw more attention to themselves. Following the local extinction of red deer in the nineteenth century, they began to return to the Lower Engadine around the time of the park's founding, and had settled in the park. The quality of the surveys notwithstanding, the downward trend of roe deer in the park noted during the interwar period was likely due to their displacement by red deer.[101] Indeed, as a result of the climbing numbers of red deer, in 1929 hunting red deer was permitted again throughout the entire canton of Grisons, a step the ENPK found worrisome. The commission intervened successfully through the cantonal government, which much to the annoyance of the commune of Zernez agreed to a ban on hunting red deer in the area between the national park and the Inn River. In the following years the Engadine side of the national park was girdled by no-hunting areas imposed by the federal state. Once these areas were included in new park contracts and additionally compensated, the communes abandoned their resistance.[102] In 1931, much to the delight of the ENPK, the Italian government also banned hunting in the area bordering Livigno, giving in addition new life to the old hope of a cross-border protected area.[103] The thus formed extensive no-hunting area provided the basis for strong growth of the local deer population.

With increasing population density, the deer began to change their behavior. Whereas the first generations of red deer had spent the entire year in the park, their successors in the 1930s developed a seasonal migratory behavior. They passed the summer months in the high areas of the park, and in late autumn crossed over the park boundaries to seek winter quarters at lower altitudes. The sparse winter food supply may well have driven the animals to make this change. On their travels and at their wintering sites they inevitably came into conflict with local forestry and agriculture. These conflicts accentuated after 1939, when in keeping with the national wartime *Anbauschlacht* ("cultivation battle") agricultural use of the land intensified and was extended to other areas. In addition, with the outbreak of the war in 1939, all hunting was stopped. To protect the fields against wildlife, plot guards were posted, whose cost was covered by both the Federal War Food Office and the ENPK.[104]

In spring of 1945 a new—or rather, forgotten—phenomenon (re)appeared: Between January and April around a hundred dead deer were found in the park region. The park commission was mystified. Because the deaths had occurred suddenly with the onset of spring, the commission assumed some connection with the exceptionally severe winter. When, three years later, another twenty deer cadavers were discovered in the national park, the ENPK asked a veterinarian to investigate the cause of the deaths. He attributed them to general exhaustion and malnutrition, thus confirming the conjecture of the ENPK. In contrast to the die-off of roe deer in 1917, the commission now stressed that the investigation had revealed evidence neither of parasitic nor bacterial disease, nor any sign of problems due to inbreeding or degeneration.[105] In short, the national park offered the deer healthy living conditions. This time, however, the ENPK did not let the topic drop, as in the following decades, the next deer die-off was never far behind.

Illustration 10. Dead red deer at the train station of Lavin in spring 1951, attracting children and photographer Rudolf Grass. Photo by Rudolf Grass.

204   *Creating Wilderness*

Indeed, further die-offs occurred in 1950 and 1953. Because the available food supply was apparently insufficient, the cantonal hunting authorities suggested decimating the deer population by holding extraordinary hunts. Among hunting circles, however, there was violent opposition. Special hunts that were not open to all hunters were seen as a betrayal of Grisons hunting tradition, the *"Bündner Volksjagd."* Consequently, the authorities briefly opened the two-day special deer hunt organized at the border of the national park in late autumn 1956 to all licensed cantonal hunters. They came in scores and killed over a hundred animals within a small area.[106] In so doing, they fulfilled the mission but also managed to arouse no small degree of indignation through their actions. The media reported the event nationwide in unflattering terms. *Die Woche* denounced the "massacre of the deer in the national park" in lavishly illustrated accounts. Even the usually reserved liberal *Neue Zürcher Zeitung* blared "Deer Slaughter in the Engadine" and referred to a "shameful massacre."[107] Leading representatives of leased hunting, such as Paul Vetterli, the editor of the *Jagdzeitung,* capitalized on the event to the fullest as a way of agitating against licensed hunting in general.[108] In the following year, the special hunt was repeated, but then discontinued due to persistent criticism. Only the ordinary hunting in September was extended by a few days, which was not enough to bother the "national park deer," which during this season were usually still in the park or in the adjacent no-hunting area.[109] The measure may even have promoted the deer stock in the park insofar as it reduced the competition in the common wintering sites. In 1962 the no-hunting areas around the park were suspended. The local deer population, however, continued to increase, and in the 1960s even exponentially (see chart 5).

The second major event of the 1950s after the failed extraordinary deer hunt was the introduction of systematic wildlife biology studies. The obvious prob-

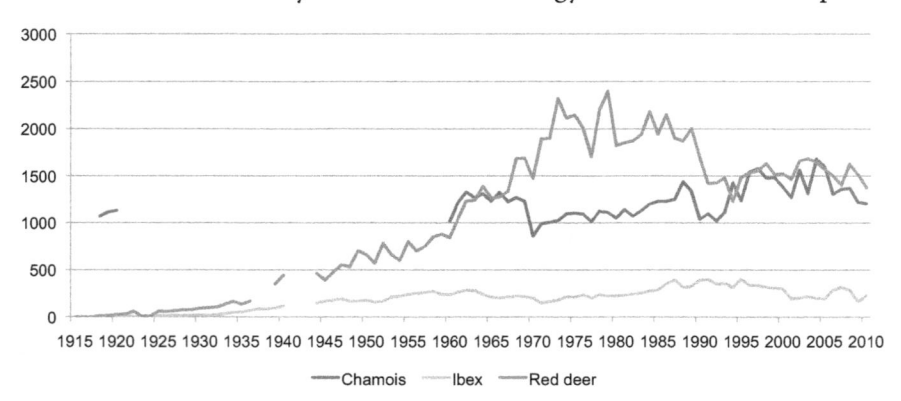

Chart 5. Development of stocks of chamois, ibex, and red deer in the Swiss National Park, 1915–2010 (the highest summer values). No reliable data are available for chamois between 1920 and 1960.[110] *Source:* SNP 2011.

lems with the red deer—the growing population, the mass die-offs, and the rise in damage by wildlife to the rural area surrounding the national park—increased interest in scientific investigations. Moreover, the founding of the Swiss National Science Foundation (SNF) in 1952 opened a new avenue to funding that enabled the launch of longer-term research projects beginning in 1954. Now the same sort of advanced wildlife research as was being done in the United States could be taken up, revealing problems similar to those experienced by American national parks with a high density of ungulates.[111] However, the presence of wildlife biologists irritated the local experts—the hunters. Dieter Burckhardt, the first wildlife biologist to work in the park, moved to Zernez in 1956 after obtaining a two-year grant from the SNF. In an analysis of the deer problem written at the end of that year, he stated that a scientific basis first had to be established to enable determination of effective and objectively sustainable control measures. To this end the cantonal gamekeepers would have to be strengthened and professionalized. Because Burckhardt expected "massive resistance among the population," he advised taking things a step at a time. The top priority must be "that every person in a position of responsibility be clear that hunting is not the exclusive province of hunters."[112]

The hunters were slow to come to this realization. In the early 1960s the hunting lobby opposed the granting of federal subsidies to wildlife biology research.[113] Mocked as the "gentry of game research" wildlife biologists were not much esteemed by local hunters. Unlike earlier scientists who only appeared for a few weeks, this new type of researchers sometimes remained on site the entire year. Relations between academic researchers and local hunters were tense, and significantly, in the mid-1960s the tension was vented in a short but heated outburst. A rumor that park authorities had shot deer calves in the region of the national park for research purposes—and even outside of the hunting season—unleashed a storm of indignation. "The national park is a thing unto itself—like hunting in Grisons. Both have established limits that must be utterly respected," complained one upset letter writer in the local press in January 1965.[114] But the rumor soon proved false. The cantonal hunting inspector had ordered the shooting and called in the park wardens as backup for his own gamekeepers.[115] The uproar that resulted showed how delicate local social relations were, the degree to which the population mistrusted the park authorities, and how poorly communication functioned. The episode also revealed how radically divided the national park and hunting were, and how clearly this division was aligned with responsibilities on either side. Any crossing of the imaginary border was fraught with incalculable danger. As a result of the affair, the canton and the national park both subsequently waived any mutual assistance in gamekeeping. The deer, in contrast, little worried about the ideological struggles of humans, moved freely back and forth across human-drawn borders and multiplied further. They adapted their behavior optimally to hunting, withdrawing during the hunting season to the safer fields of the park in daytime and at night herding into the richer pastures of the periphery to dine. The population dynamics and agility of the deer increased the pressure on humans and their rigid lines of demarcation.

Shooting in the National Park

In 1970 the problems with the deer could no longer be handled desultorily, as previously. In the preceding years the deer population had shot up rapidly. In 1960 some 800 deer had passed the summer months in the park; by 1970 that number exceeded 1,500, and by 1971 it was more than 1,800. Reports of damage caused by deer increased accordingly. While the cost of preventing and compensating wildlife damage in the canton of Grisons had long hovered around 100,000 Swiss francs, in 1972 it jumped to over 200,000 francs. In the following three years the cost reached a peak of 400,000 francs (1975); between 40 and 60 percent of the funds were spent for the "*Einflussbereich Nationalpark*" (national park sphere of influence) (see chart 6).[116]

In 1969 Jean Baer concluded that allowing the shooting of deer in the park was unavoidable. The WNPK chair and former director of the International Union for the Conservation of Nature had explored the issue with reference to other parks: "The opinion of these authorities is unanimous, for the same problem seems to exist everywhere: The principle of a national park without human intervention is no longer tenable. The deer population must be reduced."

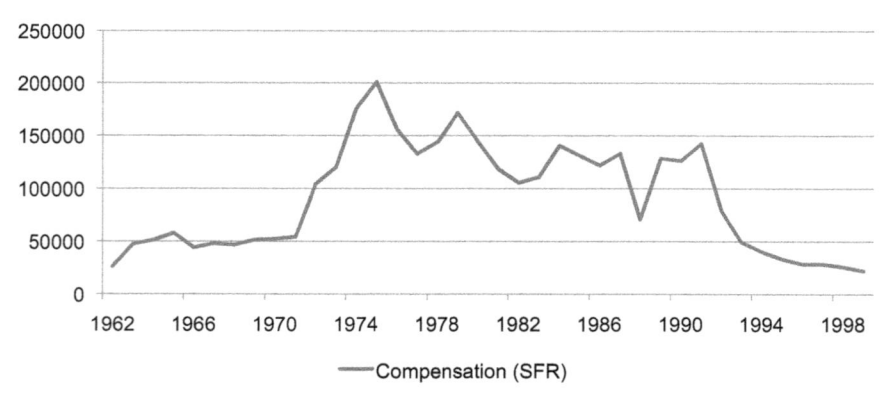

Chart 6. Cost of damage caused by wildlife in the area of the Swiss National Park and for feed in the area of Zuoz-Brail, 1962–99. The jump in expenditures clearly shows that these costs did not depend only on the number of wild animals but also weather conditions and prevention and compensation practices. Voser 1987 tried to measure the actual change in yearly losses in yield. *Source:* Haller 2002, 68.

However, his radical proposal met with very strong reservations among his colleagues in the WNPK.[117] Ironically, during the following year (1970), proclaimed European Conservation Year by Council of Europe, the issue suddenly became more acute since that spring saw the greatest winter die-off ever, as six hundred deer perished. "Although in many areas—and with the help of park wardens—intensive feeding was applied to the wintering sites, comprehensive and massive help for the distressed animals came too late, and thus in some places mass mortality due to malnutrition was unavoidable," wrote the park directorate in its annual report. Based on the experience of recent decades as well as of international comparisons, winter die-offs were to be expected every four to five years. The ENPK in turn announced that it was aware of the problem and had examined "for years ways and means to prevent [a] further rise in stock." The commission had already suggested to the cantonal authorities measures to apply in the park surroundings and also recommended them for "the park itself insofar as they are consistent with the park statute."[118] What was not consistent with the park statute was the shooting of animals in the park, which the cantonal authorities were now demanding. Instead, the ENPK recommended a whole raft of other measures: breaking up large concentrations of deer in the park prior to hunting; shooting wildlife outside the park; adapting hunting to the migratory behavior of the deer; trapping animals and transporting them away from the wintering sites; and releasing predators, which, however, would still encounter substantial resistance "outside the park."[119]

The ENPK got nowhere with its recommendations. The idea of waylaying deer at the park boundary as they left the park with the onset of winter was rejected as "un-hunterly."[120] The targeted dispersal of deer had been shown in 1971 to have little effect, serving mainly to draw the ire of park visitors. The following year the ENPK came under heavy political pressure after the federal forest inspector announced federal subsidies for reforestation in the areas around the national park contingent on reducing local deer stocks to a "level the forests could sustain." Although in July of that year the park authorities again pronounced themselves "unanimously opposed to shooting in the park," a month later they caved in and agreed to "selective shooting of sick, wounded, and weak animals in the national park under park supervision during the summer (from 1973 onward) up to a maximum of 100 animals to stabilize the local stocks." The cantonal authorities in turn ordered reduction kills outside the park, which were carried out for the first time in late autumn 1972 by local hunters under the supervision of the cantonal gamekeepers.[121] During the summer of 1973, also for the first time, "after careful selection" 67 wounded or "extremely sick" animals were shot in the park.[122] In the meantime, debates continued. The WNPK, which following lengthy discussions finally issued a statement, rejected the shootings; the park director and park wardens performed them only reluctantly.[123] The deer problem in the national park was widely reported in the national press, and in autumn 1973 Swiss TV organized a public debate that was transmitted directly into Swiss households from Zernez. By then, however, tempers had cooled and all sides showed a willingness to adopt the measures decided for wildlife kills inside the park and reduction kills outside it. To prevent further mass die-offs, a new cantonal hay regulation introduced in 1974 also contained a provision for winter feeding.

The solution entailed a classic tradeoff that required both sides—national park and hunters—to make concessions regarding their handling of deer. The legal aspects of the deer kills in the park remained shaky, and the parties were not particularly happy with the outcome, but they managed to contain their displeasure. Nonetheless, as it happened, although the measures mitigated the problem to some extent, they did not actually make it go away. The deer stocks in and around the national park continued to swell. A project carried out in the second half of the 1970s showed that the number of animals was higher than previously supposed. A new method was used—so-called night census—by which the animals were counted in spring using headlights at night when they left the forest to find food.[124] The park directorate had underestimated the "unreported cases"—the number of animals that escaped their counts. In addition, the numbers for Val Trupchun, an area of the national park that was particularly rich in wildlife, were proved false beyond the possibility of accidental error.[125] Just as park wardens in the 1920s had inflated the numbers of chamois to match the expectations of the park, now it was equally opportune to undercount deer to prevent reduction kills. In neither case were the numbers impartial, but rather a function of the political context, which the parties that produced the numbers influenced in turn.

The measures introduced, and perhaps intraspecies competition for food as well, did in fact ultimately result in a leveling off of stocks in the 1980s, albeit they remained at a level that many still considered too high. The debate reignited around the middle of the decade, though in an unexpected manner, when deer-induced damage to vegetation was condemned not only outside the park, in the communes, but within the park itself. That deer were influencing the development of plant life—and especially forest regeneration—both within and outside of the park was obviously not news. Josias Braun-Blanquet had already pointed it out in the 1920s.[126] Moreover, there was no lack of warnings of irreparable damage, which began to be heard in the 1950s.[127] But up to that point, the national park had always dismissed such fears as unfounded. The annual report of 1986 took a different tone. "*Contrary to the findings of the previous year*, certain caveats must be made regarding the general condition of the vegetation in the park. More detailed checks of the various park areas and of strongly frequented staging points and movements of deer revealed patchy conditions that give us pause."[128] The park directorate urged in vain that these occasional findings not be equated with a general inability of park vegetation to regenerate. Soon horror stories were circulating in the media about hordes of deer eating the park bare. "National Park in Danger: Deer Grazing on Protected Plants!" trumpeted a headline in a September 1986 issues of the *Sonntags-Blick,* the most widely read (tabloid) newspaper in Switzerland.[129] Although deer grazing on protected plants in no way contradicted the park's conservation principles, it was precisely these principles that were now called into question. The Zurich *Tages-Anzeiger* quoted federal hunting inspector Hans-Jörg Blankenhorn, who in the 1970s had led a research project on deer in the national park area, as saying, "It cannot be the policy of the park to allow thousands of deer to munch the entire flora to the ground."[130] The impression was one of a state of emergency that required decisive countermeasures, including revising the concept of the park. The applicable statutory provision allowing only such interventions as "immediately serve to protect the park" appeared in any event to have been more than fulfilled. Being of this mind, the ENPK ordered the most comprehensive deer shooting up to that point: In 1987, more than 150 animals were killed by park wardens and the local gamekeepers.[131] That this massive intervention was proportionate was not universally agreed. Thus, the guidelines on interventions and change in the park area, which the ENPK and WNPK labored on for the next two years, may have been a direct response to the shooting. According to the guidelines, this intervention showed how difficult the statutory provisions are to interpret.[132] The guidelines were completed in 1989. In offering a narrow interpretation of the law, the two park commissions created a written basis for future decisions.

In retrospect, one might wonder at the suddenness and the vehemence of the furore at the time. It could plausibly be related to the "*Waldsterben*" (forest dieback) debate, which was at a peak in the mid-1980s.[133] At the time, however, no one did connect the two issues; the forest damage was attributed only to the deer. Still, *Waldsterben* clearly altered the perception of forests and the degree of attention given them. Forest damage that had previously gone unnoticed was now sought and found. In the following years forest dieback was put into perspective and even wholly called into question. Forests proved more robust than the death scenarios of the mid-1980s had led people to believe. The very term *Waldsterben* vanished from analyses of forest conditions almost as rapidly as it had appeared.[134]

Research results published from the mid-1990s managed in a similarly dramatic way to cast doubt on the then current forestry doctrine on the "wildlife forest problem." High concentrations of ungulates, it was said, could indeed slow the development of forests in the national park, but posed no danger either to the current inventory and its rejuvenation or the natural reforestation of former pastures. In other words, deer had no determinant effect on the park vegetation. Regulating them was consequently incompatible with the park statutes.[135]

For permanently reducing and stabilizing the deer population throughout the region another measure was actually crucial: cantonal hunt planning, which was introduced in the 1980s. This tool, which had already been applied to ibex hunting since 1977 and had significantly been shaped by the findings of wildlife research in the national park, made it possible to combine wildlife biology principles with population statistics and hunting bags in such a way as to produce a detailed picture of a particular stock of animals destined for a required kill. It also made it possible to incorporate the tradition-conscious *Bündner Volksjagd* into a comprehensive wildlife management system based on collection and processing of aggregated data. What for decades had repeatedly failed now worked: Hunters and deer became amenable to discipline.[136] The tradeoff—the park administration's agreeing to let deer be shot inside the park—was no longer politically necessary. In 1996 the measure was repealed. The founding fathers' wish that inside the national park "no chopping or shooting should be heard" had been regranted.[137]

In concluding, it can properly be said that, following the Second World War, the Swiss National Park came under pressure more or less equally from all sides. The electricity industry was keen to exploit hydropower; increasing numbers of tourists were frequenting the park or simply passed by it on their way to their holiday destination; and the deer population flourished so successfully that they soon were perceived as a nuisance both locally and beyond, which in turn affected the park as a no-hunting zone. In each of the discourses that helped to shape these developments, the concept of total protection was called into question. But the discourses were also related. For Braun-Blanquet, the intervention represented by the exploitation of hydropower in 1958 was put into perspective by the existing "deer surplus" and the damage it posed to park flora.[138] Fifteen years later a cantonal official argued conversely that the agreement on hydropower had eroded the principle of total protection to such an extent that it now allowed interfering with the deer population, an interpretation the ENPK immediately rejected.[139] The park authorities defended total protection by revering the legacy of the founding fathers. They were very aware that they were custodians of an idea conceived for all eternity that would allow nature the freedom to restore itself and give science the opportunity to document the process. This awareness had both advantages and disadvantages. For a long time, it endowed the park authorities—whose means were otherwise limited—with a strong identity, and consequently prevented them from abandoning their acquisitions lightly. On the other hand, the park authorities struggled to accept new challenges and to deal with them in any way but defensively. The concept of total protection was designed for a stable context; but the social environment was always in motion and with it the natural conditions in the park. Adapting to change while simultaneously adhering to principles proved a difficult balancing act that was not always optimally managed. Maintaining the heterotopia of the national park required just the right mixture of idealism and realism. Only in that way could the socionatural dynamics be tamed and transformed into that temporary societal equilibrium essential to the national park as a social institution. In this respect, it would have helped if the borders between park and surroundings, between nature and culture had not been so sharply delineated, and if the national park could have been recognized for what, in effect, it was: an artificially created and maintained wilderness.

Notes

1. *NZZ*, 13 December 1958.
2. Bachmann 1999, 242–253, Gredig and Willi 2006, 197–199. To get the money together, in 1946 the Swiss Heritage Society (*Schweizerischer Bund für Heimatschutz*) and the SBN sold chocolate coins all over Switzerland. The strategy was so successful that the two organizations decided to repeat the "chocolate coin" collection on a regular basis. See Bundi 2001.
3. Engadiner Gemeinden 1958, 25–28. The commune of Zernez had allowed the first such related investigations to be carried out in 1912–14 (Parolini 2012b). However, in negotiating the 1909 Cluozza contract, it had already planned to extract a proviso regarding hydropower. See chapter 3.
4. Nachtrag vom 13 June 1920 zum Dienstbarkeitsvertrag vom 29 November 1913, Punkt 4, in Engadiner Gemeinden 1958, 19 f. SBN Archives, M 3.2, ENPK, meeting of 19 September 1919. Zernez to ENPK, 24 September 1919, in Engadiner Gemeinden 1958, 21 f. When the plans for the power plant came up again in 1926, they provoked a dispute in the ENPK over how the 1920 decision was reached. Brunies and Bühlmann in particular made mutual accusations. SBN Archives, M 3.2, ENPK, meeting of 23–24 August 1926; SNP Archives, 660.118, Bühlmann to ENPK, 5 October 1926; BAR 9500.25, vol. 7, ENPK, meeting of 21 January 1928.
5. Engadiner Gemeinden 1958, 22–25. SNP Archives, ENPK, meeting of 2–3 September 1938; GA Zernez, B 21 b, Soprastanza, meeting of 19 October 1938. The commune of Zernez later submitted its 1938 request for a waiver to the ENPK as implicit recognition of its rights.
6. See Haag 2004.
7. On the planning, see Meier 2003 and Gredig and Willi 2006, 333–349.
8. FOK Archives, WNPK, meeting of 20 January 1952, 4.
9. ENPK to EDI, 30 November 1944. Cited in Fritsche 2002, 69.
10. Handschin 1947, 83. In this respect, the WNPK bemoaned that funding not granted had frustrated a lot of research in the past, and led to the present meager research results. WNPK annual report 1947, 1. On these debates, see also Fritsche 2002, 62–77.
11. Schweizerischer Bund für Naturschutz 1947, emphasis mine. See also WNPK annual report 1945, 1, and 1947, 1; ENPK annual report 1947, 5.
12. Frey-Wyssling 1959, 8. After 2000 the value for the region of both national park tourism and the Engadine power plant was calculated at around 17 million Swiss francs each (Küpfer 2000; Parolini 2012b). At the end of the 1950s, however, national park

tourism was not so important (see below in this chapter) nor was anyone particularly aware of its potential for adding value.
13. Copiously sourced descriptions of the Spöl conflict can be found in Skenderovoic 1992; Fritsche 2002; Meier 2003; and Truttmann 2008.
14. SNP Archives, ENPK, meeting of 14 July 1956, Schlatter, Problem Nationalpark/Spölwerk, attachment to the minutes.
15. See Schweizerischer Bundesrat 1957, 22–24.
16. WNPK annual report 1956, 2.
17. Fritsche 2002, 84.
18. See Stettler 2002, 72–79. Braun-Blanquet's joy at the defeat of the power plant opponents, as expressed in the *NZZ* article cited, may well have been shared by many natural scientists. Braun-Blanquet still constituted an exception insofar as, as early as 1951 in a report for submission to the power plant designers, he had shown himself favorably inclined to their ideas even as the WNPK was still fundamentally opposed. See Fritsche 2002, 78–80.
19. Zbinden 1953; 1957.
20. Zbinden 1953, 36 and 34.
21. Ibid., 62.
22. Schweizerischer Bundesrat 1938, 999. See Schnetzer 2009.
23. Zbinden 1953, 10, 8. The *Eidgenössische Natur- und Heimatschutzkommission* is an extraparliamentary federal commission with a consultative function that has existed since 1936.
24. Zbinden 1957, 39.
25. Ibid., 37.
26. Ibid., 38.
27. See Kupper 2003.
28. Truttmann 2008. The *Lia Naira* got its name from local adversaries who claimed that its members only met in the dark.
29. See Skenderovoic 1992, 73–86; Meier 2003, 64–77.
30. For a history of the construction, see Meier 2003.
31. NA, Record Group 79, 3.1, L 66, Box 2182, Memorandum "Swiss National Park," John S. McLaughlin, NPS Region 2 Omaha Nebraska, to NPS Director, 22 November 1950.
32. Harvey 1994. For similar cases of conflicts in the Alps, see Mauz 2003 (France); Würflinger 2007 and Kupper and Wöbse 2013 (Austria); Hasenöhrl 2010 (Bavaria). A transalpine analysis of the subject has yet to be done.
33. Nash 1982, 332.
34. ENPK annual report 1958, 5.
35. Verkehrsverein Graubünden 1942; Verkehrsverein Graubünden 1968.
36. Verkehrsverein Graubünden 1942, section titled "Tierleben im Nationalpark."
37. SCNAT Archives, Box 537, Christ: Gutachten über die Gesetze der amerikanischen Reservationen, 2 May 1908. The report was published in the SNK annual report 1908–9, 43–47. But the recommendations for Switzerland were omitted, and the report ended with sentence: "Our own viewpoints, of course, are in many cases quite different; however, at this stage of preparation I will refrain from going more deeply into the matter."
38. *Basler Nachrichten*, 8 May 1908.

39. König 2000. On the history of tourism, see Schumacher 2002; Hachtmann 2007.
40. Bachmann 2005. See also the discussion in chapter 2.
41. From the comprehensive literature, see, for instance, Runte 1987, 82–105; Shaffer 2001; Sutter 2002. On Yellowstone in particular, see Magoc 1999; Barringer 2002. On Hetch Hetchy, see Nash 1982, 161–181; Runte 1990, 67–82. Kupper 2009b offers a transatlantic view as well as an introduction to the history of national park tourism.
42. Cited in Runte 1987, 93.
43. Cited in ibid., 82.
44. Cited in Sellars 1997, 28.
45. http://www.nps.gov/legacy/organic-act-of-1916.htm, accessed 4 December 2008.
46. SNK annual report 1908–9, 52–57. Schweizerischer Bundesrat 1912, 420.
47. Schröter 1918, 765.
48. Ibid., 764. Schröter, too, emphasized the differences between Switzerland and the United States, where the "national parks are considered first and foremost ... as 'playgrounds ... for the benefit and enjoyment of the people.'" He found it a "very understandable reaction against the nerveracking pace of American life."
49. At the time the NSK chose Val Cluozza as the nucleus of a future large reserve, a hut project was already in existence, initiated by Heinrich Cranz of Stuttgart, a member of the German-Austrian Alpine Association. The SNK initially supported the project. But after the Swiss Alpine Association, *Schweizerischer Alpenclub*, protested against such an intrusion into its national territory, the SNK decided to establish the huts on its own. The intervention of the *Schweizerischer Alpenclub* was part of the nationalist tendencies described in chapter 2. SNK annual report 1908–9, 33, 51 f., SCNAT Archives, Box 521, SNK Reservationenkomitee, meeting of 31 October 1908, and SNK, meeting of 16 May 1909, Protokollbuch, 21, 81 f.
50. SBN Archives, M 3.2, ENPK, meeting of 1 December 1916.
51. See GA Zernez B 21 a, records on *Chamanna da Cluoza*, for instance, Wohlwend to Bühlmann, 11 January 1919 and 19 April 1921. Similarly, BAR 9500.25, vol. 6, Zernez to EDI, 9 August 1927. The same criticism was also voiced in Scuol, SNP Archives, 152.100, Brunies: Bericht über die Sitzung der WNPK vom 13 January 1929.
52. Hotel & Pension Ofenberg, State Archives Grisons, X 23 f 3 a.
53. Maggini 1916; ENPK annual report 1919, 8. Brunies 1923. On the history of the Ofenpass road, see Gottschalk 1994.
54. BAR, E 9500.25, vol. 37: Bühlmann to Schröter, 25 February 1918.
55. ENPK annual reports 1927, 4.
56. ENPK annual report 1925, 5.
57. BAR, E 9500.25, vol. 38: Prof. Bachmann, Bericht über den Besuch im Schw. Nationalpark, 27–30 July 1928, 7 August 1928.
58. See Merki 2002, 147–167; Hollinger 2008.
59. EKW, Frequenzstatistik Strassentunnel Munt la Schera, 1970–2009.
60. Botschaft BR 1979, 709 f. On road building, see the Inventar historischer Verkehrswege der Schweiz (www.ivs.admin.ch). New tunnels built for the hydroelectric power plants were also used by pathogens and fish for traveling from the Inn to the Spöl River. Thus, in 1986 chars were discovered in the Spöl that had originated in the lakes of the Upper Engadine. ENPK annual report 1986, 18. See also the annual reports 1972, 1975, 1984.

61. SNP Archives, 156.100, Handschin, Memorandum zu Handen SBN und ENPK: Allgemeine Beobachtungen im Nationalpark, Aufenthalt 1933.
62. ENPK annual report 1933, 3 f.
63. ENPK annual report 1934, 9. Documents relating to preparation of the park rules can be found in the SBN Archives, M1. ENPK annual report 1938, 3 f.
64. ENPK annual report 1939, 13.
65. Bland 1927, 495.
66. ENPK annual report 1959, 5.
67. SNP Archives, 182.100, Schloeth: Der SNP Heute—und Morgen, 11 November 1967, 5. *Schweizer Naturschutz* 3 (1968), 54–56.
68. ENPK annual report 1971, 1–4.
69. On international national park tourism, see Butler and Boyd 2000; Eagles and McCool 2002; Frost and Hall 2009b. Statistics on American visitors can be found at www.nature.nps.gov/stats.
70. ENPK annual report 1984, 3.
71. SNP Archives, 182.100, Schloeth: Der SNP Heute—und Morgen, 11 November 1967, 1.
72. Ibid., 9–11. SNP Archives, 187.100, Schloeth, Bericht, Third international short course on Administration of National Parks and equivalent Reserves (27 August–23 September 1967 from Jackson Wyo—Gr. Canyon).
73. SNP Archives, 188.100, Schloeth, Bericht über die 2. Weltkonferenz der Nationalparks in USA (18–27 September 1972).
74. SNP Archives, 182.100, Schloeth: Gedanken zur Planung für die Zukunft des Schweiz. Nationalparkes, Sonderbericht II, Feb. 1969. SNP Archives, ENPK, meeting of 29 November 1967, 2–8; 6 March 1968, 1–5; and 14–15 July 1969, 6–12. The subject was dropped at subsequent meetings. On the earlier plans for a national park in French-speaking Switzerland, see chapter 2.
75. SNP Archives, 182.100, Schloeth: Der SNP Heute—und Morgen, 11 November 1967, 3. In 1981 he referred to a "indoctrination tourism" (Robert Schloeth: Gedanken zur Zielsetzung des Schweiz. Nationalparks, 1981). See also Schloeth 1989.
76. ENPK annual report 1981, 5.
77. SNP Archives, 137.100, Schloeth, Studienreise nach USA vom 28/1–15/3/1982. On the beginnings of nature interpretation in the American national parks, see Pitcaithley 2002; Smith 2004.
78. SNP Archives, 182.100, Schloeth: Gedanken über einen Naturpark Unterengadin, 14 April 1978.
79. SNP Archives, 900.100 Instruktion für die Parkwächter des Schweizerischen Nationalparks von 1917. Documents on the tour offerings from Pension Langen in Zernez are to be found in SNP Archives, 380.100.
80. SNP Archives, ENPK, meeting of 2–3 September 1938, 2 f., and 25 March 1939, 104. See also ENPK annual report 1938, 4.
81. SNP Archives, 182.100, Burckhardt: Gedanken zum Nationalpark, 6 December 1956, 6.
82. The survey and concept had been done in connection with the Council of Europe's renewal of the European Diploma to the Swiss National Park (originally awarded in 1967) in 1974. See the documents in the SNP Archives, 182.103, 303.101, 360.101.

83. Küpfer 2000.
84. *Schweizerische Jagdzeitung* 16 (1917). The Jagdzeitung was published by the Schweizerische Jagdschutzverein and represented the interests of the leased-hunting system. On Otto Meyer, see Schmidt 1976, 76-80.
85. Cited in *Schweizerische Jagdzeitung* 21 (1917).
86. Sarasin 1911, 4; see also SNK annual report 1909-10, 40-42; and Bachmann 1999, 198-202. On the relationship between hunting and nature protection in Switzerland, see Tschanz 1999.
87. *Schweizerische Jagdzeitung* 19 (1917).
88. Schmidt 1976, 128-158. Blankenhorn and Müller 2008; Schmid 2010. On hunting in Grisons, see Schmid 1986; Metz 1991, 487-496; Jenny and Müller 2002; Schmid 2010, 84-104.
89. *Schweizerische Jagdzeitung* 21 (1917). The same issue contained a response from ENPK secretary Bühlmann and a further response from Meyer.
90. ENPK annual report 1921, 9. This effect was also noted in African national parks. See Gissibl 2009, 379.
91. From the "standpoint of the game caring hunter," Hoffmann told the ENPK, he would also allow the shooting of those chamois bucks and goats that are known to be vicious brawlers. SCNAT Archives, Box 533, Bericht über den Aufenthalt von Dr. Karl R. Hoffmann im Nationalpark vom 25/8-10/9/1924, 6. The ENPK asked the opinion of the zoology subcommission of the WNPK on the fox intervention. SBN Archives, M 3.2, ENPK, meeting vom 18/10/1924.
92. BAR 9500.25, Bd. 38, Bericht des Oberaufsehers über die Herbstinspektion 1928, 1.
93. BAR 9500.25, vol. 7, ENPK, meeting of 24 January 1929, 1 f. WNPK, meeting of 13 January 1929, 5 f. SNP Archives, 152.100, Brunies, Bericht über die Sitzung der WNPK of 13 January 1929. BAR 9500.25, vol. 38, Bericht des Oberaufsehers über die Herbstinspektion 1928, 1; and Herbstinspektion 1929, 2-5.
94. ENPK annual report 1929, 5-7. Jean Carl, who hailed from Scuol, chaired the zoology subcommission from 1923 to 1939. He was an entomologist and since 1900 had worked at the Geneva Museum of Natural History. Revilliod 1944.
95. BAR 9500.25, vol. 9, Unterlagen zur Kommission zur Prüfung der Frage der wissenschaftlichen Erforschung der höheren Tierarten im Schweiz. Nationalpark.
96. SNP Archives, ENPK, meeting of 12 March 938, 1 f. Handschin was himself an entomologist. On his life, see Simon 2009, 145-154.
97. Interview Burckhardt.
98. On the relationship between science and national parks in the United States and in Switzerland, see Kupper 2009a.
99. See the ENPK annual reports for the 1930s. Heinrich Haller tried using various methods to retroactively determine the development of the red deer population. He ended up concluding that, prior to 1990, stocks had been underestimated. Haller 2002, 51-70.
100. BAR 9500.25, vol. 10, WNPK, meeting of 14 January 1934, 2; ENPK, meeting of 26 February 1934, 7 f. On wildlife watching in the United States, see Sellars 1997; Pritchard 1999; Wondrak Biel 2006.
101. Schmidt 1976, 259-262. Similar displacement processes may have occurred between ibex and chamois.

102. GA Zernez, B 21 a, Zernez to Kleinen Rat, 14 August 1930. On the new park contracts, see chapter 3.
103. ENPK annual report 1931, 4.
104. See the annual report for this year. During the war years, the ENPK also allowed cattle to summer on Alp Trupchun, which had been part of the national park since 1932, though they rejected other requests.
105. ENPK annual report 1948, 5 f. This assessment was confirmed in later deer die-offs. WNPK annual report 1953, 2 f. On the first deer deaths in 1945, see (in addition to the ENPK annual report) the SNP Archives, ENPK, meeting of 19 April 1945, 4 f.
106. SNP Archives, 115.100, Burckhardt. Bericht über die Extrahirschjagd vom 30/11–1/12/1956 in der Umgebung des Nationalparks, 16 December 1956. *Die Woche*, 17 December 1956. Originally, the government wanted to determine participation in the special hunt by drawing lots or through supervisory bodies.
107. *Die Woche*, 3 and 10 December 1956. *NZZ*, 12 December 1956. The Schaffhauser Arbeiter-Zeitung referred to "deer murder." *AZ Schaffhausen*, 17 December 1956.
108. For instance in the *NZZ*, 25 December 1956. On Vetterli, who incidentally had studied wildlife in the national park from 1927 to 1929 on behalf of the ENPK, see Schmidt 1976, 136 f.
109. In addition, the definition of lactating animals (which could not be shot) was loosened to increase the hunting pressure. Personal communication Hannes Jenny.
110. Beginning in 1991, numbers for roe deer were discounted owing to the unreliability of the surveys (ENPK annual report 1991, 6–9). Because deer reside manly in the border areas of the national park, their numbers in the park area fluctuate widely.
111. Burckhardt 1957. On ungulate research in the SNP, see Filli 2006. On American national park research, see Wright 1992; Sellars 1997; Pritchard 1999. A comparison of red deer management in the national parks of Yellowstone and Grand Teton, Bavarian Forest, and Swiss National Park, see Lhota 1998. In a cross-country study, Spehr attempted to differentiate historical phases of wildlife management (Spehr 1994). The result is not convincing. For application to Switzerland, see Tschanz 1999.
112. Archiv SNP, 115.100, Burckhardt, Bericht über die Extrahirschjagd vom 30/11–1/12/1956 in der Umgebung des Nationalparks, 16 December 1956, 12.
113. The spokesman was again Paul Vetterli. Schmidt 1976, 104.
114. *Der Freie Rätier*, 11 January 1965, and *Fögl Ladin*, 15 January 1965. Bündner Jägerzeitung: *Nationalparkgrenzen und Wildforschung. Konflikt mit den "Herren der Wildforschung,"* January 1965.
115. The measure was based on an understanding between the park and the canton on shared game management. Zernez Communal Archives, B 21 a, Kuster, Aktennotiz über die Besprechung vom 5/1/1965 mit Gemeinderat Zernez betreffend Missstimmung zwischen Parkhut und Bevölkerung; Stellungnahme Justiz und Polizeidep. betr. Abschuss verwaister Hirschkälber vom 29/1/1965.
116. SNP Archives, 111.102, Auslagen für Wildschaden im Kanton Graubünden, 12 March 1975; Verhütung und Vergütung von Wildschaden, 1962–1983. See Haller 2002, 60 f.
117. FOK Archives, WNPK, meeting of 22 February 1969, 2. Later Baer revised his view and rejected shooting kills in the park. SNP Archives, ENPK, meeting of 30 July 1973, 3.

118. ENPK annual report 1970, 8 f.
119. SNP Archives, ENPK, meeting of 19 June 1970, 4–7. SNP Archives, 115.102, Schloeth, Die Entwicklung des Hirschwildbestandes im Schweizerische Nationalpark und seiner Umgebung, und die möglichen Massnahmen zu seiner Regulierung, June 1971; ENPK, press communiqué, 13 July 1971. On the plans for predators, see chapter 4.
120. SNP Archives, ENPK, meeting of 19 June 1970, 5. The suggestion was made by the federal hunting inspector, Carl Desax.
121. SNP Archives, ENPK, meeting of 28 March 1972, 4, and 16 July 1972, 2–5; ENPK annual report 1972, 9.
122. ENPK annual report 1973, 7.
123. The ENPK continued to believe that the kills were incompatible with the park statute. At the same time, they asked that the statute be clarified. "The guiding principle of freely developing nature must be extended to include principles of 'preventing profound disturbance of natural development' and 'promoting natural diversity.'" SNP Archives, 115.104, Nationalparkstatut und Hirschabschüsse, Stellungnahme der WNPK, undated, 9. The negative attitude was reinforced in 1975. FOK Archives, WNPK, meeting of 15 February 1975, 2 f. However, the clarification of the statute was not effected until the end of the 1980s, when the park commission established formal guidelines to ensure the park objectives as a basis for evaluating interventions as well as changes in the park. Nationalparkkommission (ENPK) and Wissenschaftliche Nationalparkkommission (WNPK) 1989. See below.
124. Blankenhorn et al. 1979.
125. Haller 2002, 61–67.
126. Schröter 1926, 96.
127. In the 1950s Thurgau states' councilor and avid hunter Eric Ullmann uttered relevant warnings. In 1953 he called for the shooting of deer to re-establish the biological balance of the park. *NZZ*, no. 1407 (17 June 1953). Later he addressed his concerns to the Federal Council, SNP Archives, 182.100, Ullmann, Nationalpark, transcript, 13 June 1957. See also the description of Braun-Blanquet's 1958 position at the beginning of this chapter.
128. ENPK annual report 1986, 20 f. Emphasis mine. SNP Archives, 115.114, Präsidenten der Nationalparkgemeinden Zernez, S-chanf, Scuol, Valchava to ENPK, 29 November 1985.
129. Sonntags-Blick, 21 September 1986.
130. Tages-Anzeiger, 15 October 1986.
131. ENPK annual report 1987, 8 f. The legal basis is found in Art. 1, Nationalparkgesetz 1980.
132. Eidgenössische Nationalparkkommission (ENPK) and Wissenschaftliche Nationalparkkommission (WNPK) 1989, 11. The aftermath of the kills on the behavior of ungulates were still discernable several years later. Filli 1996.
133. Haefeli 1998.
134. See Anders and Uekötter 2003.
135. Krüsi et al. 1995; Schütz et al. 2000b. Summary: Haller 2006, 9.
136. See Jenny and Müller 2002. On regulation of ibex, see also Ratti 1994. The Proget d'ecologia in particular provided important scientific principles (Blankenhorn et al. 1979). The legal basis was established through revision of the hunting law at the fed-

eral and cantonal level (1986 and 1989). On the astonishing persistance of the self-image of the hunter, see Tschanz 1999.
137. Rudio and Schröter 1906, 505.
138. *NZZ*, 13 December 1958.
139. SNP Archives, ENPK, meeting of 30 July 1973, 3.

CONCLUSION

Creating Wilderness

In early 1909 when the Swiss League for Nature Protection was founded, the *Neue Zürcher Zeitung* welcomed the news: "The new league wishes to create a 'reserve' along the lines of North America's Yellowstone park. There, nature shall be left to its own devices, humans 'and their sorrows' will be kept out, and we will see how fantastically beautiful and interesting such an area can be. People will tremble in awe; cultural snobs, occasional tourists, and alpenrose pickers will be ashamed." However, the writer did wish to dispel one particular illusion, "namely, that such a park actually represents unadulterated nature. A very important piece of this nature is missing, a piece whose lack makes the entire reserve just too unnatural, the piece that nature itself willed and created, and that constitutes the culmination of its evolution: humans." No place in Switzerland remained untouched by "genus homo," wrote the journalist, asking rhetorically: "So does driving this creature from the landscape really constitute a return to nature? Hardly, unless you would argue that this expelling of humans by humans is itself a natural process." In any event, such an interpretation had not actually yet been made, and thus many would "prefer admiring nature in its truly freely developing state and virtuously observing and enjoying it where it had not been manipulated by the artificial expulsion of genus homo, where among all the mighty living creatures, the 'mightiest' would still be present. The bustle of the big city, the grinding and din of a factory, the activity in a large seaport, at a major train station, a roaring express train, an automobile, an airplane—mind you, these are all manifestations of nature unfolding and as such are truer and more real than anything to be seen in the carefully enclosed and policed nature park."[1]

Defining natural and artificial, and true and false, as the author of the 1909 *NZZ* article did, was unusual. By understanding humans to be part of nature, he turned the customary assumptions on their head. The movement of people and the grinding and din of machines were manifestations of nature unfolding at its truest and most pure, whereas the fenced and policed nature park seemed almost unnatural, artificial. However, the author also did not get around to drawing a line between nature and culture because otherwise everything would become natural, even "the expelling of humans by humans." This idea obviously pleased him little, and consequently he chose to regard the establishment of a national park-like reserve as "a sign of high culture," which aligned him with the national park promoters of the conservation movement.[2]

The strict separation of nature and culture was a precarious and highly problematic operation, and essential to the conception and development of the national park idea. At the same time, this separation was an expression of modern Western thought that had emerged over the course of the nineteenth century. The creation of the national park can be interpreted as an attempt to remedy these modern developments—which were perceived as excesses—using modern means. Three modern concepts were key to the genesis of the national park idea: duality (the division into dual categories); globalism (understanding the world as a whole); and evolution (the arrangement of world events as a sequence of developments in time). The significance of these three concepts is also reflected in the translational history of the Swiss National Park. Duality comes into play mainly in nature-culture interactions; globalism in topographical descriptors; and evolution in chronological systems. For the sake of clarity, I will treat the three topics in turn. However, they are not separate one from the other, but rather overlap. Thus, the distinction between nature and culture is made in space both at the local level (for example, the separate natural space of the national park) and the global level (for example, a division into civilized and uncivilized parts of the world). Similarly, ideas about nature influenced the timescales imposed.

The Swiss National Park was conceived as a "natural" space "protected from all human influence" that should be left entirely to its "freely developing nature" (federal decree of 1914). To this end, areas were carved out and geographical borders specified to separate these areas from the surrounding landscape. But this separation functioned only to a limited extent and certainly nowhere near the absoluteness intended by the founders as "total protection." Rather, the history of the national park was more typically characterized by border crossings and fortifications, border negotiations, and shifting borders. The predominance of this issue has historical grounds. The Swiss National Park never fenced in any "pristine" nature; the park's territory was extracted from a cultural landscape. The outlines of the park were easy to draw on a map, but less easy to realize on the ground. The national park was not an undisturbed natural enclave but an artificially created one in the middle of an "undisturbed" cultural space. As such, it was in a difficult position. Neither were the "waves of human culture flowing over the earth" (Carl Schröter) deterred by the park's borders nor was the park able to take care of itself. Two factors were often cited as contributing to this lack of autonomy: the absence of previously existing species such as predators, which would leave gaps in natural cycles that would require human intervention; and the fact that the park area did not constitute a natural ecosystem, which meant that natural processes would creep beyond the borders. However, while cross-border processes can be mitigated through clever boundary drawing and balanced composition of species, they can never be eliminated. For ecosystems that have one and the same border for all the components within them do not exist, and neither do ecosystems whose boundaries remain stable over time. As ecology learned in the twentieth century, nature is inherently dynamic. Relative stability, as expressed in a "climax state," is not the "natural" end state of "undisturbed" community, as supposed by early ecologists, but an exceptional phenomenon that requires scientific explanation.[3] The desire to keep human influence at a distance also turned out to be an illusion that, in the face of increasing use, growing pollution, and accelerating climate change, proved ever more difficult to maintain.

National parks—and here one must agree with the astute commentary of the *NZZ* in 1909—are artificial constructs. Their creation is based on long-term stable boundaries that separate the parks from their surroundings. But the conditions both in and around national parks are characterized by natural and social dynamics that almost inevitably put the park borders under pressure. At the same time, these borders create social and environmental realities that have difficulty adapting to changing conditions due to the spatial arrangement. Space-oriented nature protection is not a flexible tool, which is both its strength and its weakness. It creates conditions and resists shortsighted interventions; but it also results in path dependencies and is itself only moderately adaptive.

Globally, the national park idea was highly mobile, whereas once established, parks tended to develop considerable inertia locally. But they were also exposed to the social forces they created. If the social relationship with nature went out of balance, generally speaking the heterotopic national parks were also affected. Thus, in recent decades efforts to make the boundaries of national parks and similar protected areas less absolute have coincided with the softening of the line dividing nature and culture.[4] The terms "environment" and "sustainability," now infused with new meaning, embody this social change, which also affected the Swiss National Park, though a bit later. Although in 2000 the attempt to provide the park with a buffer zone failed, the inclusion of the national park as the core zone of the biosphere reserve *Biosfera Val Müstair* appears, ten years later, to be on firm footing.

The creation of this biosphere represents the convergence of two trends evident in the political topography of the Swiss National Park. First, in recent decades, the park has enjoyed increasing support at both the local and regional level; and second, inter- and transnational aspects have also become more significant. These trends are consistent with a mutually dependent process of globalization and localization apparent in other areas. Transnational links and international regimes already figured largely when the Swiss National Park was founded. At the time, however, they were dealt with at the national level. Federal Councilor Felix-Louis Calonder praised the national park "as a magnificent realization of a major international concept done in a fittingly national manner."[5] The term "national park," which despite substantial reservations about the US model was chosen to gain national support, had far-reaching ramifications. It shaped interest and led to expectations among park managers and scientists, locals and visitors. Although from 1914 to 1945 activities at the national level were in the forefront, in the decades following the Second World War, other levels came increasingly into focus. Among newly formed international conservation elites, which included the authoritative participation of the Swiss, the Swiss National Park was considered a prime example of a scientific national park. At the same time, local and regional voices were gradually making themselves more audible. In Switzerland these global and international activities were only recently reflected in the expanded federal act on the protection of nature and cultural heritage. The initiative for establishing "parks of national importance" was transferred to local and regional institutions, whereas the role of the federal government was limited to consultation, certification, and financial aid. Remarkably, very little emphasis was put on international compatibility—the most common nomenclature, that of the International Union for Conservation of Nature, was not adopted—and the much more federally integrated Swiss National Park was excluded from the new law. As a result, an eventual second Swiss National Park will be subject to a different law than the original park, which for its part does not meet the new conditions.[6]

In the early years, people did not speak of the Swiss National Park, but rather of one or the first Swiss national park, which would be followed by others. Only when these follow-up projects failed to materialize did the park adopt the definite article and the capital "N" and "P." The implicit message was that the park would remain a singular phenomenon. It invited interpretation as a member of a group of institutions that the federal government created only one of to serve the national interest. Examples include the Swiss National Museum, the Swiss National Library, and the Swiss National Bank. The end to this singular existence gave rise to a new question. What meaning would the term "national park" have in Switzerland in the future? What would be the relationship between the "old" Swiss National Park and any "new" Swiss national parks? These questions were excluded from the new law. But dealing with them has not been permanently tabled, only postponed.

National parks always stood for a promise of the future. The current generation, opined the *NZZ* journalist in the article cited above, can only regret "that it will not be able to share in the enjoyment to be had for a future generation." The *Naturschutzkommission* (SNK) wished the park to be a "gift to the future," although in this case the recipient was very abstract, and fundamentally timeless. For people who lived in the area around the national park, on the other hand, the future was very concrete; specifically, it concerned the next few years at most, their own destiny, and that of their children, relatives, and friends. Whereas conservationists and scientists thought in terms of natural historical timescales, the local population moved in real-world dimensions. This a priori complicated political negotiations, in which the durations for use of areas extended beyond these real-world dimensions.

But scientists also had trouble with long-termism. Research projects were designed to be carried out by several generations of researchers in succession. Once a research project was designed and implemented, there followed decades of patient, meticulous documentation of gradual changes. Scientifically valuable results critical to academic recognition consequently were often out of reach. To address this dilemma, in the 1990s researchers developed a method to expand their possibilities for disseminating results over the time period of observation. They blended data series from several plots to obtain a larger data series. That enabled them to compress the observation time by accumulating the time intervals recorded at various monitoring stations. By blending observation series that spanned several decades, they were able to build hypothetical data sets covering centuries. They effectively were able to fit time into space, and vice versa.

Given its orientation toward scientific research lasting over long periods of time, from the very beginning the Swiss National Park was unusual. Support from the global aspirations and transnational networks of individual actors, especially Paul Sarasin, helped bring the park to the attention of the world and gave it a global historical significance that only few other national parks enjoy. But its special approach also made extraordinary demands on the conception and administration of the park. In setting its objectives, the park could only remain viable if external conditions remained stable over the long term. It required a guarantee that the protection measures would endure over many decades. Consequently, establishing firm principles and solid structures was imperative.

In this respect, the founders of the national park were very successful. In comparative perspective, the uniquely high continuity that has marked the conceptual orientation of the park for over a century testifies to this. However, two interrelated disadvantages are also evident: First, both the ongoing development and expansion of the park were designed to be difficult; the latter in particular has come back to haunt the park insofar as the inclusion of local stakeholders has long been limited to the required minimum. Second, the park's intended function as a role model could not be honored to the extent desired. As the prototype of a scientific national park, the Swiss national park enjoyed a sustained degree of international attention, which was reflected in its international reputation. But it never managed to achieve the popularity and impact of the American parks. Even within its own country, it was not copied. In contrast to other countries in which the establishment of a national park was usually followed by other parks, the Swiss National Park remained a singular phenomenon. The dreams of creating national parks in the interwar period came to nothing, whereas more recent attempts were placed on a new institutional basis. In its campaign for the new Swiss parks, the federal government highlighted the touristic value of parks and referred to the Swiss National Park as the prime example. Given the park's history, this kind of advertising was irritating to say the least but on closer inspection the reasons for doing so become clear.[7] In tourism the government found an economically and politically more powerful ally than science. This converges with the significance of the Swiss National Park in global historical perspective. On the global level, the Swiss park played only a secondary role, but it has been an active and innovative one that in turn has allowed discussion of global historical issues.

A "highly interesting experiment" would be initiated, reported the author of the 1909 *NZZ* article on the planned national park. Similarly, the SNK spoke at the time of a "grand experiment." The commission believed that nature could be separated from humans in a protected space, and that nature, so isolated, would "restore its ur-nature" on its own. From the distance of a century one can say with certainty: This idea was an illusion. Primeval nature was not restored; rather, wilderness was created. In this respect, the SNK's experiment failed. Were its members still alive today, they would nonetheless probably not be discouraged. Rather, they would be proud to have initiated such an experiment, which a hundred years later is still running and is producing results that continue to generate interest.

The social experiment known as the "national park" is not yet complete, neither in the Swiss National Park nor in Switzerland, nor on the international or global stage. More national parks will be created and existing national parks will evolve, as will the connotations of the term "national park." Ideas of national park and wilderness have recently converged. Here it is important to remember—and this is perhaps one of the broader lessons to draw from the Swiss National Park—that even wilderness is not something that exists outside of society, at the periphery, where it can be conserved. Wilderness does not exist; it is created. It is not a natural condition, but a historical process. An ongoing social debate over wilderness is both a prerequisite and a justification for its existence. Demonstrating the historical particularity of wilderness and its historicity in a competent and stimulating way is a task for transnational environmental history. This book, too, is a contribution to the ongoing process of creating wilderness.

Notes

1. *NZZ*, 13 January 1909. "Blest is the wide world every where / When man and his sorrows come not near," is Friedrich Schiller (from the play *The Bride of Messina*). The

reference to humans as the mightiest among the mighty is an allusion by the author (who signed himself "Tr.") to the Greek tragedy *Antigone* by Sophocles. Five years later, the *NZZ*'s editor-in-chief, Walter Bissegger, made this passage the motto of his address to the National Council on the national park resolution, though he interpreted it somewhat differently. Bissegger quoted from Schiller's poem "The Alpine Hunter." See chapter 1. The national park idea obviously evoked authors and quotations from the educational canon of the contemporary middle-class.
2. *NZZ*, 13 January 1909.
3. See, for instance, the discussion on the concept of "punctuated equilibrium," Gould and Eldredge 1993.
4. See Zimmerer 2000.
5. *Amtliches Bulletin Nationalrat* 24 (1914), 184.
6. The law requires a core and buffer zone for national parks. The order of the list of services (a. Recreation, b. Environmental education, c. Scientific research) is reversed for the Swiss National Park. The Federal Office for the Environment nevertheless includes it under the category "National Park" (http://www.bafu.admin.ch/paerke/06579, accessed 28 September 2010).
7. Schweizerischer Bundesrat 2005, 2168.

Bibliography

Archival Sources

Archiv Schweizerischer Nationalpark, Zernez (Archiv SNP)
Verwaltungsarchiv SNP
Eidgenössische Nationalparkkommission, ENPK, Protokollbücher, 1938–
Tagebücher der Nationalparkwächter, 1910–
Archiv Schweizerische Akademie der Naturwissenschaften, Burgerbibliothek Bern, (Archiv SCNAT)
Schweizerische Naturschutzkommission SNK, Schachteln 521–537, 1906–44
Archiv Forschungskommission Schweizerischer Nationalpark, Swiss Academy of Sciences, Bern (Archiv FOK)
Wissenschaftliche Nationalparkkommission WNPK, Sitzungsprotokolle, 1917–
Archiv *Pro Natura* (Schweizerischer Bund für Naturschutz), Staatsarchiv Basel-Stadt, PA 924 (Archiv SBN)
M, Nationalpark, 1910–88
Schweizerisches Bundesarchiv, Bern (BAR)
9500.25, Akz. 1967/47, ENPK, vols. 1–38, 1892–1965
E 16, Pertinenzbestand 1849–1922, vol. 41, Nationalpark, 1915–20
E 2001 (A), vol. 444, Weltnaturschutz, 1911–13
Staatsarchiv Graubünden, Chur (StaGB)
X 8 g, Jagd, Nationalpark, 1911–
X 23 f 3 a, Natur- und Heimatschutz, Gross-Schutzgebiete, Nationalpark, 1907–
Gemeindearchiv Scuol (GA Scuol)
Politische Gemeinde (Cumün Politic)
- II B, Parc Naziunal, 1920–60
- Briefkopien, 1907–10
- Protokollbücher Politische Gemeinde, Gemeinderat und Gemeindeversammlungen, 1901–62

Bürgergemeinde (Corporaziun da Vaschins)
- Concessiun OEE, Parc Naziunal, Proget Spöl, 1957–64
- Protokollbücher Bürgergemeinde, Bürgerrat und Bürgerversammlungen, 1910–72

Gemeindearchiv Zernez (GA Zernez)
B 21, Parc Naziunal, 1908–75
C 4, Cudeschs da quint (Rechnungsbücher), 1904–50
ETH-Bibliothek, Archive und Nachlässe, Zurich
Archive, SR2: Schulratsprotokolle
Nachlässe, Hs 399: Nachlass Carl Schröter

Archiv Neue Zürcher Zeitung, Zurich (NZZ)
Digitale Archive of all issues since 1780
Nationale Archives, Washington, DC, USA (NA)
Record Group 79, Records of the National Park Service, 3.1, General Records, Foreign Parks 0-30
- Entry 7: Central Classif. Files 1907–49, 1907–32, Boxes 629, 632
- Entry 7: Central Classif. Files 1907–49, 1933–49, Box 2920
- Administrative Files 1949–71, L66: Boxes 2182, 2183

Library of Congress, Washington, DC (LoC)
Papers of John C. Merriam

Online Databases

Bundesblatt der Schweizerischen Eidgenossenschaft, www.amtsdruckschriften.bar.admin.ch
Historisches Lexikon der Schweiz, www.hls-dhs-dss.ch
JSTOR, www.jstor.org
Le Temps Archives Historiques, www.letempsarchives.ch
Memobase, Memoriav, http://de.memoriav.ch/memobase
Nature, www.nature.com/nature/archive
Schulratsprotokolle online, www.sr.ethbib.ethz.ch/digbib/home
SEALS (Server für digitalisierte Zeitschriften), http://retro.seals.ch/digbib/home
Swiss National Park Data Center, www.parcs.ch/mmds
Times Archive, http://archive.timesonline.co.uk/tol/archive

Interviews

Chasper Buchli, 30 June 2009
Martin Bundi, 8 July 2009
Dieter Burckhardt, 7 November 2007
Jon Filli, 31 May 2008
Heinrich Haller, 25 September 2007
Jürg Paul Müller, 19 December 2007
Bernhard Nievergelt, 30 September 2008
Jon Domenic Parolini, 26 September 2007
Klaus Robin, 19 August 2008
Thomas Scheurer, 29 April 2008
Robert Schloeth, 7 November 2007
Martin Schütz, 8 October 2008

Annual Reports

Eidgenössische Nationalparkkommission, ENPK, 1915–
Schweizerischer Bund für Naturschutz, 1914–
Schweizerische Naturschutzkommission, SNK, 1906–14
Wissenschaftliche Nationalparkkommission, WNPK (now Forschungskommission Nationalpark), 1917–

Statistics

Amt für Wirtschaft und Tourismus Graubünden, www.awt.gr.ch, Tourismusdaten seit 1992

Bundesamt für Statistik, www.bfs.admin.ch, Statistisches Lexikon der Schweiz

Engadiner Kraftwerke, Frequenzstatistik Strassentunnel Munt La Schera, 1970–2009.

Online Datenbasis zur Wirtschafts- und Sozialgeschichte der Schweiz. Hrsg. von Patrick Kammerer, Margrit Müller, Jakob Tanner und Ulrich Woitek, www.fsw.uzh.ch/histstat

Schweizerischer Nationalpark, Ungulate numbers

Publications

Abderhalden, Emil. 1939. *Gesamtinhaltsübersicht, Stichwort- und Mitarbeiterverzeichnis.* Berlin: Urban & Schwarzenberg.

Abderhalden, Walter. 2005. *Raumnutzung und sexuelle Segregation beim Alpensteinbock Capra ibex ibex.* Zernez: Forschungskommission des Schweizerischen Nationalparks.

Adams, William M. 2004. *Against Extinction: The Story of Conservation.* London: Earthscan.

Agrawal, Arun. 2005. *Environmentality: Technologies of Government and the Making of Subjects.* Durham: Duke University Press.

Agrawal, Arun, and Kent Redford. 2009. "Conservation and Displacement: An Overview," *Conservation and Society* 7 (1), 1–10.

Akeley, Carl Ethan. 1923. *In Brightest Africa.* Garden City: Doubleday.

Allgöwer, Britta. 1996. *Konzept für die Weiterführung des Geographischen Informationssystems des Schweizerischen Nationalparks (GIS-SNP Konzept II)*, http://gis.nationalpark.ch/pdf_snp/gis-snp_konzept_II_1996.pdf.

Allgöwer, Britta, and Peter Bitter 1992. *Konzeptstudie zum Aufbau eines geographischen Informationssystemes für den Schweizerischen Nationalpark (GIS-SNP).* Zernez: WNPK.

Allgöwer, Britta, et al. 2005. "Waldbrand—nur ein Fall für die Feuerwehr?" in *Cratschla* (2), 12–13.

AnArchitektur (ed.). 2002. *Material zu: Lefèbvre, Die Produktion des Raumes.* An Architektur, 1.

Anders, Kenneth, and Frank Uekötter. 2003. "Viel Lärm ums stille Sterben: Die Debatte über das Waldsterben in Deutschland," in Jens Hohensee and Frank Uekötter (eds.), *Wird Kassandra heiser? Die Geschichte falscher Ökoalarme.* Stuttgart: Franz Steiner Verlag, 112–138.

Anderson, Benedict 1991. *Imagined Communities: Reflections on the Origin and Spread of Nationalism.* London: Verso.

Andrews, E. D., and Leslie A. Pizzi. 2000. "Origin of the Colorado River Experimental Flood in Grand Canyon," *Hydrological Sciences Journal* 45 (4), 607–627.

Babcock, Ernest B. 1934. "Harvey Monroe Hall," *University of California publications in botany* 17 (12), 355–367.

Bachmann, Ernst, and Max Oechslin. 1950. *Der Schweizerische Nationalpark.* Basel.

Bachmann, Stefan. 1999. *Zwischen Patriotismus und Wissenschaft: Die Schweizerischen Naturschutzpioniere (1900–1938).* Zürich: Chronos.

———. 2005. "Alpenromantik und Tourismuskritik: Widerstand gegen den Boom der Bergbahnen," in Madlaina Bundi (ed.), *Erhalten und Gestalten: 100 Jahre Schweizer Heimatschutz*. Baden: hier + jetzt, 26–35.
Backhaus, Norman, Claude Reichler, and Matthias Stremlow 2007. *Alpenlandschaften: Von der Vorstellung zur Handlung*. Zürich: vdf.
Baer, Jean-Georges. 1962. "Un demi-siècle d'activité scientifique dans le Parc national suisse," *Verhandlungen der Schweizerischen Naturforschenden Gesellschaft* 142, 50–62.
Baer, Jean-Georges, et al. 1968. *Oekologische Untersuchungen im Unterengadin*, Lfg 1. Chur: WNPK.
Barbey, Auguste. 1919. "Le danger d'extension des dégâts d'insectes dans les forêts du Parc national de l'Engadine," *Journal Forestier Suisse* 1, 21–23.
Barringer, Mark D. 2002. *Selling Yellowstone: Capitalism and the Construction of Nature*. Lawrence: University Press of Kansas.
Barrow, Mark V. 2009. *Nature's Ghosts: Confronting Extinction from the Age of Jefferson to the Age of Ecology*. Chicago: University of Chicago Press.
Barth, Boris, and Jürgen Osterhammel (eds.). 2005. *Zivilisierungsmissionen: Imperiale Weltverbesserung seit dem 18. Jahrhundert*. Konstanz: UVK Verlagsgesellschaft.
Barthelmess, Alfred. 1987. *Landschaft, Lebensraum des Menschen: Probleme von Landschaftsschutz und Landschaftspflege geschichtlich dargestellt und dokummentiert*. Freiburg i. Br.: Alber.
Bauer, Nicole. 2005. *Für und wider Wildnis: Soziale Dimensionen einer aktuellen gesellschaftlichen Debatte*. Bern: Haupt.
Baur, Bruno. 2010. *Biodiversität*. Bern: Haupt.
Bayly, Christopher A. 2004. *The Birth of the Modern World, 1780–1914: Global Connections and Comparisons*. Malden: Blackwell.
Becking, Rudy W. 1957. "The Zürich-Montpellier School of Phytosociology," *The Botanical Review* 23 (7), 411–488.
Beinart, William, and Lotte Hughes 2007. *Environment and Empire*. Oxford: Oxford University Press.
Bender, Thomas (ed.). 2001. *Rethinking American History in a Global Age*. Berkeley: University of California Press.
Benson, Etienne. 2010. *Wired Wilderness: Technologies of Tracking and the Making of Modern Wildlife*. Baltimore: Johns Hopkins University Press.
———. 2012. "Demarcating Wilderness and Disciplining Wildlife: Radiotracking Large Carnivores in Yellowstone and Chitwan National Parks," in Gissibl, Höhler, and Kupper (eds.), *Civilizing Nature: National Parks in Global Historical Perspective*. New York: Berghahn Books, 173–188.
Biernacki, Richard. 2000. "Language and the Shift from Signs to Practices in Cultural Inquiry," in: *History and Theory* 39, 289–310.
Bland, G. Edith 1927. "The National Park of Switzerland," in *Annual Report Smithonian Institution 1926*, 495–503.
Blankenhorn, Hans-Jörg. 2006. "Die Rolle des Bundes," in Marco Giacometti (ed.), *Von Königen und Wilderern: Die Rettung und Wiederansiedlung des Alpensteinbocks*. Wohlen: Salm, 191–203.
Blankenhorn, Hans-Jörg, et al. 1979. *Bericht zum Hirschproblem im Engadin und im Münstertal*. St. Gallen: Anzeiger-Druckerei.

Blankenhorn, Hans-Jörg and Kurt Müller 2008. Jagd, in: *Historisches Lexikon der Schweiz*, URL: http://www.hls-dhs-dss.ch/textes/d/D13942.php (Version vom 28.01.2008)

Blom, Philipp 2008. *The vertigo years change and culture in the West, 1900-1914*, London: Weidenfeld & Nicolson.

Bowler, Peter John 1992. *The Fontana history of the environmental sciences*, London: Fontana Press.

Bowler, Peter John 2003. *Evolution: The History of an Idea*, Berkeley: University of California Press.

Bowles, Samuel. 1869. *The Switzerland of America: A Summer Vacation in the Parks and Mountains of Colorado*. Springfield: S. Bowles & co.

Bratich, Jack Z., Jeremy Packer, and Cameron McCarthy (eds.). 2003. *Foucault, Cultural Studies, and Governmentality*. Albany: State University of New York Press.

Braudel, Fernand (ed.). 1958. "Histoire et sciences sociales: La longue durée," *Annales* 13 (4), 725–753.

Braudel, Fernand. 1976. *La Méditerranée et le monde méditerranéen à l'époque de Philippe II*. Paris: Colin.

Braun-Blanquet, Josias. 1921. Prinzipien einer Systematik der Pflanzengesellschaften auf floristischer Grundlage, in: *Jahrb. St. Galler Naturwiss. Ges.*, 57, 305–351.

———. 1928. *Pflanzensoziologie: Grundzüge der Vegetationskunde*. Berlin: Julius Springer.

———. 1931. *Vegetations-Entwicklung im Schweizer. Nationalpark Ergebnisse der Untersuchung von Dauerbeobachtungsflächen*. Chur.

———. 1932. *Plant Sociology: The Study of Plant Communities*. New York: McGraw-Hill.

———. 1939. "Über die Flora des schweizerischen Nationalparks," *Schweizer Naturschutz* 5 (4/5), 60–63.

Braun-Blanquet, Josias, and Hans Jenny. 1926. *Vegetations-Entwicklung und Bodenbildung in der alpinen Stufe der Zentralalpen (Klimaxgebiet des Caricion curvulae) mit besonderer Berücksichtigung der Verhältnisse im schweizerischen Nationalparkgebiet*. Zürich: Fretz.

Braun-Blanquet, Josias, Hans Pallmann, and Roman Bach 1954. *Pflanzensoziologische und bodenkundliche Untersuchungen im schweizerischen Nationalpark und seinen Nachbargebieten*. Liestal.

Breitenmoser, Urs, and Christine Breitenmoser-Würsten. 2008. *Der Luchs: Ein Grossraubtier in der Kulturlandschaft*. Wohlen: Salm.

Brockington, Dan. 2002. *Fortress Conservation: The Preservation of the Mkomazi Game Reserve, Tanzania*. Oxford: The International African Institute.

Brockington, Dan, Rosaleen Duffy, and Jim Igoe. 2008. *Nature Unbound: Conservation, Capitalism and the Future of Protected Areas*. London: Earthscan.

Bröckling, Ulrich, Susanne Krassmann, and Thomas Lemke (eds.). 2000. *Gouvernementalität der Gegenwart: Studien zur Ökonomisierung des Sozialen*. Frankfurt: Suhrkamp.

Brunhes, Jean 1911. *Les limites de notre cage*. Fribourg: Imprimerie de l'Oeuvre de Saint-Paul.

Brunies, Steivan. 1906. *Die Flora des Ofengebietes (Südost-Graubünden): Ein floristischer und pflanzengeographischer Beitrag zur Erforschung Graubündens*. Chur: s.n.

———. 1914. *Der schweizerische Nationalpark*. Basel: Frobenius.

———. 1918. *Der Schweizerische Nationalpark*. Basel: Schwabe.

———. 1919a. *Excursiuns tres il Parc Nazionel Svizzer: üna guida pella giuventüna*. Basel: Lia Svizra.

———. 1919b. *Il Parc nazional sun terra ladina*. Basel: Schwabe.
———. 1923. *Streifzüge durch den Schweizerischen Nationalpark*. Basel: Schwabe.
———. 1928. *Unser Nationalpark und die ausserschweizerischen alpinen Reservationen*. Zürich: Beer.
———. 1930. "Davart l'influenza da la natüra grischuna sün nos pövel ladin," *Annalas* 44, 55–72.
———. 1951. "'Einbürgerung' des Alpenbären im Nationalpark?" *Terra Grischuna* (2).
Bühlmann, Fritz. 1924. "Die Entstehung des schweizerischen Nationalparks im Unterengadin," *ENPK Jahresbericht*, 1–12.
Bundi, Madlaina. 2001. *Goldene Schokolade: Die Taleraktion von Heimat- und Naturschutz 1946–1962*. Universität Zürich: Lizentiatsarbeit.
Bundi, Martin. 2006. "Projekte zur Wiederansiedlung im 19. Jahrhundert," in Marco Giacometti (ed.), *Von Königen und Wilderern: Die Rettung und Wiederansiedlung des Alpensteinbocks*. Wohlen: Salm, 77–106.
Bündnerische Vereinigung für Heimatschutz (ed.). 1907. *Das Engadiner Haus*. Schuls.
Burckhardt, Dieter. 1957. "Über das Wintersterben der Hirsche in der Umgebung des Nationalparkes," *Schweizer Naturschutz* 23 (1), 1–5.
Burger, Hans. 1950. "Forstliche Versuchsflächen im schweizerischen Nationalpark," *Mitteilungen der Schweizerischen Anstalt für das Forstliche Versuchswesen* 26, 583–634.
Bürgi, Michael, and Daniel Speich (eds.). 2004. *Lokale Naturen: 150 Jahre Thurgauische Naturforschende Gesellschaft, 1854–2004*. Frauenfeld: Thurgauische Naturforschende Gesellschaft.
Burke, Edmund, and Kenneth Pomeranz (eds.). 2009. *The Environment and World History*. Berkeley: University of California Press.
Bütikofer, Ernst. 1920. *Die Molluskenfauna des schweizerischen Nationalparks*. Zürich: Fretz.
Butler, Richard W., and Stephen W. Boyd (eds.). 2000. *Tourism and National Parks: Issues and Implications*. Chichester: John Wiley.
Cahalane, Victor H. (ed.). 1962. *National Parks—A World Need*. New York: American Committee for International Wildlife Protection.
Callicott, John B., and Michael P. Nelson (eds.). 1998. *The Great New Wilderness Debate*. Athens: University of Georgia Press.
Camenisch, Martin, and Martin Schütz. 2000. "Temporal and spatial variability of the vegetation in a four-year exclosure experiment in Val Trupchun (Swiss National Park)," in Martin Schütz et al. (eds.), *Succession research in the Swiss National Park: From Braun-Blanquet's permanent plots to models of long-term ecological change*. Zernez: Forschungskommission des Schweizerischen Nationalparks, 165–188.
Cameron, Laura, and David Matless. 2010. "Translocal Ecologies: The Norfolk Broads, the 'Natural,' and the International Phytogeographical Excursion, 1911," *Journal of the History of Biology*, Epub 30.7.2010.
Campell, E., and W. Trepp. 1968. *Vegetationskarte des schweizerischen Nationalparkes Kartenmaterial*. Chur: Nationalpark-Museum.
Carr, Ethan. 1998. *Wilderness by Design: Landscape Architecture and the National Park Service*. Lincoln: University of Nebraska Press.
Carruthers, Jane. 1995. *The Kruger National Park: A Social and Political History*. Pietermaritzburg: University of Natal Press.

Catrina, Werner. 1972. *Die Entstehung der Rhätischen Bahn*. Zürich: Juris.
———. 1983. *Die Rätoromanen zwischen Resignation und Aufbruch*. Zürich: Orell Füssli.
Catton, Theodore. 1995. *Land Reborn: A History of Administration and Visitor Use in Glacier Bay National Park and Preserve*. Anchorage: National Park Service.
———. 1997. *Inhabited Wilderness: Indians, Eskimos, and National Parks in Alaska*. Albuquerque: University of New Mexico Press.
Cioc, Mark. 2009. *The Game of Conservation: International Treaties to Protect the World's Migratory Animals*. Athens: Ohio University Press.
Clavuot, Ottavio. 2008. "Engadin," *Historisches Lexikon der Schweiz*, www.hls-dhs-dss.ch/textes/d/D8067.php (Version vom 23 October 2006)
Clements, Frederic E. 1916. *Plant Succession: An Analysis of the Development of Vegetation*. Washington: The Carnegie Institution of Washington.
Coates, Peter. 1998. *Nature Western Attitudes Since Ancient Times*. Berkeley: University of California Press.
———. 2006. *American Perceptions of Immigrant and Invasive Species: Strangers on the Land*. Berkeley: University of California Press.
Coaz, Johann, and Carl Schröter. 1905. *Ein Besuch im Val Scarl (Seitental des Unterengadin)*. Bern: Stämpfli.
Colchester, Marcus. 2003. *Salvaging Nature: Indigenous Peoples, Protected Areas and Biodiversity Conservation*. World Rainforest Movement.
Conférence Internationale pour la Protection de la Nature Berne (ed.). 1914. *Recueil des procès-verbaux*. Bern: K.-J. Wyss.
Conrad, Sebastian. 2006. *Globalisierung und Nation im deutschen Kaiserreich*. Munich: Beck.
Conrad, Sebastian, Andreas Eckert, and Ulrike Freitag (eds.). 2007. *Globalgeschichte: Theorien, Ansätze, Themen*. Frankfurt: Campus.
Conrad, Sebastian, and Jürgen Osterhammel. 2004. *Das Kaiserreich transnational: Deutschland in der Welt 1871-1914*. Göttingen: Vandenhoeck & Ruprecht.
Conrad, Sebastian, and Shalini Randeria (eds.). 2002. *Jenseits des Eurozentrismus: Postkoloniale Perspektiven in den Geschichts- und Kulturwissenschaften*. Frankfurt: Campus.
Conwentz, Hugo. 1904. *Die Gefährdung der Naturdenkmäler und Vorschläge zu ihrer Erhaltung*. Berlin: Borntraeger.
Coolidge, Harold J. 1972. "Evolution of the Concept, Role and Early History of National Parks," in Jean-Paul Harroy (ed.), *World National Parks: Progress and Opportunities*. Brussels: Hayez, 29-38.
Cooper, Frederick. 2005. *Colonialism in Question: Theory, Knowledge, History*. Berkeley: University of Califiornia Press.
Cronon, William. 1995. "The Trouble with Wilderness," in William Cronon (ed.), *Uncommon Ground: Toward Reinventing Nature*. New York, London: W.W. Norton, 69-90.
——— (ed.). 1996. *Uncommon Ground. Rethinking the Human Place in Nature*. New York: W.W. Norton.
Crosby, Alfred W. 2004. *Ecological Imperialism: The Biological Expansion of Europe, 900-1900*. Cambridge: Cambridge University Press.
Dachnowski, Alfred. 1914. "The International Phytogeographic Excursion of 1913 and its Significance to Ecology in America," *The Journal of Ecology* 2 (4), 237-245.

Daum, Andreas. 2002. *Wissenschaftspopularisierung im 19. Jahrhundert: Bürgerliche Kultur, naturwissenschaftliche Bildung und die deutsche Öffentlichkeit, 1848-1914*. Munich: Oldenbourg.
David, Adam. 1945. *Doktor David erzählt: Weitere Erlebnisse des alten "Afrikaners" und Jägers*. Basel: Friedrich Reinhardt.
Delort, Robert, and François Walter. 2001. *Histoire de l'environnement européen*. Paris: Presses Universitaires de France.
Dinzelbacher, Peter (ed.). 2000. *Mensch und Tier in der Geschichte Europas*. Stuttgart: Kröner.
Döring, Jörg, and Tristan Thielmann (eds.). 2008. *Spatial Turn: Das Raumparadigma in den Kultur- und Sozialwissenschaften*. Bielefeld: transcript.
Dowie, Mark 2009. *Conservation Refugees: The Hundred-Year Conflict between Global Conservation and Native Peoples*. Cambridge: MIT.
Drehsen, Volker, and Walter Sparn (eds.). 1996. *Vom Weltbildwandel zur Weltanschauungsanalyse: Krisenwahrnehmung und Krisenbewältigung um 1900*. Berlin: Akademie-Verlag.
Dudley, Nigel (ed.). 2008. *Guidelines for Applying Protected Areas Management Categories*. Gland: IUCN.
Dunlap, Thomas R. 1999. *Nature and the English Diaspora: Environment and History in the United States, Canada, Australia, and New Zealand*. Cambridge: Cambridge University Press.
Eagles, Paul F. J., and Stephen F. McCool. 2002. *Tourism in National Parks and Protected Areas: Planning and Management*. Wallingford: CABI.
Egli, Werner M. 2011. "Woher kommen die Findlinge: Wie die frühe Hochgebirgsforschung zur Erfindung der 'primitiven Gesellschaft' beitrug," in: Werner M. Egli and Imgrid Tomkowiak (eds.), *Berge*. Zürich: Chronos, 105–123.
Eidgenössische und Wissenschaftliche Nationalparkkommission. 1989. *Schweizerischer Nationalpark: Leitlinien zur Gewährleistung der Parkziele*. s.l.: ENPK, WNPK.
Eidgenössisches Statistisches Amt (ed.). 1923. *Eidgenössische Volkszählung 1. Dezember 1920, Heft 9: Graubünden*. Bern: A. Francke.
Eitler, Pascal, and Maren Möhring. 2008. "Eine Tiergeschichte der Moderne: Theoretische Perspektiven," *Traverse. Zeitschrift für Geschichte* 15 (3), 91–105.
Elliott, Hugh F. I. 1974. *Second World Conference on National Parks*. Morges, Switzerland,: IUCN.
Engadiner Gemeinden (ed.). 1958. *Dokumente zur Spölfrage*. Chur: Gasser & Eggerling.
Escher, Jean-Robert. 1994. *Entstehung und Entwicklung des Dürsrüti-Reservates*. ETH Zürich: Diplomarbeit.
Eser, Uta 1999. *Der Naturschutz und das Fremde: Ökologische und normative Grundlagen der Umweltethik*. Frankfurt: Campus.
———. 2003. "Der Wert der Vielfalt: 'Biodiversität' zwischen Wissenschaft, Politik und Ethik," in Monika Bobbert et al. (eds.), *Umwelt—Ethik—Recht*. Tübingen: Francke, 160–181.
Etter, Tom Michael. 1992. *Untersuchung zur Ausrottungsgeschichte des Wolfes (Canis lupus L.) in der Schweiz und den benachbarten Gebieten des Auslandes*. ETH Zürich: Diplomarbeit.
Evans, David. 1997. *A History of Nature Conservation in Britain*. London: Routledge.

Evans, Sterling. 2010. "Recent Developments in Transnational Environmental History: Labor, Settler Communities, and Comparative Histories," *Radical History Review* (107), 195–208.
Falser, Michael S. 2008. *Zwischen Identität und Authentizität: Zur politischen Geschichte der Denkmalpflege in Deutschland*. Dresden: Thelem.
Fehr, Christine, et al. 2006. *Welche Schutzgebiete braucht die Schweiz? Pro Natura Standpunkt, vom Pro Natura Delegiertenrat verabschiedet am 22. April 2006*. Basel: Pro Natura.
Feuerstein, Domenic. 1936. *Wo der Aar noch kreist . . . ein besinnliches Buch aus dem Schweizerischen Nationalpark und den benachbarten Heimatbergen*. Zürich: Ferrari.
Feuerstein, Johann. 1927. *Der schweizerische National-Park: 50 künstlerische Aufnahmen*. Zürich: Kunstanstalt Brunner.
Filli, Flurin. 1996. "Einfluss eines einmaligen Rothirschabschusses in einem Gebiet des Schweizerischen Nationalparks," *Zeitschrift für Jagdwissenschaft* 42 (4), 249–255.
——— (ed.). 2006. "Ungulate Research in the Swiss National Park: Development, Current Issues and Future Challenges," in Flurin Filli and Werner Suter (eds.), *Ungulate Research in the Swiss National Park*. Zernez: Research Council of the Swiss National Park, 9–29.
Fisch, Jörg. 1992. "Zivilisation, Kultur," in Otto Brunner et al. (eds.), *Geschichtliche Grundbegriffe*, 7. Stuttgart: Klett-Cotta, 679–774.
Flahault, Charles, Marie Henri, and Carl Schröter (eds.). 1910. *Phytogeographische Nomenklatur: Berichte und Vorschläge*. Zürich.
Fleury, Antoine, and Frédéric Joye. 2002. *Die Anfänge der Forschungspolitik in der Schweiz. Gründungsgeschichte des Schweizerischen Nationalfonds zur Förderung der wissenschaftlichen Forschung 1934–1952*. Baden: hier + jetzt.
Floericke, Kurt. 1910. "Entwicklung, Stand und Aussichten der Naturschutzparkbewegung," in Verein Naturschutzpark (ed.), *Naturschutzparke in Deutschland und Österreich: Ein Mahnwort an das deutsche und österreichische Volk*. Stuttgart: Franckh, 7–18.
———. 1913. "Entwicklung, Stand und Aussichten der Naturschutzparkbewegung," in Verein Naturschutzpark (ed.), *Naturschutzparke in Deutschland und Österreich: Ein Mahnwort an das deutsche und österreichische Volk*, 2. überarb. u. erg. Aufl. Stuttgart: Franckh, 7–18.
Ford, Caroline. 2012. "Imperial Preservation and Landscape Reclamation: National Parks and Natural Reserves in French Colonial Africa," in Gissibl, Höhler, and Kupper (eds.), *Civilizing Nature: National Parks in Global Historical Perspective*. New York: Berghahn Books, 68–83.
Forschungskommission des Schweizerischen Nationalparks. 2008. *Forschungskonzept 2008–2018 für den Schweizerischen Nationalpark und die Biosfera Val Müstair*.
Foucault, Michel. 2004. *Sécurité, territoire, population cours au Collège de France (1977–1978), Cours au Collège de France*. Paris: Gallimard/Seuil.
——— (ed.). 1994 (1967). *Des espaces autres*, in Dits et écrits, IV. Paris: Gallimard, 752–762.
Franke, Mary A. 2000. *Yellowstone in the Afterglow: Lessons From the Fires*. Mammoth Hot Springs: Yellowstone Center for Resources.
Frey-Wyssling, Albert. 1959. *Naturschutz und Technik*. Zürich: Polygraphischer Verlag.
Frey, Eduard. 1952 and 1959. *Die Flechtenflora und -Vegetation des Nationalparks im Unterengadin (Part 1 and 2)*. Liestal.

Fritsche, Stefan. 2002. *Naturschutzkonzepte Naturschutz Natur: Exkursionen an die Grenze zur Natur am Beispiel der Geschichte des Schweizerischen Nationalparks.* Universität Zürich: Lizentiatsarbeit.

Fritzsche, Bruno, et al. 2001. *Historischer Strukturatlas der Schweiz.* Baden: hier + jetzt.

Frohn, Hans-Werner. 2006. "Naturschutz macht Staat—Staat macht Naturschutz. Von der Staatlichen Stelle für Naturdenkmalpflege in Preussen bis zum Bundesamt für Naturschutz 1906 bis 2006—eine Institutionengeschichte," in Bundesamt für Naturschutz (ed.), *Natur und Staat: Staatlicher Naturschutz in Deutschland 1906–2006.* Bonn: Bundesamt für Naturschutz, 85–314.

Frost, Warwick, and C. Michael Hall. 2009a. "National Parks and the 'Worthless Lands Hypothesis' revisited," in Frost and Hall (eds.), *Tourism and National Parks: International Perspectives on Development, Histories, and Change.* New York: Routledge, 45–62.

——— (eds.). 2009b. *Tourism and National Parks: International Perspectives on Development, Histories, and Change.* New York: Routledge.

Galison, Peter. 1997. *Image and Logic: A Material Culture of Microphysics.* Chicago: University of Chicago Press.

———. 2003. *Einstein's clocks, Poincaré's maps empires of time.* New York: W.W. Norton.

Gassert, Philipp. 2012. *Transnationale Geschichte.* Docupedia-Zeitgeschichte: Version: 2.0, 29 October 2012.

Gates, Barbara T. 1998. *Kindred Nature: Victorian and Edwardian Women Embrace the Living World.* Chicago: University of Chicago Press.

Gäumann, Ernst, and Eduard Campell. 1932. "Über eine Kiefernkrankheit im Gebiete des Ofenberges," *Schweizerische Zeitschrift für Forstwesen* 83, 328–332.

Geissler, Patricia, and Josef Hartmann (eds.). 2000. "Vegetation dynamics in a moutain pine stand burnt down in 1951," in Martin Schütz et al. (eds.), *Succession research in the Swiss National Park: From Braun-Blanquet's permanent plots to models of long-term ecological change.* Zernez: Research Council of the Swiss National Park, 107–129.

Geisthövel, Alexa, and Habbo Knoch (eds.). 2005. *Orte der Moderne: Erfahrungswelten des 19. und 20. Jahrhunderts.* Frankfurt: Campus.

Geppert, Alexander C. T., Uffa Jensen, and Jörn Weinhold (eds.). 2005. *Ortsgespräche: Raum und Kommunikation im 19. und 20. Jahrhundert.* Bielefeld: transcript.

Geyer, Martin H., and Johannes Paulmann (eds.). 2001. *The Mechanics of Internationalism: Culture, Society and Politics from the 1840s to the First World War.* Oxford: Oxford University Press.

Giacometti, Marco (ed.). 2006. *Von Königen und Wilderern: Die Rettung und Wiederansiedlung des Alpensteinbocks.* Wohlen: Salm.

Ginzburg, Carlo. 1993. "Mikro-Historie: Zwei oder drei Dinge, die ich von ihr weiss," in *Historische Anthropologie* 1 (2), 169–192.

Gissibl, Bernhard. 2005. "Paradiesvögel: Kolonialer Naturschutz und die Mode der deutschen Frau am Anfang des 20. Jahrhunderts," in Johannes Paulmann et al. (eds.), *Ritual—Macht—Natur: Europäisch-ozeanische Beziehungswelten in der Neuzeit.* Bremen: Übersee-Museum, 131–154.

———. 2006. "German Colonialism and the Beginnings of International Wildlife Preservation in Africa," *GHI Bulletin* Supplement 3, 121–143.

———. 2009. *The Nature of Colonialism: Hunting, Conservation and the Politics of Wildlife in the German Colonial Empire.* Universität Mannheim: dissertation.

———. 2012. "A Bavarian Serengeti: Space, Race and Time in the Entangled History of Nature Conservation in East Africa and Germany," in Gissibl, Höhler, and Kupper (eds.), *Civilizing Nature: National Parks in Global Historical Perspective*. New York: Berghahn Books, 102–119.
Gissibl, Bernhard, Sabine Höhler, and Patrick Kupper (eds.). 2012a. *Civilizing Nature: National Parks in Global Historical Perspective*. New York: Berghahn Books.
———. 2012b. "Towards a Global History of National Parks," in Gissibl, Höhler, and Kupper (eds.), *Civilizing Nature: National Parks in Global Historical Perspective*. New York: Berghahn Books, 1–27.
Gleason, Henry A. 1933. "Review: Braun-Blanquet's Plant Sociology," *Ecology* 14 (1), 70–74.
Glutz-Graff, Robert. 1905. *Ueber Natur-Denkmäler, ihre Gefährdung u. Erhaltung*. Solothurn: Union.
Golley, Frank B. 1993. *A History of the Ecosystem Concept in Ecology: More than the Sum of the Parts*. New Haven: Yale University Press.
Gonseth, Yves, Daniel Cherix, and Aline Pasche. 2007. "Recherches scientifiques sur les invertébrés au Parc National Suisse," in Cherix et al. (eds.), *Faunistique et écologie des invertébrés au Parc National Suisse*. Zernez: Forschungskommission des Schweizerischen Nationalparks, 183–195.
Goodland, Robert. 1982. *Tribal Peoples and Economic Development: Human Ecologic Considerations*. Washington, DC: World Bank.
Gottschalk, Fadri. 1994. *IVS Dokumentation Ofenpass*. Bern: IVS.
Gould, Stephen Jay, and Niles Eldredge. 1993. "Punctuated Equilibrium Comes of Age," *Nature* 366 (18 November), 223–227.
Gradmann, Robert. 1898. *Das Pflanzenleben der Schwäbischen Alb mit Berücksichtigung der angrenzenden Gebiete Süddeutschlands*. Tübingen: Verlag des Schwäbischen Albvereins.
Graf, Friedrich Wilhelm. 2000. "Alter Geist und neuer Mensch. Religiöse Zukunftserwartungen um 1900," in Ute Frevert (ed.), *Das Neue Jahrhundert. Europäische Zeitdiagnosen und Zukunftsentwürfe um 1900*, Sonderheft 18. Göttingen: Vandenhoeck & Ruprecht, 185–228.
Graf von Hardenberg, Wilko. 2009. "Between Propaganda and Preservation: The Italian National Parks in the Alps," in *Forth Symposon of the Hohe Tauern National Park for Research in Protected Areas*, Conference Volume, 119–121.
———. 2010. Ressourcen und Konflikte als Elemente einer sozialen Umweltgeschichte des 20. Jahrhunderts: Das italienische Beispiel, in: Herrmann, Bernd (ed.): *Beiträge zum Göttinger Umwelthistorischen Kolloquium 2009—2010*, Göttingen: Universitätsverlag Göttingen, 27–46.
Grämiger, Helena, and Bertil O. Krüsi (eds.). 2000. "Balthasar Stüssi, 17 July 1908–24 October 1992," in Martin Schütz et al. (eds.), *Succession research in the Swiss National Park: From Braun-Blanquet's permanent plots to models of long-term ecological change*. Zernez: Research Council of the Swiss National Park, 27–38.
Gredig, Martin, and Walter Willi. 2006. *Unter Strom: Wasserkraftwerke und Elektrifizierung in Graubünden 1879–2000*. Chur: Bündner Monatsblatt.
Grimm, Paul Eugen. 2012. *Scuol: Landschaft, Geschichte, Menschen*. St. Moritz: Gammeter.
Grob, Hans, François Bergier, and Hans Werner Tobler (eds.). 1980. *Eidgenössische Technische Hochschule Zürich 1955–1980: Festschrift zum 125jährigen Bestehen*. Zürich: NZZ Verlag.

Grusin, Richard. 2004. *Culture, Technology, and the Creation of America's National Parks.* Cambridge: Cambridge University Press.
Guenther, Konrad. 1919. *Der Naturschutz,* überarb. und erg. Aufl. Freiburg i. Br.: Fehlenfeld.
Gugerli, David. 1998. "'Translationen' der elektrischen Übertragung: Ein Beitrag zur Revision der Geschichte technischer Innovationen," in Bettina Heintz and Bernhard Nievergelt (eds.), *Wissenschafts- und Technikforschung in der Schweiz. Sondierungen einer neuen Disziplin.* Zürich: Seismo, 195–211.
Gugerli, David, and Daniel Speich. 2002. *Topografien der Nation. Politik, kartografische Ordnung und Landschaft im 19. Jahrhundert.* Zürich: Chronos.
Gugerli, David, Patrick Kupper, and Daniel Speich. 2010. *Transforming the Future: ETH Zurich and the Construction of Modern Switzerland 1855–2005.* Zürich: Chronos.
Guha, Ramachandra. 2000. *Environmentalism: A Global History.* New York etc.: Longman.
Haag, Erich. 2004. *Grenzen der Technik. Der Widerstand gegen das Kraftwerkprojekt Urseren.* Zürich: Chronos.
Hachtmann, Rüdiger. 2007. *Tourismus-Geschichte.* Göttingen: Vandenhoeck und Ruprecht.
Hacking, Ian. 1999. *The Social Construction of What?* Cambridge: Harvard University Press.
Haefeli, Ueli. 1998. "Der lange Weg zum Umweltschutzgesetz: Die Anwort des politischen Systems auf das neue gesellschaftliche Leitbild 'Umweltschutz,'" in Mario König et al. (eds.), *Dynamisierung und Umbau: Die Schweiz in den 60er und 70er Jahren,* vol. 3. Zürich, 251–264.
Hall, Harvey M. 1929. "European Reservations for the Protection of Natural Conditions," *Journal of Forestry* 27 (6), 667–684.
Hall, Marcus. 2005. *Earth Repair: A Transatlantic History Of Environmental Restoration.* Charlottesville: University Press of Virginia.
Hall, Melanie (ed.). 2011. *Towards World Heritage: International Origins of the Preservation Movement 1870–1930.* Farnham: Ashgate.
Haller, Heinrich. 1996. *Der Steinadler in Graubünden: Langfristige Untersuchungen zur Populationsökologie von Aquila chrysaetos im Zentrum der Alpen.* [S.l.]: Ala.
———. 2002. *Der Rothirsch im Schweizerischen Nationalpark und dessen Umgebung: Eine alpine Population von Cervus elaphus zeitlich und räumlich dokumentiert,* mit Beitr. von Ralph Kühn et al. Zernez: Forschungskommission des Schweizerischen Nationalparks.
———. 2006. "Der Schweizerische Nationalpark," in Werner Konold et al. (eds.), *Handbuch Naturschutz und Landschaftspflege,* XIV-9. Landsberg am Lech: ecomed, 1–13.
———. 2009. "Ein Jungluchs auf Reisen," *Cratschla* (1), 4–13.
Hammer, Urs. 1995. *Vom Alpenidyll zum modernen Musterstaat: Der Mythos der Schweiz als "Alpine Sister Republic" in den USA des 19. Jahrhunderts.* Basel: Helbling & Lichtenhahn.
Handschin, Eduard. 1939. "Von der wissenschaftlichen Erforschung des Nationalparkes," *Schweizer Naturschutz* 5 (4/5), 55–60.
———. 1947. "Vernehmlassung der wissenschaftlichen Nationalparkkommission an den Präsidenten der eidgenössischen Nationalparkkommission," in Schweizerischer Bund für Naturschutz (ed.), *Nationalpark oder internationales Spölkraftwerk.* Basel: SBN, 81–84.
Haraway, Donna. 1989. *Primate Visions: Gender, Race, and Nature in the World of Modern Science.* New York: Routledge.

Harper, Melissa, and Richard White. 2012. "How National Were the First National Parks? Comparative Perspectives from the British Settler Societies," in Gissibl, Höhler, and Kupper (eds.), *Civilizing Nature: National Parks in Global Historical Perspective.* New York: Berghahn Books, 50–67.
Harroy, Jean-Paul. 1972a. "National Parks: A 100-Year Appraisel," in Jean-Paul Harroy (ed.), *World National Parks: Progress and Opportunities.* Brussels: Hayez, 13–20.
——— (ed.). 1972b. *World National Parks: Progress and Opportunities.* Brussels: Hayez.
———. 1993. "Contribution à l'histoire jusque 1934 de la création de l'institut des parcs nationaux du Congo belge," *Civilisations* (41), 427–442.
Harvey, Mark William Thornton. 1994. *A Symbol of Wilderness: Echo Park and the American Conservation Movement.* Albuquerque: University of New Mexico Press.
Hasenöhrl, Ute. 2010. *Zivilgesellschaft und Protest: Eine Geschichte der Naturschutz- und Umweltbewegung in Bayern 1945–80.* Göttingen: Vandenhoeck & Ruprecht.
Haupt, Sabine, and Stefan Bodo Würffel (eds.). 2008. *Handbuch Fin de Siècle.* Stuttgart: Kröner.
Hegi, Gustav. 1911. *Die Naturschutzbewegung und der schweizerische Nationalpark.* Zürich: Orell Füssli.
Heijnsbergen, P. van. 1997. *International Legal Protection of Wild Fauna and Flora.* Amsterdam: IOS Press.
Herren, Madeleine. 2000. *Hintertüren zur Macht: Internationalismus und modernisierungsorientierte Aussenpolitik in Belgien, der Schweiz und den USA, 1865–1914.* Munich: Oldenbourg.
Herren, Madeleine, and Sacha Zala. 2002. *Netzwerk Aussenpolitik: Internationale Kongresse und Organisationen als Instrumente schweizerischer Aussenpolitik 1914–1950.* Zürich: Chronos.
Hobsbawm, Eric John. 1987. *The Age of Empire, 1875–1914.* London: Weidenfeld and Nicolson.
Holdgate, Martin W. 1999. *The Green Web: A Union for World Conservation.* London: Earthscan.
Hollinger, Stefan. 2008. *Graubünden und das Auto: Kontroversen um den Automobilverkehr 1900–1925.* Chur: Desertina.
Hopkins, Antony G. (ed.). 2006. *Global History: Interactions between the Universal and the Local.* New York: Palgrave Macmillan.
Hughes, J. Donald. 2006. *What is Environmental History?*, Cambridge: Polity.
———. 2009. *An Environmental History of the World: Humankind's Changing Role in the Community of Life.* London: Routledge.
Humair, Cédric, and Hans Ulrich Jost (eds.). 2008. *Prométhée déchaîné: Technologies, culture et société helvétiques à la Belle Epoque.* Lausanne: Antipodes.
Ingold, Tim. 2008. "When ANT Meets SPIDER: Social Theory for Arthropods," in Carl Knappett and Lambros Malafouris (eds.), *Material Agency: Towards a Non-Anthropocentric Approach.* New York: Springer, 209–215.
Iriye, Akira, and Pierre-Yves Saunier (eds.). 2009. *The Palgrave Dictionary of Transnational History.* Basingstoke: Palgrave Macmillan.
Isenberg, Andrew C. 2000. *The Destruction of the Bison: An Environmental History, 1750–1920.* Cambridge: Cambridge University Press.

———. 2002. "The Moral Ecology of Wildlife," in Nigel Rothfels (ed.), *Representing Animals.* Bloomington: Indiana University Press, 48–64.
IUCN. 1994a. *Guidelines for Protected Area Management Categories.* Gland: IUCN.
——— (ed.). 1994b. *Richtlinien für Management-Kategorien von Schutzgebieten.* Gland, Cambridge: IUCN.
Jacoby, Karl. 2001. *Crimes against Nature: Squatters, Poachers, Thieves, and the Hidden History of American Conservation.* Berkeley: University of California Press.
Jarvis, Kimberly A. 2007. "Gender and Wilderness Conservation," in Michael L. Lewis (ed.), *American Wilderness: A New History.* New York: Oxford University Press, 149–166.
Jenny, Hannes, and Jürg P. Müller. 2002. *Phänomen Bündner Jagd.* Chur: Amt für Jagd und Fischerei Graubünden, Bündner Natur-Museum.
Johnson, Benjamin. 2007. "Wilderness Parks and Their Discontents," in Lewis (ed.), *American Wilderness: A New History.* New York: Oxford University Press, 113–130.
Jones, Jeannette Eileen. 2010. *In Search of Brightest Africa: Reimagining the Dark Continent in American Culture, 1884–1936.* Athens: University of Georgia Press.
Jones, Karen. 2012. "Unpacking Yellowstone: The American National Park in Global Perspective," in Gissibl, Höhler, and Kupper (eds.), *Civilizing Nature: National Parks in Global Historical Perspective.* New York: Berghahn Books, 31–49.
Jones, Karen R., and John Wills. 2005. *The Invention of the Park: Recreational Landscapes from the Garden of Eden to Disney's Magic Kingdom.* Cambridge, Malden: Polity.
Jungo, Joseph. 1972. "Der Schweizerische Nationalpark," *Schweizerische Zeitschrift für Forstwesen* 123 (9), 556–564.
Kaelble, Hartmut (ed.). 2003. *Vergleich und Transfer: Komparatistik in den Sozial-, Geschichts- und Kulturwissenschaften.* Frankfurt: Campus.
———. 2006. "Herausforderungen an die Transfergeschichte," *Comparativ* 16 (3), 7–12.
Kaiser, Dolf. 1985. *Fast ein Volk von Zuckerbäckern? Bündner Konditoren, Cafetiers und Hoteliers in europäischen Landen bis zum Ersten Weltkrieg ein wirtschaftsgeschichtlicher Beitrag.* Zürich: Verlag Neue Zürcher Zeitung.
Kalof, Linda, et al. (eds.). 2007. *A Cultural History of Animals.* Oxford: Berg.
Kathirithamby-Wells, Jeyamalar. 2005. *Nature and Nation: Forests and Development in Peninsular Malaysia,* Honolulu: University of Hawai Press.
———. 2012. "From Colonial Imposition to National Icon: Malaysia's Taman Negara National Park," in Gissibl, Höhler, and Kupper (eds.), *Civilizing Nature: National Parks in Global Historical Perspective.* New York: Berghahn Books, 84–101.
Kaufmann, Stefan. 2005. *Soziologie der Landschaft.* Wiesbaden: Verlag für Sozialwissenschaften.
Kern, Stephen. 1983. *The Culture of Time and Space 1880–1918.* London: Weidenfeld & Nicolson.
Kingsland, Sharon E. 2005. *The Evolution of American Ecology, 1890–2000.* Baltimore: Johns Hopkins University Press.
Kirchhoff, Thomas, and Ludwig Trepl. 2009a. "Landschaft, Wildnis, Ökosystem: Zur kulturbedingten Vieldeutigkeit ästhetischer, moralischer und theoretischer Naturauffassungen, einleitender Überblick," in Thomas Kirchhoff and Ludwig Trepl (eds.), *Vieldeutige Natur: Landschaft, Wildnis und Ökosystem als kulturgeschichtliche Phänomene.* Bielefeld: transcript, 13–68.

Kirchhoff, Thomas, and Ludwig Trepl (eds.). 2009b. *Vieldeutige Natur: Landschaft, Wildnis und Ökosystem als kulturgeschichtliche Phänomene.* Bielefeld: transcript.

Klautke, Egbert. 2003. *Unbegrenzte Möglichkeiten: "Amerikanisierung" in Deutschland und Frankreich (1900–1933).* Stuttgart: Steiner.

Klötzli, Frank A. 1991. "Zum Einfluss von Strassenböschungsansaaten auf die umliegende naturnähere Vegetation am Beispiel des Schweizer Nationalparks," *Laufener Seminarbeiträge* (3), 114–123.

Knöbl, Wolfgang. 2007. *Die Kontingenz der Moderne: Wege in Europa, Asien und Amerika,* Frankfurt: Campus.

Kohler, Robert E. 2002. *Landscapes and Labscapes: Exploring the Lab-Field Border in Biology.* Chicago: University of Chicago Press.

———. 2006. *All Creatures: Naturalists, Collectors, and Biodiversity, 1850–1950.* Princeton: Princeton University Press.

König, Wolfgang. 2000. *Bahnen und Berge: Verkehrstechnik, Tourismus und Naturschutz in den Schweizer Alpen 1870–1939,* vol. 2. Frankfurt: Campus.

Koselleck, Reinhart. 1994. "Fortschritt," in Otto Brunner et al. (eds.), *Geschichtliche Grundbegriffe,* vol. 2. Stuttgart: Klett Cotta, 351–423.

———. 2000. *Zeitschichten: Studien zur Historik.* Frankfurt: Suhrkamp.

Kraas, Frauke. 1992. *Die Rätoromanen Graubündens.* Stuttgart: Steiner.

Kracauer, Siegfried. 1971. *Geschichte—Vor den letzten Dingen.* Frankfurt: Suhrkamp.

Kranz, Andreas. 2009. "Die stille Rückkehr der Fischotter in den Alpen," *Cratschla* (2), 24–25.

Krasmann, Susanne, and Michael Volkmer (eds.). 2007. *Michel Foucaults "Geschichte der Gouvernementalität" in den Sozialwissenschaften: Internationale Beiträge.* Bielefeld: transcript.

Krech, Shepard, John R. McNeill, and Carolyn Merchant (eds.). 2004. *Encyclopedia of World Environmental History,* 3 vols. New York: Routledge.

Kreis, Georg. 2004. *Mythos Rütli: Geschichte eines Erinnerungsortes,* Zürich: Orell Füssli.

———. 2008. *Zeitzeichen für die Ewigkeit: 300 Jahre schweizerische Denkmaltopografie.* Zürich: NZZ Verlag.

Krüger, Tobias. 2008. *Die Entdeckung der Eiszeiten: Internationale Rezeption und Konsequenzen für das Verständnis der Klimageschichte.* Basel: Schwabe.

Krüsi, Bertil O., et al. 1995. "Huftiere, Vegetationsdynamik und botanische Vielfalt im Nationalpark," *Cratschla* 3 (2), 14–25.

Kuper, Adam. 2005. *The Reinvention of Primitive Society: Transformations of a Myth.* London: Routledge.

Küpfer, Irene. 2000. *Die regionalwirtschaftliche Bedeutung des Nationalparktourismus untersucht am Beispiel des Schweizerischen Nationalparks.* Zernez: Forschungskommission des Schweizerischen Nationalparks.

Kupper, Patrick. 2003. "Die '1970er Diagnose': Grundsätzliche Überlegungen zu einem Wendepunkt der Umweltgeschichte," *Archiv für Sozialgeschichte* 43, Umweltgeschichte und Umweltbewegungen, 325–348.

———. 2008. "Nationalparks in der europäischen Geschichte," in *Clio-online. Themenportal "Europäische Geschichte",* http://www.europa.clio-online.de/2008/Article=330.

———. 2009a. "Science and the National Parks: A Transatlantic Perspective on the Interwar Years," *Environmental History* 14 (1), 58–81.

———. 2009b. "Tourismus und Nationalparks: Eine vergleichende Geschichte der USA und der Schweiz," in Bundesamt für Naturschutz (ed.), *Wenn sich alle in der Natur erholen, wo erholt sich dann die Natur?" Naturschutz, Freizeitnutzung, Erholungsvorsorge und Sport—gestern, heute, morgen*. Bonn: Bundesamt für Naturschutz, 207–228.

———. 2009c. "Zernez, 11. November 1909, ein Meilenstein auf dem Weg zum Schweizerischen Nationalpark," *Cratschla* (2), 18–21.

———. 2010. "Grenzüberschreitungen: Zur Geschichte von Mensch und Tier im Schweizerischen Nationalpark," *Histoire des Alpes* 15: Mensch und Wildtiere, 229–245.

———. 2014. "Transnationale Umweltgeschichte," in Manfred Jakubowski-Tiessen (ed.), *Beiträge zum Göttinger Umwelthistorischen Kolloquium 2012–2013*. Göttingen: Universitätsverlag Göttingen, 77–88.

Kupper, Patrick, and Anna-Katharina Wöbse. 2013. *Geschichte des Nationalparks Hohe Tauern*. Innsbruck: Tyrolia.

Kurth, Alfred, A. Weidmann, and F. Thommen. 1960. *Beitrag zur Kenntnis der Waldverhältnisse im schweizerischen Nationalpark*. Zürich: Beer.

Küster, Hansjörg. 2009. *Schöne Aussichten: Kleine Geschichte der Landschaft*. Munich: Beck.

Lansel, Peider. 1936. *Die Rätoromanen*. Frauenfeld: Huber.

Latour, Bruno. 1987. *Science in Action: How to Follow Scientists and Engineers through Society*. Cambridge: Harvard University Press.

———. 1993. *We Have Never Been Modern*. New York: Harvester Wheatsheaf.

———. 2005. *Reassembling the Social: An Introduction to Actor-Network-Theory*. Oxford: Clarendon.

Lefebvre, Henri. 1968. *La vie quotidienne dans le monde moderne*. Collection Idées, Paris: Gallimard.

Lefebvre, Henri. 1974. *La production de l'espace*. Paris: Anthropos.

Lekan, Thomas M. 2004. *Imagining the Nation in Nature: Landscape Preservation and German Identity, 1885–1945*. Cambridge: Harvard University Press.

Lekan, Thomas, and Thomas Zeller (eds.). 2005. *Germany's Nature: Cultural Landscapes and Environmental History*. New Brunswick: Rutgers University Press.

Leonhard, Jörn, and Ulrike von Hirschhausen. 2009. *Empires und Nationalstaaten im 19. Jahrhundert*. Göttingen: Vandenhoeck & Ruprecht.

Leopold, A. Starker, et al. 1963. *Wildlife Management in the National Parks: The Leopold Report*. Advisory Board on Wildlife Management.

Levi, Giovanni. 1992. "On Microhistory," in Peter Burke (ed.), *New Perspectives on Historical Writing*. University Park: Pennsylvania State University Press, 97–119.

Lewis, Michael. 2003. *Inventing Global Ecology: Tracking the Biodiversity Ideal in India, 1945–1997*. New Delhi: Orient Longman.

——— (ed.). 2007a. *American Wilderness: A New History*. New York: Oxford University Press.

———. 2007b. "Wilderness and Conservation Science," in Lewis (ed.), *American Wilderness: A New History*. New York: Oxford University Press, 205–222.

———. 2012. "Globalizing Nature: National Parks, Tiger Reserves, and Biosphere Reserves in Independent India," in Gissibl, Höhler, and Kupper (eds.), *Civilizing Nature: National Parks in Global Historical Perspective*. New York: Berghahn Books, 224–239.

Lhota, Simone. 1998. *Rothirschmanagement in vier Nationalparkregionen im Vergleich*. Leopold Franzens Universität: Diplomarbeit.

Louter, David. 2006. *Windshield Wilderness: Cars, Roads, and Nature in Washington's National Parks*. Seattle: University of Washington Press.
Luck, Georg. 1923. *Jägersagen und Jagdgeschichten*. Bern: Bircher.
Lüdi, Werner. 1954. *Die Neubildung des Waldes im Lavinar der Alp La Schera im Schweizerischen Nationalpark (Unterengadin)*. Liestal: Lüdin.
Lüdtke, Alf. 1993. *Eigen-Sinn: Fabrikalltag, Arbeitererfahrungen und Politik vom Kaiserreich bis in den Faschismus*. Hamburg: Ergebnisse Verlag.
———. 2002. "Eigensinn," in Stefan Jordan (ed.), *Lexikon Geschichtswissenschaft: Hundert Grundbegriffe*. Stuttgart: Reclam, 64–67.
Lüer, Rolf. 1994. *Geschichte des Naturschutzes in der Lüneburger Heide*. Niederhaverbeck: Verein Naturschutzpark.
Luhmann, Niklas. 1989. *Vertrauen: Ein Mechanismus der Reduktion sozialer Komplexität*. Stuttgart: Ferdinand Enke Verlag.
MacKenzie, John M. 1997. *The Empire of Nature: Hunting Conservation and British Imperialism*. Manchester: Manchester University Press.
Maggini, Giovanni. 1916: *Der Schweizerische Nationalpark aus der Vogelschau*. Basel: Frobenius AG.
Magoc, Chris J. 1999. *Yellowstone: The Creation and Selling of an American Landscape, 1870–1903*. Albuquerque: University of New Mexico Press.
Maier, Charles S. 2000. "Consigning the Twentieth Century to History: Alternative Narratives for the Modern Era," *American Historical Review* 105 (3), 807–831.
Manning, Patrick. 2003. *Navigating World History: Historians Create a Global Past*. New York: Palgrave Macmillan.
Mark, Stephen R. 2005. *Preserving the Living Past: John C. Merriam's Legacy in the State and National Parks*. Berkeley: University of California Press.
Marks, Robert B. 2010. "World Environmental History: Nature, Modernity, and Power," *Radical History Review* (107), 209–224.
Marvin, Garry. 2009. "Wölfe im Schafspelz: Eine anthropologische Sicht auf die Beziehungen zwischen Menschen und Wölfen in Albanien und Norwegen," in Dorothee Brantz and Christof Mauch (eds.), *Tierische Geschichte: Die Beziehung von Mensch und Tier in der Kultur der Moderne*. Paderborn: Schöningh Paderborn, 364–378.
Mathieu, Jon. 1994. *Bauern und Bären: Eine Geschichte des Unterengadins von 1650 bis 1800*. Chur: Octopus.
———. 2006. "The Sacralization of Mountains in Europe during the Modern Age," *Mountain Research and Development*, 343–349.
———. 2011. *The Third Dimension: A Comparative History of Mountains in the Modern Era*. Cambridge: White Horse Press.
Mathieu, Jon, and Simona Boscani Leoni (eds.). 2005. *Die Alpen! Zur europäischen Wahrnehmungsgeschichte seit der Renaissance*. Bern: Peter Lang.
Matthey, Willy. 2007. "Les invertébrés de la pelouse alpine à Carex firma au Parc National Suisse: Revue des travaux effectués de 1976 à 1984 au Munt la Schera," in Daniel Cherix et al. (eds.), *Faunistique et écologie des invertébrés au Parc National Suisse*. Zernez: Forschungskommission des Schweizerischen Nationalparks, 5–68.
Mauch, Christof. 2004. "Introduction: Nature and Nation in Transatlantic Perspective," in Mauch (ed.), *Nature in German History*. New York: Berghahn Books, 1–9.

Mauz, Isabelle. 2003. *Histoire et memoires du parc national de la Vanoise. 1921–1971: La construction.* Grenoble: Revue de geographie alpine.
McCormick, John. 1995. *The Global Environmental Movement.* Chichester: Wiley.
McIntosh, Robert Patrick. 1985. *The Background of Ecology: Concept and Theory.* Cambridge: Cambridge University Press.
McNeill, John R. 2000. *Something New Under the Sun: An Environmental History of the 20th-Century World.* New York: Norton.
Meier, Martina. 2010. *Die Einstellung der Lokalbevölkerung zum Schweizerischen Nationalpark.* Universität Zürich: Masterarbeit.
Meier, Robert. 2003. *Die Engadiner Kraftwerke: Natur und Technik in einer aufstrebenden Region.* Baden: Schweizerischer Wasserwirtschaftsverband.
Mels, Tom. 1999. *Wild Landscapes: The Cultural Nature of Swedish National Parks.* Lund: Lund University Press.
Merchant, Carolyn. 1984. "Women of the Progressive Conservation Movement: 1900–1916," *Environmental Review* 8 (1), 57–85.
Merki, Christoph Maria. 2002. *Der holprige Siegeszug des Automobils, 1895–1930: Zur Motorisierung des Strassenverkehrs in Frankreich, Deutschland und der Schweiz.* Vienna: Böhlau.
Merrifield, Andy. 2006. *Henri Lefebvre: A Critical Introduction.* New York: Routledge.
Messerli, Jakob. 1995. *Gleichmässig, pünktlich, schnell: Zeiteinteilung und Zeitgebrauch in der Schweiz im 19. Jahrhundert.* Zürich: Chronos.
Metz, Christian. 1990. *Der Bär in Graubünden: Eine Dokumentation.* Disentis: Desertina Verlag.
Metz, Peter. 1991. *Geschichte des Kantons Graubünden,* Band 2. Chur: Calven.
Meyer-Holzapfel, Monika. 1963. "Wiederansiedlung von Bären in der Schweiz?" *Schweizer Naturschutz* (4), 98–100.
Middell, Matthias. 2005. "Universalgeschichte, Weltgeschichte, Globalgeschichte, Geschichte der Globalisierung—ein Streit um Worte?" in Margarete Grandner et al. (eds.), *Globalisierung und Globalgeschichte.* Vienna: Mandelbaum, 60–82.
Miles, John C. 2009. *Wilderness in National Parks: Playground or Preserve.* Seattle: University of Washington Press.
Miller, Perry. 1967. *Nature's Nation.* Cambridge: Harvard University Press.
Milnik, Albrecht. 1997. *Hugo Conwentz: "Naturschutz, Wald und Forstwirtschaft".* Berlin: Bässler.
Mitchell, W. J. T. 1994. "Imperial Landscape," in Mitchell (ed.), *Landscape and Power.* Chicago: University of Chicago Press, 5–34.
Muir, John. 1901. *Our National Parks.* Boston: Houghton Mifflin.
Müller-Schneider, Paul, and Jürg P. Müller. 1981. "Zur Geschichte des Bündner Natur-Museums," in Stiftung Dr. M Blumenthal (ed.), *Festschrift zur Eröffnung des Bündner Natur-Museums.* Chur, 5–7.
Müller, Urs. 2001. *Wie funktioniert Partizipation bei Naturschutzvorhaben in der Schweiz? Untersucht am Beispiel der Erweiterung des Schweizerischen Nationalparks.* Geographisches Institut Universität Zürich: Diplomarbeit.
Müller, Urs, and Michael Kollmair. 2004. "Die Erweiterung des Schweizerischen Nationalparks: Der Planungsprozess 1995–2000, betrachtet aus partizipationstheoretischer Sicht," *disP—The Planning Review* (159), 44–51.

Nadig, Adolf (Dikussionsleiter). 1940. "Diskussionsgruppe B: Naturforschung und Naturschutz, Science Naturelles et Protection de la Nature," *Actes Soc Helv Sc Nat* 120, 79–99.

Nadig, Adolf, Willi Sauter, and Heinrich Zoller. 1999. *Oekologische Untersuchungen im Unterengadin: Versuch einer Synthese*. Zernez: WNPK.

Nash, Roderick. 1970. "The American Invention of National Parks," *American Quarterly* 22 (3), 726–735.

———. 1980. "The Confusing Birth of National Parks," *Michigan Quarterly Review* 19 (2, Spring), 216–226.

———. 1982. *Wilderness and the American Mind*. New Haven: Yale University Press.

Nationalparkgesetz. 1980. Bundesgesetz vom 19. Dezember 1980 über den Schweizerischen Nationalpark im Kanton Graubünden, SR 454.

Neumann, Roderick P. 1998. *Imposing Wilderness: Struggles over Livelihood and Nature Preservation in Africa*. Berkeley: University of California Press.

———. 2005. *Making Political Ecology*. London: Hodder Arnold.

NHG. 2008. Bundesgesetz über den Natur- und Heimatschutz (NHG), SR 451, vom 1. Juli 1966 (Stand am 1. Januar 2008).

Nicolson, Malcolm. 1989. "National Styles, Divergent Classifications: A Comparative Case Study from the History of French and American Plant Ecology," *Knowledge and Society* 8, 139–186.

Nievergelt, Bernhard. 1966. *Der Alpensteinbock (Capra ibex L.) in seinem Lebensraum: Ein oekologischer Vergleich verschiedener Kolonien*. Hamburg: Parey.

———. 1980. *Arbeitspapier zuhanden der Kommission zur wissenschaftlichen Erforschung des Nationalparks*. Zürich: 14 March 1980 (unpublished).

Oelschlaeger, Max. 1991. *The Idea of Wilderness: From Prehistory to the Age of Ecology*. New Haven: Yale University Press.

Olwig, Kenneth R. 1995. "Reinventing Common Nature: Yosemite and Mount Rushmore—A Meandering Tale of a Double Nature," in William Cronon (ed.), *Uncommon Ground: Toward Reinventing Nature*. New York: W.W. Norton, 379–408.

Osterhammel, Jürgen. 2001. *Geschichtswissenschaft jenseits des Nationalstaats: Studien zur Beziehungsgeschichte und Zivilisationsvergleich*. Göttingen: Vandenhoeck & Ruprecht.

——— (ed.). 2008. *Weltgeschichte*. Stuttgart: Steiner.

———. 2009. *Die Verwandlung der Welt: Eine Geschichte des 19.Jahrhunderts*. Munich: Beck.

Pallmann, Hans, and Erwin Frei. 1943. *Beitrag zur Kenntnis der Lokalklimate einiger kennzeichnender Waldgesellschaften des Schweizerischen Nationalparkes (Fuorn)*. Aarau: Sauerländer.

Pardé, L. 1935. "Visite de quelques parcIl nationaux de l'Europe centrale," *Revue des eaux et forêts* (June/July), 485–497, 585–593.

Parolini, Jon Domenic. 1995. *Zur Geschichte der Waldnutzung im Gebiet des heutigen Schweizerischen Nationalparks*. Zürich.

———. 2012a. *Vom Kahlschlag zum Naturreservat: Geschichte der Waldnutzung im Gebiet des Schweizerischen Nationalparks*. Bern: Haupt.

———. 2012b. "Wasserkraftnutzung und Naturschutz: Der Schweizerische Nationalpark und die Spölkraftwerke," in Ferdinand Schanz et al. (eds.), *Ergebnisse aus 70 Jahren Gewässerforschung im Schweizerischen Nationalpark*. Zernez: Forschungskommission des Schweizerischen Nationalparks, 99–108.

Pedrotti, Franco. 2005. *Notizie storiche sul Parco Nazionale dello Stelvio.* Temi.
Phillips, Adrian. 2004. "The History of the International System of Protected Area Management Categories," *Parks* 14 (3), 4–14.
Pickering, James H. 2005: *America's Switzerland: Estes Park and Rocky Mountain National Park, the Growth Years.* Boulder: University Press of Colorado.
Pitcaithley, Dwight T. 2002. *National Parks and Education: The First Twenty Years.* http://www.cr.nps.gov/history/resedu/education.htm.
Potthast, Thomas. 2004. "Die wahre Natur ist Veränderung: Zur Ikonoklastik des ökologischen Gleichgewichts," in Ludwig Fischer (ed.), *Projektionsfläche Natur: Zum Zusammenhang von Naturbildern und gesellschaftlichen Verhältnissen.* Hamburg: Hamburg University Press, 193–221.
——— (ed.). 2007. *Biodiversität—Schlüsselbegriff des Naturschutzes im 21. Jahrhundert?* Bonn-Bad Godesberg: Bundesamt für Naturschutz.
Pritchard, James A. 1999. *Preserving Yellowstone's Natural Conditions: Science and the Perception of Nature.* Lincoln: University of Nebraska Press.
Pro Natura. 1999. *Pro Natura Schutzgebietsstrategie: Skizze einer nationalen Schutzgebietsstrategie*, vom Pro Natura Delegiertenrat am 11. Dezember 1999 verabschiedet. Basel: Pro Natura.
Pyne, Stephen J. 2004. *Tending Rire: Coping with America's Wildland Fires.* Washington, DC: Island Press.
Radkau, Joachim. 1998. *Das Zeitalter der Nervosität. Deutschland zwischen Bismarck und Hitler.* Munich: Hanser.
———. 2008. *Nature and Power: A Global History of the Environment.* Washington, DC: German Historical Institute.
Radkau, Joachim. 2011. *Die Ära der Ökologie: Eine Weltgeschichte.* Munich: Beck.
Ranger, Terence O. 1999. *Voices from the Rocks: Nature, Culture & History in the Matopos Hills of Zimbabwe.* Oxford: James Currey.
Ratti, Peider. 1994. "Stand von Hege und Erforschung des Steinwildes im Kanton Graubünden (Schweiz)," *Zeitschrift für Jagdwissenschaft* 40, 223–231.
Regensberg, Friedrich. 1912. "Naturschutzparke in den Kolonien," in Verein Naturschutzpark (ed.), *Naturschutzparke in Deutschland und Österreich: Ein Mahnwort an das deutsche und österreichische Volk.* Stuttgart: Franckh, 54–57.
Reich, Justin. 2001. "Re-Creating the Wilderness: Shaping Narratives and Landscapes in Shenandoah National Park," *Environmental History* 6 (1), 95–117.
Reichholf, Josef. 2008. *Stabile Ungleichgewichte: Die Ökologie der Zukunft.* Frankfurt: Suhrkamp.
Reiger, John F. 1986. *American Sportsmen and the Origins of Conservation.* Norman: University of Oklahoma Press.
Reubi, Serge. 2011. *Gentlemen, prolétaires et primitifs institutionnalisation, pratiques de collection et choix muséographiques dans l'ethnographie suisse, 1880–1950.* Bern: Peter Lang.
Revel, Jacques (ed.). 1996. *Jeux d'échelles: La micro-analyse à l'expérience.* Paris: Gallimard.
Revilliod, Pierre. 1944. "Jean Carl (1877–1944)," *Verhandlungen der Schweizerischen Naturforschenden Gesellschaft* 124, 311–320.
Rheinberger, Hans-Jörg. 2001. *Experimentalsysteme und epistemische Dinge: Eine Geschichte der Proteinsynthese im Reagenzglas.* Göttingen: Wallstein.

Rheinberger, Hans-Jörg, and Michael Hagner (eds.). 1993. *Die Experimentalisierung des Lebens: Experimentalsysteme in den biologischen Wissenschaften 1850/1950.* Berlin: Akademie Verlag.
Richards, John F. 2003. *The Unending Frontier: An Environmental History of the Early Modern World.* Berkeley: University of California Press.
Riederer, Raphael. 1996. *Untersuchungen über die Sukzessionsvorgänge in den Lavinaren nördlich der Alp La Schera im Schweizerischen Nationalpark.* Universität Bern: Diplomarbeit.
Risch, Anita C. 2004. *Above- and Belowground Patterns and Processes Following Land Use Change in Subalpine Conifer Forests of the Central European Alps.* ETH Zürich: Dissertation.
Robertson, Roland. 1995. "Glocalization: Time-Space and Homogeneity-Heterogeneity," in Mike Featherstone et al. (eds.), *Global Modernities.* London: Sage, 25–44.
Robin, Klaus, Jürg Paul Müller, and Thomas Pachlatko. 2004. "Das Projekt zur Wiederansiedlung des Bartgeiers in den Alpen ist 25-jährig: Ein Überblick," *Der Ornithologische Beobachter* 101 (1), 1–18.
Roeder, Carolin Firouzeh. 2012. "Slovenia's Triglav National Park: From Imperial Borderland to National Ethnoscape," in Gissibl, Höhler, and Kupper (eds.), *Civilizing Nature: National Parks in Global Historical Perspective.* New York: Berghahn Books, 240–255.
Roelcke, Volker. 1999. *Krankheit und Kulturkritik: Psychiatrische Gesellschaftsdeutungen im bürgerlichen Zeitalter (1790–1914).* Frankfurt: Campus.
Rohkrämer, Thomas. 1999. *Eine andere Moderne? Zivilisationskritik, Natur und Technik in Deutschland 1880–1933.* Paderborn, Zürich: Schöningh.
Rohner, Jürg. 1972. *Studien zum Wandel von Bevölkerung und Landwirtschaft im Unterengadin.* Basel: Helbing & Lichtenhahn.
Rothman, Hal. 1989. *Preserving Different Pasts: The American National Monuments.* Urbana: University of Illinois Press.
Rübel, Eduard. 1940. *Carl Schröter, 1855–1939.* Zürich: Beer.
Rudio, Ferdinand, and Carl Schröter. 1906. "'Naturschutz' in der Schweiz, Notizen zur schweizerischen Kulturgeschichte, 19," *Vierteljahrsschrift der Naturforschenden Gesellschaft in Zürich* Jg. 54, 502–508.
———. 1909. "Naturschutz in der Schweiz und anderswo, Notizen zur schweizerischen Kulturgeschichte, 27," *Vierteljahrsschrift der Naturforschenden Gesellschaft in Zürich* Jg. 54, 480–504.
Runte, Alfred. 1987. *National Parks: The American Experience.* Lincoln: University of Nebraska Press.
———. 1990. *Yosemite: The Embattled Wilderness.* Lincoln: University of Nebraska Press.
Rütimeyer, Leopold. 1924. *Ur-Ethnographie der Schweiz.* Basel: Helbing.
Ryser-Degiorgis, Marie-Pierre, et al. 2009. "Detection of Mycoplasma Conjunctivae in the Eyes of Healthy, Free-Ranging Alpine Ibex: Possible Involvement of Alpine Ibex as Carriers for the Main Causing Agent of Infectious Keratoconjunctivitis in Wild Caprinae," *Veterinary Microbiology* 134 (3–4), 368–374.
Sachs, Aaron. 2007. *The Humboldt Current: A European Explorer and His American Disciples.* Oxford: Oxford University Press.
Sandlos, John. 2005. "Federal Spaces, Local Conflicts: National Parks and the Exclusionary Politics of the Conservation Movement in Ontario, 1900–1935," *Journal of the Canadian Historical Association* 16 (1), 293–318.

———. 2007. *Hunters at the Margin: Native People and Wildlife Conservation in the Northwest Territories.* Vancouver: UBC Press.
Sarasin, Fritz. 1907. "Über die niedrigsten Menschenformen des südöstlichen Asiens," *Verhandlungen der Schweizerischen Naturforschenden Gesellschaft* 90 (vol. 1), 225–247.
———. 1928–29. "Paul Sarasin, 1856–1929," *Verhandlungen der Naturforschenden Gesellschaft in Basel* 40 (2), 1–28.
Sarasin, Paul. 1910. *Weltnaturschutz.* Basel: Birkhäuser.
———. 1911. *Ueber nationalen und internationalen Vogelschutz, sowie einige anschliessende Fragen des Weltnaturschutzes.* Basel: Helbing & Lichtenhahn.
———. 1914. *Über die Aufgaben des Weltnaturschutzes.* Basel: Helbing & Lichtenhahn.
———. 1917. *Die Ausrottung des Fischotters in der Schweiz.* Basel: Birkhäuser.
Sarasin, Paul, and Fritz Sarasin. 1905. *Reisen in Celebes ausgeführt in den Jahren 1893–1896 und 1902–1903.* Wiesbaden: Kreidel.
Schama, Simon. 1995. *Landscape and Memory.* London: HarperCollins.
Schatzki, Theodore R. 2003. "Nature and Technology in History," *History and Theory: Studies in the Philosophy of History* 42 (4), 82–93.
Scheurer, Thomas (ed.). 2000a. "The history of botanical studies and permanent plot research in the Swiss National Park," in Martin Schütz et al. (eds.), *Succession research in the Swiss National Park: From Braun-Blanquet's permanent plots to models of long-term ecological change.* Zernez: Research Council of the Swiss National Park, 9–25.
Scheurer, Thomas. 2000b. "Mehr Dynamik im Spöl," *Cratschla* (2), 2–9.
Schläpfer, Daniel. 1960. *Der Bergbau am Ofenpass (Pass dal Fuorn): Eine wirtschaftsgeographische Untersuchung im Unterengadin und seinen Nachbartälern.* Liestal.
Schloeth, Robert. 1961. *Markierung und erste Beobachtungen von markiertem Rotwild im schweizerischen Nationalpark und dessen Umgebung.* Liestal: Lüdin.
———. 1970. "Grossraubwild in Graubünden?" *Bündner Wald* 23 (6), 269–273.
———. 1976. *Der schweizerische Nationalpark.* Zofingen: Ringier.
———. 1989. *Die Einmaligkeit eines Ameisenhaufens: Tagebuch aus dem Schweizerischen Nationalpark.* Gümligen: Zytglogge.
Schmid, Christian. 2005. *Stadt, Raum und Gesellschaft: Henri Lefebvre und die Theorie der Produktion des Raume.* Stuttgart: Steiner.
———. 1986. *Die Jagd in Graubünden: Von der Jagd als Nahrungsmittelgrundlage zur Jagd als Freizeitbeschäftigung: Der Wandel des Jagdwesens vom Übergang der Jagdhoheit an den Kanton 1873 bis nach dem Ersten Weltkrieg.* Universität Zürich: Lizentiatsarbeit.
Schmid, Raphael. 2010. *Wenn Wildtiere verschwinden: Jagd und Wild in der Geschichte der Schweiz 1798–1970:* Diss Univ Bern, 2009.
Schmidt, Alexander. 1997. *Reisen in die Moderne: Der Amerika-Diskurs des deutschen Bürgertums vor dem Ersten Weltkrieg im europäischen Vergleich.* Berlin: Akademie Verlag.
Schmidt, Philipp. 1976. *Das Wild der Schweiz: Eine Geschichte der jagdbaren Tiere unseres Landes.* Bern: Hallwag.
Schmoll, Friedemann. 2004. *Erinnerung an die Natur: Die Geschichte des Naturschutzes im deutschen Kaiserreich.* Frankfurt: Campus.
Schneider, Jost. 2006. "Zucht in Gehegen und Aussetzungen bis 1938," in Marco Giacometti (ed.), *Von Königen und Wilderern: Die Rettung und Wiederansiedlung des Alpensteinbocks.* Wohlen: Salm, 109–160.

Schnetzer, Dominik. 2009. *Bergbild und Geistige Landesverteidigung: Die visuelle Inszenierung der Alpen im massenmedialen Ensemble der modernen Schweiz.* Zürich: Chronos.

Schorta, Andrea. 1988. *Vez l'alp da Grimmels.* Chur: Octopus-Verlag.

Schreiber, Martin. 2004. *Der historische Bergbau bei S-charl im Unterengadin: Untersuchungsergebnisse über das Blei- und Silberbergwerk und dessen Beziehungen zum Tirol.* Chur: Südostschweiz Buchverlag.

Schröder, Iris, and Sabine Höhler. 2005. "Welt-Räume. Annäherungen an eine Geschichte der Globalität im 20. Jahrhundert," in Iris Schröder and Sabine Höhler (eds.), *Welt-Räume. Geschichte, Geographie und Globalisierung seit 1900.* Frankfurt: Campus, 9–50.

Schröter, Carl. 1902. *Die Vegetation des Bodensees, enthaltend die Characeen, Moose und Gefässpflanzen.* Lindau i.B.: Joh. Thom. Stettner.

Schröter, Carl. 1910. "Der erste schweizerische Nationalpark Val Cluoza bei Zernez," *Heimatschutz* Jg. 5 (Heft 3), 17–24.

———. 1918. "Der schweizerische Nationalpark im Unterengadin," *Die Naturwissenschaften* 6 (52), 761–765.

———. 1920. "Der Werdegang des schweizerischen Nationalparks als Total-Reservation und die Organisation seiner wissenschaftlichen Untersuchung," *Denkschriften der Schweizerischen Naturforschenden Gesellschaft* LV, II-VIII.

———. 1924. "Die Aufgaben der wissenschaftlichen Erforschung in Nationalparken," in Emil Abderhalden (ed.), *Handbuch der biologischen Arbeitsmethoden, Abt. 11: Allgemeine Methoden zur Untersuchung des Pflanzenorganismus.* Berlin: Urban & Schwarzenberg, 387–394.

———. 1926. "Die wissenschaftliche Erforschung des Schweizerischen Nationalparks," in Naturforschende Gesellschaft Graubünden (ed.), *100 Jahre Naturforschende Gesellschaft Graubünden: Erweiterter Jahresbericht,* 64. Chur: Naturforschende Gesellschaft Graubünden, 85–108.

Schulte Fischedick, Kaat, and Terry Shinn. 1993. "The International Phytogeographical Excursions, 1911-1923: Intellectual Convergence in Vegetation Science," in Elisabeth Crawford et al. (eds.), *Denationalizing Science: The Contexts of International Scientific Practice.* Dordrecht: Kluwer Academic Publishers, 107–131.

Schulze, Hagen. 1994. *Staat und Nation in der europäischen Geschichte.* Munich: Beck.

Schumacher, Beatrice. 2002. *Ferien: Interpretationen und Popularisierung eines Bedürfnisses, Schweiz 1890-1950.* Vienna: Böhlau.

Schumacher, Beatrice. 2005. *Engagiert unterwegs: 100 Jahre Naturfreunde Schweiz, 1905–2005.* Baden: hier + jetzt.

Schütz, Martin, et al. (eds.). 2000a. "Predicting the development of subalpine grassland in the Swiss National Park: How to build a succession model based on data from long-term permanent plots," in Schütz et al. (eds.), *Succession research in the Swiss National Park: From Braun-Blanquet's permanent plots to models of long-term ecological change.* Zernez: Research Council of the Swiss National Park, 207–235.

——— (eds.). 2000b. *Succession research in the Swiss National Park: From Braun-Blanquet's permanent plots to models of long-term ecological change.* Zernez: Research Council of the Swiss National Park.

Schwarz, Angela (ed.). 2005. *Der Park in der Metropole: Urbanes Wachstum und städtische Parks im 19. Jahrhundert.* Bielefeld: transcript.

Schweiz Statistisches Bureau (ed.). 1907. *Die Ergebnisse der Eidgenössischen Volkszählung vom 1. Dezember 1900, Band 3: Die Unterscheidung der Bevölkerung nach dem Berufe.* Bern: Lack & Grunau.

Schweizerischer Bund für Naturschutz (ed.). 1947. *Nationalpark oder internationales Spölkraftwerk: Stimmen zur Erhaltung des Schweizerischen Nationalparkes im Unterengadin, Appels pour sauver le Park National Suisse de la Basse-Engadine.* Basel: SBN.

Schweizerischer Bund für Naturschutz and Schweizer Heimatschutz (eds.). 1964. *Das Talerwerk 1964 für den Schweizerischen Nationalpark.*

Schweizerischer Bundesrat. 1912. "Botschaft des Bundesrates an die Bundesversammlung betreffend die Beteiligung des Bundes an der Errichtung eines schweizerischen Nationalparks im Unterengadin (Kanton Graubünden), vom 9. Dezember 1912.," *Bundesblatt* (5), 415–426.

———. 1914. "Nachtragsbotschaft des Bundesrates an die Bundesversammlung betreffend die Errichtung eines schweizerischen Nationalparkes im Unter-Engadin, vom 30. Dezember 1913.," *Bundesblatt* (1), 13–26.

———. 1938. "Botschaft des Bundesrates an die Bundesversammlung über die Organisation und die Aufgaben der schweizerischen Kulturwahrung und Kulturwerbung, vom 9.12.1938.," *Bundesblatt* 90 (2), 985–1035.

———. 1957. "Botschaft des Bundesrates an die Bundesversammlung betreffend die Genehmigung eines zwischen der Schweizerischen Eidgenossenschaft und der Italienischen Republik abgeschlossenen Abkommens über die Nutzbarmachung der Wasserkraft des Spöl, vom 28. Juni 1957.," *Bundesblatt* 109 (2), 1–56.

———. 1959. "Botschaft des Bundesrates an die Bundesversammlung über den schweizerischen Nationalpark im Kanton Graubünden, vom 15. Mai 1959.," *Bundesblatt* 111 (1), 1317–1344.

———. 2005. "Botschaft zur Teilrevisionüber den Natur- und Heimatschutz (NHG) vom 23. Februar 2005," *Bundesblatt* 1 (11), 2151–2170.

Schweizerischer Nationalpark (ed.). 1998. *Auf den Spuren der Bären: Zur Vergangenheit und Zukunft der Braunbären in der Schweiz.* Chur: Desertina.

——— (ed.). 2001. *Es brennt im Schweizerischen Nationalpark: was nun?* Zernez: SNP.

Scott, James C. 1998. *Seeing Like a State: How Certain Schemes to Improve the Human Condition Have Failed,* New Haven: Yale University Press.

Sellars, Richard W. 1997. *Preserving Nature in the National Parks: A History.* New Haven: Yale University Press.

Selmi, Adel. 2009. "L'émergence de l'idée de parc national en France: De la protection des paysages à l'expérimentation coloniale," in Raphaël Larrère et al. (eds.), *Histoire des parcs nationaux: Comment prendre soin de la nature?* Versailles: Editions Quae, 43–58.

Shaffer, Marguerite S. 2001. *See America First: Tourism and National Identity, 1880–1940.* Washington, DC: Smithsonian Institution Press.

Sheail, John. 2010. *Nature's Spectacle: The World's First National Parks and Protected Places.* London: Earthscan.

Sieferle, Rolf Peter. 1999. "Einleitung: Naturerfahrung und Naturkonstruktion," in Rolf Peter Sieferle and Helga Breuninger (eds.), *Natur-Bilder. Wahrnehmungen von Natur und Umwelt in der Geschichte.* Frankfurt: Campus, 9–18.

Siegenthaler, Hansjörg. 1993. *Regelvertrauen, Prosperität und Krisen: Die Ungleichmässigkeit wirtschaftlicher und sozialer Entwicklung als Ergebnis individuellen Handelns und sozialen Lernens.* Tübingen: Mohr.

Sievert, James. 2000. *The Origins of Nature Conservation in Italy.* Bern: Lang.

Simon, Christian. 2009. *Natur-Geschichte: Das Naturhistorische Museum Basel im 19. und 20. Jahrhundert.* Basel: Merian.

Skenderovic, Damir. 1992. *Die schweizerische Umweltschutzbewegung in den 1950er und 1960er Jahren: Oppositionen und Aktionen.* Universität Freiburg: Lizentiatsarbeit.

Smith, Diane Marie. 2004. "What One Knows One Loves Best": *A Brief Administrative History of Science Education in the National Parks, 1916–1925.* Montana State University: MA thesis.

Smith, G. F. Herbert. 1947. "Nature Protection in Great Britain," *Nature* (4066, 4 October), 457–459.

Snow, Charles P. 1967 (1959). *Die zwei Kulturen: Literarische und naturwissenschaftliche Intelligenz.* Stuttgart: Klett Cotta.

Spehr, Christoph. 1994. *Die Jagd nach Natur: Zur historischen Entwicklung des gesellschaftlichen Naturverhältnisses in den USA, Deutschland, Grossbritannien und Italien am Beispiel von Wildnutzung, Artenschutz und Jagd.* Frankfurt: IKO.

Speich, Daniel. 2008. "Switzerland," in Guntram H. Herb and David H. Kaplan (eds.), *Nations and Nationalism: A Global Historical Overview, Volume I (1770–1880).* Santa Barbara: Abc-Clio, 244–255.

Spence, Mark David. 1999. *Dispossessing the Wilderness: Indian Removal and the Making of the National Parks.* New York: Oxford University Press.

Sprecher, Georg. 1942. *Die wirtschaftliche und finanzielle Entwicklung der Bündner Gemeinden: Ein Beitrag zur Wirtschaftskunde der Gebirgskantone.* Chur: Schuler.

Star, Susan Leigh, and James R. Griesemer. 1989. "Institutional Ecology, 'Translation' and Boundary Objects: Amateurs and Professionals in Berkeley's Museum of Vertebrate Zoology, 1907–39," *Social Studies of Science* 19, 387–420.

Steinberg, Theodore. 2002a. *Down to Earth: Nature's Role in American History.* New York: Oxford University Press.

———. 2002b. "Down to Earth: Nature, Agency, and Power in History," *The American Historical Review* 107 (3), 798–820.

Stemmler, Carl. 1932. *Die Adler der Schweiz.* Zürich: Grethlein.

Stettler, Niklaus. 2002. *Natur erforschen. Perspektiven einer Kulturgeschichte der Biowissenschaften an Schweizer Universitäten 1945–1975.* Zürich: Chronos.

Stremlow, Matthias. 1998. *Die Alpen aus der Untersicht. Von der Verheissung der nahen Fremde zur Sportarena. Kontinuität und Wandel von Alpenbildern seit 1700.* Bern: Haupt.

Stremlow, Matthias, and Christian Sidler. 2002. *Schreibzüge durch die Wildnis: Wildnisvorstellungen in Literatur und Printmedien der Schweiz.* Bern: Haupt.

Sutter, Paul S. 2002. *Driven Wild: How the Fight against Automobiles Launched the Modern Wilderness Movement.* Seattle: University of Washington Press.

Takacs, David. 1996. *The Idea of Biodiversity: Philosophies of Paradise.* Baltimore: Johns Hopkins University Press.

Tanner, Jakob. 2004. *Historische Anthropologie zur Einführung.* Hamburg: Junius.

Tanner, Jakob, and Angelika Linke. 2006. "Amerika als 'gigantischer Bildschirm Europas,'" in Angelika Linke and Jakob Tanner (eds.), *Attraktion und Abwehr: Die Amerikanisierung der Alltagskultur in Europa*. Cologne: Böhlau, 1–33.
Tansley, Arthur G. 1939. "Obituary: Carl Schröter, 1855–1939," *The Journal of Ecology* 27 (2/August), 531–534.
Tarnuzzer, Christian. 1911. "Ein Naturschutzpark in der Schweiz," *Süddeutsche Monatshefte* 8 (2), 246–254.
———. 1916. "Die officielle Exkursion der Schweizerischen Naturforschenden Gesellschaft in den Nationalpark am 9. August 1916," *Verhandlungen der Schweizerischen Naturforschenden Gesellschaft* 98 (Teil 1), 217–234.
Taylor, Joseph E., III. 2008. "Boundary Terminology," *Environmental History* 13 (July), 454–481.
Thurler, Louis. 1910. *Chalamala: Comédie lyrique en 3 actes (Musique de Emile Lauber)*. Estavayer-le-Lac: Butty.
Trepl, Ludwig. 1987. *Geschichte der Ökologie: Vom 17. Jahrhundert bis zur Gegenwart*. Frankfurt: Athenäum.
Trom, Danny. 1995. "Natur und nationale Identität: Der Streit um den Schutz der 'Natur' um die Jahrhundertwende in Deutschland und Frankreich," in Etienne François et al. (eds.), *Nation und Emotion: Deutschland und Frankreich im Vergleich, 19. und 20. Jahrhundert*. Göttingen: Vandenhoeck & Ruprecht, 147–167.
Truttmann, David. 2008. *"Die andere Stimme aus dem Unterengadin": Die Lia Naira und ihr Widerstand gegen den Bau der Engadiner Kraftwerke*. Universität Zürich: Lizentiatsarbeit.
Tschanz, Christoph. 1999. *Zwischen "Männerfreiheit" und "eindringendem Sichbeschäftigen mit den Geschöpfen der freien Wildbahn": Die Jagd als Raum sozialer Repräsentation und als Projektionsfläche des gesellschaftlichen Verhältnisses zur Natur in der Schweiz 1900–1965*. Universität Zürich: Lizentiatsarbeit.
Tyrrell, Ian. 2012. "America's National Parks: The Transnational Creation of National Space in the Progressive Era," *Journal of American Studies* 46 (1), 1–21.
Uekötter, Frank. 2007. *Umweltgeschichte im 19. und 20. Jahrhundert*. Munich: Oldenburg.
———. 2010. "Umwelt- und Ressourcenprobleme," in Hans-Ulrich Thamer (ed.), *Globalisierung: 1880 bis heute*, WBG Weltgeschichte 6. Darmstadt: WBG, 373–402.
UNEP-WCMC (ed.). 2008. *Annual Report on Protected Areas: A Review of Global Conservation Progress in 2007*. Cambridge: UNEP-WCMC.
van der Windt, Henny. 2012. "Parks without Wilderness, Wilderness without Parks? Assigning National Park status to Dutch Man-made Landscapes and Colonial Game Reserves," in Gissibl, Höhler, and Kupper (eds.), *Civilizing Nature: National Parks in Global Historical Perspective*. New York: Berghahn Books, 206–223.
van Laak, Dirk. 2004. "Kolonien als 'Laboratorien der Moderne'?" in Sebastian Conrad Sebastian and Jürgen Osterhammel (eds.), *Das Kaiserreich transnational: Deutschland in der Welt 1871–1914*. Göttingen: Vandenhoeck & Ruprecht, 257–279.
Van Schuylenbergh, Patricia. 2009. "Albert National Park: The Birth of Africa's First National Park (1925–1960)," in Marc Languy and Emmanuel de Merode (eds.), *Virunga: The Survival of Africa's First National Park*. Tielt: Lannoo, 64–73.
Verein Naturschutzpark (ed.). 1910. *Naturschutzparke in Deutschland und Österreich: Ein Mahnwort an das deutsche und österreichische Volk*. Stuttgart: Franckh.

Verkehrsverein Graubünden (ed.). 1942. *Kleiner Führer durch den Schweizerischen Nationalpark.* Chur: Bischofberger.
—— (ed.). 1968. *Kleiner Führer durch den Schweizerischen Nationalpark.* Samaden: Engadin Press.
Vischer, Wilhelm. 1946. *Naturschutz in der Schweiz.* Basel: SBN.
Voigt, Annette. 2009. *Die Konstruktion der Natur: Ökologische Theorien und politische Philosophien der Vergesellschaftung.* Stuttgart: Steiner.
Voser, Peter. 1987. "Einflüsse hoher Rothirschbestände auf die Vegetation im Unterengadin und im Münstertal, Kanton Graubünden," *Ergebnisse der wissenschaftlichen Untersuchungen im Schweizerischen Nationalpark* 82, 143–220.
Voth, Andreas. 2007. "National Parks and Rural Development in Spain," in Ingo Mose (ed.), *Protected Areas and Regional Development in Europe: Towards a New Model for the 21st Century.* Aldershot: Ashgate, 141–160.
Wagner, Peter. 1995. *Soziologie der Moderne: Freiheit und Disziplin.* Frankfurt: Campus.
Wakild, Emily. 2012. "A Revolutionary Civilization: National Parks, Transnational Exchanges, and the Construction of Modern Mexico," in Gissibl, Höhler, and Kupper (eds.), *Civilizing Nature: National Parks in Global Historical Perspective.* New York: Berghahn Books, 191–205.
Walter, François. 1996. *Bedrohliche und bedrohte Natur: Umweltgeschichte der Schweiz seit 1800.* Zürich: Chronos.
——. 2004. *Les figures paysagères de la nation: territoire et paysage en Europe (16e-20e siècle).* Paris: Ecole des hautes études en sciences sociales.
——. 2005. "La montagne alpine: Un dispositif esthétique et idéologique à l'échelle de l'Europe," *Revue d'Histoire Moderne et Contemporaine* 52 (2), 64–87.
Warming, Eugen. 1896. *Lehrbuch der ökologischen Pflanzengeographie: Eine Einführung in die Kenntnisse der Pflanzenvereine.* Berlin: Borntraeger.
Warren, Louis S. 1997. *The Hunter's Game: Poachers and Conservationists in Twentieth-Century America.* New Haven: Yale University Press.
Weber, Darius. 1990. *Das Ende des Fischotters in der Schweiz.* Bern: BUWAL.
Weber, Max. 1922 (1904). "Die Objektivität sozialwissenschaftlicher und sozialpolitischer Erkenntnis," in Max Weber (ed.), *Gesammelte Aufsätze zur Wissenschaftslehre.* Tübingen: Mohr, 146–214.
Weber, Wolfgang E. J. 2001. "Universalgeschichte," in Michael Maurer (ed.), *Aufriss der Historischen Wissenschaften, Band 2: Räume.* Stuttgart: Reclam, 15–98.
Weiner, Douglas R. 1988. *Models of Nature: Ecology, Conservation, and Cultural Revolution in Soviet Russia.* Bloomington: Indiana University Press.
Werner, Michael, and Bénédicte Zimmermann. 2006. "Beyond Comparison: Histoire Croisée and the Challenge of Reflexivity," *History and Theory* 45 (1/February), 30–50.
Wernli, Michael, et al. 2009. *Besucherzählung Schweizerischer Nationalpark.* Bern: Forschungskommission des Schweizerischen Nationalparks.
Whisnant, Anne Mitchell. 2008. "The Scenic is Political: Creating Natural and Cultural Landscapes along America's Blue Ridge Parkway," in Christof Mauch and Thomas Zeller (eds.), *The World beyond the Windshield: Roads and Landscapes in the United States and Europe.* Athens: Ohio University Press, 59–78.

White, Richard. 1991. *The Middle Ground: Indians, Empires, and Republics in the Great Lakes Region, 1650–1815*. Cambridge: Cambridge University Press.
———. 1995. "'Are You an Environmentalist or Do You Work for a Living?': Work and Nature," in William Cronon (ed.), *Uncommon Ground: Toward Reinventing Nature*. New York, London: W.W. Norton, 171–185.
———. 1999. "The Nationalization of Nature," *Journal of American History* 86 (3), 976–986.
Wild, Markus. 2008. *Tierphilosophie zur Einführung*. Hamburg: Junius.
Wilkins, Thurman. 1998. *Thomas Moran: Artist of the Mountains*. Norman: University of Oklahoma Press.
Winiwarter, Verena, and Martin Knoll. 2007. *Umweltgeschichte: Eine Einführung*. Cologne: Böhlau.
Wissenschaftliche Nationalparkkommission. 1986. *Dauerbeobachtungsflächen im Gebiet des Schweizerischen Nationalparks*. Zürich: WNPK.
——— (ed.). 1987. *Materialien zur bisherigen und zukünftigen Nationalparkforschung*. Zürich: WNPK.
———. 1990. *Forschungskonzept Nationalpark: Grundsätze und Leitlinien zur Nationalparkforschung 1989*. Zürich: WNPK.
Wissenschaftliche Nationalparkkommission and Nationalparkdirektion (ed.). 1991. *Waldbrand im Schweizerischen Nationalpark: Ergebnisse der Klausurtagung vom 2./3. Juli 1991*. Zürich: WNPK.
Wöbse, Anna-Katharina. 2003. "Lina Hähnle—eine Galionsfigur der frühen Naturschutzbewegung," in Stiftun Naturschutzgeschichte (ed.), *Naturschutz hat Geschichte*. Essen: Klartext, 113–130.
———. 2004. "Als eine Mode untragbar wurde: Die Kampagnen gegen den Federschmuck im Deutschen Kaiserreich," in Dorothea Deterts et al. (eds.), *Federn kitzeln die Sinne*. Bremen: Übersee-Museum, 43–50.
———. 2006a. "Naturschutz global—oder: Hilfe von aussen. Internationale Beziehungen des amtlichen Naturschutzes im 20. Jahrhundert," in Bundesamt für Naturschutz (ed.), *Natur und Staat: Staatlicher Naturschutz in Deutschland 1906–2006*. Bonn: Bundesamt für Naturschutz, 625–662.
———. 2006b. "Paul Sarasins 'anthropologischer Naturschutz': Zur 'Größe' Mensch im frühen internationalen Naturschutz. Ein Werkstattbericht," in Gert Gröning and Joachim Wolschke-Bulmahn (eds.), *Naturschutz und Demokratie!?* Munich: Martin Meidenbauer, 207–214.
———. 2012a. *Weltnaturschutz: Umweltdiplomatie in Völkerbund und Vereinten Nationen 1920–1950*. Frankfurt: Campus.
———. 2012b. "Framing the Heritage of Humankind: National Parks on the International Agenda," in Gissibl, Höhler, and Kupper (eds.), *Civilizing Nature: National Parks in Global Historical Perspective*. New York: Berghahn Books, 140–156.
Wondrak Biel, Alice. 2006. *Do (not) Feed the Bears: The Fitful History of Wildlife and Tourists in Yellowstone*. Lawrence: University of Kansas Press.
World Conservation Monitoring Centre. 1990. *1990 United Nations List of National Parks and Protected Areas*. Gland: IUCN.
———. 1998. *1997 United Nations List of Protected Areas*. Gland: IUCN.

Worster, Donald. 1985. *Nature's Economy: A History of Ecological Ideas.* Cambridge: Cambridge University Press.
Wright, George M., Joseph S. Dixon, and Benjamin H. Thompson. 1933. *Fauna of the National Parks of the United States. A Preliminary Survey of Faunal Relations in National Parks.* Washington, DC: U.S. Govt. Print. Off.
Wright, R. Gerald. 1992. *Wildlife Research and Management in the National Parks.* Urbana: University of Illinois Press.
Würflinger, Roland. 2007. *"Kultur statt verwilderte Natur": Der Widerstand gegen die Errichtung des Nationalparks Gesäuse.* Universität Wien: Diplomarbeit.
Zbinden, Hans. 1953. *Das Spiel um den Spöl: Grundsätzliches zum Kampf um den Nationalpark.* Bern: Herbert Lang.
———. 1957. "Der Schweizer Naturschutz vor erweiterten Aufgaben," *Schweizer Naturschutz* 23 (2), 33–40.
Ziegler, Ursula. 2002. *Prozessschutz vor dem Hintergrund der Ideengeschichte des Naturschutzes.* TU Munich: Diplomarbeit.
Zimmerer, Karl S. 2000. "The Reworking of Conservation Geographies: Nonequilibrium Landscapes and Nature-Society Hybrids," *Annals of the Association of American Geographers* 90 (2), 356–369.
Zoller, Heinrich. 1964. *Flora des schweizerischen Nationalparks und seiner Umgebung.* Chur: Nationalpark-Museum.
Zuanon, Jean-Paul. 1995. *Chronique d'un "parc oublié": Du parc de la Bérarde (1913) au parc national des Ecrins (1973).* Grenoble: Revue de Géographie Alpine.

Index

A
Abderhalden, Emil, 197
absolute protection. *See* total protection
Adams, Charles C., 158
aesthetic, 22–25, 41, 69, 125, 157, 181
Africa, 30, 60–61, 83, 98–99, 101n7, 119, 122, 157, 215n90
Agrawal, Arun, 71, 99, 106
Akeley, Carl, 157
Albert, Parc National (Belgian Congo), 60, 73, 157, 173n79
Albright, Horace M., 158
Aldrovandus, Ulysses, 64
Aletsch (reserve), 45, 92, 105n67
Almen, Peter von, 39, 64
Alps, 22–25, 111–112, 129–130, 186, 189–190
amphibians, 148
animals
    domestic, 16, 117, 122, 177
    harmful and useful, 126, 132, 198
    killing/shooting of, 129, 152, 162, 199, 207, 215n91, 217n127
Antarctica, 31
anthropological nature protection, 74
anti-Americanism, 51
ants, 148
Arabia, 58
archeology, 43, 74
Ardez, 92
Argentina, 68n70
art history, 43, 55
Asia, 56, 58, 73, 98–99
Association of Nature Parks (German and Austrian), 60
Association pour la protection des plantes (Swiss), 52, 64
Australia, 20, 68n70
Austria, 21, 26–27, 31, 33, 49, 58, 64n7, 68n70, 76–77, 107, 126, 128, 156, 189, 212n32, 213n49
authenticity, 29, 150
automobile, 5, 78, 156–157, 186, 188–191, 219
    ban on, 189

B
Bächler, Emil, 111
Bachmann, Hans, 64
Bachmann, Stefan, 64n4, 65n19
Baer, Jean, 14n35, 61, 206, 216n117
Barbey, Auguste, 146
bark beetles, 122
Basel, 40, 44–45, 55, 59–60, 66n34, 68n64, 74, 81, 97–99, 118–119, 171n44
Bavaria, 49, 212n32, 216n111
bear, 24, 41, 45, 49, 64n8, 66n41, 82, 85, 94, 126–130, 135nn60–63, 178, 185, 187
    grizzly, 163
bearded vulture, 64, 130–131– 185
Belgian Congo, 60, 73, 157
Belgium, 60–61, 68n70, 157
Belle Epoque, 16, 77
Bergamo, 79
Bern, 11, 39, 41, 45, 52, 58, 66n34, 74, 97–99, 113, 154, 171n44
Bernard, Charles, 61
Bezzola, Rudolf, 82, 89
biocenosis (biocoenose), 42, 140–143
biodiversity, 1, 73, 130, 168, 171n40
biosphere reserve, 106n97, 168, 221
birds, 24, 29–30, 46, 130–131, 148, 156, 162, 185
Bischoff, Joannes, 96

bison, 30, 34, 53
Bissegger, Walter, 15, 16, 24, 29, 33, 34, 64n5, 225n1
Blankenhorn, Hans-Jörg, 209
block glacier, 146
borders, 6, 8–9, 22, 49, 59–60, 79, 83, 93, 96–97, 103, 107–108, 111, 113, 115, 117–118, 121, 132, 139, 142, 158, 177, 182–83, 189, 202–206, 211, 216, 220–221
    border patrol, 121, 201
botany, 8, 45, 55, 139–140, 145, 147–149, 150, 151, 155, 159, 162–163, 165
boulders (glacial erratics), 23–24, 83
Bowles, Samuel, 21
Brail, 75, 206
Braudel, Fernand, 16, 34n6
Braun-Blanquet, Josias, 140, 142, 145, 147–150, 163–166, 174nn110–111, 175–176, 210, 212n18, 217n127
breeding
    of bearded vulture, 130
    of butterflies, 162
    of ibex, 111–113
Breslau (Wrocław), 81
British settler colonies, 7, 33
Brockington, Dan, 17
Brockman-Jerosch, Heinrich, 147
Brunhes, Jean, 25
Brunies, Steivan, 42, 44–45, 67n53, 80–83, 90, 93–94, 97–98, 102n33, 103n47, 118–120, 131, 133n6, 134n33, 134n35, 135nn37–38, 146–147, 189, 200–201, 211n4
Brussels, 14n35, 60–61, 170n10
Buchli, Christian, 26
buffer zone, 101, 221, 225n6. See also core zone
Bühlmann, Fritz, 57, 67n45, 92–94, 113, 115, 120, 134n35, 144, 160, 210, 211n4, 215n89
Bundi, Martin, 98, 227
Bündner Verkehrsverein, 188
Burckhardt, Dieter, 197, 205, 227
Bütikofer, Ernst, 193, 199

C
Cahalane, Victor H., 61–62
California, 140, 158
Calonder, Felix-Louis, 27, 221
Campell, Eduard, 105n77
camping, 185, 187
Canada, 5, 20
Canfield, David, 183
capitalism, 30
Carl, Jean, 201, 215n94
Catlin, George, 35n13
cattle, 42, 77, 107, 216n104
Celebes (Sulawesi), 56, 68n66, 74
Central America, 61
Ceylon, 56, 74
Chaix, André, 146
Chaix, Émile, 196
Chalamala, Louise, 39
chauvinism, 120
China, 58
Chodat, Robert, 171n44
Christ, Hermann, 41–42, 44–45, 51, 64n5, 64n11, 65n26, 185–186
Chur, 1, 77, 84, 117, 153, 188
Cinuos-chel, 80–81
civilization, 1, 5–6, 8, 12n21, 20, 24, 28–33, 41, 53, 56, 67n59, 73–74, 117, 122
Clements, Frederic E., 141–142, 164, 174n110
climate, 34n6, 135n51, 143, 152, 164, 178
    change, 221
Cluozza log cabin, 46–47, 121
Coaz, Johann, 41–42, 45, 47–48, 65n18, 66n27, 66n37, 91, 103n49
colonization, 6, 143
Colorado River, 161, 184
commerce, 18, 21, 77, 113
compensations, 85, 87, 91–93, 97, 99, 106n83, 126, 175–176, 206
complete protection. See total protection
computer, 163, 166, 168
Comte, Auguste, 164
Congo. See Belgian Congo

conservation movement, 3, 15–17, 25–30, 33–34, 40–42, 59–60, 66n34, 72, 112, 186, 199
Convent of St. Johann, 129
Convention on Biological Diversity, 168
Conwentz, Hugo, 31–33, 59
Coolidge, Harold J., 61–62, 68n81
Cooper, William, 151
core zone, 70, 101, 197, 221. *See also* buffer zone
Correvon, Henry, 52, 64n2
Cowles, Henry C., 151, 167
Cramer, Carl, 139
Cranz, Heinrich, 213n49
Crater Lake National Park, 125
Curie, Marie, 28
Czechoslovakia, 61, 107

D
Dachnowski, Alfred, 170n13
damming, 8, 132, 161, 175–177, 184
    Ova Spin, 179–182
    Punt dal Gall dam, 173n92, 190
Daniels, Mark, 187
Danzig (city), 31
Darwin, Charles, 25–26
David, Adam, 119, 134n34
Debarges, Henry, 38–39, 64n2
decolonization, 99
deer
    fallow, 125
    roe, 128, 185, 198–203, 216n110
deer, red, 8, 115, 122, 125, 128, 147, 185, 207
    population, 129–132, 160–163, 175–176, 200–210, 216n105
    shooting in Swiss National Park, 206–209, 217n123
Defert, Henry, 156
democracy, 19, 49, 99
Denmark, 68n70
Desax, Carl, 217n120
German Association for the Protection of Birds (*Deutscher Bund für Vogelschutz*), 46

Diels, Ludwig, 141
Dietschi, Urs, 181
Dinosaur National Monument, 183
diseases, 122, 135n45, 135n49, 149, 197, 199, 203. *See also* rabies
Duerst, Ulrich, 201–202
Duffy, Rosaleen, 17
dying out, 8, 160, 198–199, 203–205, 207–208. *See also* extinction

E
eagle, 24, 130
Echo Park, 8, 183–184
ecology, 39, 65, 132, 139–141, 149, 163–168, 221
    moral ecology, 65n19, 116–117, 132
    synecology, 140
Ecology (journal), 159, 174n110
ecosystem, 62, 68n83, 100, 109, 116, 140, 168, 220–221
edelweiss, 23, 29
education, 77, 81, 157, 159, 188, 194, 225n6
Einstein, Albert, 28
electricity industry, 8, 82, 177–178, 182, 210. *See also* damming; Engadiner Kraftwerke
elephant, 30
emotion, 71, 95, 97–99
empire, 2, 11n3, 27, 51, 60
Enderlin, Florian, 66n27
Engadine
    Lower, 15, 41, 45, 49–50, 59, 64n8, 75–79, 93, 96, 102n23, 107, 109, 123, 126, 129, 147, 161, 172n59, 175, 177–178, 197, 201
    Upper, 75, 77–79, 102n23, 111, 176, 188, 213n60
Engadiner Kraftwerke, 121, 161, 173n92, 177, 182
Enlightenment, 22, 25, 27
ENPK (Eidgenössische Nationalparkkommission) 48, 50, 70, 81, 92–98, 111,–115, 119–132, 142, 146–147, 151–152, 159–162, 177–180, 189–192, 196–203, 207–210,

environment, 3, 9, 24, 31, 49, 65n17, 71–72, 80, 99, 106n92, 112, 120, 122, 130, 140, 150–151, 210, 221
environmental history, 12n22, 13n26, 13n28, 35n22, 35n31, 36n40, 49n17, 116, 224
environmentality, 9, 71, 99
equilibrium, 116–117, 131–133, 136nn82–83, 141–142, 175–176, 211, 225n3
  biological balance, 175, 217n127
ETH Zurich (federal polytechnic), 11, 148–149, 162
ethnology, 43, 55, 74, 101n12
Europe, 1, 3–4, 12n21, 19–22, 25–33, 35n15, 35n22, 36n40, 42–43, 47, 54–59, 67n49, 73–75, 78n20, 83, 98, 107–108, 130, 140–141, 146, 157–158, 164, 189, 214
European Conservation Year 1970, 207
Everglades National Park, 65n14
evolution, theory of, 5, 38–39, 74, 101n12, 138, 141, 147, 160, 190, 200, 219–220
exploitation, 3, 8, 20, 22, 48, 62, 68n83, 99, 113, 144, 176–178, 182, 186, 188, 210
expulsion of humans, 4, 17, 72–75, 219
extinction, 24, 29, 32, 34, 49, 74, 113, 129, 136n71, 168, 202. See also dying out

F
farmers, 79, 81, 89–90, 95, 128, 141
fauna, 8, 29–30, 38, 42, 49, 97, 112, 123, 130, 138–139, 143, 147–148, 158, 161, 185, 188, 190–191, 200–201
Federal Commission for Nature and Heritage Protection, 181
feeding
  stations, 115, 207
  winter, 115, 208
fence, 41, 122, 162, 173n99, 219–220
Feuerstein, Domenic, 99
Feuerstein, Johann, 99
fieldwork, 74, 160, 162, 164–165
Finsteraarhorn, 45
fire, 14n35, 17, 123–124, 161, 185, 191
  management, 123–124

First World War, 3, 6, 16, 29, 34, 44, 47, 50, 55, 59, 61, 63, 76, 118–119, 126, 128, 133n7, 156, 160, 171n30, 176, 186, 189
Fischer, Eduard, 171n44
Fischer-Sigwart, Hermann, 64n5
fish, 30, 82, 148, 167, 173n92, 213n60
fishing, 20, 24, 35n26, 85, 119, 125, 185, 187
Flahault, Charles, 140, 149, 151, 170n10
Floericke, Kurt, 54, 64n7
flora, 8, 23, 29, 41–42, 45, 49, 81, 97, 107, 112, 123, 125, 136n82, 136n84, 138–140, 148–149, 158–159, 161, 163–164, 173n92, 185, 188, 190, 200, 209–210
folklore, 74, 92, 97
forest
  history, 143, 171n34
  reserves, 43, 65n18
forestation, 151, 207, 209
forestry, 22, 24, 42–43, 48, 66n27, 75, 79, 84, 91, 94–95, 121–122, 146, 162, 188, 203, 209
  Federal Institute for Experimental Forestry, 146
fortress conservation, 73–74
Foucault, Michel, 6, 71, 101n3
fowl, 123
fox, 123, 130–131, 200, 215n91
  reduction of, 123, 131
France, 31, 58, 60, 156, 158, 212n32
Freud, Sigmund, 28
Frey, Eduard, 147
Friends of Nature, 65n25
frontier, 4, 30, 192
fundraising, 21, 46, 129
future. See posterity
future generations, 30, 92, 187, 221

G
Galison, Peter, 172n60
game, 23, 30, 33, 82, 95, 107, 112, 119, 175–176, 180, 198–201, 205, 215n91, 216n115
  cantonal gamekeepers, 205, 207, 209
garden, 23, 32–33, 52–53, 141, 148, 202
Gäumann, Ernst, 135n45, 162

Geistige Landesverteidigung, 97, 180–181
Gemuseus-Riggenbach, Rosina, 66n34
genetics, 116, 148, 168
Geneva, 38–39, 44, 52, 63, 64n2, 140, 146, 162, 171n44
geography, 8, 55, 82, 142, 145
geology, 8, 55, 145–146
German Association for the Protection of Birds, 26, 46, 66n29
Germany, 26, 31, 33, 35n31, 36n34, 36n54, 51, 54, 58, 141, 155, 197
Gessner, Conrad, 64n2
Gessner, Ulysses, 38–39, 64n2
geyser, 18–20, 30, 32
Giacometti, Robert, 98
GIS (geographical information system), 76, 87, 163, 169, 183
glacier, 23, 42, 113, 146, 151
Glarus, 44
Gleason, Henry, 174n110
global history, 3, 5, 9–10, 16–17, 35n25, 35n31, 75, 187, 223–224
globalism, 220
globalization, 2–3, 15, 27, 32, 56, 221
Glutz, Robert, 32–33, 43, 65n18
Gnehm, Robert, 148
goat, 64n2, 110, 122, 189, 215n91
Goethe, Johann Wolfgang, 22
Gotthard, 77
Gradmann, Robert, 141
Gran Paradiso, 111, 113, 156,
Grand Canyon National Monument, 32
Grass, Curdin, 111, 123
Grass, Gian J., 102n33
Grass, Rudolf, 203
Graz, 55
grazing, 16, 48, 79, 93–95, 103n42, 122, 130, 135n51, 141, 148, 162, 175, 199, 209
  over-, 8, 208–209
Great Britain. *See* United Kingdom
Great Smoky Mountain National Park, 65n14
Griesemer, James, 172n60
Grimsel, 45
Grisons, 11, 34, 52–53, 66n27, 67n47, 76, 78, 82, 85, 91, 96, 98, 105n76, 106n85, 113, 115, 118, 135n60, 176, 178, 184, 189, 195, 199, 202, 205–206, 215n88
Gross Glockner Park, 107

H
habitat, 18, 68n83, 113, 132, 151
Haeckel, Ernst, 38, 140
Hagenbeck's Zoo, Hamburg, 52–53
Hähnle, Lina, 46, 66n29
Hall in Tyrol, 175
Hall, Ansel F., 158
Hall, Harvey M., 158
Hall, Marcus, 65n17
Haller, Albrecht von, 22
Haller, Heinrich, 169, 197, 215n99, 227
Hämmerle, Andrea, 98
Handschin, Eduard, 122, 150, 178, 190–194, 210, 215n96
Harder Wildlife Park, 110
Harroy, Jean-Paul, 61, 154
Heer, Oswald, 140
Hegi, Gustav, 34, 37n69
Heierli, Jakob, 64n5
Heim, Albert, 64n5, 65n19
Heim, Roger, 61
herbarium, 148
Herder, Johann Gottfried von, 36n37
heritage, 21, 28, 30, 36n40, 41, 43, 45, 52, 65n17, 65n19, 73, 100, 129, 176, 179, 181, 186, 222
Hetch Hetchy, 184, 186, 213n41
heterotopia, 6–7, 23, 117, 211, 221
Hoffmann, Karl R., 200, 215n91
Holland. *See* Netherlands
human interference, 6, 118, 128, 133, 141–142, 151, 186
human rights, 72–73
humanity, 6, 27
Humboldt, Alexander von, 31, 56
Hungary, 58, 68n70, 126
hunting, 16–17, 20, 23, 85, 115, 125, 198–210
  lease-based, 198–210
  no-hunting zone, 83, 87, 89, 93–95, 106n85, 112, 202, 204, 210

regulation of, 85, 91, 128–129, 198, 209
See also poaching
Huxley, Julian, 60, 61

I
ibex, 109–116
    breeding of, 111–113
    hunting of, 111–113, 210
    reintroduction of, 84, 93, 105n72, 110–113, 129, 158
Iceland, 19–20
identity
    cultural, 19, 156
    national, 7, 22, 26, 54, 99
Igoe, Jim, 17
imperialism, 26–27, 56, 59, 98
India, 58, 71, 99
indigenous peoples, 5, 17, 20, 53, 73–74, 97, 154, 158, 181
    Declaration on Rights of Indigenous Peoples, 73–74
Inn River and Valley, 75–77, 93–94, 142, 202
Innsbruck, 76
International Nature Protection Conference
    Bern 1913, 74, 175
    Brunnen 1947, 61
    Fontainebleau 1948, 61, 109
International Office for the Protection of Nature, 60
International Phytogeographic Excursion, 140
International Union for Conservation of Nature (IUCN), 11, 14n35, 61–63, 68n91, 69n84, 100, 109, 133n9, 136n86, 154
International Union for the Protection of Nature (IUPN), 61
internationalism, 27, 59
invertebrates, 147–148, 185, 201
Isenberg, Andrew, 116
Italy, 21, 26, 31, 36, 76–77, 83, 111, 117–118, 128, 156, 158, 175, 177, 182, 190, 202

J
Japan, 26, 58, 62, 163
Jenny, Hans, 147, 162

K
Karwendel Park, 107
Kiefer-Hablitzel, Charles, 74
Kiefer-Hablitzel, Mathilde, 74
Knopfli, Walter, 148
Kohler, Robert, 149–150
Könz, Jachen, 98
Koselleck, Reinhard, 34n6
Kozhevnikov, Grigorij Alexandrowitsch, 154, 155
Kracauer, Sigfried, 13n27
Kreis, Georg, 65n16
Kurth, Alfred, 151, 161

L
La Punt-Chamues-ch, 59, 105n69
laboratory, 8–9, 138, 142–143, 147–152, 156, 160–162, 167–168, 172n60, 172n76
landscape, 1, 7–8, 13, 19–22, 25–26, 29–33, 36n40, 36n54, 41–42, 45, 51, 53, 61–62, 68n83, 70, 73, 75, 97, 100, 117, 125, 130, 141, 149, 151, 156, 167, 178, 181, 187, 196, 219–220
    cultural landscapes, 21, 73, 100, 141, 181, 220
Landwirtschaftliche Versuchsanstalt, 149
    Institute for Experimental Agriculture, 149
Langen, Hermann, 109–112, 114, 118–121, 146, 188–189, 197–198
Langen's wife and children, 121, 188–189
Lansel, Peider, 52–53, 67n53, 98, 106n89
larch, 41
Latour, Bruno, 12–13, 153, 166
Lavin, 70, 87, 92, 98, 103n51, 203
League of Nations, 60, 108
Lefebvre, Henri, 7, 13n24, 28
Lega Nazionale per la Protezione dei Monumenti Naturali, 27, 31
Legler, David, 49
Leopold, Aldo, 116

Lia Naira (Black League), 182, 212n28
liberalism, 5, 204
lichen, 147, 164
life reform, 28
Linné, Carl von, 164
livelihood, 80
livestock, 20, 48, 80, 122, 128, 130
Livigno (town, valley), 111, 118, 121, 131, 182, 190, 202
local
    acceptance, 7, 72, 90–91, 99, 128
    actors, 73, 80, 82, 89, 99
    participation, 72, 96–98, 100, 197, 222
    population, 7, 73–75, 79, 98–101, 120, 126, 128, 179, 223
London, 11, 19–20, 30, 60
Luchetta, 120
Lüdi, Werner, 165
Lüdtke, Alf, 116
Lüneburger Heide, 31
lynx, 125, 128–130, 132, 185

M
Madagascar, 157
Maier, Charles, 5
mammals, 147, 185
mapping, 5, 139, 145, 160, 163, 170n36
materialism, 6, 29–31
Matterhorn, 43–44, 52, 65n19, 186
Matthey, Willy, 137
media
    press, 19–20, 27, 39, 44, 52, 64n2, 109, 120, 128, 136n63, 175, 184, 186, 198, 205, 208–209
    radio, 163, 183, 184
Merriam, John C., 157–158, 173n79, 227
meteorology, 143, 145–146,
Mexico, 73
Meyer, Otto, 198–199
Meylan, Charles, 147
middle class, 19, 22, 25, 27, 40, 51, 73, 82, 186, 225n1
migration
    of animals, 8, 116, 125–126, 128–129, 202, 207
    of humans, 51, 77
military (troops), 20, 29, 93, 156, 161, 180, 189, 198
Miller, Perry, 21
Minahassa, 56, 58
mining, 20, 24, 101n17, 171n34
Möbius, Karl August, 140
modernity, 2, 5–6, 12, 26–29, 117, 132, 181, 220
Mohr, Otto, 82, 96, 104n52
monitoring, 49, 111, 118–119, 121–124, 131, 138, 141, 150–151, 156, 165–168, 192, 223
Montana, 18
Montpellier, 140, 149
Moscow, 154
moss, 148, 164
Mother Earth, 6
Mount Rainer, 22
mountain pine, 41, 175
mugo pine, 95
Muir, John, 28, 186
Müller, Jürg P., 227
Munt la Schera tunnel, 183, 190
Müstair, 76–77, 93, 101, 102n23, 120, 129, 168, 190

N
Nadig, Adolf, 148, 150
Napoleon Bonaparte, 76
Nash, Roderick, 3, 18, 34n8, 67n59, 184
national park
    American model, 3, 7, 17, 20, 29–34, 43, 52, 54, 63, 73, 108–109, 185, 196, 222
    idea of, 3–7, 9, 15–18, 34n8, 34n10, 35nn13–15, 39, 47, 53– 54, 59, 61, 71, 73, 112, 118, 124, 156–57, 180, 186, 220–21, 224, 225n1
    invention of, 9, 16, 13n35
    as label, 53, 73, 100, 199
    Swiss model, 3, 7, 10, 54, 59, 63, 107–109, 155–156, 223
nationalism, 19, 21, 27, 39–40, 54, 59, 63, 80, 213n49
nationalization, 3, 49, 59, 63

nation-state, 2, 11n3, 21–22, 26–27, 36n43, 39, 58–59
natural
  dynamics, 168, 206, 211
  history, 19, 23, 26, 31, 117, 152
  monument, 29–33, 40, 58, 196
  resources, 8, 22, 48, 186
nature
  freely developing, 8, 70, 112, 133, 138, 156, 161, 217n123, 219–220
  primeval, pristine, 4–6, 38, 40, 42–43, 46, 49, 53, 73, 124–125, 141, 154, 220, 224
  restoration of, 4, 12n13, 28, 40, 42–43, 52, 65n17, 125, 141, 175, 210, 224
  unspoiled, 20, 24–25, 29, 73
  ur-nature, 4, 6, 125, 135n56, 224
Nature (journal), 108–109
nature-culture separation, 6–7, 12n22, 13n23, 122, 211, 220
Nazi, 180
Netherlands, 26, 31, 60–61, 68n70, 73, 158
Neurath, Otto, 24
New Zealand, 20
Newton, Isaac, 28
Niagara Falls, 19, 35n15
Nievergelt, Bernhard, 135n47, 137–138, 168, 227
North America, 26, 31–33, 53, 81, 101n7, 219
Norway, 61, 68n70
nudism, 191

O
Obwalden, 129
Ofengebiet, 41–42, 44–5, 79, 81–83
Olgiati, Velerio, 100
Omaha, Nebraska, 183
otter, 129–130, 136n71,

P
Pallmann, Hans, 147, 162
paradise, 53, 131
parc national de la Bérarde, 60, 156
Paris, 60, 157

Parks of National Importance, 100, 222
partial protection, 107, 133
pasture, 48, 79, 90–91, 95, 105n82, 130, 151, 206, 209
pathology, 120, 148–149
patriotism, 19, 23, 27, 32, 80, 97, 110, 192
Peter and Paul Wildlife Park, 110–111, 113
Pictet, Arnold, 162
Pieniny, bi-national park, 107
Planck, Max, 28
plant communities, 41, 142, 163–164, 174n110
plant sociology, 140, 142, 149, 152, 163, 174nn110–111
plants. See flora
poaching, 49, 58, 111, 115, 117–119, 121, 131
Poland, 107, 158
pollution, 221
pony, 189
Portugal, 68n70
Poschiavo, 76
posterity, 49, 58, 74
postwar period, 9, 61, 162, 168, 180, 182, 194
pragmatism, 179, 181
predator, 23, 49, 66n41, 82, 103n37, 112, 117, 123, 128–132, 175, 199–200, 207, 217n119, 220
  reward for killing of, 130, 199
prehistory, 55, 75
Pro Nationalpark foundation, 98
Pro Natura. See SBN
process protection, 133, 136n86
property rights, 79, 166
Protestantism, 77, 120
Prussia, 21, 30–31, 39

R
rabies, 123, 129, 135n47
radio tracking, 163, 184
railways/railroad, 30, 44, 65n19, 77–79, 82, 85, 102n20, 102n23, 104n61, 185–186
Rauch, Men, 96
Rauch, Otto, 95, 105nn80–81

recreation, 4, 42, 54, 62–63, 106n87, 109, 157, 159, 184, 187, 194, 196, 225n6. *See also* tourism
Reinalter, Romedi, 119–121
religious sites, 17
reptiles, 148
Reserves Committee (SNK), 11n10–11, 45–46, 64n11, 66n27, 80–81, 107, 199, 212n37
Revel, Jacques, 9
Rhaetian Railway, 153, 188
Rheinau, 179
Riis, Paul B., 97
Rikli, Martin, 148, 171n42
Robin, Klaus, 121, 169, 197, 227
Rocky Mountain National Park, 22, 32, 183, 187
Rohn, Albert, 148, 171n44
Romandy. *See* Switzerland, French-speaking
Romansh. *See* Switzerland, Romansh-speaking
romanticism, 4, 25, 27, 112
Röntgen, Wilhelm Conrad, 28
Roosevelt, Theodore, 32 34, 36n39
Roten, Heinrich von, 67n42
Rousseau, Jean-Jacques, 22, 25–26
Royal Academy (UK), 32
Rübel, Eduard, 140
Ruchet, Marc-Emile, 44, 46, 82
Runte, Alfred, 18–19, 66n37
Russia, 30, 140, 154–155, 172n69
Rütimeyer, Leopold, 74–75
Rütli, 21
Rytz, Walter, 148

S

Salis, Adolf von, 176–177
salt licks, 111–112, 115–117, 131, 200
Sami, 21, 73
Samnaun, 77
San Francisco, 186
sanctuary, 4, 6, 15, 34, 50, 66n34, 184, 188
Sarasin, Eduard, 148

Sarasin, Fritz, 42, 44–46, 55–56, 58, 68n65, 74
Sarasin, Paul, 26n44, 40, 42–43, 45–48, 50, 52, 55–58, 60, 63, 64n2, 64n5, 65n13, 68n65, 74, 89, 92–94, 103n40, 108, 129, 144, 146, 148, 154, 162, 198, 223
SBN (Schweizerischer Bund für Naturschutz), 10, 46–48, 51, 60–61, 65n18, 81, 92–97, 100, 109, 121, 126–127, 130, 137, 144–145, 177–184, 190–192, 196–197, 201–202, 211n2
scale
  large-, 7, 31, 33, 59, 100, 122, 140, 164
  small-, 33, 140, 164
S-chanf, 47–50, 92, 102n23, 103n47, 103n53, 104n63, 119–121, 182
Schardt, Hans, 339
Schatzki, Theodore, 13n23
Scheurer, Thomas, 137, 227
Schiller, Friedrich, 29, 224n1
Schillings, Carl Georg, 64n7
Schloeth, Robert, 98, 105n77, 128–130, 160, 162, 169, 192–197, 227
Schobinger, Josef Anton, 82
Schröter, Carl, 6, 11, 28–29, 41–42, 45, 47, 49–51, 53, 63, 64n5, 65n18, 66n28, 81, 83, 90, 92, 108, 112, 125, 132, 133n4, 139–142, 144, 148–150, 152, 155, 158, 160, 166, 170n7, 170nn10–11, 188–189, 213n48, 220
Schütz, Martin, 220, 228
Schweizerische Volkspartei (SVP), 71
Scientific Park Commission (research program 2008–2018), 168
Scuol, 11, 47–48, 50, 77–78, 80, 82, 85, 87, 89–97, 99, 102n19, 102n23, 103n51, 104n52, 104n63, 105n64, 105n76, 105nn81–83, 107, 112, 115, 121, 144, 182, 213n51, 215n94
seasonal, 20, 61, 79, 102n28, 149, 152, 195, 198, 202, 204–206
Second World War, 60, 63, 71, 73, 85, 113, 132, 145, 160, 161–162, 176–177, 180, 182, 192, 210, 222
"See America First" campaign, 187

Semper, Karl, 55
Senn, Gustav, 171n44
Serrardi, Christel, 104n58
sheep, 79, 105n82, 122, 130
Shelford, Victor E., 151, 167
Shenandoah National Park, 65
Siegenthaler, Hansjörg, 16
Sils Lake, 176, 184
Smithsonian Institution, 191
SNG (Schweizerische Naturforschende Gesellschaft), 40, 42–45, 48, 50, 55, 64n5, 67n47, 96, 144–148, 178, 189
SNK (Swiss Commission for Nature Protection), 40–55, 59, 63–64, 75, 80–85, 89–93, 98, 107–108, 112, 117, 120, 139, 146, 154, 176, 186, 188, 224
Snow, C. P., 12n22
socialism, 5, 49, 65n25
Société pour la Protection des Paysages, 26
soil, 135n51, 143, 145, 147, 152, 162, 164, 175, 181
Sophocles, 15, 224n1
Soviet Union, 154–155
Spain, 68n70, 133n7
species
  endangered, 30, 130
  invasive, 197
  native and alien, 125
Spöl River, 8, 93, 100, 113, 132, 160, 173n92, 175, 177, 213n60
springtail, 190
spruce, 41
Spyri, Johanna, 64n2
St. Gallen, 110–110, 113, 119
St. Moritz, 77–80, 125
Stampa, 176
Star, Susan Leigh, 152–153, 172n60
Station Internationale de Géobotanique Mediterranéenne et Alpine, 149
statistics, 22, 102n22–23, 160, 165, 192, 195, 201, 210, 214n69
Stelvio National Park, 21, 118, 156
Stemmler, Carl, 130
stone pine, 175
Strict Nature Reserve, 62–63, 109, 136n86, 172n70

Stüssi, Balthasar, 165–166
sub-alpine, 113, 139, 163
subsistence, 4, 58, 77, 80
succession, 141–142, 151, 166
Suhner-Müller, Gottfried, 128
sustainability, 70, 92, 99, 126, 187, 198–199, 205, 221
Sweden, 21, 31–32, 42, 55, 67n60, 68n70, 73, 83, 103n39, 155
Swiss citizenship, 120
Swiss Forest Association, 43, 45
Swiss government (Federal Council), 22, 27, 38, 43–48, 50, 54, 58, 67n47, 67n60, 80, 82, 85, 91–92, 96, 98, 100, 103n47, 104n61, 104n63, 112, 139, 145, 146, 178–181, 190, 217n127, 221
Swiss Heritage Society, 43, 211n2
Swiss national day, 50, 70
Swiss National Park
  accessibility, 6, 19, 21, 23, 41–42, 52, 73, 99, 157, 185–186, 189, 192
  administration, 8, 49, 98–101, 117, 154, 162, 169, 194, 197, 210
  authorities, 71, 73, 93, 98–100, 112, 115, 122, 124–125, 131, 179, 197, 199–200, 205, 207, 210
  contracts, 70, 82–85, 92–96, 104n59, 121, 126, 177–182, 202, 211n3, 216n102
  as model (see national park)
  museum, 153, 188
  as scientific national park, 8, 62, 154, 159, 222–23
  wardens, 67n56, 84, 109–121, 131, 134nn31–35, 141, 146–147, 188, 191–192, 196–201, 205, 207–210
Swiss National Science Foundation, 145, 160, 205
Swiss Parliament, 15, 34, 47
  Council of States, 49
  National Council, 15, 24, 49, 64n7, 92, 98, 104n61, 113, 225n1
Swiss Society of Prehistory, 75
Swiss Writer's Association, 180
Switzerland
  French-speaking, 50, 96, 105n67, 196

German-speaking, 11n8, 37n56, 50, 64n7, 82, 155, 171n30, 199
Italian-speaking, 50
Romansh-speaking, 45, 50, 67n47, 77–78, 82, 97–98, 146
Sydney, 20

T

Tamangur forest, 65n18
Tansley, Arthur G., 140
Tarasp, 77, 90, 92–93, 104n55, 106n83
Tarnuzzer, Christian, 53
Tatra bi-national park, 107, 133n1
Tavrü, cooperative of, 66n33, 85, 92, 94–95, 107
technology, 25–27, 44, 163, 168, 176, 181
Tenger, Eduard, 201
Thellung, Albert, 148
Thompson, E. P., 116
Thurler, Louis, 64n2
Ticino, 50, 128
Tienhoven, Pieter van, 60
Töndury, Gian, 82
total protection, 8, 108, 111, 133, 138, 154
tourism, 1, 5, 8, 19, 22–25, 29–30, 32, 35n15, 42, 44, 52–53, 77–80, 89–90, 97, 108, 118, 126, 128, 131–132, 155–156, 160–161, 169, 176, 184–188, 191–197, 202, 210, 211n11, 213nn39–41, 214n69, 219, 224
    hotels, 21–22, 42, 4, 65n13, 90, 95, 104n57, 126, 160, 186–189, 197
    tourism/hospitality industry, 25, 95, 155, 186
transect, 165
transhumance, 79–80, 96
transnational, 1, 9, 13n26, 27, 33, 108, 221–224
Trentino, 118, 126–128
Triglav national park, 107, 133n1
trout, 126, 131
Tscharner, Blasius, 118, 134n30
Tschudi, Niklaus Friedrich von, 112
Twa (people), 73
Tyrol, 77, 79, 175

U

Uehlinger, Arthur, 244
UK National Trust, 26
UK Society for the Preservation of the Wild Fauna of the Empire, 26
Ullmann, Erich, 360
UN Conference Rio de Janeiro 1992, 168
ungulates, 128, 135n51, 169, 185, 205, 209, 217n132
United Kingdom, 26, 36n53, 58, 60–61, 109, 158
United States (US), 3–8, 11n10, 17–19, 21, 26, 29–30, 32–33, 35n31, 36n53, 42, 44, 51, 58, 60, 65n14, 66n37, 73, 103n37, 124, 140, 157, 162–163, 184–186, 188– 189, 194, 196, 201, 205, 213n48, 215n98, 215n100
University of Zurich, 81, 137, 139, 165
urban parks, 19–20
US Congress, 17–18, 32, 184
US Department of the Interior, 182
US National Academy of Sciences, 61
US national forests, 41
US National Park Service, 11, 12n13, 23, 61, 106n87, 124, 157, 182, 187, 196

V

Valais, 50
Valtellino, 79
vegetation, 8, 41, 123, 135n51, 139, 146, 151, 160, 162–166, 175, 208–209
Vereeniging tot Behoud von Natuurmonumenten, 31
veterinary, 122, 200–203
Vetterli, Paul, 204, 216n108
Victor Emmanuel III, 156
Vinschgau, 76
visitors, 4–5, 8, 30, 46, 50, 53, 62, 69, 84, 108, 119–120, 124–125, 128, 159–161, 176, 185, 188–195. *See also* tourism
Vonmoos, Jon, 96
vulgarization, 186
vulture. *See* bearded vulture

W

Wagner, Peter, 27–28

Waldsterben, 209
war. *See* First World War and Second World War
Warming, Eugenius, 140
water power. *See* electricity industry
waterfall, 18, 32, 42
Weber, Max, 164, 174n111
Wetekamp, Wilhelm, 30–31
Widmann, Josef Viktor, 39–40, 64n2
Wilczek, Ernest, 64n5, 171n44
wilderness, 1, 3–8, 11nn8–9, 12n13, 29–30, 42, 45, 53, 62, 73, 82, 100, 121–122, 157–158, 182, 184, 211, 224
wildlife
    biology, 116, 197, 210, 204–205, 210
    losing fear of humans, 121–122, 128, 200
    management, 8, 85, 115, 199, 210, 216n111
    research, 159, 162–163, 169, 201, 205, 210
    statistics, 200–201, 210
    study of, 130, 139, 142–143, 145, 200
    See also fauna
WNPK, 130, 135n49, 137–138, 142–147, 152–153, 160, 165–166, 171n29, 171n36, 178–179, 190, 200–202, 206–207, 209, 211n10, 212n18, 215n91, 216n105, 217n123
wolf, 126, 129, 136n66, 185
women, 28–29, 36n53, 121
World Conference on National Parks (first), Seattle 1962, 61
World Conference on National Parks (second), Yellowstone and Grand Teton National Parks 1972, 17–18, 34n10, 61, 69n83
world history, 5, 13n28
Württemberg, 49

Würzburg, 55
WWF (World Wildlife Fund), 129
Wyoming, 18

Y
Yard, Robert Sterling, 187
Yellowstone National Park, 3, 17–21, 29–34, 34n10, 35n13, 36n54, 53, 73, 97, 124, 136n63, 154, 163, 185–186, 196, 213n41, 216n111, 219
Yosemite State and National Park, 19, 35n13, 158, 184, 186
Yugoslavia, 107

Z
Zapovedniki, 154–155
Zbinden, Hans, 180–181
Zemp, Josef, 44
Zernez, 10–11, 42, 45–48, 53, 66n34, 70–71, 75–80, 82–85, 87, 89–94, 96, 98–100, 102n23, 102nn26–27, 103n45, 104nn62–63, 105n77, 106n83, 110, 112–113, 118–119, 122, 134nn31–32, 154, 160, 176–177, 182, 189, 191–192, 195, 197–198, 202, 205, 208, 211n3, 211n5, 214n79, 216n115
Zimmerli, Natanael Georg, 112, 115
Zoller, Heinrich, 159
zoology, 8, 32, 38, 41, 45, 55, 61, 64n2, 130, 137, 139, 147, 151, 154, 158, 162, 171n37, 201–202, 215n91, 215n94
Zschokke, Friedrich, 45, 48, 65n5, 139, 141, 144, 147
Zurich school of plant ecology, 140, 149
Zurich Zoo, 128
Zurich, 11, 34, 38, 41, 45, 67n51, 81, 120, 128, 137, 139–140, 148–149, 162, 165, 171n44, 191, 209

Milton Keynes UK
Ingram Content Group UK Ltd.
UKHW020027180823
427053UK00002B/2